Visions of the
American West

Visions of the
American West

GERALD F. KREYCHE

THE UNIVERSITY PRESS OF KENTUCKY

Library of Congress Cataloging-in-Publication Data
Kreyche, Gerald F.
    Visions of the American West.

    Bibliography: p.
    Includes index.
    1. West (U.S.)—History.   I. Title.
F591.K75   1989   978   88-26176
ISBN 0-8131-1642-2   ISBN 0-8131-0197-2 (pbk.)

Contents

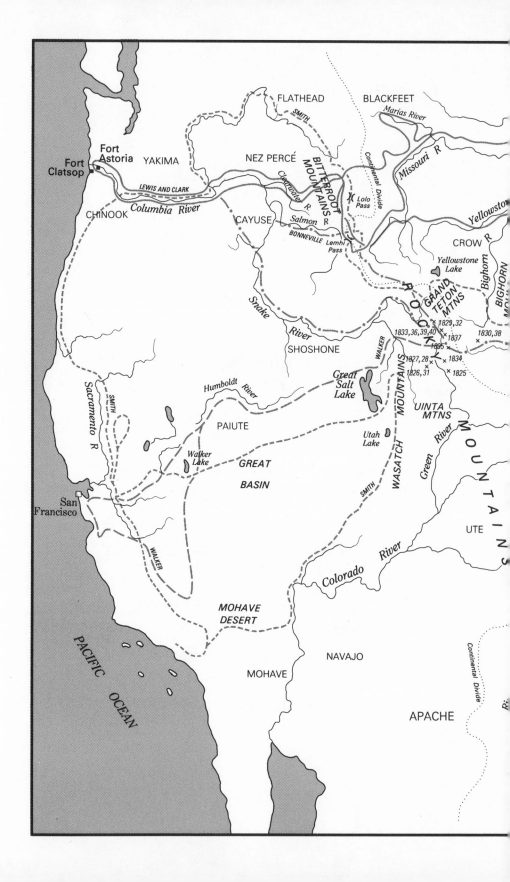

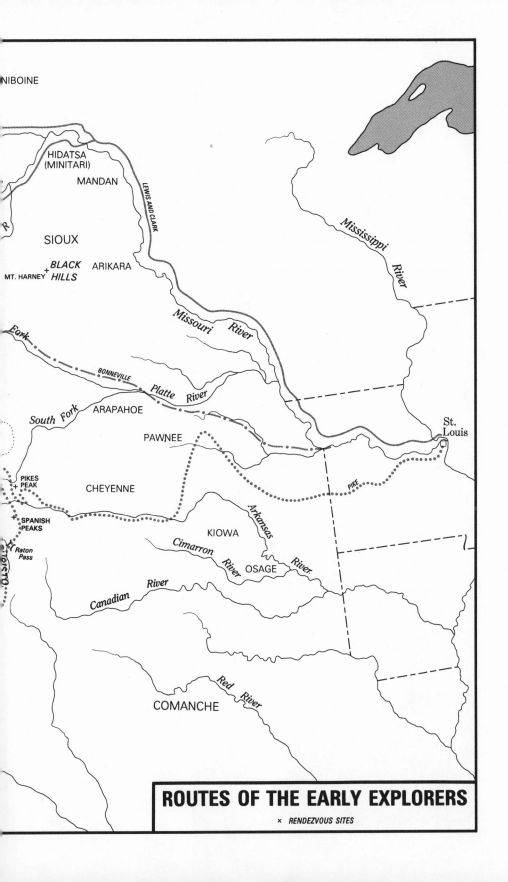

ROUTES OF THE EARLY EXPLORERS

× *RENDEZVOUS SITES*

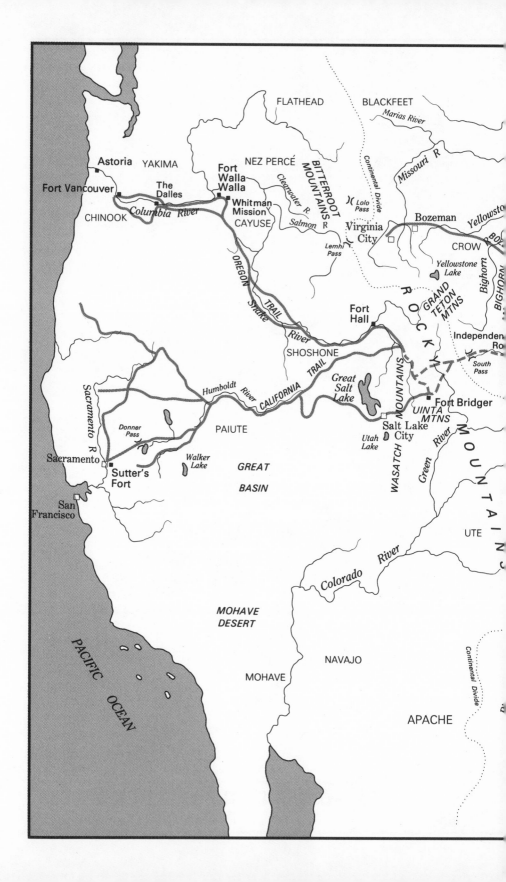

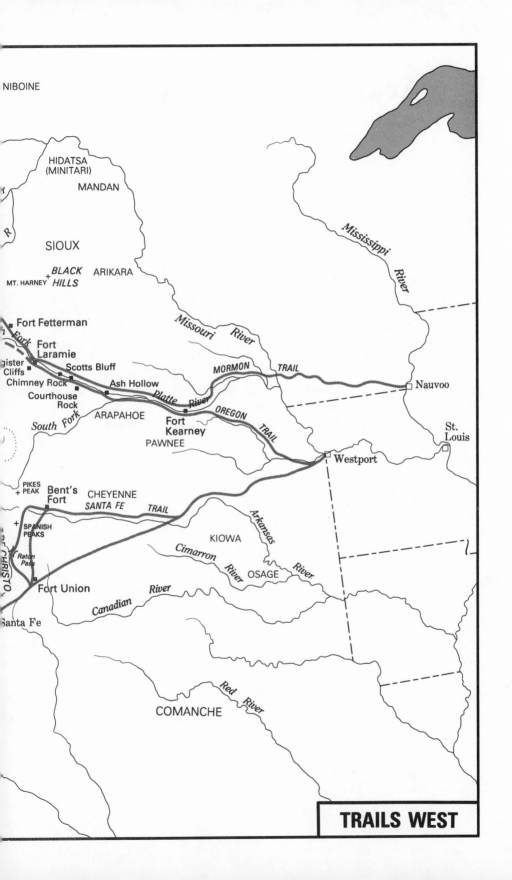

NIBOINE

HIDATSA
(MINITARI)

MANDAN

SIOUX

BLACK
MT. HARNEY + *HILLS*   ARIKARA

Fort Fetterman

Fork Fort
Laramie
gister   Scotts Bluff
Cliffs
Chimney Rock   Ash Hollow   MORMON   TRAIL
Courthouse
Rock   Platte   River
South Fork   ARAPAHOE   OREGON
Fort   TRAIL
Kearney
PAWNEE

PIKES
+ PEAK   Bent's   CHEYENNE
Fort   *SANTA FE*   TRAIL

+ SPANISH
PEAKS

Raton
Pass

Fort Union   River

Canadian

Santa Fe

KIOWA   Arkansas
Cimarron   River
River   OSAGE

COMANCHE   Red   River

Mississippi   River

Missouri   River

Nauvoo

St.
Louis

Westport

TRAILS WEST

Acknowledgments

I am grateful to De Paul University for making available a research grant that enabled me to complete this work. Deep thanks also go to Virginia Waller, who made invaluable editorial suggestions and provided the drawings. I owe a special debt to Murdoch Matthew, whose editing expertise and sensitivities have added immensely to this work; and to Larry Brence for his cartographic skill.

This book grows out of thirty years of wandering the West nearly every summer. I am grateful to my six children for their companionship and for their fresh and individual perspectives on all our experiences. Finally, I thank my wife, Eleanor—for everything.

Prologue

The West as History and Myth

Countless studies on the American West have taken the point of view of history, psychology, sociology, anthropology, and various other disciplines. Seldom, however, has the West been written about from the perspective of a philosopher.

As a philosopher, I want to call attention not only to the history, but more especially to the very spirit of the American West, a spirit which though uniquely American has moved people the world over. I realize that the term *spirit* may seem ethereal and vague, but, like ideas themselves, which often suffer equally under that criticism, spirit, ideas, and dreams always have moved the entire world. Christianity and capitalism, though radically opposed, are examples of the power of dreams and ideas. A contemporary example of this power was Martin Luther King's "I have a dream," the speech which vitalized and impelled the Civil Rights movement. So it was with the movement West; it was essentially the quest of spirit for the realization of a dream, the American dream.

One of the major purposes of this book is to illustrate the various visions that were part of that dream—visions that eventually produced the American West.

Beginning with the Lewis and Clark Corps of Discovery mandated by Jefferson, the initial vision was the exploration of a new land. Quite literally, Americans wanted to know the geographical content of their country and what opportunities it offered. The mountain men who followed (indeed, some were members of the corps) were propelled west by a vision of adventure and profit from the fur trade. Subsequently, they and others came into contact with the Native Americans' vision of their own world, a world in which the white man was a trespasser—and conqueror. The Indian's vision was of a holistic and harmonious unity, in which natural and religious elements were cut of the same cloth, and man was a part of, rather than apart from nature. Conflict between the two visions was inescapable.

The goldseekers heard the siren of quick and untold wealth calling, beckoning, encouraging, and finally driving them west as though each were a Midas redivivus. The missionaries, in their own way as single-minded as the goldseekers, were propelled west by the quest of souls. At all costs, they would christianize the savage, whether noble or not.

Those who took to the trails were inspired by different visions. Some, hell-bent for trade, took off along the Santa Fe trail and found, variously, riches and death. The vision quest for religious freedom in a land to be called Deseret drew the Mormons to make their own trail with handcart brigades that captured the imagination of the world. The Oregon trail and its extension, the California trail, were created by people with visions of rich agrarian opportunity.

The army of the West had its vision prescribed for it, to be the protectors and peacemakers on the frontier. Yet before that role could be realized, death and deprivation would first pave the way.

Finally, after the Civil War, the vision of free land brought the ex-soldier, the poor and the dispossessed, and the land-hungry cattle baron to the West. Accompanying the herds was the cowboy looking for work and romance. Seldom did he find both.

This book, then, is about visions and constitutes a kind of philosophical reflection on the West, on what it offered, not only to Americans but to the world. It is my hope that this work will open to the reader a perspective on the movement west that heretofore has not been portrayed, or if so, only sparingly. Not that the book offers a full-fledged philosophy of the American West; that would be a lifetime task and I have only suggested an outline.[1] Yet the possibilities for such a project are at least indicated in this work.

To any careful student of the West, it should be patent that the region was there, an opportunity available to a special people with a special philosophy of life whom it would transform and who, in turn, would transform it. These were persons who wanted to test, in the most rigorous way, the newly founded democratic principles of their nation. Common motivations drew them west. Europeans came to escape the tyranny and persecution and the tired and rigid values of the old world. Yet, like Americans who came from the East, they burned passionately to fulfill their dreams. These dreams were of prospering by their own efforts in a totally new environment. They didn't know how it would come about but they were determined to make for themselves a better, more satisfying mode of existence. The Mormons are a fine example of this, and countless Americans moving west today are driven by the same motivation.

Those who went westering were a curious lot who always wanted to see the other side of the mountain, and they eagerly anticipated glowing new adventures in what seemed to them a virgin land.[2] The move west was their opportunity to prove themselves by heroic deeds and accomplishments. Above all, they went west seeking a place where they could control their own destiny.

Another purpose of this book is to retell the major events of the nineteenth-century American West, not merely as history but as a human story. There the West poignantly reveals its own triumphs and defeats, its own pride (often bordering on hubris) and pathos.

Every culture produces a distinguishing philosophy or philosophical outlook. This book suggests that in the American West there was and continues to be a distinctive ethos, a special character, a tone and guiding belief, forever setting it apart from those of the eastern United States.

One benefit of familiarizing ourselves with the western experience is that we come to know more about ourselves as Americans. Bruce Rosenberg, for example, points out that folkloric literature of the West is a study of archetypes—the mountain man, the pony express rider, and the lonely prospector. The "boy general" Autie Custer and John Frémont the Pathfinder both fit this genre. They are important, for perusing them reveals ourselves to ourselves. They serve as vehicles for our own ego projections, ourselves in heroic guise. They give hope and evidence that, in this great land, anyone can succeed. Lack of pedigree is no barrier to success, and egalitarianism rules the day. Studies of Western folklore, then, reveal the American pride in energy, endurance, persistence, speed, commitment, and dumb luck.[3]

As Wallace Stegner points out, the western experience is not only regional but is at once primordial and universal. Witness how the pulse quickens at mention of the following: tumbleweed, rodeo, high plains, cowboy, grizzly, coyote, sod house, frontier, mountain man, Custer, Sitting Bull, Crazy Horse, and countless other expressions associated with the American West. Each conjures an image and communicates excitement. In its own manner, each speaks of life, struggle and death, failure and success, fame and anonymity, and all point to matters worthy of philosophical reflection.

It is my stubborn contention that in westering, the veneer of the sophisticated Easterner was sloughed off. What now stood in sharp outline was the frontiersman and later the pioneer. What the West helped produce through this process was a new, virtually unique, and authentic man—a *homo Americanus*. The West brought forth a being truly free—not just a Patrick Henry, who was still English, free but also inhibited. Instead, the West gave rise to a Jim Bridger, the fabled mountain man who could neither read nor write but knew where the beaver were, knew the mountains and their passes and topography like the back of his hand. The West gave rise to a Kit Carson, another illiterate who held his own with other mountain men

and trail blazers and rose to an army colonelcy. The West gave us a
Buffalo Bill and an Annie Oakley, both of whom brought Old World
Europe to its feet in adulation. The West had no Paul Revere, but it
did have a Portugee Phillips who in December 1866, when Fort Phil
Kearny was besieged by Red Cloud's Oglala Sioux, rode 236 miles
through snow and subzero cold to reach Fort Laramie for help. In
varied ways, the West excelled in promoting this distinctive American
character.

I take it as patent that movements are related to ideas, that the
two interact, and that each reciprocally modifies the other. I find
support in Frederick Jackson Turner's thesis that the frontier shaped
the pioneer as much as the pioneer shaped the frontier. It is also true
that the gun or the plow or the windmill shaped the West as much
as the West shaped them.

Today we can relive the West and at least vicariously make it our
experience as well. In a sense, the vicarious experience sometimes
may be better: actuality passes by one time only but vicarious experiences can be relived time and time again. Witness the durability of
myths in cowboy and Indian movies and the countless paperbacks
by authors such as Zane Grey, Karl May, Louis L'Amour, and others.
They all make an unconscious appeal to something basic in each of
us, latent in the collective unconscious.

The Western spirit thus reveals itself as both metaphysical and
mythical, two elements essential to the makeup of all life that is pe-
culiarly human. Walt Whitman picked up this theme of the West,
giving form to its own philosophy, when he wrote, "The metaphysics
and music fit for the New World, before being finally assimilated,
need first and feeding visits here [the great American West]."[4] What
I hope to convey with this presentation of the West is a greater appreciation of freedom, self-reliance, and individualism, all seemingly
in short supply today and all issues for philosophical reflection.

So that the reader may appreciate the spirit of this book, permit
me to stress the sometimes forgotten truism that America literally was
a new world, a new culture. The United States was a nation on the
move and showed little concern for the *status quo*, since the nation's
needs were nearly all dynamic. Never did the nation pause to reflect
on what it had accomplished, so frenzied were its efforts to effect
further change and further growth. Bridges had to be built to carry
the traffic of commerce, deserts had to be crossed to reach the promised land, and mountains had to be penetrated to capture untold
wealth in furs and gold. American pragmatism ruled the day: growth
was not so much linear as it was episodic and dialectical, taking quan-
tum leaps from plateau to plateau, all befitting the youthful character
of the nation.

To blink an eye was to witness a new stage, for, as history shows, America grew in gulps. Established as a nation in 1776, it acquired in 1783 practically all the territory from the Appalachians west to the Mississippi and the land south of the Great Lakes to the Gulf of Mexico. The purchase of France's Louisiana land in 1803 brought in another full third of the continent. Florida was bought in 1819. In 1845 Texas was annexed, and in 1846 the Oregon Country was added. Finally, in the next eight years the Mexican Cession and Gadsden Purchase gave us California and the present Southwest, fairly completing the present continental boundaries of the lower forty-eight.

This growing in gulps also was typical of the various short-lived enterprises that accompanied the geographical growth. The fur trade, for example, which began with the Lewis and Clark expedition, reached its zenith in 1825 with the establishment of the rendezvous system. By 1840, the trade in beaver petered out, giving way to buffalo hide, much as the pony express and the stagecoach gave way to the telegraph and the railway. The gold rush quickly ran its California course and the miners moved on to Nevada, Montana, Colorado, and elsewhere. With many of its energies exhausted in this country, the search for gold spread from the United States territories to the Fraser River in British Columbia and on up to the Klondike. The great cattle drives and the cowboy era were ushered in shortly after the Civil War. Lasting fewer than twenty-five years, the axiom that characterized previous enterprises marked this one as well: "Get in and get out!"

The rise of the West thus was characterized by a series of contradictory drives—toward subjugation and freedom, exploitation and exploration, destruction, conservation, and liberation. Understood as a dialectical struggle attempting to produce a new synthesis, the process offers endless polarities. Among these opposing forces were Roman Catholic and Protestant, white man and red man, American and Mexican, Gentile and Mormon, farmer and cattleman, Irish and Chinese, Indian tribe and Indian tribe, and above all, man and nature. Yet these struggles helped develop the West's distinctive character and left their imprint on all who went there.

In all its movements, Americans relied on both innovation and past experience, but the emphasis was on change and adaptation. Novelty marked each step of the way in the development of the West. Individualistic fur trapping was unified by the organization of fur companies that, with William Ashley, set up improved systems of doing business by establishing the rendezvous arrangement. Changing methods were used to wrest gold from the earth. First there were placer methods (panning), then pick and shovel work, sluice boxes, hydraulic means of washing down banks, and, last, dredging streams. In each case, brawn gave way to brain. Small ranchers particularly suffered change as absentee landlords or large business corporations took over vast acreages of land in the West.

Americans were moving toward goals, but these were not goals understood in the traditional manner of some ultimate end, some *summum bonum* or highest good. Rather, what moved these people was what John Dewey called having at all times an *end in view*. This end in view, subject to constant revision, was dictated variously by ever-changing needs and opportunities. Originally, the West may have been carved out of an old way of life but the old ways were soon transcended.

What informal philosophy developed out of the West was a living and existential philosophy, not a schoolbook set of propositions. Such a philosophy provided a vision that shaped a people and shored up a nation. Grounded in the gut experience of pioneers, it provided further steel for Americans seeking to forge their own identity.[5] As more than one author has observed, the West is the most American part of America!

It might be said that the people who stayed in the East did so in order to *do*, and those who went West did so in order to *be*. The difference between doing and being is a philosophical, a metaphysical distinction, if ever there was one. Alkali dry plains, arroyos with their frequent gully washers, fast rivers, vast distances, fantastic natural formations, and mountains which had "fourteener" peaks—these made the difference.

The West was a place to ennoble the common man, to strike out on one's own, to go back to the wild and savage for a renewal of vitality, to lead the strenuous life, and to sing the praises of America. Welcome to the American West!

1. Lewis and Clark
The Corps of Discovery

Thomas Jefferson, although a believer in an agrarian democracy, also was an exponent of an aristocracy of talent. He himself was interested in virtually everything, and his many talents were equal to those interests. This remarkable president must be understood as a product of the Enlightenment, whose ideas and philosophical principles he adopted and adapted to fit the needs of America. Among those fundamental ideas was an absolute confidence in the sufficiency of mankind, the thought that whatever the odds, man could make it on his own. This fit well with the Deism of the time. Jefferson had equal confidence, also born of the Enlightenment, that human reason was able to govern everything, provided that it was tempered in the crucible of hard experience. Lastly, the Enlightenment led him to a total commitment to the reality of human freedom and its promulgation.

Jefferson's eagerness to know what lay west of the Mississippi and Missouri rivers was no mere desire to satisfy curiosity about the unknown. His interest lay always in the practical implications that knowledge can give. He found himself in basic agreement with Francis Bacon's dictum that knowledge and power meet in one. In typically American fashion, Jefferson wanted to know in order to do. As early as 1762, territory west of the Mississippi, excepting coastal areas and the Southwest, had been ceded to Spain by its previous owner, France. Soon after taking power, however, Napoleon wanted it back and, in 1800 with the Treaty of San Ildefonso, he forced Spain to return the coveted property.

The Mississippi River long had constituted the western border of the United States, and neither Jefferson nor other Americans were much concerned when Spanish territory was on the other side, for the military threat of a lethargic Spain was small. Still, the border was there, a visible barrier and limit, perhaps even an offense to the youthful United States.

Jefferson's personal concern for this vast land area west and north was deep-rooted. As early as 1784, seventeen years before he became president, Jefferson conferred with George Rogers Clark, the American Revolutionary War general and surveyor, about exploring the land west, even though the United States had no claims to it. Pursuing this goal in 1786, Jefferson actually engaged a former marine to *walk* through that land. His name was John Ledyard, and he had been at Nooka with the renowned navigator Captain Cook. Ledyard prepared for the trip by going to Europe: he planned to go from *west to east!* Starting from Russia, he would walk through Alaska, down Canada, and across the Louisiana land. As a kind of warm-up, Ledyard actually walked from Stockholm to St. Petersburg, 1,400 miles in seven weeks. Continuing, he travelled as far as Irkutsk, Siberia, before Russian imperial troops were called to halt him. The Russians sent him to Poland and his great adventure ended.

Undaunted by this setback—Jefferson would not consider it a defeat—the future third president of the United States arranged for André Michaux to explore the land. Michaux was a French scientist whose specialty was botany, a subject close to Jefferson's heart. The plan, instigated in 1792, preceded by one year the crossing of the Canadian continental divide by the great Alexander Mackenzie.

As vice-president of the American Philosophical Society, Jefferson pressured some funding from that august body to help sponsor the trip. Even George Washington was talked into a $25 donation. Alexander Hamilton and Jefferson himself each contributed $12.50, and soon a grand total of $128.50 was collected for the journey. Unfortunately, rumors spread that Michaux was a French intelligence officer, and this project, too, fell by the wayside. Still wedded to the notion of traversing the area, Jefferson bided his time, planting suggestions here, winning friends there, and at last in 1801, the year of his inauguration, he was able to take more direct action. What occurred strains the meaning of the word *serendipitous*.

For some time, England, France, and Spain had been vying for supremacy among the European powers. Napoleon hoped to gain against England by establishing a strong force in the Caribbean, then to move his troops from there into the Louisiana land. This worried Jefferson. To have Spain on the doorstep was one thing, to have a militaristic France was quite another. Americans needed access to New Orleans at the Mississippi delta, for it was the trade route for all western commerce. Clearly, its closure to trade and traffic would be totally unacceptable to the United States. Jefferson hinted strongly that he would move troops into the area if there were an outbreak of war.

The transfer of the land to France had actually cancelled the Pinckney Treaty of 1795 that guaranteed America's right to ship through the port and off-load and on-load there. Seeking to protect port rights, perhaps even to purchase the port of New Orleans itself, Jefferson sent negotiators to the French. The timing scarcely could have been more propitious, for while discussions were taking place, Napoleon's Caribbean troops, although victorious in overthrowing the dictatorship there, actually were defeated in nonmilitary battle with yellow fever. With their ranks decimated, Napoleon, still determined to spite England, now offered to sell not just New Orleans but the entire Louisiana land. Astounded, and with very little dickering, the American delegation bought the land for an even then paltry sum of approximately fifteen million dollars, the official transfer taking place on March 8, 1804. Yet even before this event, Jefferson had made more detailed plans for exploring the area and had set some in motion. In 1802, he asked the local Spanish officials how they might view American exploratory activity in the area. The major purpose, he assured them, was the humanistic goal of "adding to the knowledge of geography." Their reply, as expected, was unfavorable. This must have been a testing of the waters by Jefferson, for as early as May 1801 he had learned that the land now was under title to the French.

Despite Spain's reply, January 18, 1803, found Jefferson badgering Congress for appropriations to conduct such an exploration. He explained that the United States needed more territory, since the Indians were reluctant to give up further lands. Jefferson also wanted to introduce the western Indian to "agriculture, to manufactures, and civilization." Because of his Enlightenment convictions, he respected the Native American "as a member like himself of the universal body of men." He firmly believed the Indian "to be in body and mind equal to the White man."[1] As to how the red man could be helped, Jefferson declared, "Commerce is the great engine by which we are to coerce them and not war."[2]

Justifying to Congress his request for funding the mission, Jefferson argued:

An intelligent officer, with ten or twelve chosen men, fit for the enterprise and willing to undertake it, taken from our posts where they may be spared without inconvenience, might explore the whole line, even to the Western Ocean, have conferences with the natives on the subject of commercial interests. . . . While other civilized nations have encountered great expense to enlarge the boundaries of knowledge by undertaking voyages of discovery . . . our nation seems to owe to the same object, as well as to its own interest, to explore this the only line of easy communication across the continent, and so directly traversing our own part of it. The interests of commerce place the principal object within the constitutional powers and care of Congress, and that it should incidentally advance the geographical knowledge of our own continent cannot but be an additional gratification.[3]

Congress listened to the president's plea and then penuriously appropriated $2,500. (In fact, the expedition was to cost over $38,000, one of the first cases of governmental cost overrun.) Jefferson's endeavor was already taking steps to put the money to use, for a month before his inauguration in 1801, he had made a singular appointment of a private secretary. The secretary's name was Meriwether Lewis, an army captain and man of many skills and talents—but spelling was not one of them. No matter, for what Jefferson had in mind was not someone to transcribe presidential correspondence but a man to put together a transcontinental exploratory party, keep a careful and detailed record in the field, and report back to the president. All these plans Jefferson would detail in his secret message to Congress *two years later*. Lewis started to formulate his plans for executing the wishes of the president, and Jefferson's long-held dream of exploring the continent to the Pacific was inching toward reality.

Already well-known to Jefferson, Lewis came from a high-born Virginia family. On the occasion of Washington's call to put down the Whiskey Rebellion, Lewis, then aged twenty, joined the army, eventually winning a regular captaincy. He fought in the Indian wars under General "Mad" Anthony Wayne and, during that stint, as an ensign under Captain William Clark. Lewis and Clark respected each other but at the time had no inkling of how deep and enduring that respect and friendship would become, or how it might be put to the test.

Jefferson assigned his beloved Louisiana exploration project to Lewis and placed full confidence in him. That confidence is witnessed by Jefferson's own praise for Lewis. Writing in the introduction to the Biddle editions of the expedition journals, he enumerates and lauds Lewis's many virtues, declaring, "with all these qualifications, as if selected and implanted in nature in one body for this express purpose, I could have no hesitation in confiding the enterprise to him."[4]

Lewis, now given full authority to organize and carry out the project, requested that the former Captain William Clark, no longer on active status, be reinstated in the Army with that rank as coleader of the expedition. Jefferson concurred and Lewis asked Clark to "participate with me in its fatiegues, it's dangers and it's honors." Declared Lewis, "There is no man on earth with whom I should feel equal pleasure in sharing them as with yourself."[5] Clark replied he would "cheerfully join." The pact was sealed, but unknown to Jefferson, the army refused the full captaincy for Clark. Nonetheless, Lewis designated Clark as captain and cocommander; the expedition's men so regarded him and the journals so record him. Deeply disappointed by the lack of official confirmation, Clark took it in stride.

Like Lewis, William Clark also came from a well-known Virginia family. William's oldest brother, George Rogers Clark, had won fame for the family, and from him William picked up a good knowledge of the natural sciences. William also was a fair student of history, and the more he read, the more he came to dislike all things British.

Although historians frequently refer to Lewis as the "diplomatic and commercial thinker," and Clark as the "negotiator,"[6] a more recent study convincingly argues that "Clark was as much a diplomatic and commercial thinker as Lewis."[7] In addition, Clark's experiences as an engineer and surveyor would prove invaluable to the expedition.

Lewis, who was twenty-eight when the expedition set out, was a bit more formal than Clark and certainly more introspective. Possessed of strong scientific interests, Lewis was an acute observer of flora, fauna, and minerals—sometimes to the detriment of his health, for often he tasted specimens to assist him in placing them taxonomically. A number of them were mildly poisonous, but Lewis continued the practice.

Thwaites called him "a philosopher who enjoyed the exercise of writing," but he never ceased to be a leader of men. He seemed to feel it a weakness to show or confide his feelings to any other than his peers, and the journals support this view of him. Appearing aloof, Lewis constantly struggled to understand women, Indians, his dog Scannon, and perhaps even himself. In the journals he refers to Scannon only as "the dog."[8] Thus, although Lewis was a leader, he was also very much a private man.

Clark was no less a disciplinarian than Lewis but was more outgoing and warm in human relations. He looked at the Native American not so much as a savage (Lewis's view) but, Jefferson-like, as a "child of nature." Clark not only was understanding of their diverse cultures; he was sympathetic to them. In the good sense of the term, he was amused with the Indian, and many of them let down their guard with him. He came to be a father figure, combining firmness with kindness, tolerance with discipline. Unlike Lewis, he came to enjoy eating dog, rather than devouring it only out of necessity. Further, he didn't mind the lack of salt that caused others often to grumble. In short, he was an adaptable man.

Lewis and Clark complemented each other in nearly every way. While the individuality of each stands out clearly, they always operated as a team, as though they were a single leader with differing characteristics. One would lead the exploration one day, and on the

following day the other would take his turn. Only when one was sick
did the other continue leading, almost with an air of guilt. This leapfrogging pattern was typical, and the journals give no evidence of
any genuine disagreement.[9]

As they planned their mission, Lewis stayed in the East and Clark
went to the frontier city of St. Louis. Lewis took instructions in such
diverse subjects as botany, zoology, medicine, and navigation. He
also arranged for supplies from the Harper's Ferry Armory, even
directing the artisans there to design a portable and collapsible iron
boat frame to be covered with skins and used to float the rivers west.
It turned out to be the most disastrous piece of equipment on the
expedition. Weighing a hundred pounds and thirty-six feet long when
extended, it never worked. Lewis abandoned it by the great falls of
the Missouri.

At Pittsburgh, Lewis oversaw the construction of a twenty-two-
oar keelboat that would be floated down the Ohio River and eventually to St. Louis; from there, it would take the expedition up the
Missouri. The keelboat was armed with swivel guns fore and aft that
fired shrapnel-like charges of metal fragments. Its deck was layered
so that its storage places and cabins could form fortifications, which
capability was to prove useful. Work on the keelboat was always
behind schedule and might have served notice to an intense and
frustrated Lewis of what the future was to hold. He used the delay
to recruit men, making no commitments and accepting them at first
only on a trial basis.

Meanwhile, Clark did the same kind of recruitment at his St. Louis
post. He also purchased and gathered supplies, some of which were
obtained from a Manuel Lisa,[10] who would become a major figure in
the fur trade and, indeed, a later partner with Clark in a fur trade
venture. The supplies included food and medicine (a considerable
amount of which was the opiate laudanum), and various scientific
instruments like sextants, thermometers, and compasses. There also
were packs of military coats (for Indians), paints, fishhooks, awls,
and weapons. Not to be forgotten were various grades of Jefferson
medals to be given to important and cooperative chiefs. One hundred
gallons of whiskey were taken along—for use among expedition
members only.

The Corps of Discovery, as it was to be called, was composed of
a melánge of "robust, helthy, hardy" men who were distinguished
by uncommon courage and uncommon skill. All were single: nine
were chosen from among Kentucky's best woodsmen, fourteen were
soldiers, and two were French river experts. Pay for privates was five
dollars a month and for sergeants, eight. The company also included
a hunter-interpreter and Clark's strapping black body-servant, York.

Lewis and Clark themselves would complete the twenty-nine on the official list. On the first part of the journey, to the winter quarters at Fort Mandan in present-day North Dakota, they would be assisted by sixteen extra men. Thus forty-five persons would begin the adventure, travelling in the keelboat and two pirogues (dugout canoes).

Clark set up first camp at Wood River (Fort Dubois), located where the giant Missouri and Mississippi rivers merged into one (serving almost as a symbol of Lewis and Clark themselves). Lewis joined the company there after catching up on last-minute details in the East. Finally, spring was in full bloom and the rivers were flowing at their highest. It was time to make the movement west.

On May 14, 1804, the intrepid Lewis and Clark began a journey that would take them to the delta of the mighty Columbia River on the Pacific Ocean. In reaching their destination, they would strengthen the United States' claim to what was later known as Oregon land, first claimed by Captain Gray and his Columbia crew in 1792. Both claims would later undergird the agitation for "Fifty-four/forty or fight!" and add to the nation the states of Oregon and Washington. The entire American movement west could be rightly viewed as "an affirmation of democracy and a doctrine of geographical determinism."[11] The phrase "manifest destiny" had yet to be coined but, as a belief that stimulated the epic adventure, it already was forcibly present.

Both captains as well as the sergeants kept journals, and two privates also penned some notes along the way. On the day of departure, Clark wrote in his journal, "I set out at 4 o'clock P.M., in the presence of many of the neighbouring inhabitents, and proceeded on under a jentle brease up the Missourie."[12] Only four miles were made that first day but they effectively served as a shake-down cruise for the approximately seven thousand miles to go. The men were fully aware that the expedition would take some two years; such a time away from loved ones was not unusual in those days. Whalers out of Boston commonly spent two years before the mast, and ships sailing from the East around the Horn to the Columbia and northward often were gone three years.

Although reports of other expeditions indicated the vastness of the unexplored land Lewis and Clark were about to enter, no one was quite sure how great the distance was from one point to another, nor what lay between. The Missouri itself, with its serpentine turns and doublebacks, was twenty-five hundred miles long and wended its way through canyons, mountains, deserts, and breaks. After the Missouri, the trip to the Pacific still was considerable; the continental divide was only the highest of several parallel mountain ranges that had to be crossed. Even today, Europeans, and indeed many Americans who never have been West, fail to comprehend that the distance from Berlin to Moscow is the same as from Chicago to Denver, and Barcelona is no farther from Moscow than Chicago is from San Francisco.

The voyage of discovery began with enthusiasm among all, and it is fair to say that, by and large, it retained that enthusiasm throughout. If ever there were an *esprit de corps*, this group had it. This spirit was due both to the careful selection of its men and to the special character and qualities of its leaders. They set a tone that contributed largely to the success of the venture.

Up they went now, up the mighty Missouri that whites called "Big Muddy" and Indians "the river that screams at all others." While pack horses leisurely walked along the river banks, the 55-foot square-sailed keelboat and accompanying pirogues fought for every inch of progress, bucking the mighty downstream current. Full of surprises, the river with its floating islands of flotsam was ever threatening to stove in the bow of the keelboat or overturn the pirogues. Almost regularly, cut banks fell into the mainstream, adding to its muddy color and creating maelstroms, as the river pursued its eternal effort to straighten its way. Bloated carcasses of buffalo floated by, a symbol of death to the unwary. Far upstream, the "hump-back cows" had been betrayed as the thawing ice they hoped to cross on had broken through.

Sand bars were everywhere and constantly changing, crumbling apart and washing away only to reappear near a bank in the river. Several times when the expedition left an island where it had camped the night before, the men would look back to see the land completely disintegrate. They thanked Providence that these were only close calls and not tragedies.

Anyone who has tried to paddle upstream knows the effort that must go into making any progress, and the corps used various means to go forward as the river tried relentlessly to drive them back. When the breeze was favorable, the sail would be hoisted, but even then, the twisting of the river meant that the boat always was tacking, first in one direction, then in another. The winds were gusty rather than constant, and they always had to be alert so that the sail did not luff or the boom swing around, cracking open the head of an innocent victim. Coming gusts advertised their presence on the river with a series of small waves. Yet although the boatmen watched the water carefully, often sudden gusts nearly threw the craft onto the banks. Many times the keelboat became entangled in submerged brush and overhanging trees.

With no wind, or with unfavorable ones, the oars were put to work—backbreaking work, for they often snagged in the ever-present flotsam on the river. Where the water was sufficiently shallow, long poles would be thrust into the river, their tips reaching down to its bed, and men would push with all their weight as they walked forward on a ribbed deck, repeating the action hundreds of times a day. When all else failed, or sometimes in conjunction with other modes of propulsion, the men resorted to the bone-wearying cordelle, which meant towing the boat by hand using long ropes attached to the mast and bow. These ropes were often more than two hundred yards long. Sometimes the keelboat was cordelled by men walking in the water near the banks or, when possible, on the banks themselves.

In the river, there always were snags and, frequently, snakes. There, too, mosquitoes seemed to lie in wait to attack their prey, whether man or beast. On occasion, bluffs had to be climbed and the boat towed from their very pinnacles. Yet, as Lewis and Clark and the sergeants would record in the most frequent passage in their journals, "We proceeded on!"[13]

Rain plagued much of this early spring journey as the company passed the villages of various tribes, first the Maha (Omaha), then the Osage, Kansas, Otoes, Ponca, Sioux, Arickara, Mandan, and Gros Ventre. When the explorers stopped in some of the major villages as ambassadors of good will, they counselled peace and presented gifts such as medals and tobacco twists. All of these tribes knew the white man and traded with him and, with a few exceptions like the Sioux, offered little challenge to the expedition.

The first real tragedy struck the group near Council Bluffs. There, Sergeant Floyd, who had been suffering from abdominal pains and a fever, grew weaker and weaker. He died on August 2, 1804, probably of a ruptured appendix, and was buried near Sioux Falls. Clark wrote in tribute to Floyd, "This man at all times gave us proof of his firmness and Determined resolution to doe Service to his Countrey and honer to himself after paying all the honor to our Deceased brother we camped in the Mouth of floyds River about 30 miles wide, a butifull evening."[14]

Because of floods in later years, his body was reinterred and the grave is now on a high bluff marked by an impressive obelisk. Given the state of medicine at the time, nothing could have been done for him even had he fallen ill closer to medical help. The saddened men hoped the death was not a portent of things to come. Fortunately it was not, for, remarkably, no one else died during the two-year trek.

Floyd's death necessitated the election of a new sergeant, and that honor and rank fell to Patrick Gass, a carpenter-soldier, whose pay with the promotion accordingly was raised from five to eight dollars a month.

The expedition continued up the Missouri. In this area, the band encountered Indians who told of pygmy Indians living nearby armed with poisoned arrows. The story sounded so convincing that the explorers went nearly a dozen miles out of their way to see the pygmies. The captains found nothing but a vacant hill. Today a marker some thirty miles northwest of Sioux City identifies the spot, which is called Spirit Mound.

Now about six months into its trek, the expedition was beginning to look for a place to winter. For obvious reasons, they did not want it to be in Sioux lands, for these Indians were a warlike and domineering people. In previous confrontations with them, the Sioux backed off only when the expedition offered small-arms fire and threatened them with the imposing swivel guns.

On November 2, 1804, the expedition settled into winter quarters near the mouth of the Knife River where it empties into the Missouri. This was the land of the Mandans and was about thirty miles north of present-day Bismarck. Here the men built a triangular fort and named it Fort Mandan. The bitter winter to come demanded a sufficient store of food and firewood, so they gathered what supplies they could to trade for Mandan corn. Despite the harshness of the weather, the winter break provided a respite from the arduous river travel, and the general camaraderie cheered up the party. The Indians enjoyed the white man's presence and both sides were hospitable to each other.

Throughout the expedition, several factors, some almost accidental, helped to win and keep the friendship of the Indians. Among these was Clark's personal servant, York, a huge strong man, full of good humor and ready for any activity, serious or frivolous. Indians had never seen such black skin color before and could scarcely believe it was not a dye. York's tight, curly "buffalo hair" also fascinated them and many looked upon him as a minor deity. Some even offered York a tryst with their wives, a signal honor, and York found he could hardly refuse this generosity, although other soldiers shared this as well. Some historians claim that over a period of time, fifty descendants came out of such liaisons. Lewis and Clark themselves were invited to partake of these affairs but, using all their diplomatic skills, they resisted. The situation is detailed in the journals with more than a few implied chuckles.

Music always brings people together, as was demonstrated when Peter Cruzatte brought out his fiddle. The Indians delighted in the jigging of the whites, so different from their own stomping dances. Cruzatte was part Indian, which may have helped his cause. Although blind in one eye, he was an excellent hunter whose skills were exceeded only by his abilities as a versatile frontiersman and river man.

Clark himself was a wonder to the Indians for his flaming red hair. He employed their own medicines and introduced the red man to white medicine. Throughout the journey, he was a physician of last resort, using laudanum that may not have cured many diseases but with its opium base surely relieved many symptoms. For this, the Indians and whites were grateful.

One of the men of the expedition was something of an acrobat and entertained everyone by walking on his hands. Try as they might, few Indians learned to duplicate this feat and they enjoyed all the more watching the antics of the whites.

Great fascination was aroused by the famous airgun brought with the expedition. It fired without a flash (no black powder smoke or loud discharge) and was fairly accurate within short range. This "big medicine" provoked wonder, even though it hardly was practical, since it had to be pumped up to five hundred times for each shot.

To a nontechnological people, the art of the blacksmith was miraculous, and John Shields, an enlisted man, was one of the best. He could make tools such as axes from discarded metals and saved many a broken rifle that otherwise would have been cast aside. This, together with Lewis's foresight in bringing extra rifle parts, insured that the corps always had a good supply of working arms.

Travel to the land of the Mandans had been largely uninformative, as this route already had been well-traversed by whites. Of the route from the Mandan villages north, however, whites knew little, and the commanders pressed the Mandans for all information they could deliver on that part of the country. The Indians told of a place of great falls (now Great Falls, Montana) many moons ahead. Indeed, the falls proved so mighty that the river dropped some four hundred feet. A few Indians also told of an eagle nest near the falls. Sure enough, the nest was there and demonstrated the accuracy of Indian information. This kind of detail was exactly what the explorers wanted and needed. They also culled additional knowledge of what lay ahead from trappers wintering at the fort or just passing through. One thing they learned from these *coureurs des bois* was that the expedition would need horses when moving from the Missouri to the Columbia River Basin. Unlikely though it seemed, serendipity would provide the horses at the needed time.

One of the temporary inhabitants of the Mandan village was an experienced trapper who had been employed by the Northwest Company, at that time a rival of the Hudson's Bay firm. The trapper, Toussaint Charbonneau, about forty years old, was accompanied by an Indian wife (like many trappers of the day, he had several). Although he spoke no English, he was fluent in a number of Indian languages, among which were Hidatsa and Gros Ventre. The woman was a Snake (Shoshone), whose tribal grounds were near the origins of the Missouri where the expedition was going. When she was a child of ten, she was captured by the Hidatsa, sometimes called Mini-tari, who traded her to Charbonneau. Told of her tribal background, Lewis and Clark wanted to know more about her and what she might know about the area toward which they were headed. They knew her as Sacajawea, which they thought meant "Birdwoman."[15] She indicated that her father was a Shoshone chief. She spoke Shoshone and, because of her life with the Hidatsa, their language as well. Now sixteen years old, she was pregnant with her baby due in the dead of winter. If the story of her background were true, thought the captains, she could be very useful in procuring horses from her people. Her husband's linguistic skills also would be valuable, so they bargained with the Charbonneaus to accompany the Corps of Discovery. Financial compensation proved adequate incentive, and Charbonneau and Sacajawea agreed to join.

The expedition soon to head out of Fort Mandan now included a red woman, a black man, some mixtures, and whites of various stripes. Added to this melánge would be Sacajawea's baby, born February 11, 1805. The young Indian woman had a difficult labor and for a while, life for her and the baby seemed touch and go. Clark rendered what assistance and medicines he could, but nothing helped until Sacajawea suggested some ground-up rattles from a rattlesnake. Whether these rattles were medicinal or not, immediately after she took the potion the baby was delivered and named Toussaint Baptiste. Clark and, indeed, most of the expedition took a liking to the child and gave him their own special nickname of Pomp, short for Pompey. Clark's affection for the lad and association with him was to be life-long. A rock formation along the Missouri was named in the child's honor and still is known today as Pompey's Pillar.

While the presence of a woman and child might seem excess baggage on such an expedition, the very opposite was true. Their accompaniment immediately signified to other tribes that this was no war party, which would have left women and children behind.

Although Sacajawea long was credited with a detailed geographical knowledge of the up-river area and supposedly led Lewis and Clark to the headwater country, this could not have been the case. When she was kidnapped, her captors had taken her along a different route. Nonetheless she proved helpful in conveying her knowledge of useful herbs for food and medicine. And when her husband, a strangely timid and clumsy man, knocked some of Clark's important scientific instruments overboard, Sacajawea, to the everlasting gratitude of the red-haired captain, saved them. Despite the romantic framework in which some biographers have falsely put her, it is fair to say that "after truth has been sorted from fiction, Sacajawea emerges as a courageous and admirable person in her own right, with no need of embellishment."[16] Clark acknowledged her worth symbolically by naming a tributary of the Mussellshell River after her. Later, Clark legally adopted her son, Baptiste, whose life was to be as fascinating and adventuresome as his mother's.

As the long siege of winter at last was broken, the corps readied itself for the next leg of the journey by dismissing the men brought along to assist in building the fort and getting supplies this far. The keelboat was loaded with wondrous new specimens that had been collected up to now. These were sure to please the insatiable appetite of Jefferson for such things. It was Jefferson who had directed that the expedition be as much a scientific one as exploratory. The journals of Lewis and Clark contain as much description of the environment they encountered as record of events and travails. Geographical location, topology, measurement of distance, readings of latitude and longitude, barometric pressure and temperature recordings—all were part of the work of the corps. Onto the returning keelboat went "barking squirrels" (prairie dogs), "beardless goats" (pronghorn antelope), prickly pear cactus, and various samples of minerals and plants. Also taken back were letters to families and messages to the president. This would be the last communication of the group with the outside world.

Additional dugouts were carved from cottonwood trees as the main party prepared to face and chart the unknown. Those going ahead to the Pacific numbered thirty-three and included Charbonneau, Sacajawea, and their baby. Lewis reflected on the mission ahead:

Our vessels consisted of six small canoes, and two large perogues. This little fleet altho' not quite so rispectable as those of Columbus or Capt. Cook, were still viewed by us with as much pleasure as those deservedly famed adventurers ever beheld theirs; and I dare say with quite as much anxiety for their safety and reservation. We were now about to penetrate a country at least two thousand miles in width, on which the foot of civilized man had never trodden; the good or evil it had in store for us was for experiment yet to determine. . . . [I entertain] the most confident hope of succeeding in a voyage which I had formed a da[r]ling project of mine for the last ten years, I could but esteem this moment of my departure as among the most happy of my life. The party are in excellent health and sperits, zealously attached to the enterprise, and anxious to proceed not a whisper of murmur or discontent to be heard among them, but all act in unison, and with the most perfect harmony.[17]

The corps headed out on April 7, 1805, and soon entered buffalo country. Food for the expedition was not a present problem; Clark recorded herds of as many as ten thousand animals. After the meager and monotonous diet at the fort, the men welcomed the choice meats of buffalo tongue, buffalo hump, and beaver tail. Buffalo intestines provided a gourmet treat, *boudins blanc.*[18]

Even Lewis's giant Newfoundland dog, Scannon, got caught up in the excitement and jumped into the river to drag an unlucky swimming antelope to the men in the boat. He went after beaver also but nearly lost his life when one of the rodents bit through an artery on his leg. Fortunately, Lewis was able to halt the bleeding and the dog recovered. Evidence indicates that Scannon made the entire trip, eventually returning to St. Louis with the men.

Scannon was the envy of many Indians who wanted to barter for him. Once he was dognapped. Indian admiration was not for the dog as a possible pet, for dogs never served that function in the red man's society. Rather, they served three useful purposes. Like horses, they could shoulder a loaded travois, helping to move articles from camp to camp. They acted as campground sentinels, warning of approaching strangers. And dogs were considered an excellent eating delicacy. Not all Indians ate dog, however, and those along the Columbia River chided and ridiculed Lewis and Clark for doing so.

By now, most of the men had worn out their regular clothes and were dressed in the skins of elk or deer. Such clothing could be quite functional if the skins first were properly smoked and tanned. Less well prepared skins became stiff and uncomfortable and would shrink and toughen when wetted. When such moccasins became soaked, the leather would tighten on the foot, causing intense pain by cutting circulation of the blood. Moccasins that lost their shape with wetting produced blisters and callouses. Wet rawhide did have its uses, however, and was employed as a binding agent for broken rifle stocks, splints, and various other needs.

"Musquetoes were troublesum," reported the captains, and were a constant plague, for the expedition generally camped and travelled in and around water and the lowlands. No one ever became used to them, and passage after passage in the journals tells how they made life miserable for the men. On occasion, the swarms forced the men to break camp earlier than scheduled, without the sleep needed for the coming day. Better to work and make progress rather than be eaten alive, argued the captains, and, to a man, the troops agreed. Scannon, the dog, was equally bothered and would whine in anguish throughout the night. The "musquetoes" would disappear only when a fresh breeze set in, and every hint of such a coming wind was greeted with thanks. The family *Culicidae* certainly shared top honors among reports in the journals.

Farther north, the country grew increasingly wild, and grizzlies started to make their frightening appearance, specially in the willows along the banks of the river. Without question, they were the omnipresent monarchs of the land, and the Indians both feared and admired their prowess.[19] So impressed by them were the red men that the grizzly was the only animal on which coup could be counted. That is, if an Indian killed, wounded, or touched one, he could mark this honor on a coup stick.

The first few confrontations of the soldiers with *ursa horribilis* led the men, including Lewis, to believe that the Indians had exaggerated the strength and ferocity of these omnivorous and opportunistic eaters. After all, the men were equipped with updated Harpers Ferry 1803 flintlock rifles. Further meetings with the bears, however, engendered considerable more respect for this huge animal. On April 29, 1805, Lewis wrote dismissingly that "the Indians may well fear this animal equipped as they generally are with their bows and arrows or indifferent fuzees, but in the hands of skillful riflemen they are by no means as formidable or dangerous as they have been represented."[20] Less than two weeks later, however, Bratton, one of those walking along the river bank, came running toward the men hollering that he had just shot a grizzly, which despite a considerable wound had chased him for some distance. Organizing a party, Lewis pursued the bear, finding it in the brush and dispatched two balls to the animal's brain. Describing it as a "monstrous beast," Lewis commented, "these bears being so hard to die reather intiamedates us all; I must confess that I do not like the gentlemen and had reather fight two Indians than one bear."[21] (The journals also referred to the grizzlies as the "white bear" or "silver tip," for the end of the hairs had a whitish tinge and glistened under certain light conditions.)

The spring weather was unpredictable. High winds and rain, often with hailstones up to seven inches in diameter, pelted them from time to time. Cloudbursts often caught them in the open, and on one such occasion, when Clark and Sacajawea were walking in a ravine, the rain turned into a real gully washer. The rush of water in the ravine nearly overtook the girl, threatening to drown her, when Clark pulled her out not a second too soon. A number of expensive and important instruments were lost to the rushing water, but later most were found a half-mile downstream.

Although the men had the health of backwoodsmen, many suffered occasional bouts of the ague with its accompanying fever and chills. (Ague was a generic term which included a touch of malaria or simple neuralgia with its aching sensation. Fortunately, whatever the malady was, it usually went away as quickly as it came.) Clark had chronic rheumatism in his neck and suffered greatly whenever dampness set in. Like the others, he also was plagued with boils, which produced up to a half pint of fluid when drained. One carbuncle on his ankle temporarily disabled him and he was embarrassed to be unable to walk with the men and do his share. Dysentery could strike anyone at any time; much of it was due to drinking alkaline-laden waters or the muddy water of the Missouri. Dietary changes produced the same effect as their fare went from almost exclusively meat to the heavy starches of prairie turnip and camas lily and finally to fish.

Nevertheless, the company proceeded on, past the meeting of the Yellowstone and Missouri rivers to the confluence of the Missouri and Marias rivers.[22] Whenever they encountered such a meeting of two large rivers, it was difficult to know which was the main trunk and which was the tributary. On this occasion, the men were convinced the Marias was the Missouri and therefore the one to be followed. Lewis and Clark disagreed but allowed the men to explore their judgment while the captains went their own way. In a few days, the other group discovered their error and followed the trail back to the leaders of the expedition. The willingness of the two captains to give the men a hearing and test their mistaken hypothesis increased, if possible, the respect the men had for them. Few had the temerity to challenge Lewis and Clark's good judgment again.

Working its way up the Big Muddy, the expedition now could hear a roar of mighty waters and knew they were approaching the great falls spoken of by the Mandans. Arrival there brought a magnificent view of cascading streams and rainbow mists. Delight, however, was tempered by the knowledge that they would have to make a killing portage around the falls. Undaunted, the men set to work cutting down cottonwood trees and slicing through their trunks to make crude wheels to place under materials for transport. Caches were buried under dirt and brush to hide the expedition's precious supplies for the way back. A sign of the planning that went into the expedition was the leaden flasks that held powder and were sealed with the lead itself. These could be put anywhere in the river and retrieved when needed. The materials served as their own container. The men were only too happy to cache the hundred-pound collapsible boat frame, one of Lewis's very few innovations that never worked: it sank every time it was put to the test.

The expedition reached the point above the falls where they again embarked on the water, grateful after the backbreaking work of an eighteen-mile portage. Now the Missouri took a turn to the southwest

and soon led them to its source, the forks of three rivers, which
the explorers named the Jefferson, the Madison, and the Gallatin (the
latter honoring the secretary of the Treasury). Having reached the
headwaters of the Big Muddy, one part of their mission was accomplished. No white man had set foot there before, and the nation's
geographical knowledge was deeply enriched. Unknown to the corps,
they were only a short distance north and west of the natural wonders
of what was to become the most famous national park in all the world,
Yellowstone.[23] They were entering an area more and more familiar
to Sacajawea, for they were adjacent to her homeland. The pulses of
all quickened with this indication, for the men knew that horses now
would be their means of transport. No more rowing, poling, or wea-
rying cordelling. At last they would *have* a beast of burden instead of
being one. (Had they known what was in store as they crossed the
Bitterroot Mountains, they might not have been so eager to abandon
their former mode of transport, despite its hardships.)

The business at hand was to contact Indians, preferably Sacajawea's people, and then to barter successfully for the Indians' most
priceless possession, horses. In pursuing its goal, the corps decided
to follow the Jefferson Fork. Lewis went on ahead to check it out,
with Clark to follow shortly, watching for signs left by Lewis. At one
turnoff, Lewis marked the spot by placing some skins on the ground
indicating the direction to take. Additionally, Lewis left a note speared
on a newly broken willow branch placed in the ground. Lewis also
ordered one of his hunters, George Drouillard, to lag behind to reconnoiter and do some hunting.

Clark, following after, veered away from Lewis's path, for he did
not find the skins or the stick with the note on it. Happily, Clark did
come across Drouillard, who put the red-haired captain on the correct
trail. Clark also was worried about a hunter who had been sent to
look for game. He was George Shannon, the youngest member of the
expedition. The captain was piqued because the same lad had been
lost for fifteen days once before. Being lost twice would never do for
a member of the corps! A trumpet was sounded and shots were fired
to guide the young soldier to the camp but to no avail. As things
turned out, no rebuke was warranted for Shannon went up the correct
branch (that Clark had missed) and, aware of Clark's error, located
the party anyway. By so doing, he proved decisively that he had
become a full-fledged woodsman, equal to the best of the group.[24]

Meanwhile, although concerned about Clark's delay, Lewis decided not to wait any longer but to push ahead with his contingent
hoping to make Indian contact. Now on the west slopes of the continental divide, the group spotted one Indian on what Lewis covet-

ously described as an "elagant horse." Before the party could hail
him, however, the Indian fled, supposing the strangers to be enemies.
Disappointed with the near miss, Lewis and his men mused that
where there was one Indian, there were likely to be others.

Soon Lewis's party saw several more Indians. They were women.
This time, fearing that these Indians also would flee, they laid gifts
on the ground and then retired some distance. Timidly at first, then
more boldly, several approached and took the gifts. Lewis, still some
distance away shouted, "Tab-ba-bone," the Shoshone word for
"white man." (A slight mispronunciation would render the meaning
not as "white man," but as "stranger" or "alien." If the word was
mispronounced, it would explain the initial reluctance of the Indians
to approach the white men.) To back up the claim, for his face and
hands looked as dark as any red man's, the captain rolled up his
sleeves to show his white arms. More Indians gathered but, not fully
convinced, one, Cameawhait, who proved to be the chief, nevertheless cautiously came up to talk. Lewis identified himself as best he
could and said that shortly another white party would join them.
Lewis urged the chief to stay to meet this new party. Cameawhait
and his men grew increasingly nervous and reluctant, fearing that it
all was some ambush or devilish trick planned by the hated Blackfeet
who were out to slaughter the Shoshone. To reassure the chief and
as a sign of good faith, the captain presented the chief with the cocked
hat and overshirt he was wearing. Momentarily appeased, the chief
accompanied Lewis to where he was supposed to meet Clark. To the
consternation of both Indian and white man, Clark was not yet there.

The chief now was certain this was a trap. Lewis considered this
the moment to show supreme good faith; he gave the Indian his own
gun, telling the chief to use it if his enemies appeared instead of the
white men. Further, made bold by the desperation of his situation,
Lewis offered himself as the target if he spoke with a forked tongue.
For the success of the expedition, the Indian's trust and help was
crucial.

To Lewis's great relief, and no doubt to the relief of the Indians,
Clark and his outfit appeared. As evidence that fact often is stranger
than fiction, Sacajawea, who had been travelling with Clark's group,
now began to suck frantically on her fingers. She was telling the
Indians in sign language that they were her people, that she was
suckled by them. As she approached some of the women, she recognized one as a woman who had been kidnapped with her and had
escaped. Almost at the same moment, the other recognized Sacajawea
and the two fell into each other's arms, tears of joy streaming all the
while. As if this were not surprise enough, when Sacajawea was taken

into the council to serve as interpreter, she recognized the chief as her own brother! The emotions of all, red and white alike, overflowed as all went to celebrate their good fortune in the camp of the Shoshones.

United now and under the happiest of circumstances, the two captains tried to understand how they had missed signals so that any future rendezvous might be more timely. After talking things over, they surmised that panthers had taken the skins and a beaver had walked off with the green stick and its attached note. The captains agreed that they would never again use a green stick, as this proved to be a beaver delicacy.

Although the Shoshones had a reputation as hard traders and nothing was dearer to their hearts than horses, the return of Chief Cameawhait's sister induced them to provide Lewis and Clark with the needed horses. Many of the men in the expedition thought they were near the end of their journey, perhaps having no more than a hundred miles to go after easily crossing the continental divide at Lemhi. (MacKenzie had crossed the divide in less than a thousand steps. What the explorers did not know was that the divide is considerably closer to the Pacific at MacKenzie's crossing than at theirs.) Yet clearly they could not be so near the ocean, for then the Shoshone would have known white men before, because traders would surely have come short distances inland. Still, there were grounds for optimism, because the presence of salmon, a salt water fish, in the Indian camp bespoke the ocean. At least the Indians seemed to have contact with salt water fishermen. As facts turned out, salmon spawn far from the ocean in fresh water streams, and the corps had several mountain ranges to cross, including the mighty Bitterroot range. Indeed, the most arduous part of their journey still lay ahead. They had entered the Shoshone camp on August 11 and would not reach even the Columbia River for two long months.

In camp with the Indians for a week, Lewis observed his birthday. He was becoming reflective, a mood that would become more evident as the trip continued. Even his attitude toward the Indians and his own men seemed to undergo a subtle change. On his birthday, we find the following rather long passage:

This day I completed my thirty first year, and conceived that I had in all human probability now existed about half the period which I am to remain in this Sublunary world. I reflected that I had as yet done but little, very little, indeed, to further the hapiness of the human race, or to advance the information of the succeeding generation. I viewed with regret the many hours I have spent in indolence. . . . [I resolve in the] future, to redouble my exertions and at least endeavor to promote those two primary objects of human existence, by giving them the aid of that portion of talents which nature and fortune have bestoed on me; or in future, to live for mankind, as I have therefore lived for myself.[25]

With the party ready to move west again, Clark took some men to reconnoiter the Lemhi River to the Salmon River. Soon it was evident the Salmon was not the way to go; even today the Salmon's wildness earns it the name "river of no return." Realizing they needed a guide to lead them north out of the Bitterroots, they persuaded a reluctant Shoshone named Toby to accept the assignment, together with his four sons and one other Indian. The route they took, over a hundred miles north of the village, came to be known as the Lolo Trail. (This may have been named after a trapper called Lawrence, whose name was mispronounced by Indians.) The Bitterroots were well named for they provided the most bitter experiences for the expedition. Packhorses slid off cliff-hugging trails into yawning canyons. Crippled, they had to be dispatched and their packs tediously brought up the cliffs to be added to the already overburdened backs of other horses. The strenuousness of the crossing in the snow is well captured in John Clymer's painting "Lewis and Clark in the Bitterroots."

The original reluctance of Toby and his sons deepened as the hardships increased and two of the boys ran off to return to their people. Shortly thereafter Toby and the others did the same, leaving the expedition completely on its own. Sacajawea, however, remained with the expedition instead of staying with her people. Whether she did so freely is difficult to say, but evidence suggests she enjoyed the adventure, perhaps even insisting on continuing.

Making their way as best they could, they were confident that if the Indians could get through those mountains, the white man could do the same. Indeed, the success of the venture was as much a product of resolute will as of intelligence and planning. Never in the journals is there any indication of wavering at any time in the task at hand.

After some days, the corps found a new tribe of Indians, later to be known as the Flatheads (not because their heads were flat but rather because their identity was so indicated in sign language). The troops found the language of these newly met Indians absolutely incomprehensible. Luck was with the adventurers, however, as one of the Flathead lads knew the tongue of the Shoshone, so communication was possible after all. In order for the captains to renew their supplies, "the bargaining went like this: Clark would make an offer in English. Private LaBiche translated it to French. Charbonneau translated from French to Minitari. His wife, Sacajawea changed this to Shoshone, which the boy rendered in Flathead!"[26]

Successful in this most circuitous of bargaining, the company moved on to the Clearwater River, which flowed into the Snake River, which emptied into the final flow of the Columbia. Three times, the group mistakenly thought they had reached the Columbia, but they did not do so until October 16, 1805. The men rejoiced knowing that from here it would be downstream to their destination, the great Pacific Ocean.

More and different tribes of Indians were encountered now, among whom were the most destitute yet met. Of some, Lewis observed that their poverty of material possession was matched only by their paucity of morals. Although these small tribes occasionally killed an elk or deer, they subsisted largely on a diet of fish, particularly salmon and sturgeon.

Among these Indians were the Clatsop, Chinook, and Salish who mostly used only spears to procure the fish, occasionally putting out some few primitive fish traps called weirs. The Indians were astounded when they saw the white men employ nets, capturing in one drop some five hundred fish. The camps were as unkempt as their inhabitants and the journals record the disgust of the captains at such human misery. Joining the plague of mosquitoes, fleas abounded everywhere and infested everyone. It was the corps' first total encounter with this pestilence and spreader of disease and it was too much even for those hardy soldiers. To rid their garments of fleas, the men spread out their clothes on dying embers and watched with delight as the heat drove the fleas from their hiding places in the seams. Lewis and Clark reflected at length in the journals on such misery and offered abundant Enlightenment analysis of it.

The most common malady among these Indians was sore eyes, usually eventuating in blindness at an early age. Such blindness was so common that it was accepted as a part of life. The causes of the condition were several, one of which was the constant and irritating reflection of sunlight off the water where they made their daily living. (Unlike the Eskimo, they did not protect their eyes from the glare by using split goggles.) The heavy smoke pollution in their dwellings was another factor as was their habit of rubbing their eyes with serrated leaves of grass. Instead of providing relief, the rubbing cut the eyeballs and made them permanently blind.

Feeling great sympathy, Clark prepared an ointment that offered, if not a cure, at least considerable easing of discomfort. Here more than anywhere else, Clark won his reputation as a great medicine man, and sometimes his practices came as a welcome placebo. Clark often employed the sweatbath, the Plains Indians' treatment for nearly any malady, and with it worked a near miracle on one arthritic and crippled old Indian. Clark also was not beyond using magic to impress the natives with the white man's power, and he worked his magnetic compass for all it was worth.

Leaving this place of human degradation, the corps encountered Indians who exhibited metal trinkets on their bodies and who possessed some forged tools. These could only be gotten from white traders and the signs were most welcome, for they indicated to the explorers that their journey west was nearing its end. A final and convincing bit of evidence was the use by the Indians of a number of white man cuss words. This was the *pièce de resistànce*.

Rain became a near constant, but the discomfort it caused by soaking bed rolls, making steady sleep a near impossibility, was tempered by the observation that increasingly the river ebbed and flowed with the tides and the water became increasingly salty. To avoid tidal rises, the men were forced to bed down on rocks next to the river, in clothing thoroughly sodden from the rains. Their spirits remained high despite their misery as they knew they were reaching their western terminus. On November 7, 1805, Lewis declared in his journal, "Great joy in camp we are in *view* of the Ocian [actually the 'great bay of the river'] this great Pacific ocian which we been so long anxious to See."[27]

Now the men quickly constructed Fort Clatsop (restored as a national historic site located near present-day Astoria) to protect themselves from the coming winter. At all times the fort was run as a military post, with limited numbers of Indians allowed in during the day and turned out at night. Having come so far, the captains would not relax any vigilance that might endanger the mission. Life was confined and tedious at the post and food was scarce, the hunters travelling far and wide in search of the little game the forests contained. Often even these skilled woodsmen came back empty-handed to a disappointed fort.

Using Fort Clatsop as a base of operations, Lewis and Clark sent parties out on various excursions to learn of the environs. An interesting passage in the journals tells of a huge whale washed up on the shore some miles away. This event excited the normally placid Sacajawea and, despite the captains' protests, she insisted on going with a party of salt-makers to see the leviathan. It proved to be one of the high points of her journey. The men and Sacajawea returned with salt, and the troops rejoiced at getting this seasoning once again. (Interestingly, few western Indians used salt and were surprised that the white men would spoil their meat with it.)

The winter stay proved damp and uncomfortable, and many questioned the location of the fort. The constant storms and wind made even Clark lament, "O! how horrible is the day waves brakeing with great violence against the Shore throwing the water into our Camp, etc."[28] Yet they kept up their spirits, thinking of the coming spring departure and the journey home. On Christmas Day, all the men exchanged presents, but Clark noted, "we would have Spent this day the nativity of Christ in feasting, had we any thing either to raise our Sperits or even gratify our appetites, our Diner concisted of pore Elk Spoiled that we eate it thro' near necessity, Some Spoiled pounded fish and a fiew roots."[29]

The long wait for spring and return to civilization was spent in making preparations for the journey. New clothes were made and old ones mended, and equipment was carefully checked. There always remained the possibility that a ship might appear on the coast and return them home by sea, for there was some traffic along the shore. Indeed, one ship, the Lydia, did anchor briefly and its captain enquired of the Indians if they knew anything about the Corps of Discovery. The Indians told him the corps had already gone. Whether this was an outright lie or only a mistaken belief is hard to determine, but it surely must have been a disappointing moment when Lewis and Clark heard about it. They could have been saved a tough return trek of thirty-five hundred miles.

The advent of spring in the third week of March brought more wind and rain but did not discourage the troops who were waiting only for one day of decent weather to start back. Lewis reflected in his journal what must have been the thoughts of all: "Altho' we have not fared sumptuously this winter and spring at Fort Clatsop, we have lived quite as comfortably as we had any reason to expect we should; and have accomplished every object which induced our remaining at this place except that of meeting of travelers who visit the entrance of this river."[30]

Finally, on March 23 and with few regrets, the Corps of Discovery bid farewell to Fort Clatsop and headed for home, continuing to trade along the river. Here they encountered the most severe Indian attempts at thievery. The reason was clear; the red men surmised that the troops would not be back and thus what was pilfered now would bring no later retribution. The objects of theft were not only the expedition's axes, knives, guns, and utensils, but even Lewis's dog, Scannon. In a rather trying moment, Lewis ordered his men, if "insulted" by the Indians to put them to instant death; clearly, the leader's patience was wearing thin.

At last arriving at the junction where they must leave the river and travel by land, the need for horses became pre-eminent again. None was available here, but the captains knew that if they had beads to trade, these could be bartered for horses later. Seeking such beads they offered their canoes to the Indians, who, although very desirous of the craft, at first declined, believing they would inherit the canoes when the whites had to abandon them in their overland journey. To dash this hope, a soldier was ordered to chop up a canoe, thereby decisively indicating that none would be left in usable condition if a trade was not effected. The Indians quickly got the message and a bargain for beads was struck.

It might be supposed that the tired but successful expedition would make a beeline for home, but the conscientious captains would not have it so, desiring rather to accumulate more information. Hence, where they had previously crossed into the Beaverhead Valley, they split into three groups, each taking a different route to a rendezvous at the confluence of the Missouri and Yellowstone rivers, near present-day Fort Buford. One group was designated to go south, retracing the trail that brought them west. Clark, with Sacajawea in his company and aided by her knowledge of the local area, took a middle route that brought them to the Bozeman Pass and shortened considerably the distance required by travel over the Lolo Trail.

Lewis's party travelled again to the area of the great falls, unearthed the cache of supplies, then moved northward along the Marias River. The purpose was to determine if the river might prove a usable route in transporting furs from Canada down the Missouri.

For the first two of the separate groups, travel was without incident, but Lewis and his men were not so favored. Trespassing in Blackfeet country, the group was almost asking for trouble and it soon came. The Blackfeet had a reputation for fierceness and were the terror of the surrounding tribes. They had a weapons advantage over the other tribes: their contacts with the Hudson's Bay Company and the Northwest Fur Company had given them access to muskets (fuzzees) and the white man's superior firepower.

On July 27, 1806, Lewis's group was camped on the Marias when it spotted a small party of Blackfeet. Lewis did not know whether the Indians were an isolated party or the advance of a larger band, but he invited them to smoke and presented them with some flags and medals. The Indians repaid his good will with an attempt to pilfer a gun and run off with the expedition's horses. (On this occasion, Lewis had relaxed his guard, failing to post adequate sentries.)

Ruben Fields, one of two brothers on the expedition, caught one of the Blackfeet in the act of stealing the soldier's gun and, in the struggle to prevent this, stabbed the Indian to death. Lewis himself saw another Indian trying to steal a horse. Pursuing the thief, he ordered him to halt. When the man did not respond, the captain leveled his pistol and "at a distance of thirty steps shot him in the belly." Badly wounded, the Indian crawled behind a rock where several other red men had forted up. Despite the odds against him, Lewis wanted to follow the Indian, but in his haste to pursue, he had forgotten his bullet pouch and so was out of ammunition. It was Lewis's second act of carelessness. Perhaps Lewis was wearing down.

Turnabout being fair play, Lewis's men began to run off Indian ponies. Lewis himself returned to the Indian stabbed by Fields, the body still holding in its hand a flag of friendship given by Lewis and having around its neck one of the expedition's medals. Taking the flag in a gesture of defiance, Lewis left the medal on the Indian so "they might be informed who we were." This incident set the stage for what since has been an almost perpetual enmity between Blackfeet and Americans. This animosity was further inflamed when Americans began to trade guns to the Crows, enabling them to fight on more even terms with Blackfeet, their hereditary tribal enemies.

Worried that the small party of Indians, now scattered, might be the advance of a larger one, Lewis and his men quickly packed their horses and rode virtually nonstop sixty miles toward the Yellowstone meeting point. Taking only a short rest, they proceeded another thirty miles before feeling safe from pursuit.

The next trouble did not involve an external foe. On August 11, there occurred what Lewis suspected to be a case of an enlisted man wanting to shoot his captain. Lewis and the hunter, Cruzatte, both dressed in elk skin, went into the brush looking for deer or elk. Lewis saw an elk and fired on it; suddenly he felt a ball of lead pass through his own buttocks. Thinking he was shot by an Indian, he ran back to his group, where he soon learned that he had been shot by Cruzatte. The one-eyed hunter apparently had mistaken Lewis in elk garb for an elk, although Lewis had strong doubts about the excuse and apparently harbored resentment against Cruzatte from that time on. Although the captain's wound was painful, no artery or bone was hit. For some time, Lewis had to lie prone in the pirogue while they headed downstream to rendezvous with Clark.

Travelling down river now, Lewis's group met two Illinois trappers, Joseph Dixon and Forest Hancock, who were looking for beaver. They told of meeting Clark's party earlier, so Lewis knew he was not far behind his partner. Lewis gave the trappers additional supplies and went on to a joyous reunion with the others at the appointed confluence. Clark tended Lewis's wound, which already was on the mend, and together they moved downstream to the Mandan village country.

There, they were joined by the two Illinois trappers, who had decided they were too inexperienced to go farther north. The two had a proposition for John Colter, one of the expedition's hunters; they asked him to accompany them on their way north. Colter was tempted, and when they offered him a partnership in the enterprise because of his valuable knowledge about the beaver country ahead, he knew what he wanted to do. Colter petitioned to leave the expedition and, as he was the only one to do so, permission was granted. Colter headed back again to the high country wilderness with his new-found trapper friends.[31]

The rest of the group continued down river until they came to the Mandan village where they had wintered over a year and a half earlier. The captains asked the Mandans to send some chiefs with the expedition to meet President Jefferson and establish good relations between red men and white men. The Indians at first were sly and thought this a good opportunity to get rid of a few habitual troublemakers, but when the captains learned of this, the Indians gave up a reputable chief and some families more representative of the tribe.

Here at the Mandan village, Charbonneau, Sacajawea, and their boy, Toussaint Baptiste (Pomp), parted from the expedition, the translator/guide/trapper receiving between four and five hundred dollars for his services. Pomp now was sixteen months old and the darling of Clark, who offered to take the boy to St. Louis and adopt him. The Charbonneaus refused, but Clark invited them to visit him any time at his St. Louis residence.

Taking leave of the Mandan village, the corps continued down the Missouri, passing the house of the aging and nearly blind Daniel Boone, a symbol of how old generations must give way to the new. During the fourth week in September 1806, the party reached St. Louis, bringing to a successful end the more than two-year voyage of discovery. The city was taken by surprise, since no word had emerged from the deep wilderness since the support troops had returned over a year before and most of the citizens believed the corps members were lost or dead. After an enthusiastic celebration, the mundane activity of writing further reports to Jefferson and others commenced.

In retrospect, it is safe to say that: "Lewis and Clark established in the West the moral ascendancy over the Indian the French *coureurs des bois* once had enjoyed, and though this ascendancy would have periods of ebb and flow, depending on the character of the white men who went among the Indians, those who entered the West from this time on, down to and including the mountain men, could maintain themselves there and travel with immunity among the tribes to the extent that they shared the willingness of Lewis and Clark in the ultimate emergency to shoot the works whatever the cost."[32]

A gratified and generous Congress authorized double pay for all members of the expedition, additionally granting each 320 acres of land and giving a number of letters of commendation. Lewis and Clark each received $1,228 as well as land grants of 1,600 acres apiece.[33]

At the breakup of the expedition, the men went their various ways. Some remained in the army, others farmed the land they had received, even buying unwanted land from fellow corps members not interested in farming. One, Alexander Williard, lived to the ripe age of eighty-eight, dying near Sacramento, California.

Two of the most useful men of the expedition, Potts and Drouillard, returned to the high country and the trapping trade; both died at the hands of the Indians. The youth, Shannon, whom Lewis berated for getting lost, took up law, became a judge, and then a Kentucky senator. Sergeant Gass also made his mark in law, both as a judge and as a U.S. district attorney. He lived the longest of the group, dying at age ninety-nine on April 30, 1870.

A fascinating mystery surrounds the post-expedition history of York, Clark's inherited black body-servant slave. Contemporary scholarship investigating the puzzle of what happened to York affirms that York was not freed from slavery at the end of the expedition, as might have been expected given Clark's opposition to perpetual servitude.[34] Indeed, Clark already had freed another of his slaves, so one is left to wonder why York was not freed after two years of danger and service in the wilderness.

York remains a shadowy figure and was not even listed on the roster of expedition members sent to the secretary of war on January 15, 1807. Because he was a servant and of slave status, such recognition was not required. What is clear, however, is that although "nowhere in any of the journals, including Sergeant Gass's [who had an intense dislike for blacks], is there any derogatory remark made about him,"[35] some kind of falling-out must have occurred between Clark and York before 1811 and possibly even earlier.

York certainly remained a slave of Clark's for some years after the expedition, during which time he was reduced from the "highly favored status of body-servant to one of the lowest slave positions, a hired-out slave."[36] Sometime after 1808 he was freed by Clark. When the noted author Washington Irving visited Clark in 1832, he claimed that York no longer could cope with his freedom and came close to being a lazy bum. Irving says the former slave died in Tennessee, but others reported that he died while residing with the Crow Indians.

Clark, in an upward phase of his career, was appointed governor of the Missouri Territory and tendered the post of Indian Agent. He also was appointed brigadier general of the militia—not bad for a bogus captain! Having good political connections, Clark now was enticed into a fur company partnership with Manuel Lisa, a fascinating entrepreneur and pioneer in the western trade. Clark's office was

was a busy one, and the most pleasant of his duties was dealing with the Indians and trying to ameliorate their problems. Clark married a childhood friend, Julia Hancock, and named one of his children from that union Meriwether Lewis. After Julia's death, he married her cousin, Harriet Kennerly. Clark died in 1838, a well-respected and humane person.

Lewis was appointed governor of the Louisiana Territory but apparently the appointment ill-suited him, for he had increasing administrative, political, and personal problems. He knew that he probably would not be reappointed to the post and this contributed to the bouts of depression to which he seemed prone.

As he headed toward Washington in an attempt to clear up his difficulties, October 10, 1809, found him on the Natchez Trace in a heavy rainstorm that made travel extremely uncomfortable. He and his small entourage stopped at Grinder's Stand, a small settlement in Tennessee just south of the Duck River and east of the Tennessee River. The place contained a cabin in which Lewis slept and a barn where the men stayed. What happened next is not clear. "According to Mrs. Grinder, Lewis had a few drinks, talked to himself, then asked his men for a bearskin and buffalo robe and retired to his room. Shortly thereafter, she heard a pistol shot in his room and a heavy thud. Then there was another shot, and Lewis appeared at her door crying that he was wounded and asking for water."[37]

The landlady called his men and they found him with two wounds, one in his side, another in his head. The wounds proved fatal and Lewis died at age thirty-five. Some suggest he was the victim of a robbery attempt, which certainly was possible at that time along the Trace. However, the official declaration was that Lewis committed suicide, and that most likely is the truth of the matter. He was buried in Tennessee and is remembered not for the circumstances of his death but for his life of duty, leadership, and love of country.

2. The Mountain Men

To Risk a Skin for a Skin

Some lived into their late seventies, dying in bed with a roof over their heads; others met their end on the arid and inhospitable high plains in the very bloom of life. They all belonged to the exclusive genre of *voyageurs*, whether they were hunters or explorer-entrepreneurs or boatmen paddling a pirogue or bateau into the unknown wilderness. Yet within this genre of voyageurs, one group knew themselves as the elite. They were the mountain men who plied their trade under the terse motto *Pro pelle cutem*, to risk one's skin for a skin! This was the official motto of the Hudson's Bay Company, but it applied to mountain men-trappers everywhere.

Although towns and lakes and forests were named after these trappers, the trappers themselves are little remembered today. Nonetheless, their feats were bigger than life and their legends are at the heart of the folklore of the American West. They not only trapped and explored but acted as guides for armies, missionary groups, and emigrants. They helped the United States government establish territorial claims by assisting topographers and cartographers. They were the American demigods whose travels and travails made them the New World counterpart of the Homeric Odysseus. They were the forerunners of a nation changing stride, moving from the birthpangs of the "Spirit of '76" to the adolescent messianism of "Manifest Destiny."

What brought them to the mountains was *Castor canadensis*, commonly known as the beaver. For three hundred years, long before the Lewis and Clark expedition, beaver hats had been in vogue among both army troops and style-conscious civilians. As Europe had long since run out of beaver, the demands for pelts were considerable. By 1800, one hundred thousand skins a year were needed to keep up with demand. Great fur companies such as the Hudson's Bay Company, the Missouri Fur Company, the Nor'westers, Astor's American Fur Company, and the Rocky Mountain Fur Company sprang into existence to profit from, if not to capture, the trade.

Although the fur pelts of other animals also were sought, the beaver "plus," that is, prime pelt, was the most desired. It long was the standard unit of currency and fetched in trade the hides of three martens, or one fox, or one moose, or two deerskins.[1] Hudson's Bay Company even issued various denominations of wooden coins imprinted with their value in beaver pelts; they were good in trade at most fur posts.

A profitable sideline of the beaver market was the castoreum, drawn from the sex glands of the animal, both male and female. The castoreum had long been regarded as a cure-all for colic, epilepsy, frostbite, and hysteria. Interestingly, modern chemical analysis shows that it contains salicylic acid, a main ingredient of aspirin. Today the chief use of castoreum is as a perfume base.

The beaver was sought along the banks of the rivers, slow-running streams, and flooded meadows where it lived.[2] The flooded meadows, as is well known, were its own work. An industrious pair of beavers might build up to six dams in a single summer. Their techniques included wedging a line of sticks in a stream bed to collect debris; they would then weave in other material and plaster it all with mud. They could carry the mud in their forepaws, a feat only recently photographed. They could cut down three-inch aspen trees (a favorite food, along with the sweet cottonwood) in less than a minute. In time, they dropped trees as large as two and a half feet in diameter across a stream. They needed no special instinct to do this—the branches naturally grew toward the open sky over the water and this weight would drag the trunk down in that direction.

The beavers' throats were protected from woodchips and splinters by flaps of skin behind their ever-growing, self-sharpening incisors. Blood vessels dilated to seal their lungs during the quarter-hour they could spend underwater. The stocky animals weighed between thirty and seventy pounds. They never stopped growing, however, and some were as large as a hundred pounds. Their large flat tails, slapped against the water, made a danger signal audible for a half-mile; the tails were sought by trappers as a great gastronomical delicacy.

Indians caught beaver by tearing open the tops of the domed lodges built in the still water behind the dams and spearing any animals that had not fled through the underwater exits; in winter, the Indians chopped through pond ice and set nets. These methods provided food and pelts but not in quantities that would satisfy the white men. To turn beavers into fortunes, traps were needed.

Walking downstream some distance above the lodge and being careful to leave no human scent, the trapper would bait the end of a stick with a mixture of castoreum and oil of juniper or camphor gum carried in a flask on his belt. A small amount of the strong-smelling stuff was enough. The stick was set into the bank like a fishing pole and, directly beneath, a pan trap was placed on the stream bottom. The chain attached to the trap was staked down in deep water away from the bank.

Approaching from underwater to investigate the scent of a strange beaver in its territory, the quarry would step on the pan of the trap and be caught by the spring action of the jaws. In danger, the beaver would retreat to the deepest part of the stream where, unable to free itself, it would drown. The benefit to the trapper was that the beaver carcass was hidden from predators who might eat it on land and that the hide was preserved from deteriorating. On occasion, a neophyte might not anchor the trap's chain in water sufficiently deep. The beaver would then remain alive, often gnaw off the pinioned leg, and escape, crippled but still functional.

The halcyon days of early nineteenth century beaver trapping were few and beaver themselves quickly became scarce. One reason for this was the unrestrained trapping, which made poor men rich. Another was the effort of British interests to wipe out beaver in the Northwest so that the disputed Oregon Territory would not be so eagerly claimed by the United States. A third and decisive reason was the introduction of the silk hat in the western world in the mid-1840s. This stylistic change sounded the final death knell for the beaver trade.[3]

But who were these men of the woods and mountains, these gods about whom so much lore and legend have been written? Why should we be interested in these *coureurs de bois* who sought the soft gold for only three or four decades nearly a century and a half ago?

The answer is quite simple: we cannot know who we are as Americans unless we are familiar with our roots. In our age of mediocrity and half effort, it is important to see that America was not always so and need not continue to be so. It makes scant difference to us whether we are newly arrived boat people or whether our ancestors' pedigrees date back to the Mayflower. It is a sad commentary that we need to be reminded that, despite our commonality with much of the rest of the world, there is an *esprit* and a uniqueness that we share as Americans. As the philosopher George Santayana put it so well, "To be American is of itself almost a moral condition, an education, and a career." It is to have "the right stuff!"

Every nation needs an awareness of its mythic roots and its archetypal heroes from which it can draw its strength and sense of continuing identity as a people. Greece had its Olympian gods, England its heraldic kings, Egypt its pharaohs, and Israel its biblical patriarchs. America had no such gods or royalty but, at various times, different persons have filled that role, and it was one given to the mountain men from 1800 to 1850.

The terms *archetypal* and *mythic* may seem nonempirical and to have only a poetic resonance about them, so perhaps I should clarify my meaning. By archetypal, I refer to a prototype or model. By mythic, I do not mean fairy tale but something closer to the Greek sense of *mythos*, a kind of flexible vehicle or story containing a fundamental truth. In this sense, the mythic is always symbolic, but it is not less than real; in some ways it is more than real, for it is at the heart of everything that is vitally human. Fundamentally, we are symbolic beings who live in a combination of myth and history. A dialectic obtains between them, for myth always is seeking to become history and history always is seeking to become myth. Facts quickly pass; symbols endure. Meaning, as symbolic, has shades of vagueness that call for continual interpretation; hence, symbols renew themselves differently in different generations.

An example or two may be helpful. The mythic George Washington—the George Washington who lives in the hearts of his countrymen—is more important to us today than the historical figure who lived in 1776. It is his spirit that is alive and continues to be life-giving to Americans. Many Christian theologians make the same point about the Jesus of history and the mythical Christ of the believing community. It is the Christ in which the community believed (and to some extent itself reproduced) that has primary import today. Whether we speak of Washington, Christ, Robin Hood, Joaquin Murietta, Harriet Tubman, or any other inspiring person, we must realize that while there is a historical base for each, that person is for us today essentially and exactly what we have made of them. Nothing important is lost in this and much is gained. This is why we need to study folklore as well as fact, for folklore stands as its own type of fact, and a mighty one at that. The West offers life-sustaining spirit to the rest of the country, indeed, to much of the world that is fascinated with its history and geography. This American West offers a spirit of raw vitality, of largess, of magnificence in its great shining mountains, its stark deserts, its windy high plains, and, above all, its big sky.

The West and its heroes, then, have played important roles in the American Dream. To know the West we must understand those who contributed to it. Permit me to press a bit further this connection between dream and vision, myth and symbol. As Willa Cather, author of *Death Comes for the Archbishop*, put it, the West, like America itself, was dreamed into reality. Visionaries dreamed cities, dreamed a railroad, and dreamed a united nation. Ultimately the dream produced reality itself and that reality in turn became another dream—in the case of our nation, and in our mythic consciousness, the American Dream.

Carl Jung, the Swiss psychiatrist and exponent of unconscious archetypes, also argued that a dream is a living myth and a myth is a living dream. The importance of the two is that they both have strong power to transform our own character.

Dreams and myths do not make reality less real. If anything, they make it more real and more than real, for the real lasts but a moment, whereas myths, dreams, and visions endure through generations. Any true feeling for the West has always partaken of both dream and reality. Walt Whitman attested to this when he visited the great prairies of the West and declared himself impressed by "that vast Something, stretching out its own unbounded side, unconfined which there is in these prairies, combining the real and the ideal, and beautiful as dreams."[4]

As a country coming to be in the era of the mountain men, America's truth had the stamp of the American character. Its truth was not something ready-made, waiting to be plucked by some speculative mind. This was the "truth" of the Old World mentality. America's truth was a truth in the making and essentially *in* the making, for its truth was a consequence of the dialectical interplay of man and nature rather than some *a priori* verity. Things were not true in and of themselves but became true through our interaction with them. This position later was articulated by John Dewey and William James, both thoroughly American and thoroughly philosophers.

Given such a perspective, the nature, yes, the very construction of truth largely depended on the kinds of materials put into it. In part, at least, the truth for this period of America lay in the ingredients of the mountain men themselves—in their courage, their resourcefulness, their persistence, and their will to survive, and more than to survive, to endure and eventually to prevail.

Perhaps we can get a better feel for this period of American history if we look at a bit of the gestalt background against which it took place. America was moving, flexing its muscles and coming into its own, the rising star of the New World, a grand experiment. America presented the first opportunity for mankind to start from zero, because the established civilized world, although it might attempt to modify its structures, could never completely free itself from its longstanding cultural presuppositions. In truth, America was a new world in every sense of the term and the Old World was caught up in its excitement, despite being thousands of miles removed, although in ensuing years it did not stay removed. Thousands of newcomers participated actively in the American venture; royalty, noblemen, and commoners came to find out what a new world was like, participating in its making and falling in love with what they saw.

Tocqueville and others reported and supported what was going on. European romanticism found a new home, and artists like Alfred Jacob Miller, Thomas Moran, Albert Bierstadt, Karl Bodmer, and George Catlin (and later Remington and Russell) kept the spirit of idealism alive.

In religion and philosophy, transcendentalism supplanted the Deism of the early founding fathers. (Deism maintained that although God created the world, he had left it to take care of itself. Providence and divine government no longer ruled man's world, for man had come of age and now could govern himself.) In transcendentalism, God was a kind of oversoul, a part of cosmic unity, Whitman's "vast something." He was present to all men, not as a personal, providential, and loving God, but as a kind of inner spirit. Not through the intellect but rather by a gut feeling, aided by imagination and intuition, did one come to realize this sense of the "lower case" divine. Close to a *deus ex machina*, God was brought in at man's will to service whatever needs arose, and this outlook fit exceedingly well the notion of a grass roots democracy. Emerson, Thoreau, Whitman, and many others pushed its cause. Read Whitman's *Leaves of Grass* and there you will find extolled the simple, humble, and, above all, natural life. Belief in the common man was the center around which this country was built. As Whitman claims, "Our American superiority and vitality are in the bulk of people, not in a gentry like the old world. Other lands have their vitality in a few, a class, but we have it in the bulk of the people. . . . the average of the people is immense."[5] This notion sat well with a nation that boasted increasingly of its democracy and self-reliance.

Within the period, then, the mountain men partook of a larger movement whose intentionality they carried and transmitted but which they only dimly perceived. They were like a young boy seeing a neighborhood girl and feeling for the first time some strange and wondrous stirrings. He is dimly aware of these, but has scant notions about their cause or implications. It was the rise of Spirit (*Geist*) in history, and now it was America's turn to play a starring role in the theatre of change.

The first sign of growth within what is now the territory of the United States was the birth of the great fur companies. The American enterprises followed the lead of the venerable Hudson's Bay Company[6] and the Nor'westers,[7] both governed by European interests. Our own efforts were prompted by the opening of the West through the Louisiana Purchase. Its vast and uncharted reaches offered immense trapping possibilities.[8]

In 1807, the mysterious, almost furtive, Manuel Lisa of St. Louis established a fur post and fort at the confluence of the Yellowstone and Bighorn rivers, on the edge of the notorious country of the Blackfeet. (Some of his employees were ex-Lewis and Clark men.) In 1809, together with William Clark, Andrew Henry, and Pierre Chouteau, Lisa established the Missouri Fur Company.

In 1811, John Jacob Astor, whose ships traded from New York to the Orient, established the American Fur Company, the Columbia branch of which was known as the Pacific Fur Company. The companies were immortalized in a book, *Astoria*, by no less distinguished a writer than Washington Irving, already well-known in Europe for his short stories "Rip Van Winkle," "The Legend of Sleepy Hollow," and others. Irving was a personal friend of Astor, and his writings are a primary source of the fur trade movement. Irving's *The Adventures of Captain Bonneville*, about an army officer on leave to establish a trading post in Wyoming, is another classic study of this era.

Astor launched expeditions to establish his company on the Columbia River. One group went overland and the other by ship around the Horn. The story of the first group is one of the most fascinating and heart-wrenching in the annals of the fur trade. The trek was headed by Wilson Price Hunt, a 27-year-old American. Other principal members of this expedition were Alexander McKay (sometimes spelled McKae), who earlier accompanied Mackenzie on the crossing of the continental divide and who had been an employee of the Nor'westers, along with Ramsey Crooks and David Stuart. (Stuart's nephew, Robert Stuart, would make the ocean voyage.) Each of the principals was given five of the one hundred shares financing the enterprise, Astor controlling fifty shares. They were accompanied by French *éngages*.

Near the Wyoming-Idaho borders, the group could find little food, so they split into two smaller parties headed by Hunt and Crooks. At times, the men were forced to eat their own leather garments and to drink their own urine. Chowder was made by scouring the river banks for dried fish bones and pounding them into a powder that was mixed with water. Each going its own way, neither party found a way to cross the mountains but, incredibly, they met each other by chance on opposite sides of a river. They reunited and found an Indian village that gave them food and supplies. They split up again, the two groups finally reaching Astoria, one in January 1812, the other in May. Seven stragglers from one group came to the post nearly a year later.

The journey by sea was no less adventuresome. After a seven-month voyage around the horn, the ship, named the *Tonquin*, arrived at newly established Astoria in 1811. The dangers of the trip had only begun, however. As a small boat was launched in the treacherous estuary of the Columbia, eight men were lost by drowning. Then the ship, rather than waste time waiting for the rest of the overland group to arrive, sailed north for trading. While at Nooka, it was boarded by Indians who became hostile and massacred the white men. One sailor, undiscovered, in a final act of desperation and defiance, managed to blow up the ship, killing himself and the Indians aboard. All the weapons and supplies for Astoria were lost. Astor sent a second supply ship, the *Lark*, but it too met disaster, shipwreck in the Hawaiian Islands. A third vessel, the *Beaver*, finally arrived. Hunt boarded it and travelled north to trade with the Russians. He obtained seal pelts, a precious commodity the world over, and went to Hawaii with his cargo. There he disembarked while the *Beaver* made the usual run to Canton, China, picking him up on the way back. This indeed was world trade!

Meanwhile the Astorians started to build distant forts in the Northwest for trading purposes. One of the men, John Clark, established a post at Spokane, where he boastfully showed Indians two silver goblets, saying that only important chiefs used them. The Indians promptly stole the silver. Clark held the entire Indian village responsible and, when the thief who stole them was discovered, had him hanged as an example of Astorian summary justice. Understandably, the Indians were angered rather than subdued. Had the Astorians followed the example of the Hudson's Bay Company in dealing with the Indians, they would have fared better.

When news of the War of 1812 reached the Astorians, it was clear that, with Britain fighting the United States, they could not hope to retain their foothold at the mouth of the Columbia. The surrounding British were too powerful and had a warship waiting nearby. Accordingly, Astor's men sold the post to the Nor'westers for fifty-eight thousand dollars, of which fourteen thousand was back pay for the employees. Those who had come to Astoria overland now prepared for the trek home. Although their mission so far had been ill-fated, nonetheless valuable lessons were learned and Astor was to grow rich from the education.

In one of the great missed opportunities of history, the returning men followed east what later was to become the Oregon Trail, and never realized that they had found the long-sought way through the mountains. The Astorians travelled over South Pass in Fremont County, Wyoming, a saddle in the mountains slightly over seven thousand feet in altitude. The crossing was so easy that only the change in direction of the water flow gave evidence that the divide had been conquered. Knowledge of this pass would enable settlers in wagon trains to come to the Oregon country. Other routes to Oregon were through tortuous passes where only horses and mules but not wagons could go. (Recall the difficulties of Lewis and Clark in the Bitterroots.) When South Pass became known, civilization quickly rushed to the Northwest, for the nation was eager to establish itself there. But no one took notice of its discovery, and it remained unknown to the whites until 1824, twelve years after the Astorians had crossed it from west to east. The mountain man Jedediah Smith is credited with its "effective discovery," and he learned of it from the Indians who lived thereabout.

The fur trade developed rapidly now, taking off on its thirty-year trajectory. The year 1821 witnessed the inauguration of a new firm that was to change old ways of doing business. It was the firm of General William Ashley and Major William Henry. Ashley was a first-class entrepreneur who had been highly prominent in Missouri politics with a commission from the militia. Henry had been active in the fur trade and had worked with Ashley for a while in an enterprise that produced lead and powder in Missouri mines during the War of 1812. The firm entered the fur trade competition with the oft-quoted advertisement:

TO ENTERPRISING YOUNG MEN

The subscriber wishes to engage ONE HUNDRED MEN, to ascend the river Missouri of its source, there to be employed for one, two or three years. For particulars enquire of Major Andrew Henry near the Lead Mines, in the County of Washington, (who will ascend with, and command the party) or to the subscriber at St. Louis.

WM. H. ASHLEY

Few applicants knew what they might be getting into. On the way up the Missouri, thirteen of the Ashley-Henry men were killed and nine wounded. The up-river trip now was dangerous, for the Arickara (who had been peaceful enough with Lewis and Clark) now wanted to control all passage up stream and imposed fees for transit. And beyond the Arickara waited the Blackfeet. The fur traders would not give in to blackmail, and this effectively closed for some time the Missouri River to the trade. This was indeed a serious blow to the entrepreneurs, for while some of the furs were taken by white men's traps, many were procured by trade with the Indians. Indeed, as far back as 1802, Congress had forbidden whites to trap in Indian lands. Congress also required that licenses be issued to whites engaged in bartering so that the august legislative body would know what was going on in the West. The intent was good, but the law was not rigorously enforced.

Another law ineffectively enforced was the prohibition of whiskey in Indian trade. One way of getting around this prohibition was to carry whiskey (sometimes pure alcohol) for the *éngages*, who were legally entitled to it. Then, in the wilderness, it was diluted and used for barter. For a time, some of the forts on the upper Missouri, far from the reach of regular government inspection, had their own stills and produced alcohol in volume. Knowing alcohol's debilitating effect on Indians and on the fur trade itself, the Hudson's Bay Company tried long and hard not to trade in whiskey but eventually had to accommodate itself to the competition. (We now know that Indians are highly susceptible to alcohol because their bodies differ in enzyme makeup from those of whites.)

The whites really did not want to trade for Indian-caught beaver skins; they wanted to trap the beaver themselves, as they were unhappy with the careless manner in which Indians dressed the pelts. Often the red man damaged a good hide, making it virtually worthless on the market. Until taught otherwise, Indians frequently slit the hide along the upper backbone rather than at the belly bottom.

For a number of reasons enmity was growing between the Indians (especially the Arikara) and whites. Ashley called in the army under the command of Colonel Leavenworth to undo the river blockade, but the affair was a fiasco. Ashley never forgave what he regarded as the ineptness and indecision of the colonel.

But, Ashley's genius finessed the problem of going upstream by choosing to move overland for beaver. This developed into the famous fur trade rendezvous system that held sway from 1825 to 1840. Essentially, the system set up meeting places in the far West at which trappers, Indians, and fur companies all would converge for their mutual benefit. The system made it unnecessary for trappers to come out of the wilds each year, thereby saving everyone time and effort. The rendezvous enabled the trappers to remain in the mountains as long as they liked. The trading caravans often were made of former trappers who wanted to experience the other end of their business, and many of the most famous mountain men played both roles simultaneously—Jim Bridger, the Sublette brothers, Andrew Henry, Jedediah Smith, and others.

The first rendezvous took place in 1825 on Henry's Fork of the Green River in northeastern Utah. Such meetings generally were scheduled for early summer, the mountain man's leisure period, when beavers were molting and their pelts not worth taking. The timing of the meetings also was dictated by the flow of western rivers, with the mountain spring runoff just reaching the plains waterways.

The full rivers allowed the companies to float their fur packs downstream in a quicker, safer, and less laborious way than if they proceeded by pack mule. The Platte River, with its two forks near the border of Colorado and Nebraska, was one such river that demanded an early float, for by midsummer, as one Westerner described it, the stream was "a mile wide, an inch deep, too thin to plow, and too thick to drink."

In addition to rendezvous sites chosen along the Green River (called by Indians the Siskadee or Sagehen River) and its many beaver-rich tributaries, other places were selected.[9] Among these were the Popo Agie in the valley just south of the massive Wind River range, which more or less constitutes the eastern border of present-day Grand Teton National Park. Another favorite meeting place was the sheltered Pierre's Hole in Idaho, near present-day Driggs, just west of the Tetons. The fame of this site was established by the Battle of Pierre's Hole at the 1832 rendezvous, in which a number of trappers and Indians were wounded and killed.[10]

The agreed-upon place for rendezvous was determined a year in advance. The meetings provided an opportunity for mountain-bound trappers and Indians alike to get rid of "tipi fever" and to let off steam. The rendezvous was a major social occasion featuring trading, gouging, shooting matches, horse and mule racing, gambling of different sorts, and general debauchery.[11]

Although the first rendezvous formally lasted but a day, Ashley went to great lengths to assure its success. His representatives preceded him and stayed on after the trade day itself. The affair was a true Bacchanal and most trappers were broke and in debt to the company before they returned to their trade. It was not an "easy come" but it was an "easy go." Even this early in the history of our country, the trappers and Indians were caught in a company store credit system, often with disastrous results.

Frequently the company made more profits by selling goods to the trappers than by selling the beaver pelts back in St. Louis. Although prices for merchandise varied at each rendezvous and even in different transactions at the same meeting, figures from the 1825 meeting give an idea of the costs. Beaver pelts brought around $3 a pound, but sugar and coffee sold for $1.50 a pound. Fishhooks went for $1.50 a dozen. Tobacco commanded a price of $3 a pound, lead $1, and powder $2. Blue bolts of cloth sold for $5 and scarlet for $6 a yard. Ashley made a profit of between forty and fifty thousand dollars from this first rendezvous.[12]

Having made one fortune, Ashley staged another rendezvous in 1826 and made a second killing. Thereupon he sold his enterprise to Smith, Jackson, and Sublette, who eventually formed a new company, the Rocky Mountain Fur Company. Later partners in this company were such colorful characters and sterling mountain men as Jim Bridger and Tom Fitzpatrick. A number of other companies involved in the fur trade, including Astor's American Fur Company, only played further variations on the established theme.

What was the makeup of those men who worked the traps and risked a skin for a skin and from where did they come? They were Scots, French, British, Canadians, Spanish, and Americans. A number were blacks, mixtures of black and white, and further mixtures of red and white. To facilitate trade, many intermarried with the Indians, the same man often having different wives in different tribes. This could prove expensive, for there was an adage that when one married an Indian, one married the whole tribe. Interestingly (as is sensitively brought out in Michener's *Centennial*), what began as a marriage of convenience frequently turned into a deep and meaningful relationship. The trappers, whatever the color of their skin, were accepted by the Indian culture, in contrast to the nonacceptance of the Indian by the white culture. A good example of this was the ready welcome of York, Captain Clark's black servant in the Corps of Discovery. Another was the title of Crow chieftain given the black mountain man Jim Beckwourth. Similarly Edward Rose, of black and white parentage, was highly respected by Indian and white alike.

But whether or not the mountain man married into the tribe, he took on Indian ways, including the Indian view of life. He knew that in the beginning he was only a pupil of the wilderness with the Indian as the master. One of the greatest compliments one could pay a mountain man is the title of a sketch by Remington of two trappers meeting in the mountains, the one exclaiming, "I mistook ye fur an Indian!"

Like the Indian, they scalped, smoked *kinnikinic* (a kind of red willow bark), and would gorge sumptuously on dog, beaver tail, marrow bones, and buffalo tongue and hump. Their favorite food was the boudins, part of a buffalo's intestine with its contents of half-digested food. Two trappers would stretch out the intestines and, starting at the middle in a kind of pinching action, squeeze the contents into their mouths, much as youngsters might do with a straw containing the last dregs of a malted milk shake. Very likely the trappers and the youngsters acted with the same gusto and satisfaction.

But when food was scarce, they learned to live on blood taken from their own mules. They learned, as did Lewis and Clark, to search creeks for fish bones that could be powdered and used to make a nourishing chowder. They ate the inner bark of the Ponderosa pine and drank its sap. They even ate their own leather clothes. To survive, they did whatever they had to do.

All in all, the mountain man was a man of excess. His excesses were a way to practice one-upmanship over the Indian. In drunkenness, revelry, fighting, cheating, gambling, shooting, trapping, and living off the land, he learned to out-Indian the Indian.

Like the Indian, though, the mountain man saw life as a single fabric that combined the sacred and the profane or, as the Swiss psychiatrist Carl Jung (a great student of the American Indian culture) put it, the dream and the waking state, the intellect and the imagination. This is perhaps why many of their stories seem outlandish to us and were called "tall tales" by contemporaries. We will examine some of these accounts when we come to Jim Bridger.

The speech of the mountain men was the patois of the area— French, Spanish, Indian, and American. They added to it new corruptions such as *foofawraw* (trinkets, earrings, beading, anything that might prove attractive to an Indian woman), *booshway* (for boss or *bourgeois*), *sack of possibles* (basic equipment carried on a trapping venture), and *topknot* (scalp).

The colloquialisms so abounded as to require translation. For example: "Well hos! I'll dock off buffler, and then, if thar's any meat that 'runs' that can take the shine outen 'dog,' you can slide." (Translation: Well friend, I'll [take exception to] buffalo, and then if there's any meat afoot that surpasses dog, you're crazy.)[13]

Some of the mountain men were members of a virtually preliterate society, knowing neither how to read nor to write. Jim Bridger, for example, who like Kit Carson was a later chief of scouts for the United States Army, could only make an X for his name. Carson himself was little improvement, for his greater literary ability consisted exclusively in writing his name. (He did eventually learn the basics of reading and writing—after the age of fifty.) But like members of societies having only an oral tradition, the illiterate mountain man could expertly memorize long passages read by others, even from Shakespeare and the Bible. However illiterate some were, they all "read sign"— nature's story—in flowing narrative.

In addition, mountain men were familiar with the sign language of the Plains Indians, itself a kind of lingua franca. For example, a slashing motion across the arm signified the Cheyenne, noted for mutilating the arms of their victims. The same motion across the throat indicated the Sioux, for a similar reason. (The Sioux, who called themselves "friends" or "allies," were given the name Sioux, "cutthroat," by their Ojibway/Chippewa enemies. The name stuck.) A quick waving of the hand back and forth, sometimes in a pumping motion, was a question of who, what, when, how, and where. Making a constant circle above the forehead with a finger indicated craziness, while two index fingers cocked at each side of the head signified buffalo. A waving motion of the hand could be either a snake or the Shoshone tribe or a fish, depending on the context. Communication by this means was almost as effective as the fully developed language of the deaf.

Captain Stansbury, who in 1850 asked Jim Bridger for advice on a route that later was to become part of the Union Pacific Railway path, tells of the mountain man having a conference with some Sioux and Cheyenne: "Bridger held the whole circle, for more than an hour, perfectly enchanted and evidently most deeply interested in a conversation and narrative, the whole of which was carried on without the utterance of a single word . . . exclamations of surprise and interest, and the occasional laughter, showed that the whole party perfectly understood."[14]

Many of the mountain men, of course, were well educated by any standard and frequently kept detailed and useful journals and maps. This was particularly true of Alexander Mackenzie (who, in 1793, was the first man to cross the North American continent north of Mexico), Lewis and Clark, Jedediah Smith of the Rocky Mountain Fur Company, Captain Bonneville, and Osborne Russell. (The latter was with Nathaniel Wyeth, the New England ice dealer and mountain newcomer who wanted to make a fortune in furs and Pacific salmon but was outwitted by the more experienced mountain men.)

Educated or not, the mountain man carried a certain mystique and was viewed at this end of the age of romanticism as a Charlemagnean paladin. But one of their own, Nathaniel Wyeth, characterized the mountain men simply as "a majority of scoundrels." Whatever the extremes, let it be said that "of all the frontier images, the probably least twisted by the passage of time and the subtle metamorphosis of rosy rearward vision is that of the mountain man."[15] He dominated the Western scene during his short span of prominence, 1810 to 1845. Without question, he was the most genuine folk hero and archetype of the American West because he was real and his exploits were real and few were unable to identify with him. Nevertheless, many years passed before literature and scholarship devoted attention to the mountain man and his times. Although there were some classic studies, like Chittenden's *The American Fur Trade of the Far West*, not until the 1920s were the mountain men and their sphere of influence rediscovered.

Curiously, it was the early painters (in an age before photography) who celebrated the mountain man as a perfect expression of man dominating the wilderness yet living in harmony with it. Among them were Alfred Jacob Miller, Albert Bierstadt, and George Catlin. They knew the mountain men at first hand and faithfully recorded them, while a generation later other artists continued this romance with the image of the mountain man. The paintings of William Ranney, Frederic Remington, and Charlie Russell capture the same authenticity.

As Donald Pike puts it, "At the core of each painting is the mountain man, finite and recognizable, living a life so simple in form, so exciting to contemplate, and yet so hard in its consequences as to need no fictional embellishment."[16] Indeed, the artist in painting the mountain man communicated more than an individual likeness: the artist presented the universal archetype. He reflected "the self-image of a nation growing up proud of its roots, often awed by its accomplishments even occasionally appalled by individual actions, but inevitably pleased with sharing its heritage. [The mountain man] emerges as a strong, self-reliant character, calm in repose, awesome in his potential for violence, and entirely at home in the wilderness."[17]

Now let us focus in on a few representative American mountain men, if only in vignette, in order to understand how and why they might be regarded as demigods, a breed apart from ordinary mortals.

The saga of the Western mountain man begins with John Colter, a hunter-scout who was a member of the Lewis and Clark Expedition. Colter was born around 1775, probably in Virginia, possibly in Pennsylvania. An accomplished woodsman almost six feet in height, he was recruited by Meriwether Lewis when Lewis was in the East making arrangements for the transcontinental trek. Colter joined the expedition on October 15, 1803, as a private and at all times was a testimony to Lewis's skill as a judge of men. Unfortunately, Colter kept no journals, and little biographical information about him is known. Merrill Mattes, a regional historian for the National Park Service, describes him as a "phantom explorer" and "the American Ulysses."[18] The western writer Aaron Stevens observes, "The Colter story is a collection of scattered facts, secondhand accounts, and a considerable amount of legend, crossing the years 1804-1810."[19] Nonetheless, there is enough evidence to portray his abilities as a mountain man.

Basically, Colter was a reliable loner, often serving as advance scout of the group to which he was attached. An expert hunter, muscular and with great endurance, he also had a feel for the land. He could find the main channel on the rivers and judge where the mountain passes might be. He was the first of the Lewis and Clark men to return to the mountains. As the expedition was about to begin its final descent of the Missouri toward an unsuspecting St. Louis, Colter joined forces with two Illinois trappers and headed back into the Yellowstone country. He spent the winter of 1806 with the two neophyte trappers, most probably on the northwest fringes of the upper

Yellowstone River, but nothing certain is known about his sojourn with the Illinois adventurers.

In spring 1807, Colter started canoeing down the Missouri to return to civilization at last, but changed his mind again. This time he encountered Manuel Lisa's newly organized company of trappers coming upstream. Recognizing the value of Colter's experience and information about the area to which they were headed, they, too, persuaded him to join them and return to the mountains. Colter helped to set up Fort Raymond (Manuel's Fort) on the confluence of the Bighorn and Yellowstone rivers. Anxious to establish trading ties with the various Indian tribes and to learn more about the geography of the remote country and its potential for beaver treasures, Lisa sent Colter out alone on one of the most remarkable odysseys in all recorded history. Drawing on accounts of a conversation of Henry Brackenridge with Manuel Lisa, Stevens describes Colter's journey:

In the dead of winter, alone with a thirty-pound pack, snowshoes, a gun and ammunition, this man moved off the boundaries of all existing maps and into the unknown of some of America's most rugged wilderness. His exact course is unknown, but he probably traveled a circuitous route for upwards of five hundred miles. The place names through which he passed still identify today with the great sweeps of wild free country. He was the first white to travel the upper valley of the Bighorn, first to walk the Wind River Range, first to see the Tetons and to enter Jackson Hole, first to see the headwaters of the Snake, and first to see the wonders of the Yellowstone country.[20]

In short, Colter discovered passes into and out of the later Yellowstone National Park and the Tetons, moving from Montana into Wyoming and Idaho and back. He was the first white to see Yellowstone Lake, the largest freshwater lake in North America at that altitude, and to tell of the wonders of the geysers and Yellowstone phenomena. With his journey completed, "he had more first-hand knowledge of the American West than any man alive."[21] Some physical evidence of his trip remains. His initials were found on a tree in the area by Theodore Roosevelt's hunting guide in 1889; and a carving of a human head on a rhyolite block of stone with the inscription of "John Colter, 1808," was found in Pierre's Hole, just west of the Tetons.[22]

Returning to Lisa's post, Colter again trapped and explored the surrounding area populated by the Blackfeet and their enemies the Flatheads and Crows. Getting mixed up in one of the frequent skirmishes in 1808, Colter took an arrow of the Blackfeet in the leg. Not long after, he and Daniel Potts (another ex-Lewis and Clark man) were captured by the Blackfeet near the Three Forks area (where the

Jefferson, Madison, and Gallatin rivers join to form the Missouri). Colter accepted capture, but Potts, trying to resist, was shot full of arrows, his body looking like a hive of porcupine quills. Colter was relieved of his weapons and stripped naked as the Indians offered him a chance to run for his life against their best warriors. It was a deadly challenge frequently offered by the Indians to their prisoners, with the expectation that the fleeing man would be caught forthwith. This game was one of the more amusing ways to toy with a victim before they administered the *coup de grace*.

Given a slight head start, Colter outdistanced all of the Blackfeet but one, even though Colter's bare feet were pierced by cactus thorns. His single pursuer at this point could not narrow the gap and so hurled his spear at Colter, barely missing. Colter picked up the spear as the Indian came on and gutted his pursuer with it. This was adding insult to injury, killing a man with his own weapon, and the rest of the Blackfeet were so furious that they pursued Colter with added vengeance. To elude them, Colter jumped into the Jefferson River, hiding under one of its many brush piles—a floating island of twigs and leaves (not a beaver lodge, as is sometimes described). Persistent though they were, the Blackfeet could not find their prey and went back to mourn their own loss of a brave, one more grievance stored in their memory against Americans.

Naked and armed only with the spear he retrieved from the Indian, Colter walked and ran several hundred miles over the next seven days to the safety of Manuel's Fort. Finally, in spring 1810 and after six years in the high country, he decided he had had enough of the mountain life. He put the final touch on his many journeys by paddling alone two thousand miles down the Missouri. He subsequently married and set up a home near Dundee, Missouri, and never returned to the mountains. With his vast geographical knowledge, he assisted his former chief, William Clark, in filling in details of a void on the famous Clark-Biddle map of the West, published in 1814. Colter died in 1813, probably from a liver ailment. It is ironic that while he eluded death from animals, Indians, and wilderness, civilization may have done him in. Doubly ironic, the Missouri grave of this first of the great American mountain men was erased in 1926 when the railroad pushed a right-of-way over the spot.

"In the exploration of the American West," Jedediah Smith, whose appropriate middle name was Strong, is "overshadowed only by Meriwether Lewis and William Clark."[23] We can understand this tribute from the scholar Dale Morgan when we appreciate that Smith was the "first to find and recognize the natural gateway to the Oregon country; first overland traveler to reach California; first to cross the

Sierra Nevada [from west to east]; first to traverse the Great Basin on its most direct and desert route; first to travel overland from California to the Columbia!"[24] In Smith's decade as a fur trader, trapper, and explorer, he travelled well over fifteen thousand miles of the most rugged terrain in the West and he did it largely by foot and horse.

Born the sixth of fourteen children in the state of New York in 1799, he was descended from several generations of New Englanders. In some ways Smith was typical of mountain men; he was lean in body, about six feet tall, and a born leader. He was also very different in many respects. Fairly well educated for the time, he read and wrote well, as attest his letters to William Clark, the secretary of war, his family, and others. He kept journals and records, never smoked, and drank only an occasional glass of wine. Deeply religious, he was inseparable from his Bible, which he knew exceedingly well. Intensely patriotic, he did all he could to assist his country with the political and geographical information he acquired. A man of little humor, he was all business and, like his Yankee forebears, sought to make his mark in life as an entrepreneur.

By 1822, he had been drawn as by a magnet to St. Louis, jumping off point for all mountain men. In response to Ashley's newspaper advertisement calling for "100 young men," he joined up and spent the greater part of his first year with other Ashley-Henry men on the Mussellshell River where it feeds into the Missouri. In spring 1823, while Ashley was making his way with supplies up river, Andrew Henry, having troubles at the Mussellshell, sent Smith downstream to tell Ashley to send the horses and supplies immediately to the Mussellshell post.

Almost at once, however, it was Ashley who needed Henry's help. The turnabout came when Ashley ran into the Arickara village, where Indians halted his boats and attacked the men. In this first great struggle for river traffic rights, as noted previously, thirteen of Ashley's men were killed and a large number wounded.[25] Smith arrived in time to join the fight, acquitting himself well. His leadership and bravery were noted by Ashley, who asked Smith to return to Henry and bring help for overcoming the Arickara blockade. As mentioned earlier, Ashley called on the army under Colonel Leavenworth to protect American persons and property. The forces of Leavenworth from the south and those of Smith and Henry from the north, together with some other traders from a following Missouri Fur Company group headed by Joshua Pilcher, converged below the Arickara village. They split into two brigades, Smith in charge of one. The village was punished, but not enough to satisfy the fur men, and Leavenworth was accused of doing only the absolute minimum.

With the river passage still doubtful, Ashley was forced to revise his plans. To seek an overland route, he sent Smith and a group of men west of the Black Hills and then north and west to the fur country. They were working their way toward the area of Dubois, Wyoming, a hundred miles east of the sky-reaching Wind River range, a known beaver habitat with its many streams. On the way, Jedediah was thoroughly mauled about the face and neck by one of the fabled whitetips—a grizzly bear. His scalp, ear, and face were all severely lacerated by the four-inch claws, and Smith had to be sewed up immediately or die from loss of blood. This task was undertaken with mending needle and thread by a member of the party, James Clyman, who was to achieve fame nearly equal to the best known of the mountain men. Although patched up enough to travel, Smith carried the scars of this encounter the rest of his short life.

On their way to the Wind River, they ran out of water, and after several dry days the group spread in all directions to search for the life-giving liquid. (No respectable mountain man would bother to carry a canteen in the mountains—if he couldn't find water there, he shouldn't be a mountain man in the first place. But water on the high arid plains was something else again.) Smith and two others set out in one direction, Clyman in another. When Smith's two companions became exhausted, he buried both in sand up to their necks to reduce evaporation of moisture from their bodies and went on alone. He found a waterhole—and also Clyman, newly arrived. Smith rushed back with some water to the buried partners, revived them, and brought them to the hole.

Later, near northern Idaho, Smith and his men ran into Hudson's Bay Company competition. (Hudson's Bay had been working over the entire Northwest and the Snake River basin, going as far south as northern Utah.) A Hudson's Bay man with Iroquois trappers had enemy Indians on his trail and needed protection.[26] Smith struck a bargain, forcing the Hudson's Bay men to sell him their fur pelts in return for protection and transit to the company's Flathead Post in northern Montana near Flathead Lake. Business was business!

Near the post, Smith met the famed Alexander Ross of Hudson's Bay, who was being replaced by the strange but indomitable Peter Ogden. Smith accompanied Ogden to the July 1825 rendezvous, picking up others on the way. This was Ashley's first mountain gathering and it took place on Henry's Fork of the Green River near where Wyoming cuts into the northeastern border of Utah. Smith had obtained a sizable nine thousand pounds of beaver that assured Ashley passage on the road to riches. Smith floated the cargo back to St. Louis, where he became a partner in the Ashley enterprise. In scarcely a month's time, however, he once again was headed for the mountains and beaver. This time he went all the way to southern California, then owned and occupied by the Spaniards. On the way he met a group of apparently peaceful Mohave Indians who let the large party pass without incident. In California, Smith found that the Spanish were always looking over their shoulders, justly suspicious of America's lean and hungry look.

The Spanish authorities told Smith to go out the way he came in. Instead, he and his group went north to the San Joaquin River valley which was teeming with the soft gold of the beaver, accumulating fifteen hundred pounds of pelts. He also encountered more political difficulties, and leaving some men behind to cache the beaver, Smith and two companions crossed the rugged Sierras, going east. Lack of water plagued them in the great basin of Nevada and Utah, where many rivers like the Humboldt turn into sinks; that is, they disappear underground, only to reappear elsewhere. He came back in time to meet at the Bear Lake rendezvous.

A fortnight later he set out with eighteen men for his beaver cache and the men he had left behind in California. On the way, he met the same tribe of Mohave Indians who had been friendly earlier. This time, however, when he took part of his men and material across the river, the Indians attacked those waiting behind to be ferried, killing all nine. The Mohaves then went after Smith and the men on rafts in the river, but their attack was repelled. The loss of men and materials was grievous, but Smith and what was left of his group went on to meet his men on the Stanislaus River in the San Joaquin valley.

The Spanish got word of his second arrival and, doubly suspicious and peeved, decided to do something about it. Smith tried to explain his case to the officials, but they wanted to send him for questioning to the governor in Monterrey. After delicate negotiations between the mountain men, the Spanish, and several American sea captains plying the nearby waters, Smith was allowed to post a bond and was given an exit visa. He sent word to his San Joachin party to bring their pelts and meet him near San Francisco. Selling the beaver to a sea captain for four thousand dollars, the mountain men got re-outfitted and headed north to explore. July 1827 found Smith on the Umpqua River, on his way to the Willamette River and valley in Oregon—one of the great terminals of later Oregon Trail migration. Leaving the main body of his men with his supplies on the Umpqua, Smith and two companions reconnoitered the area for a feasible route to the north. On their return, Smith's party was shot at by Indians and, when they neared the camp site, they saw that the men had been slaughtered. Only one man, Arthur Black, had escaped, fleeing north to Ft. Vancouver, the fur post where the great physician-fur trader John McLoughlin was chief factor.

Smith and his companions took the same route, arriving on August 10, 1827, two days after Black. McLoughlin, one of the most honorable men in the history of the fur trade, extended his hospitality and sent out a party of his own men with Smith to try to recover the stolen pelts and equipment. In this, they were partly successful. McLoughlin purchased the recovered pelts from Smith and charged nothing for his services.[27] For his part, Smith secretly was making extensive notes on the Hudson's Bay Company operations and British activities in the Pacific Northwest for a report to the United States secretary of war. (Smith acknowledged the factor's magnanimity in his correspondence to the States.)

Smith and Black left Vancouver in March 1829 and headed for Flathead Post to meet Smith's company partner, David Jackson. Smith and Jackson then left for the 1829 Popo Agie rendezvous to meet the third partner of the enterprise, William Sublette. Arriving late, they missed the group but knew that another meeting was to be held at Pierre's Hole later that summer. They headed in that direction, because trading plans for the coming year had to be made and they had only three to four hundred miles to go and across two mountain ranges!

Later that year, Smith and his men, guided this time by the redoubtable Jim Bridger, ventured into the notorious Blackfeet country. In 1830, the following year, Smith's men again made rendezvous at the Popo Agie. There, Smith, Sublette, and Jackson sold their company to Bridger, Fitzpatrick, Fraeb, Gervais, and Milton Sublette, brother of William. This new grouping came to be known as the Rocky Mountain Fur Company and it, too, would have an exciting but checkered history.

Smith returned to Missouri but decided in 1831 to guide a caravan to Santa Fe, with many wagons carrying his own goods, over the trail that had been established a decade before. For some distance they followed the usual route along the Arkansas River. This headed toward the two Spanish Peaks that marked the turnoff for Raton Pass and the trail to Santa Fe. To shorten the journey, they decided to take the Cimarron Cutoff across the dreaded Llano Estacado, or staked plains. This was so named because the early Spanish marked the distant water holes with stakes to guide any intrepid travelers who might risk this route.

Searching for water, Smith and Fitzpatrick went in advance of the train. The first hole they came to was dry, and Fitzpatrick stayed there to direct the wagon train. Smith went on ahead to look for a wet hole and did not return. The party had to proceed to Santa Fe without him. There they saw some Indians flaunting some of Smith's weapons. Questioned, the Indians said they obtained the weapons from passing Comanches. The Comanches told of waiting at a wet hole for buffalo when a white man arrived. There was a short fight in which Smith killed the chief but then was riddled with arrows and left dead on the spot. He was thirty-three.

At the time of his death, Jedediah Smith knew more than anyone else about the geography of the West from the Missouri River to California and from Mexico to the Columbia River. As Western writer Harvey L. Carter said of him: "Among the mountain men, in many ways he stands alone, and it was alone that he died."[28]

Let us now turn to a third mountain man. His name was Jim Bridger and all acknowledge that he was one of the best, although he did have some peculiarities, such as a weakness for tall stories. It was said of his friend Moses "Black" Harris that "lies tumbled out of his mouth like boudins out of a bufler's stomach."[29] The same flattering accusation was leveled at Jim Bridger.

"They said I was the damnedest liar ever lived. That's what a man gets for telling the truth."[30] Those are Jim Bridger's own words, and people didn't know whether to believe him or not. Was it true that he knew a place where a river ran both east and west? Was it true that he had seen a "putrefyed" forest with "putrefyed" birds? Was it true that one could bring up a fish from a cold mountain stream, throw it over one's shoulder still on the line into a boiling stream, and cook it for supper? Was it true that one could fire a Hawkens rifle at seeing a visible deer, not knowing that the deer was actually behind one's back? The answers to these questions are all Yes! Well, partly yes. At Two Ocean Pass in southeast Yellowstone National Park lies a marsh from which waters flow in both directions, one to the Pacific, the other to the Atlantic. Not far from Tower Junction in the same park are the remnants of a forest of petrified trees, many of their trunks still standing, left that way after the ash and dirt which covered them blew away. Also in the park are springs whose waters are superheated, coming out of the ground with a temperature above the boiling point. Virtually next to them and forming various confluences are ice-cold glacial streams. Finally, there is a wall of obsidian rock (a glossy lava), which reflects what is behind the person who is looking at it. Bridger saw them all; he just embellished these phenomena a bit in telling others about them.

Without question, Jim Bridger—also known as "Old Gabe," or "Blanket Chief" and sometimes as "Big Neck" because of his goiter— is the most beloved, popular, and well-remembered of the mountain men. He also was among the best two or three in the profession.

Like John Colter, Bridger was born in Virginia. The time was 1804, the momentous year that witnessed the beginning of the Lewis and Clark Expedition. Increasingly, St. Louis was the village that beckoned those who sought opportunity, and Bridger's family (his father had experience in surveying) was drawn by this call as well. Shortly after moving there, however, Bridger's parents died and Bridger became a blacksmith's apprentice, an experience that was to serve him well all of his long life. He was described in his prime as tall, lean, humorous, and kind, and a photograph taken in his later years conveys that impression. The spirit of adventure seized him when he heard of Ashley's advertisement for men to go up the Missouri. We know that he heard about it because throughout his entire life he never learned to read.

Hired by Ashley, Bridger soon revealed a prodigious and almost photographic memory for topography. One of his biographers claimed he could "hold in mind" the detailed lay of the land of the whole northwestern quarter of the continent.[31] A similar tribute was paid by the newspaper *Missouri Republican* on October 24, 1851: "This man is a perfect original. He seems to have an intuitive knowledge of the topography of the country, the courses of streams, the directions of mountains, and is never lost, wherever he may be."[32] Bridger's reputation for knowing the land was such that, where he took wagons through, other guides did not hesitate to follow.[33] Additionally, Bridger showed a gift for learning Indian languages, especially the sign language, in which he was an expert.

Yet Bridger did not burst from the womb a full-grown mountain man. He learned his trade, sometimes in painfully embarrassing lessons. On the second Ashley-Henry trip up the Missouri in 1823, Hugh Glass, a cantankerous old independent trapper but a member of the party, wandered off and got mauled by a grizzly so badly that he appeared all but dead when he was found. Rather than delay the voyage, Henry asked Bridger and another trapper to wait with the dying man and bury him when he expired. The young Bridger and his companion waited and waited, but old Glass tenaciously held on to life despite showing no signs of improvement. Since Indian attack was always a danger in that country, the two men decided to leave Glass, whose death seemed both certain and imminent. Catching up with the group, they reported that Glass had finally died. The expedition mourned the loss, although, given Glass's character, not too sadly, and proceeded upstream.

As matters turned out, Glass regained consciousness and tended his wounds until he could crawl. The death watch had left him without weapons or supplies, but he had his wallet, which contained a razor. With it, Glass could make a spark on flint and produce a fire. Warmed, he obtained food by chasing wolves away from a buffalo calf they had downed nearby. Getting stronger daily, Glass gradually hobbled and walked to Fort Kiowa, 350 miles away. It was one of the great feats of survival in all history. It did not sweeten his disposition, however, and needless to say, Glass exploded with resentment when he confronted his death-watch caretakers and would-be undertakers some months later.

Bridger "greened" with the Henry trips. While still in Ashley's employ in 1825, he discovered the Great Salt Lake, speculating that it was an inland extension of the Pacific Ocean. When Ashley sold out to Jackson, Smith, and Sublette, Bridger hired out as the guide of the new enterprise and later bought into it as a reorganized company. He was at the Pierre's Hole rendezvous and subsequent battle in 1832; afterward he took his men north to Blackfeet country for trapping. Another group tried to follow, thinking to capitalize on Bridger's knowledge, but to shake the unwanted followers Bridger led them on a not-so-merry chase farther and farther into dangerous territory. On this venture, Bridger took two Blackfeet arrows in the back. His partner pulled out one of them, but the three-inch iron barb on the other arrow remained.

The 1835 rendezvous on the Green River was attended by Dr. Marcus Whitman, a missionary-physician. Whitman and another missionary, Samuel Parker, were there to obtain a guide and explore the possibility of opening up missions among the Flatheads and Nez Percé around the Willamette Valley. The rendezvous was a major one and was described by both Parker and Whitman in their journals. Present in addition to the trappers were some two thousand Shoshone, hundreds of Flatheads and Nez Percé, representatives of the Hudson's Bay Company, and the missionary entourage.

Whitman, on learning that Bridger had carried an arrow point in his back for two years, offered to remove it. The operation was a tedious affair and Parker gave a good description of it. "The arrow was hooked at the point by striking a large bone, and a cartilaginous substance had grown around it."[34] Surgery was done with the audience of thousands observing as if from an arena. When the doctor expressed surprise that infection had not done Bridger in, Bridger replied, "Meat don't spile in the mountains." After Bridger was repaired, Indians and trappers alike lined up for medical attention, no longer afraid after witnessing the doctor's skills. All in all, it was a busy afternoon.[35]

Bridger's knowledge of Indian ways, as well as Indian good will to him (excepting, of course, among the Blackfeet and Gros Ventre), was due in part to his adopting much of their mode of life and many of their customs, even sharing many of their beliefs. He also successively married a Flathead, a Ute, and a Snake and had children by all. From these liaisons he gained an impressive knowledge of Indian ways which benefited him a number of times. Once Indians captured a mountain man, Joe Meek, and threatened to kill him unless he led them to Bridger. The Indians hoped to capture the entire Bridger party of trappers together with their equipment. Meek told the Indians exactly where Bridger was and informed them that he had only 40 men with him. Meek had no fear for his fellows' safety; he knew that Bridger actually was accompanied by 240 men. When the Indians found Bridger and discovered their enemies' superior strength, they changed plans, demanding a ransom in supplies in return for Meek. Bridger called for a smoke and negotiations, asking the Indians to send a subchief as their representative. They did, and Bridger, holding the subchief as a bargaining chip, exchanged him for Meek, as the Indians wondered what had happened.

The 1830s in the United States were marked by a depression leading to the panic of 1837. Beaver prices were off and Bridger and others could see that the days of the beaver trade were numbered. More and more Bridger looked for other ways of earning a living. One of his ventures was Fort Bridger in southwestern Wyoming, which he started in 1843 as a supply depot for emigrants on the Oregon Trail. There travellers could exchange several tired oxen for one fresh one. Bridger fattened up the spent animals and traded them to the next caravan for a handsome profit. Bridger's blacksmithing skills were also in demand for wagon and weapon repair.

For a number of reasons, Bridger found himself in conflict with the Mormon immigrants to the south. The Mormon leader, Brigham Young, even disputed Bridger's priority as discoverer of the Great Salt Lake. In 1853, Young's avenging angels, the Danites, burned and looted the fort, occupying it until 1857. Bridger filed suit with the U.S. government, claiming a loss of a hundred thousand dollars (exaggerated), but was unsuccessful. The facts concerning the entire incident remain unclear.

After 1857, Bridger leased the fort to the army but that did not end his troubles. The government refused to pay the amount Bridger wanted for rent. It would be nearly fifty years before the slow machinery of Washington finally settled the debt—in 1899 his heirs received six thousand dollars.

As Bridger's reputation grew, his services were increasingly sought by civilian wagon masters and the army alike. For example, he served as a guide for a party blazing a new route to the Virginia City goldfields, following the west side of the Bighorns and avoiding the bloody Bozeman trail through the dangerous Indian country east of the mountains.

Then too he served variously as guide to Captain Raynolds, who mounted an expedition to explore the Yellowstone region for the U.S. government. Bridger held the army post of chief of scouts for six months during the Powder River expedition of 1865-67, and he was a scout for the learned Colonel Carrington who commanded the beleaguered Fort Phil Kearny, laid siege by the Oglala Sioux Red Cloud. Bridger also served as guide for several fur companies trekking West and the many missionaries who accompanied them. He became a lifelong friend of Père Pierre Jean De Smet, the Belgian Jesuit who in 1840 founded the Catholic Pacific Northwest mission chain. (Some of the original buildings still stand on the French-speaking Flathead reservation.)

The busy Bridger assisted the former army engineer Captain E.L. Berthoud (for whom Berthoud Pass, west of Denver, is named), in mapping a stage route from Denver to Salt Lake. The mountain man also proved of help to General Grenville Dodge in building the transcontinental railroad. Dodge was so impressed with Bridger that he wrote a biography of him.

Captain Gunnison (for whom Gunnison Canyon in west central Colorado is named), no mean engineer and map maker himself, paid tribute to Bridger: "His graphic sketches are delightful romances. With a buffalo skin and a piece of charcoal he will map out any portion of this immense region, and delineate mountains, streams, and the circular valleys called 'holes' with wonderful accuracy."[36] And Bridger accepted with relish the assignment as guide for General Johnston, sent by the United States to forcibly install a governor in Utah during the Mormon "War" in 1857. Bridger's frequent periods of service to the army ended when he was sixty-four in the year 1868.

Between the obligations mentioned above, Bridger managed to help organize and guide parties of en courrant European nobles who were flocking to this country's West. In 1837, Bridger was painted by the renowned artist Alfred Jacob Miller, a guest of Sir William Drummond Stewart, the Scottish millionaire adventurer and sometime author. Both attended the rendezvous on the Green River that year. As a humorous gesture of thanks to Bridger, Stewart gave the mountain man a suit of armor—just the garb for roasting days on the plains and frosty evenings in the high country!

Bridger also guided the English nobleman Sir George Gore, who in 1854 traveled the West in style—champagne, servants, and all accouterments necessary for the life of luxury. Thus supplied, Gore's entourage spent two years in the area.

Rheumatism and gradual loss of vision at last forced Bridger to retire to Westport, Missouri, where he lived among some of his children and friends until his death at the age of seventy-seven in 1881. His beloved West remembered him with towns, forests, and wilderness areas all bearing his name.

Lastly, we must recall another mountain man, a friend and successor to Bridger. On October 6, 1826, the following advertisement appeared in the newspaper, *Missouri Intelligencer*:

Notice is hereby given to all persons.
That Christopher Carson, a boy about 16 years old, small of his age, but thickset; light hair, ran away from the subscriber, living in Franklin, Howard County, Missouri, to whom he had been bound to learn the Saddler's trade. . . . One cent reward will be given to any person who will bring back the said boy.[37]

This short and stocky young man was the storied Kit Carson. Before he died, however, he was to turn from runaway saddle apprentice into "Mountain man, scout, soldier and Indian agent."[38]

Born in Kentucky in 1809, Carson was caught up in the spirit of the times and saw his future allied to the movement West. Running away from his saddlemaker-employer, David Workman (the name is telling), Carson joined a caravan leaving Independence, Missouri, for Santa Fe. From Santa Fe, Carson wandered north toward Taos, the meeting place for the Southwest trappers, known as the Taos trappers. There, Carson learned the trade of the mountain man under the tutelage of an elder and experienced trapper, Matthew Kincais.

For the next several months, Carson travelled with one caravan to El Paso and another to Chihuahua in Mexico. A man of excellent wits, Carson remembered what he saw and where he went. His first major opportunity for development as a trapper came when he met the celebrated mountain man, Ewing Young. Attaching himself to Young's group, Carson earned his keep by doing odd jobs, including rendering service as a cook for the outfit. During the years 1828-1831, he accompanied Young on a trip to California where he again learned and remembered. He came of age on this trip not only in years but as a mountain man, for he added to his skills as a trapper the geographical and practical know-how that he needed. His immensely detailed knowledge of the entire Southwest was to stand him in good stead in future years.

For a while, Carson worked as a buffalo hunter, out of Bent's Fort, called the "Castle of the Prairies," as indeed it was, situated on the American side of the Arkansas River near La Mar, Colorado.[39] From there he explored the spine of the Rockies as he made trips to the country's northern border.

There was a rough and ready camaraderie among many of the most famous mountain men, and Carson fit hand in glove with this group. He personally knew most of his famous contemporaries, often working as a free trapper with different outfits that included Bridger, Fitzpatrick, Fontenelle, Meek, Walker, and segments of the Hudson's Bay Company.[40] As a result of these experiences, he now knew well the Unita Mountains, the great basin areas of Utah and Nevada, the Oregon country, and the valley of the Yellowstone.

By mountain standards, Carson was a simple person, a short man among sixfooters. People who met him knowing only his reputation found it hard to believe that this modest man was their hero. Nonetheless, his fame grew. Although myth had something to do with his popularity and the nation did need heros in the West to promote its expansionist doctrine, Carson's legend has a firm foundation in facts.

For example, in the early 1830s, he pursued an Indian horse thief for over a hundred miles and won back the horse. About the same time, his party of six men was attacked by several hundred Comanches. Carson, seeing that he and his men could not escape by fleeing, took the quick and decisive action of slitting the throats of their mules, making a fort out of the carcasses. The copious oozing of animal blood continually spooked the Indian ponies when their masters charged the makeshift fort against a small but withering fire. Three of the defenders fired their weapons at all Indian charges and three worked only at reloading the guns. The Comanches finally tired of their futile siege and retired from the action, leaving forty-two dead.

In 1849, Carson accompanied a mission to rescue a white woman held captive by the Indians. The commander of the group hesitated before charging the camp, despite Carson's warning that any delay would give the Indians a chance to put an arrow into the woman's heart. After the camp was finally invaded, the woman's body was still warm when Carson got to it. In 1851, Carson himself was captured by Indians; as they were about to tomahawk him to death, another Indian recognized Carson as a friend and halted the action, giving Carson his release.

Particularly well publicized was an incident that occurred at the 1835 Green River rendezvous—the one at which Dr. Whitman removed the arrowhead from Jim Bridger's back. The event was recorded by the missionary Samuel Parker, who was busy filling his journal with his wonderment at the Western men and the mountains. A huge Frenchman whose name sounded like "Shunar," took delight in beating up on his countrymen and boasted that if any Americans dared to challenge him he "would take a switch to them."[41] Carson accepted the challenge, and Parker described the scene:

[Shunar] mounted his horse with a loaded rifle, and challenged any Frenchman, American, Spaniard or Dutchman, to fight him in single combat. Kit Carson an American told him if he wished to die, he would accept the challenge. Shunar defied him. Carson mounted his horse, and with a loaded pistol, rushed into close contact, and both almost at the same instant fired. C's ball entered S's hand, came out at the wrist and passed through the arm above the elbow. Shunar's ball passed over the head of Carson; and while he [Carson] went for another pistol, Shunar begged that his life might be spared.[42]

Carson himself related that the two men were so close when they fired that Shunar's ball passed through his hair, giving him a minor powder burn by one of his eyes.

Like many mountain men, Carson married into the Indian tribes. After his first wife, an Arapaho, died, he married a Cheyenne. Some say that she divorced him, Indian style. Then at the age of thirty-three he married a third time, taking a Taos girl who was only fifteen years old.

Already well known to the other mountain men, Carson became a national figure in the 1840s. His chief publicist was Captain John C. Frémont, whom he met accidentally on a boat going up river on the Missouri. Frémont confided that he was looking for a guide, and Carson said that he could do the job. Thus began a notable friendship and association. Frémont's wife, Jessie, was the gifted daughter of the apostle of the Westward movement, Senator Thomas Hart Benton of Missouri.[43] This closely knit family embraced Carson and everyone benefited.

Carson served Frémont as guide on three separate expeditions, all of which were well-publicized. (Ironically, it was Frémont whose popular nickname became the Pathfinder.) Carson soon became the leading figure in the dime novels of the time (as Buffalo Bill would later find fame at the pen of Ned Buntline). Carson particularly enjoyed having others read to him of his heroics but was bashful about mentioning them himself; he sometimes suggested, although not too strongly, that they be toned down.

An incident that took place on one of the Frémont expeditions was typical of the exploits that attracted an eager public. The party was hailed by a Mexican man and a boy, who told how Indians had taken their horses and kidnapped others of their group, including two women. Frémont could not stop but asked for volunteers to track down the Indians. Carson and a man named Godey stepped forward. Frémont's *Memoirs* give this account of the story:

The time, place, object and numbers considered, this expedition of Carson and Godey may be considered among the boldest and most disinterested which the annals of western adventure, so full of daring deeds, can present. Two men, in a savage desert, pursue day and night an unknown body of

Indians into the defiles of an unknown mountain—attack them upon sight, without counting numbers, and defeat them in an instant—and for what? To punish the robber of the desert, and avenge the wrong of Mexicans whom they did not know. (As an epilogue, it was determined that the Indians numbered 30 and they did mutilate and kill the rest of the party they seized.)[44]

After his work with Frémont, Carson continued to find adventure and to hold responsible posts. He was caught up in the Mexican War. In 1846, he guided General Stephen Kearny and his Army of the West in their march that ended in the capture of Los Angeles.

Like other mountain men and most who went west, Carson sought to make his fortune. In 1853, together with others, he drove a large herd of sheep to California. Costing Carson and his men fifty cents apiece, the sheep sold for ten times that figure. Carson also dictated (and embellished) his memoirs, hoping to cash in on his popularity. Unfortunately, because of his functional illiteracy, he left no written documents to help investigating scholars who sought to put out an authentic biography.

When the Civil War began, Carson's services again were in demand by the army. In this period, he rounded up the Mescalero Apaches and destroyed the lodges of Comanches and Kiowa at Adobe Walls, in an action sometimes called the First Battle of Adobe Walls. In 1864, he was given a command of nearly a thousand men to rout the Navajo from their redoubt in Canyon De Chelley in northeastern Arizona. These Indians had been raiding and plundering whites with impunity. Carson attacked them with a Sherman-type scorched earth policy, invading the side box canyons where the early Anasazi made their dwellings. Carson's forces killed the Navajo's horses and sheep and burned their orchards wreaking complete devastation on them. Over two thousand were captured and marched to Basque Redondo near Fort Sumner in New Mexico. It was the Navajo's own Trail of Tears. (Four years later, the Navajo were allowed to return to Canyon De Chelley with its thousand-foot sheer walls and a wash running through the bottom, to be reunited with the spirits of the ancient ones who once inhabited the area. There they still live in hogans and wicki-ups by Spider Rock, Antelope House, and the ancient cliff dwellings, raising fruit trees, sheep, goats, and horses. Two hundred thousand strong, the Navajo have come to be the largest tribe of Indians in the United States.)

Although Carson was responsible for a great number of Indian deaths—certainly more than any other mountain man—he always had respect for Indians and their way of life. Particularly he was fond of the Utes. His reports and recommendations to the government tried to soften policy toward the red man. Carson served as Indian agent to the tribes of northern New Mexico from 1853 to 1861, and the records indicate that his administration was fairly successful. However, his inability to write and his distaste for bureaucracy, together with political problems, made his tenure a difficult one.

His health failing, in 1868 Carson was sent for medical attention to Fort Lyon in southeast Colorado. Knowing that death was near, the scout, soldier, and mountain man asked for a last meal of buffalo steak and coffee and a smoke from a clay pipe. He was buried in Taos, the heart of the Sangre de Cristo Mountains, and a wrought iron fence was placed around his cemetery plot. His home in Taos is kept as a shrine, and a short distance away is the Kit Carson Museum with an extensive and interesting collection of memorabilia.

The mountain men captured the imagination of their own era, and their appeal continues strong today. Their exploits speak to the human desire for freedom, the need to establish one's independence and worth by one's own efforts. During our country's earliest years, the mountains beckoned, but while they offered fame and fortune, they were also unforgiving of mistakes. It was an elite who mastered them, an elite not of family lineage or book learning but of physical prowess and intimate knowledge of the wilderness.

Rough as it was, the mountain men exhibited the morality of an elite (*Hernmoral*) where today we feel oppressed by a morality of the masses (*Herdenmoral*). Theirs was a time of simplicity, when strength and skill alone could bring triumph over adversity, when the blacksmith was able to cope with the highest technology. Perhaps their spirit survives in today's computer whiz kids and the corporate raiders of Wall Street, but however high the stakes risked by those entrepreneurs, their exploits do not move us as did those of the men who gladly risked their skin for a skin.

3. The Plains Indians

As Long as the Grass Grows and the Water Flows

The Indianhead penny was introduced in 1859 and replaced by the Lincoln penny fifty years later. The Native American also was honored on the buffalo-backed nickel, but that too has disappeared. The fate of these coins seems to reflect the fate of Indians themselves. Although elements of the glory days of the eighteenth and nineteenth centuries continue to be evident among Indians today, their high culture and distinctive presence are disappearing in North America.

We are accustomed to speak of "the Indian" whether we mean the Algonquians of the Northeast, the Seminoles of the South, or the Apaches of the West. But there is, of course, no archetypal Indian. Native Americans varied widely in culture and language (more different languages were spoken in the Western Hemisphere than anywhere else on earth) and included physical differences as great as those between Swedish and Turkish peoples.

Recent ethnologists see the Indians' physical diversity as clues to their origins. It is generally agreed that America was settled by way of Asia during one or more of the times when low sea levels made the Bering Straits a fifty-mile stretch of dry land. The unsettled question is when the migrations occurred. New evidence is constantly pushing back the date. The current consensus has human occupation of the hemisphere beginning about thirty thousand years ago. Some ethnologists suggest that the migration occurred in three main waves.[1] The first resulted in most of those now regarded as Indians. The second brought the ancestors of the Eskimo and Aleuts. The third accounts for the Navaho and Apache and some Northwest tribes like the Tlingit.

Whatever truth is reflected by this theory, much mystery still surrounds the Indians' origins. Despite the Native American's resemblance to Mongolian peoples—straight black hair, high cheek bones, copper-colored skin, sparse facial and body hair—the differences are also striking. Mongolians lack the Roman nose common among American Indians; Indians lack the epicanthic eyefold that gives northern Mongolians their oriental appearance.[2] And, despite their physical variations, "one amazing thing was discovered . . . all the different tribes from Canada to South America are related racially": they have the same blood type—type O, with M and Rh-positive factors present.[3]

The nomadic life of the immigrants left little evidence of the routes they took or of their experiences along the way. The best indication of their movements is the distribution of languages. Words in the vocabulary of Western Indians denote an Eastern Algonquian source: *moose*, an Algonquian word meaning "twig eater" is common in the West. Curiously, many language similarities are not found continuously along possible migration routes but vanish and reappear at intervals (some seem to pop up every thousand miles). The Athabaskan word *dine* or *dene*, for example, is found throughout both Americas but with major geographical gaps between appearances. *Dene* means "the people" or even "the chosen ones," and is used as the name of the group. Lewis and Clark were surprised to hear Northwest Indians calling themselves "chosen ones," a title the explorers associated with the ancient Hebrews. (Mormons might not have been surprised, however, for they consider Indians to be descendants of the lost tribes of Israel, citing as evidence similarity between certain words in Hebrew and Aztec.) This sort of ethnocentric identification is common among early peoples. The Eskimo designation *Innuit* has a similar connotation; the Sioux regard themselves as "the friends," "allies," or generally "us folks," and so do the Arapaho, the Cheyenne, the Apache, the Navajo, and others.

At the time of Columbus, there may have been as many as two million Indians living in what is now the United States. How many there are at present is hard to determine; intermarriage has muddled the determination of who is and is not an Indian, and different agencies use different criteria. The Navajo, the largest tribe today, have nearly two hundred thousand members; the Sioux are next with forty-five thousand. Altogether, there are over two hundred and sixty reservations scattered throughout the land.

Although there were white people who understood that the Native Americans possessed rich and complex cultures, many judged the "savages" by the standards of their own civilization and found them wanting. They considered that a land with no roads, cities, or armies was empty and in need of such things, which they were eager to supply. Inhabitants who had left so little mark on the countryside seemed to be living like animals; they could be displaced as pests, like the grizzly and cougar. At best, whites saw Indians as Rousseau's "noble savage," an innocent child of nature uncorrupted by the civilization that was fast encroaching on him. At worst, like the conquistadors in South America, they regarded the natives as wild creatures without souls to be slaughtered as they did animals. (A Papal declaration that the natives indeed were human beings possessing souls lessened the killing but did not halt it.)

Today we have abundant evidence of the high culture attained by many Indian tribes. We have only to look at the League of the Iroquois in which the Mohawk, Oneida, Onondaga, Cayuga, and Seneca nations banded together to regulate the commerce of their region. The mysterious mound builders of the Ohio knew considerable geometry, theoretical and applied.[4] The builders of the Medicine Wheel in the northern Bighorn Mountains of Wyoming showed astronomical acuity. And we must note the Pueblo builders and their predecessors, the Anasazi, with their "sun dagger" astronomy in Chaco Canyon, not to mention the high civilizations of the Aztecs, Incas, and others. If these were savages, we are all savages.

During the eighteenth and nineteenth centuries, the great plains were populated largely by eight major tribes. "They were the Blackfoot bands, the Crows, and the Assiniboin on the northern Plains; the Dakota or Sioux, the Cheyenne, and Arapaho in the central region; and the Comanche and Kiowa in the south."[5] Many of these peoples acknowledged a vague and distant kinship, such as the Sioux and some Cheyenne, and many shared a language group that is called Siouan. Kinship, however, did not imply friendship: the bitter and hereditary enemies, Crow and Blackfoot, spoke related languages. Often the source of enmities was clashing territorial claims. The Sioux claimed the land bordered by the Tetons on the west, the Platte River on the south, the Missouri on the east, and the Yellowstone on the north—an ambitious sweep that occasioned much conflict.

Before the eighteenth century, life on the plains required constant effort. Gathering food and fuel, preserving meat for less abundant times, providing clothing and shelter—all were done with stone or bone tools, all transportation was by foot. One factor brought about major changes in this way of life. The agent of change was the horse.

At one time, North America had been home to horses, elephants, and camels, as well as other large mammals including a two-story ground sloth. These disappeared rapidly at the same time that human beings were spreading over the continent. Researchers suspect that the invaders hunted down all the large animals for food. Therefore, when the Spanish brought horses to the continent, the natives had never seen their like. Some of the Spanish mounts escaped and thrived in the new environment. Sometime after 1730 the horse appeared on the high plains. The Dakota called it Šúŋka, "big dog," and the Lakota called it Šúňka Waken, "mystery dog." Just as the automobile altered the way of life for Americans in this century, so did the horse for the Plains Indians in the eighteenth century. The Indian, who never had the wheel, took passionately to the horse and the mobility that it offered. Many braves owned a hundred or more of these useful animals. They served many purposes—as beasts of burden to drag a travois, as special buffalo-running mounts, and as war horses.

Indians needed large numbers of horses because they wore them out rapidly. Fed off the land, Indian ponies did not have the vitality and endurance of those fed and held by whites.[6] In winter, when grass was scarce, Indian women fed the horses with bark stripped from cottonwood trees that lined the creek and river banks. This expedient provided little nourishment but helped the animals to survive. With the horses in a weakened condition, few raids were conducted during the winter months.

The plains at that time were seas of grass supporting vast herds of buffalo, more properly known as the American bison.[7] The buffalo was the staff of life for the Plains Indian, who regarded it as the most holy of animals. The buffalo dominated the land, affecting it in surprising ways. Constantly bothered by flies and fleas, buffalo rolled on the ground for relief.[8] When the ground was wet, they would get a cover of mud on their hide to protect them from being flea-bitten. The wallowing of many buffalo produced a depression, called a wadi. With rain, these shallow pits became miniature water holes on the dry plains, serving as a source of life for other animals. Indeed, many a plainswise Indian as well as white man was saved from dying of thirst by these water pockets.

The wadis also provided cover on the bare flat plains, so humans could stalk an animal (or another human) by hiding in the depression. Buffalo have a keen sense of smell, and any hint of danger on the wind sends them moving. Hunters moved from wadi to wadi downwind as soldiers from foxhole to foxhole. This technique was employed at the Battle of Beecher Island in 1868, when several scouts made their way through Indian lines to seek reinforcements.

The plains buffalo, on which the Indian depended, largely lived in two major herds, one in the north, the other in the south. Not true migrators, the brutes only moved around in their own territories. Around 1800, there were approximately one hundred million of the shaggy beasts on the plains.

The American bison is a large animal weighing up to twenty-five hundred pounds. It has huge shoulders and a large hump, supported by slender legs. Meaty and nutritious, it is rich in vitamins and proteins. Rather dimwitted, buffalo tend to congregate in groups. When hunters using long-range rifles would kill the group leader, the herd would mill around for a long time, unable to move away from danger until a new leader was chosen. Hunters called this leaderless gathering a "stand," and they would slaughter up to fifty of the indecisive beasts before they would flee.

For the Plains Indian, the buffalo-running horse was the key to a better life. Where previously game could be taken only after a time-consuming stalk, always with the danger of failure, the brave could now pursue buffalo on horseback with almost guaranteed success. The revolution in hunting was completed by the newly available iron-barbed arrow, a greatly more efficient weapon. Using the horse and the iron-tipped arrow, the Plains Indian entered a new era.

Consider the contrast with the situation of the woodland Indian, dependent on smaller game. A rabbit would yield at best a pound of dressed meat. A deer might offer a hundred pounds, an elk over three hundred, and the rare moose perhaps eight hundred pounds of tough and tasteless meat.[9] The average buffalo dressed out at a thousand pounds, and its taste and nutritional value were superior to nearly anything else available. Compared with beef, buffalo has 50 percent less cholesterol, 70 percent less fat, and 30 percent more protein. Beriberi, a disease caused by deficiencies of thiamine and vitamin D in a diet lacking fruit and vegetables, was virtually unknown to those who ate the buffalo, as was scurvy.

The buffalo, of course, provided much more than food. Its nonedible parts proved immensely useful. The sinew was used for thread and bowstrings; the ribs were used for sleds, and the fur wool was carded or twisted to produce ropes. Indians employed the paunch, scrotum, bladder, and intestines as containers.[10] The horns, cut longitudinally, were made into spoons. Gallstones were processed for medicine paint and the bile served as a spicy mustard. Indians, usually the women, even used the carcass for a gigantic blood-soup bowl, casting hot stones into it with everyone then imbibing.

The buffalo were so plentiful that Indians could hardly conceive that the population of the beasts might be killed off and become extinct. When this nearly happened, the unbelieving Indians explained that the buffalo simply had gone back into giant earth caves (from which they were believed to have come originally) and would return when things were better.

The buffalo were the Plains Indians' link to life itself. During the Indian Wars of the 1860s and 1870s, General Sheridan, trying to eradicate the Native American, told his armies, "Kill, skin and sell until the buffalo is exterminated, as it is the only way to bring about a lasting peace and allow civilization to advance."[11] Interestingly, this dependence was noted as early as 1852, by Pierre De Smet, the great Jesuit missionary to the Indians. He wrote to the editor of the *Précis Historiques*; they will "close their sad existence as the bison and the other animals on which they live, vanish."[12]

For a century, beginning around 1780, the Sioux, who were the fiercest of the warriors of the plains, came into their glory. Using the leisure provided by the horse and its ability to run down the plentiful buffalo, they now became expert in the practice of war. They became so proficient that the Black Hawk War ended in Illinois in 1832 largely because Chief Black Hawk didn't want to cross the Mississippi and confront the Sioux. Surrender to the whites was preferable.

The Sioux were typical in many ways of the Plains Indians. They lived mostly in tipis, although others, like the Mandans, resided in permanent large earth lodges. The Mandans were agriculturally oriented, growing beans, corn, and squash, and did not depend exclusively on the hunt for sustenance. There was an enmity between them and the Sioux, and the Mandans kept constant watch from the roofs of their earth lodges for Sioux raiding parties. Their concern increased as crops started coming to harvest.

The Sioux tipi was an ingenious lodging. Composed of about eight cow buffalo skins sewn together, with a number of lodgepoles for support, it more than adequately served its purposes. Eminently portable, the tipi could be assembled or taken down for a move in about fifteen minutes (a task usually left to the women). The entrance flap was placed facing east, away from the strong and ever-blowing dusty westerlies. The eastern orientation also had symbolic meaning—that was the direction where the great father sun and giver of life came up in the morning. Nearly all Indian dwellings, whether hogans, wickiups, or earth lodges, followed this pattern. When cold weather came, a fire was tended in the center pit of the tipi, the smoke rising up and out through the upper vent. In rain or snow, this vent could be closed by pulling a cord that hung down the center lodge pole. In summer, good ventilation was had by simply rolling up the bottom of the tipi cover and tying it in place with thongs. Inside the tipi were placed hammock-like beds, which resembled seats with backrests. All essential goods and weapons were within a moment's reach. All in all, life in the tipi was quite comfortable.[13]

If the occupants of the tipi were not well-to-do, they dismantled the smoked and softened hides after about a year's use and made clothing from them. Indians who were more prosperous preferred hides which had been worked over and softened with the animal's brains as part of the tanning materials. Nevertheless, both types of hides stayed pliable, even when subjected to a drenching rain.

Each tipi sheltered six to eight inhabitants, generally members of the Indian's extended family. It was a place of sanctuary as well as a home, and its violation by others brought quick retribution. Sometimes it even served as a sepulchre; the dead would be left inside as the village moved on. (At other times, corpses were placed on scaffolds.)

It was a great tribulation when a village had to abandon its tipis when fleeing an enemy, because the tipi was permeated with a sacred character. If, as Edgar A. Guest wrote, "It takes a heap of living to make a house a home," this was even more true of the dwelling of the Indians, whose views were holistic.[14] Among them, there was no more distinction between the sacred and the profane than there was between intellect and imagination, or between the conscious and the unconscious state of being awake or dreaming. The world was one of connectedness. As one author put it, "Their being-in-the-world is unequivocally a being-in-relations-with. . . . The Siouan world view [is one] of being-as-belonging."[15]

The base of a tipi, of course, formed a circle and thus was a constant reminder of the sacred, for the circle was a figure of the sacred. For the Indian, life itself was circular and all nature followed the circularity of the seasons. The paths of the sun and the moon were circular. In sacred rites and dances, the hoop or holy circle was embodied. Indians never wanted to live in log cabins or white man's houses, for these were unnaturally square or rectangular.

The tipi was painted with various symbols suggesting religious beliefs or the deeds and character of its inhabitants. Typical sacred symbols on the tipi were the silhouette of a crow, a holy bird that talks like a human and communicates with one's relatives in the nether world. Embellished on the tipi might be a figure of the crescent moon or the sun and its life-giving rays. A long-stemmed pipe might signify that its warrior inhabitant once led a war party. A painted human hand could signify that the warrior had earned a high "coup" by physically striking his enemy.

In setting up a tipi village, various high ranking persons were given choice locations, indicating their levels of distinction. When different tribes camped together, each was given its special place in the camp. For example, Sitting Bull's people were assigned to the entrance of the village at the Little Bighorn, for his tribe was known as "Keepers of the Gate," or more literally, "Those who camp on the horns of the hoop" (that is, the camp circle). They were responsible for screening people coming into and going out of the camp.

The Indian found supplies in unlikely places. Where wood was scarce, as it usually was on the plains except for the cottonwood trees along the waterways, the buffalo chip was used as fuel. (One mountain man remarked that when Indians cooked a steak over the chips, there was no need to use pepper.) The omnipresent droppings served other purposes as well. Dried and pulverized, they made a highly efficient odor- and urine-absorbing mattress for babies. When moss was available, it served a similar purpose. Since many mosses were medically sterile, they also were used to treat wounds and to stanch bleeding, much like our own modern gauze.

The status of women among the tribes was almost as varied as the tribes themselves. With some, women had an honored place on the council or at least were listened to by the council. With the Sioux, the woman was under the protection of Hanwi, the moon. The woman also was honored by the tradition that the sacred pipe had been given to the Sioux by the White Buffalo Calf Woman. In some instances, however, beatings and abuse were the woman's lot. In some tribes, a woman was worth something between a horse and a dog.

Women were more valued among one tribe encountered by Père De Smet, the missionary. He was among some Oglalas who had just been humiliatingly vanquished by their enemy, the Crows. The Crows had kidnapped Red Fish's daughter. As De Smet tells the story:

[Red Fish] presented himself at Port Pierre on the morrow of my arrival. The object of his journey was to obtain the liberty of his daughter, through the mediation of the officers of the fort; he offered eighty fine buffalo-robes and his best horses for her ransom. In his visit to me, his tears coursing down his cheeks, and heart-broken with grief, he thus addressed me, while sobs often interrupted his utterance: "Blackgown, I am a most unhappy father! I have lost my beloved daughter. Pity me, for I have learned that the medicine of the Blackgown is powerful before the Great Spirit."[16]

De Smet assured the man of his prayers. When Red Fish returned to his village, he found that his daughter had escaped and once more was with his people. The entire tribe praised the power of the white man's Great Spirit. Indian women had property rights that included the tipi and household goods. An Indian friend once told me, "a husband in the dog house would throw his moccasins inside the tipi to see if he then might come inside. If they were thrown out by the woman, he knew his time for reconciliation was not yet at hand."

In clothes, a woman always was fully covered, her hair generally done up in two long braids. Her ability in crafts was a matter of public display and often had a bearing on her eligibility for marriage. Crow women, members of one of the wealthier tribes, were noted for their bead and quill work. They were quite appealing to mountain men, who considered them the elite among the tribes. Favorite among the beads, generally obtained by trading, were the blue colors which represented the blue sky. Preferred were the large quality beads manufactured in Venice, a center for such merchandise; Czechoslovakia later competed in this remunerative trade. The mountain man who had such quality "foofaraw" in his "possibles" sack was lucky indeed.[17]

The Indian woman scraped skins, gathered fuel and berries, and dug for edible roots. Cooking, sewing, and socializing with the other women were part of her daily routine. Apparently, a popular topic of discussion was the sexual prowess of the village men; we are told that the women were in no way prudish among themselves. "Mores varied from tribe to tribe. The Cheyenne and Sioux placed a high, in some cases, almost psychopathic value on premarital chastity—for women—while the Crow and Arikara found this of little concern. . . . In general, sexual relations were much freer, easier and more permissive" than in white culture.[18] Although men had to purify themselves through the sweat bath, the women were exempt, for they were purified each lunar month with the menses.

In certain tribes, marriage was a nonevent; in others it followed carefully prescribed rituals. In one ritual, the brave obtained a flute which was used almost exclusively for courting. He played it in the village or on a nearby hill, where its notes would waft down to the young woman's tipi. The suitor was the butt of many jokes, as are young men in our own society when they begin to give marriage serious thought.

As maiden and youth entered courtship they were allowed to speak under a blanket draped as an awning over their heads, in front of her parent's lodge. A prospective bride made her preparations for marriage by erecting a tipi and collecting the various household appurtenances needed for married life. These were placed in the center of the camp as a kind of bridal display.

The father of the bride would tether a number of horses around the bridal tipi to let the suitor know how many horses he wanted in exchange for his daughter. The desired number usually was twice the amount the father put there. When the suitor had brought the requisite number of horses to the spot, the young couple went into the tipi together and were considered married. Of course, it was understood that when the brave married the girl, he virtually married the whole family. When white men married Indian women they found that they were responsible not only for the family but virtually for the tribe itself! Many had not anticipated this and no doubt it gave many some pause at the thought of marriage.

Many Indian women preferred white suitors because, coming out of a more benign culture, whites often (but not always) treated women better. At the 1838 rendezvous, Mrs. Smith, wife of a missionary, described the two Indian wives of Captain Andrew Drips, a well-known mountain man and their leader and guide. She confided to her diary:

They are trimmed off in high style, I assure you. The oldest wife rides a beautiful white horse, her saddle ornamented with beads and many little ginglies. A beautiful white sheepskin covering for the horse, cut in fringes one and a half yards deep, ornamented with collars and a great number of thimbles pierced in the top and hung to the fringe like little balls, making a fine gingle as she rides along, then comes the rider with her scarlet blanket, painted face and handkerchief on her head sitting astride. This is the fashion of the country. The second wife acts as an attendant.[19]

Many of the relationships between white man and Indian woman were loving and stable, but others simply were a matter of convenience, giving the white an entrée into trading with the village. Indeed, such marriages were virtually a condition of employment for some workers of the Hudson's Bay Company.

Many whites considered marriage with an Indian maiden almost utopian. According to numerous testimonials, Indian women made not only "interesting lovers but marvelous lodgekeepers, home economists and mothers."[20] Jim Bridger, as we have seen, married a Flathead, a Ute, and a Snake. Similarly, Joe Meek, Joseph Walker, and Kit Carson married into the tribes.

One of the problems faced by a married Indian woman was that should her husband be killed, whether in battle or otherwise, there would be no one to support her and her family. For some women in the poorer tribes, widowhood could prove disastrous, and struggle though they might, unless someone "adopted" them and shared their largess, they often faced certain death. The economics of a marginal people required this kind of severity, and all Indians knew it. Life was not fair. The situation was somewhat ameliorated through polygamy, a virtual necessity among peoples where, because of wars and the danger of the hunt, women always outnumbered men. There was a kind of substitute for the Jewish Levirate Law at work here.

In most tribes divorce was permitted. Although marital transgressions might be winked at, if the woman was unhappy in her marriage she would simply take her husband's belongings and place them outside the tipi. Given this public evidence of her displeasure with the union, he, in turn, would take back the horses given as a present to the father-in-law. Thus was marriage dissolved.

Taking back what was given, whether in marriages or in any other transaction, was quite common and there is much to justify the term

Indian giver. Nevertheless, the Indians had a complex code of giving not understood by whites. The phrase has a legitimate and benign meaning, in that the recipient understands that something given can always revert to the giver if the giver needs it again. When things are given, in other words, they aren't necessarily given for good!

The husband too could divorce his mate just as easily. If he discovered that his wife was unfaithful, he usually had the right to cut off her nose or ear to mark her infidelity.

All Indians loved their offspring dearly, and contrary to white practice, disciplining youngsters was strongly frowned upon. In contemporary language, Indian parents were extremely permissive. Even today, where Indian youngsters attend school with whites, teachers may be specially instructed not to discipline their charges in any way, verbal or otherwise.

Although the tribe had no formal school system, the extended family and, indeed, the entire village served this function. Boys were taught their roles as braves by hunting, vision-seeking (going alone into the wilderness to discover their course in life), and taking part in various other tasks their status demanded. All entailed proper attitudes to others. The games they played often mirrored the adult life to come. Instead of the "3 Rs," they learned all the subtleties of *reading sign*—how to interpret landforms to find water, how to find and understand traces of human and animal passage, how to scan sky and horizon for indications of weather, and other things of that sort.

The Indian brave was taught by his culture to shun manual labor, for matters manual and laborious were regarded as women's work. It was beneath male dignity to farm, haul wood, pick berries, or clean up the campground. Braves also disdained trapping. Sitting Bull, the Uncpapa Sioux, spoke for all in expressing his opinion of whites to an interviewer: "I don't want anything to do with a people who make a brave carry water on his shoulder, or haul manure."[21]

The domestic tasks shunned by braves were learned by the girls as they grew up. No one questioned the roles of the sexes and the division of labor as they followed in the path marked out by their ancestors. But conventions were not so rigid as they may sound, for, if gender roles were firmly determined, the Indians recognized more than two possibilities.

Every camp had its number of what the French called *berdache*— what we might call gays, transvestites, and hermaphrodites, except that these terms imply social roles foreign to Indian culture. The *berdache* were completely accepted, not as braves but on their own terms, being allowed to do as they preferred. Often they dressed in women's garb and did the general work of women. As different, they were considered holy (*wakan*) and even functioned as "name givers." This general lack of prejudice extended to blacks and other non-Indians, who on a number of occasions were fully accepted into the tribe.

Contrary to the stereotype of the stern and taciturn Indian, the brave was a great talker and could command his emotions at will, laughing uproariously at one moment and weeping to the heavens the next. He enjoyed camp games, beginning in youth when he became skilled at tossing a lance through a rolling hoop. A form of lacrosse also was played. All the pastimes engaged in by the brave or would-be brave promoted skill and strength as a warrior. An inveterate gambler, the brave would bet on any kind of game—dice, cards, horseracing, and the shell game. He would risk the very highest stakes, often his wife and entire belongings.

In battle, the brave always sought honors to "count coup." (The French word *coup* means a "blow" or "strike.") Individual acts of bravery enabled him to notch his coup stick, which he might carry about later or place in front of his lodge for all to see. This was our equivalent of medals presented to soldiers for acts of heroism. Interestingly, as we saw earlier, although normally coup could be counted only on human opponents, honor also was earned by wounding or killing a grizzly.

There were low order and higher order coups. Until whites learned of this, they were puzzled when an Indian would lance a soldier already killed by another brave. The explanation was that the second Indian would gain some coup credit. The aim in war was not necessarily to kill or even to defeat, but rather to obtain coup honors. Thus, a brave who physically touched his opponent had a higher coup than one who pierced him with a lance. Lesser honor was given those who shot the opponent with a bow and arrow.

Prompted by coup fever to gain distinction in his village, the brave tended to be an individualist in battle and sought his coup honors without respect to other considerations. His concern was not the outcome of a battle so much as his personal glory. This lack of organizational discipline frequently wreaked havoc on the tribe's common good; individuals often had to have their impetuosity held in check. This was accomplished by strong threats of punishment directed at those who broke ranks and went off on their own. There were special Indian police units, such as the famed Cheyenne dog soldiers, to help restrain the show-offs.

The Plains Indian's wealth was displayed in the number and quality of horses he owned; consequently, horse stealing raids were frequent. The Indian prized above all a good warrior steed and a buffalo-running horse. Going into battle, both man and steed would be painted to terrify the enemy, much like ancient Celts and African blacks in their battles and rituals. This was sound psychology; some

Remington sketches of Indians on the warpath convey a sense of how intimidating they must have been to enemies. Nor were the Indians alone in using this ploy. The river steamer the *Western Engineer* was described in the *St. Louis Enquirer* for June 25, 1819:

The bow of the vessel exhibits the form of a huge water serpent, black and scaly, rising out of the water from under the boat, his head as high as the deck, darted forward, his open mouth vomiting smoke and apparently carrying the boat on his back. From under the boat, at its stern, issues a stream of foaming water, dashing violently along. . . . Neither wind nor human hands are seen to help her, and to the eye of ignorance, the illusion is complete that a monster of the deep carries her on his back, smoking with fatigue, and lashing the waves with violent exertion.[22]

Of course, the pair of swivel guns carried by the steamer lent reality to the painted menace and helped it reach its destination on the Upper Missouri. (Major Chenault's Flying Tiger squadron in the Indo-China theatre of the Second World War employed the same effects.)

The brave was an excellent horseman, and many army officers called them the best light cavalry units ever encountered. Riding his compact horse, the brave with reasonable accuracy could unleash a string of arrows at an enemy, leaning almost completely hidden under the horse's neck.

Fighting, however, was not done in white man's ways. If, on the way to battle or a raid, the brave encountered an unfavorable omen (such as an owl or hoot of an owl, a bird viewed as an omen of death in some tribes), he would turn and go back, willing to wait for other and more auspicious times. Almost any unusual event (the equivalent of our breaking a mirror or walking under a ladder) could deter action. Generally, every brave accepted his fellow's interpretation and respected it, claiming the right so to act himself at another time. The exception was when the village with its women and children was in danger. Then the braves held their ground even to the death.

As indicated earlier, the Indian warrior seldom fought for total victory; his main object was to win coup and to humiliate the enemy. He might use the least force possible to achieve the humbling of the enemy. On one occasion, the Crow were reported to have beaten back some Oglalas with sticks and willow reeds, the latter already demoralized and in retreat.[23] Almost never did the Indian commit the time and forces necessary to lay siege, even though it might have seemed in his favor to do so. The guerrilla tactics of hit and run were his forte and he became impatient when a battle dragged on. (There were notable exceptions, which we will discuss in Chapter 7.)

Occasionally, an older warrior might prove his bravery and win respect for his entire tribe from the enemy by placing a stake in the ground and tying his leg to it with a length of cord as evidence of his intention to fight to the death. An outstanding act of pure heroism, it echoed the Indian battle dictum, "Any day for a warrior is a good day to die." Yet rules of the ritual did allow for friends of the staked man to rescue him if possible.

Battles and raids usually were conducted in warmer weather, as cold and snow greatly restricted mobility. There was a kind of unwritten agreement to refrain from fighting at these times, although sporadic skirmishes and raids took place. The U.S. Army finally took advantage of this winter-weakened condition and began to pursue winter campaigns against Indians. Custer's Battle of the Washita is an example, but fighting on the high plains in winter proved to be nearly as formidable an undertaking for the army as for the Indians.

Spring and fall would find the brave riding into battle stripped down to his loin cloth or even stark naked. There was a good reason for the lack of dress. When a bullet, arrow, or lance hit clothing, it thrust the foreign matter into the wound, and infection was almost certain. Indians knew no modern medicine, but they did realize that a clean wound was not as bad as a dirty one.

One of the accouterments of the brave going into battle was a buffalo rawhide shield. Soaked in water and highly tightened by shrinking, it was practically as hard as iron, although it weighed considerably less. Musket balls and some bullets, striking it at an angle, would easily glance off. The same was true for lance thrusts. Rawhide thus soaked and dried was so strong that strips of it were used to repair broken instruments. Wrapped around a broken lance or rifle stock and set, the binding scarcely could be removed. Indians in the Southwest used such rawhide thongs for all sorts of craftwork and repair. (Readers of adventure stories know the usefulness of rawhide in dealing with a prisoner staked to the ground. Wetting thongs tied around the neck or wrist assured progressive tightening of the bonds until the prisoner choked to death or had blood circulation to the extremities blocked off.)

In addition to the bow, lance, and war club (some made of a simple stone tied to a stick, others with a spike or broken blade emerging from the head), many Indians also had muskets. These often were trade items obtained from white trappers; others were spoils of war. The musket itself was not particularly accurate because its barrel was not rifled (grooved) to spin the ball as it came out the muzzle. The weapon was even less accurate in the hands of Indians than whites because shortage of ammunition meant that Indians got little practice in marksmanship. Some believed that it wasn't the bullet that killed but the sound directed at the target! In order to keep the Indian dependent, whites tended not to trade such necessary accessories as lead and bullet molds.

On the plains, the tomahawk was not much used in battle but still was a desired trade item, particularly when made with a blade at one end and a pipe at the other, the stock being hollowed with a draw hole. Many contests in "throwing the hawk" were held in camp. A good and effective throw that would bury the blade in a victim had the "hawk" rotate one and a half times in approximately eighteen feet. Unlike throws that utilize the breaking action of the wrist to impart momentum, the wrist remains uncocked in throwing the "hawk." (Modern horseshoe players use the same one and a half toss.) The regular trade tomahawk had a hardwood handle about eighteen inches long with a piece of heated strap iron tightly wrapped around one end. Just before closing the ends of the strap iron, a blade was inserted at its edges and then iron and blade were effectively welded together. Curiously, although smithing is a fairly simple operation, Indians from the early days of Lewis and Clark were in awe of ironsmithing and themselves never mastered the art.

De rigueur for battle was the scalping knife, which offered convincing evidence of the bearer's purpose and prowess. In scalping, the warrior would press his knee on the prone victim's back, grab the hair at the forehead, and lift it, all the while pulling severely in order to cut a clean line into the top of the scalp. Removing the bloody mess, the brave would wave it in the air triumphantly and send forth a bloodcurdling cry. (Only a representative piece of scalp needed to be taken, not the whole covering.) Many victims were scalped while still alive, and the few who survived remembered it as an intensely painful experience. One survivor was a railroad worker who with others was scalped during an Indian attack and left for dead. In fleeing from white reinforcements, however, the Indian dropped his trophy and the victim recovered it. Later the scalp found its way to a museum in Omaha where it was displayed. Most scalps were taken back to the Indian village and there displayed on a scalp pole, advertising their owners' prowess.

Scalping was a time-honored custom among Plains Indians. Archeologists recently uncovered a huge pit near Cow Creek, South Dakota, holding five hundred Indian skulls, all of which had been scalped. This site dates back to the thirteenth century. (The early date conflicts with theories that Indians learned scalping from the whites.) In colonial times, Governor Knight of New Amsterdam paid for Indian scalps. In 1837, the state of Chihuahua in Mexico also paid for scalps, an Apache warrior's scalp bringing a hundred dollars, an Indian woman's fifty, and a child's twenty-five. The bounty was withdrawn when officials realized that many Mexicans were being scalped by bandits, since Mexican hair resembled Apache hair.

When the warrior came home with his coups, he would hire a town crier or caller before entering the village. The crier usually was an old man who was given some gifts in return. He announced exploits of the brave, and the village much enjoyed the story of the battle or fight, praising the brave for his courage and success. If the fight occurred near the village, the women and children would mutilate the victim, cutting off parts, slicing through muscles, and the like, to make sure the dead warrior could not function again in the afterlife. The victorious warrior himself might take a part of the body, usually a macho sex symbol, and wave it when going into the next battle to show his power. Sometimes the severed scrotum and penis were stuffed in the victim's mouth to indicate Indian disdain for the victim.

Mutilation of victims was a common practice. Apaches would even pound in the heads of enemy babies and swing them into nearby cacti. Later, some white soldiers adopted the practice, out of hatred of the alien enemy or the emotion of the moment.

One of the most notorious documented mutilations was that visited upon troops from Fort Phil Kearny in 1866 where over eighty men were ambushed and killed.[24] Here is the report of John Guthrie who helped load the bodies: "We walked on top of their internals and did not know it in the high grass. Picked them up, that is their internals, did not know the soldier they belonged to, so you see the cavalry man got an infantry man's guts and an infantry man got a cavalry man's guts."

The official report of the fort's Commander was more graphic:

Eyes torn out and laid on the rocks; noses cut off; ears cut off; chins hewn off; teeth chopped out; joints of fingers; brains taken out and exposed; hands cut off; feet cut off; arms taken out from sockets; private parts severed and indecently placed on the person; eyes, ears, mouth and arms penetrated with spear-heads, sticks and arrows slashed to separation with knives; skulls severed in every form, from chin to crown; muscles of calves, thighs, stomach, breast, back arms and cheek taken out; punctures upon every sensitive part of the body, even to the sole of the feet and palms of the hand. All this does not approximate the whole truth.[25]

Indians mourned their own losses. When a member of the tribe was killed in the battle, an immense wail would go up in the village.

In one public ritual of grief, the immediate male relatives of the warrior would slash their chests; the women would cut their hair and often chop a joint off a finger (usually the little one) or sometimes an entire finger.[26]

If any prisoners were taken, they might be tied to a stake and tortured by the squaws and children, who would stone them and jab them with sticks until death relieved the victim. Some prisoners were turned into slaves and, to prevent their running away, their hamstrings might be severed. The prisoner was left able to limp and perform manual labor.

The warrior's bravery was illustrated particularly in the buffalo hunt.[27] Before setting out, Indians would call upon the sacred to assure a successful hunt. Drawing an outline of the buffalo on the ground, they would throw spears at it. (Interestingly, prehistoric men drew outlines of wisent on the cave walls in southern France, perhaps hurling their spears at it in a similar ritual.) Another way to encourage a successful hunt was for braves to offer their wives' sexual favors to old men and even strangers in the camp.

A successful hunt could be conducted in various ways. One technique was to build an open corral or find a box canyon into which the buffalo would be stampeded. Stones would be placed on both sides of the path leading to the enclosure; the buffalo was hesitant to step over the barrier and would follow the lines of demarcation. (A similar technique was used for pronghorn, which were the Plains Indians' second greatest source of food.) Indians at the rear and sides of the herd would make noise, and the excited and confused buffalo would be directed into the enclosure and killed at will.

Another variation was to stampede buffalo over a cliff or into a gully, killing or injuring many of the animals. Such a mass killing was witnessed by the artist George Catlin, who lived with the Mandans in the 1830s. He tells of the Sioux killing fourteen hundred buffalo in this way, taking only the tongues to trade to whites for but a few gallons of whiskey. There are a number of cliff falls in the West, especially in Montana, where even today thousands of bones give mute but eloquent testimony to this wasteful practice. Whatever romantics may suppose, ecology was not a byword with the Indians.

Another way of procuring buffalo was to don wolf skins and approach the herd, rising up and firing arrows into the prey. This was quite effective, for buffalo herds were used to the presence of wolves and had little fear of them. Wolves attacked only the very young, the very aged, or the infirm. They did so by biting through the hamstrings, thereby crippling the animal. A herd could afford such losses.

Instead of a wolf-skin covering, Indians might wear a buffalo calf skin and make a bleating sound, enticing buffalo to investigate what seemed to be one of their young in trouble. When the buffalo approached, the Indian had a good opportunity to make the kill.

The most dangerous way to hunt buffalo was to ride a specially trained buffalo horse right alongside the herd, or even directly into it. Many an Indian was killed when his horse stumbled in a prairie dog hole, tossing its rider beneath the thousands of pounding hooves. Riding next to or in the herd, the Indian would fire his arrows from his short bow with devastating effect. Sometimes, hitting no obstructive bones, the arrow went directly through the entire body. Arrows made the animal bleed more freely than bullets, although large calibre bullets might produce a greater shock effect. When using guns, the animal had to be shot "in the lights" (lungs), because the skull was so thick that a bullet or ball often flattened against it, never penetrating the brain. Arrow-stricken animals would wander off to die of hemorrhage and could be tracked later. Hunters would stay with the herd and increase the kill.

The bows used were less than four feet long, the arrows slightly over two feet. Each arrow bore the mark of its owner, so the winner of the prize could easily be determined. The prize was not the buffalo, which was shared by the village, but rather the honor for getting the food. Once the hunt was over, women and youngsters old enough to be useful would get to work skinning the animal and cutting its carcass into portable pieces of meat. Many started immediately by devouring the favorite delicacies such as the intestines and their half-digested food (boudins), the hump fat (fleece), the tongue, and the first two ribs. Thrusting their hands into the innards, they would seize chunks of liver, fat, and various organs and stuff them into their mouths. (So delicious were the buffalo to the Indians that in the spring breakup on the Missouri, when carcasses floated on ice chunks, they would risk life and limb to swim out and get masses of the half rotted and green flesh for eating.)

The body cavity of the buffalo, as we have seen, could be used as a kind of kettle. Various fluids and meats from the body would be cooked in it by heating stones and throwing them into the brew. Thigh bones would be cracked to get at the rich blood-building marrow inside. Such moments truly were times of plenty.

Jerky was made by cutting the meat into thin strips which would be laid in the sun or hung on drying racks. Several days of such weathering produced a nutritious and highly portable preserved food.

The hide would be taken back to the village and staked out by the women. It would be cleaned with sharpened bones used as scrapers, often taken from the buffalo or other animals. Shoulder blades were the best. The scraping eliminated pieces of fat and meat and thinned the hide. Next, the brains of the animal were rubbed into the hide to soften, tan, and preserve it. Finally, the hide would be thrown over a leather rope put up much like a clothesline and seesawed back and forth by two women, working it until it was soft and pliable.

As a part of every hunt, the hunter paid his respect to the buffalo persons who gave of themselves so that the tribe might live. This was done by leaving behind some food or piece of the animal. This courtesy was performed in fishing as well, and was an indication of gratitude for nature's bounty.

Anything that serves a vital human need may be designated as sacred, as, for example, the sun, a river or lake, or the land itself. The buffalo sustained the life of the Plains Indians and became as much a part of their culture as it was a part of nature. (As we have seen, the Indians made no effort to distinguish between themselves and nature, and so what was cultural was also seen as natural.) Accordingly, the buffalo was personified in a sacred figure, the White Buffalo Calf Woman. The buffalo headdress became a part of religious rituals and the skull itself was used in the Sun Dance Ceremony. These will be discussed later in this chapter.

The pronghorn, which still is plentiful in the high plains, also were objects of the hunt. This small, beautiful, and delicate-seeming creature is the fastest ungulate in North America. Its speed approaches sixty miles per hour and it seems to fear no four-legged creatures. Pronghorn spook easily at two-legged man, however, and hunting these elusive creatures required a special set of techniques. Because they are immensely curious, a hunter would lie hidden in the high grass and wave a cloth or shoe so that only it was visible. The pronghorn would come closer and closer to investigate and finally approach within range of an arrow or rifle.

Back in the village, life was lively and noisy, as children, dogs, and people went about their daily activities. Dogs were the Indians' original domestic animals and remained extremely useful even after the advent of horses. In any semi-permanent dwelling area, the need for law and order forced the inhabitants to insure justice. But in handling transgressions within their own tribes, the Indians had a system of justice very different from that of whites. Exile often was an effective punishment and deterrent; transgressors might be barred from the camp for days on end, although they were sometimes permitted to come back at night. Exile also might be absolute, with death the penalty if the criminal returned. But more often than not, the Indians did not think of crimes as committed against the community so much as against the individual who was aggrieved. To balance the scales of justice, it was usually enough to satisfy that individual, provided that both perpetrator and victim could agree on what was fair in retribution.

Each village had not one but several chiefs. One might be an administrator or tribal leader in organization; he worked with the people, rather than being set off king-like apart from them. Another was a war leader, and a third was the medicine man. Chief Joseph of the Nez Percé, for example, was more or less an administrator, and Sitting Bull of the Uncpapa Sioux was a medicine man, although he also served as a war leader. Although the medicine man ordinarily was not a chief, his influence was great and he was frequently consulted by young braves seeking a vision to tell them their place in life.

For the most part, chiefs retained their position only with the tacit consent of the others. Medicine men had to be successful in order to retain their positions; their lives might be endangered if they did not effect their cures. They were resident psychiatrists, physicians, charlatans, pharmacists, and counsellors all rolled up in one. They kept their secrets to themselves and, in this way, often lived to an old age. Only then would they take on apprentices, for to do so earlier would be to lose their hold over the people.

We must give them credit because, in addition to ceremony, the medicine men knew the value of certain herbs, many of which later became known and used by whites. For toothaches, wild licorice or the leaf of yarrow often eased the pain, and a decoction of the roots of burdock served as a remedy for pleurisy. The same roots also acted as a diuretic and were used for mild kidney ailments such as soreness in that area. The roots of wild black current berries provided stronger medicine for more severe kidney infection. Goldenrod, mixed with hot water, could be employed to induce the perspiration especially important to the ritual sweat bath ceremony. (Usually the bath itself brought about sufficient sweat, however.) To alleviate sore eyes from the smoke-filled tipis, the medicine man resorted to a strong and effective potion derived from the root of the Canadian anemone. Applied externally and taken internally, it was a useful eyewash. Cow parsnip was used for convulsions and as a poultice for boils. Those who broke tribal taboos might be forced to bathe in an extraction of the strong wild sage. The plantain root gave relief from hemorrhoids, and the simple juice of the leaves of ground ivy helped alleviate nasal congestion and headaches. Lastly, young braves made themselves into dandies with perfume from the fruit of prickly ash. The pharmacognosy of the Indians was exceptional, but their ability to deal with bone fractures was limited. Although there was some attempt at setting bones when limbs were broken, the results were usually poor and many Indians remained lifelong cripples.

The hygienic habits of Indian tribes differed greatly. Cleanliness was especially important to many of the Plains Indians, who took daily baths in the river even in winter. Other tribes, like some in the Northwest encountered by Lewis and Clark, were near the animal level. Lice were fairly constant companions everywhere. People would pick them out of each other's hair and then crack them between their teeth. Placing clothing on a smoking mound would drive the pests from the garments. Although individuals who survived all the dangers of illness, injury, and infestation sometimes went on to live long lives, the average Indian lifespan was only thirty years. Today, when the lifespan of people in developed nations is in the seventies, for the Native American it is only forty-five.

Once in contact with whites, the Indians suffered all sorts of serious illnesses, many of which were only minor inconveniences for whites, whose immunity had been built up through generations of exposure. Indians even died from chicken pox and measles; venereal diseases were rampant. We recall that Lewis and Clark found Northwest Indians infected with venereal disease by the sailors who visited them. Nonetheless, evidence suggests that although such diseases may have been exacerbated by white contact, they also were indigenous to Indians.

Of all the ills that befell the Plains Indian, smallpox was the greatest disaster. One of man's most dreaded diseases, it can be traced back as far as the twelfth century B.C.: the mummy of the Egyptian ruler Ramses V bears witness to its ravages. It conquered the Aztecs more swiftly than the arms of Cortez. Popularly known as the Red Death, it travelled up the Missouri River in 1837 on the steamer *St. Peter's*; cases of the disease among the crew were discovered above Fort Pierre. The steamer captain apparently thought only of finishing and profiting from his commercial venture. Hence, he proceeded on to Fort Clark and Fort Union.[28]

There is a story that smallpox spread to the Indians at Fort Clark when an infected blanket was stolen from the ship. In any event, the first death from the disease was reported there one month later; it then spread to neighboring Sioux, Minitari, and Gros Ventres. At first, Arickaras, who had built up a degree of immunity from previous contact, were scarcely affected. It was almost as though they had been vaccinated, although vaccine was unavailable in the wilderness. (The vaccine being used in the East was unreliable; the colonial preacher Jonathan Edwards was vaccinated upon becoming president of Princeton University in 1758 and died a month later.) With the advent of the killer disease, tribes fell out with each other; some declared that the whites were in collusion with the temporarily immune Arickaras to reduce the power of the other tribes, especially the Mandans. A Mandan chief painted by Catlin was bitter. His name was Four Bears or Máto-Tope.

Ever since I can remember, I have loved the Whites. I have lived with them ever since I was a boy and . . . I have never Wronged a White Man, on the Contrary I have always Protected them from the insults of others. . . . The 4 Bears never saw a White Man hungry, but what he gave him to eat, Drink, and a Buffalo skin to sleep on. . . . I was always ready to die for them. Which they cannot deny. I have done everything that a red Skin could do for them, and how they repaid it! . . . I do not fear Death my friends. You Know it, but to *die* with my face rotten, that even the Wolves will shrink with horror at seeing Me, and say to themselves, that is the 4 Bears the Friend of the Whites— . . . Rise all together and Not leave one of them alive.[29]

Of over eight hundred Mandans, only thirty survived. And many whites said good riddance.

The *St. Peter's,* having reached the Assiniboin post at Fort Union, actually discharged a smallpox victim there, and the plague spread to that tribe. Attempts to inoculate some with the live virus met with mixed success. Scattering, the Assiniboin spread the disease, although a number killed themselves. Over six hundred lodges housing four to five persons each were decimated. Only eleven hundred Assiniboins survived the plague. Next, a band of Blackfeet came down river to trade with the whites. Waved off, they thought the whites were tricking them in order to trade with others instead, so the Blackfeet persisted in entering the fort trading area and caught the disease.

For some time, the post did no trading at all because their customers had died off. Between 1837 and 1840, the epidemic cost approximately seventeen thousand lives among the Indians. This disaster changed the tribal power structure of the Plains Indian and also created a new smallpox mythology. The new myth, like all myths, helped people to live with what they could not understand.[30]

Many other diseases endured by the Native Americans were caused by poor sanitation. Cholera was associated with filth and struck the larger villages with nearly total devastation. During epidemics, we are told that the stench from the feces and decaying corpses of dogs, horses, and humans was so bad that many villages had to move almost as soon as they set up camp. In any event, Indians, who were hunters rather than gatherers and farmers, had to move their villages frequently because, after a while, game became scarce in their vicinity and their horses ate up all the forage.

Dysentery was rampant and had a variety of causes. Some cases were the result of bad hygiene and others of food insufficiently cooked or laden with greases and fats. Contributing in no small way to this debilitating condition were alkaline-impregnated waters that later proved a curse to white travellers as well.

Following contacts with white fur traders, alcoholism became a constant problem to the Indian, whose constitution was extremely vulnerable to its ravages. Drug abuse was relatively unknown at that time; peyote was used, but mostly in religious ceremonies. (Today drug abuse is as rampant among Indians as whites. Alcoholism is even worse; some Indian leaders cite the addiction at a 70 percent rate.)

Winter was especially hard on the Plains Indians. This is shown by the names they gave to its worst months, "month of the popping trees"—that is, the weather was so cold that the sap in trees froze and expanded, exploding trees like a cannon. The north winds, unbroken by any mountain range, regularly produced wind chill factors of minus 120 degrees. The Indians' remarkable food invention, pemmican, often was all that got them through the winter—that and the jerked meat prepared during the warmer months. But jerked meat, only about one-sixth the weight of the fresh meat from which it was derived, had the drawback of becoming dry and difficult to chew. In dampish weather, too, it tended to absorb water, losing its weight advantage for travel and becoming likely to decay.

The answer to the problem of food storage was pemmican. It was made by pulverizing the jerky and nearly filling a skin bag about the size of a flour sack. The sack was then poured full of liquid marrow fat, which seeped through the jerky. The bags were stitched closed, sealed with tallow, and pressed flat to a thickness of five inches. Each bag weighed about one hundred pounds. Stored in this manner, pemmican could lie unspoiled for over a century.

Several types of pemmican were made, one a lighter grade for summer use and another a heavier variety for winter. Both were mixed with berries. Opinions differed on the mixture's palatability; some swore by it, others swore at it, but regardless, it was a good food staple. Its low weight was welcomed by all involved in frequent transport. French Canadian trappers and voyageurs, who consumed (sometimes by guaranteed contract) up to eight pounds of meat a day, were "satisfactorily" reduced to one and a half pounds of pemmican. Kaiser Wilhelm fed it to his German troops in the First World War, and Commodore Perry used it in his polar expeditions. Remembering the Second World War, it might be considered an effective "K" or "C" ration.[31]

Communication was a major problem in the West. Although many Indian languages were only variations of a dialect, others were radically different. For example, the difference between Spanish and Portuguese is not great, but between them and Finnish or Chinese there is virtually nothing in common. Similarly, the three major dialects of Sioux—Dakota, Nakota, and Lakota (the D-N-L dialects)— are closely related and are spoken in that order, travelling east to west. But the Athapaskan languages of some Northwest Indians, to which Navaho is closely related, were a major puzzle to Lewis and Clark, who found the guttural sounds almost impossible to imitate. Like Dutch, they seemed to an outsider not so much a language as a disease of the throat.

But necessity inspires invention, and the celebrated sign language of the plains came to the rescue. It was especially useful in communicating not only between various Indian groups but between Indians and whites, as well. It took some learning on all sides but it was quite effective. Experts estimate that in the nineteenth century there were over 110,000 sign-speaking Indians in the United States.[32]

As we have seen, tribes might be designated by special sign characters. Sioux were indicated by passing one's fingers across one's throat, signifying "cutthroat," because the Sioux commonly engaged in such practice. To make the same sign across the arm would indicate Cheyenne, who mutilated their victims. A waving hand motion could indicate a Snake (Shoshone), or, in another context, the animal snake or a fish. Pawnees were represented with two fingers, one held on each side of the temple to indicate wolf, their animal totem. Arapahoes, who often tattooed themselves, were signified by rapidly tapping one's chest to imitate tattooing. Flatheads were signed by placing one's hands across one's forehead with finger tips touching. Sucking one's fingers, as Sacajawea did when she met her people, showed that one was born in that tribe. To bring both arms up and put them down as if laying a blanket on the ground signified a desire to trade.

Misinterpretation was always a real and sometimes disastrous possibility. For example, in early times, to prove they were friendly, Indians might ride into a white man's camp firing off their single-shot muskets. Whites then shot at the Indians, thinking they were being attacked. In fact, the Indians were showing they came in peace because with their weapons fired, they were defenseless.

The Indians, having no written language, preserved their history through petroglyphs (carving on rocks) and pictographs (painting on skins and other surfaces). There were also storytellers who sometimes used pictographs. The Sioux along the Missouri preserved their tribal memories through a "Big Missouri Winter Count."[33] One person was chosen to be the tribe's historian, usually a hereditary honor. Choosing one event considered the most important from each year, he then would paint a picture of it on a deer or buffalo skin. This skin would be handed down with its interpretation to his successors. The "Big Missouri Winter Count" began in 1796 and continued until 1926. One example preserved in the Sioux Indian Museum in Rapid City, South Dakota, is a series of drawings on a single large hide.

It is interesting to compare what the Indian considered important during a given year and what the whites chose for the main event. For example, the skin records a successful horse stealing foray (1796), a cold winter (1824), a year of great plenty (1857), and the death of a minor chief (1877). The Custer battle is not depicted but the birth of quadruplets is noted (1905). A few years are skipped, when nothing important happened in the Indian historian's judgment.

As Indian and white contact increased, new Indian words, phrases, and signs were created to meet the needs. This was scarcely a problem since their languages already were rich and descriptive ones. For example, the Sioux referred to the snow-capped Rockies as the "great shining mountains" and the Grand Canyon as the "upside down mountain;" the mighty Missouri, *mnisose*, is equivalent to our "Big Muddy." As we learned earlier, months were designated by descriptions characteristic of the seasons. January was the time of "popping trees" (strong cold), and April was the "moon time," when the green grass comes up. May was the time of "pony shedding."

Things related to white culture also could be signified descriptively. Whites may have called the railroad the "iron horse" but to the Indians it was "many wagons, no horses." Infantry were "walk-a-heap" and cavalry were "long knives." Artillery were "guns that shoot twice" (once out of the muzzle and once exploding on its target). Custer was known as "Yellow Hair" or, because of his seeming good fortune, "Son of the Morning Star."

The Sioux language, strictly speaking, has no tenses of future and past; hence one must pay particular attention to the context to determine its reference. This often gave rise to confusion with whites in treaty making. The language also reflected the assumption that everything is related somehow in complexes that are grouped together by association rather than logic. For example, all round objects are related. The Lakota word for *seed*, *su*, appears in the words for hail—*wasu*, "snow seed," and bullet, *mazasu*, "metal seed." A European might see little or no logical connection between hail and bullets but, to the Sioux, they both belong to the "seed" or "seed-like" family. The ancient Sioux saw a Wittgensteinian "family resemblance" here.[34]

Indians were great orators, and whites as well as Indians knew it to be impolite to interrupt the speaker. Patience was essential for sometimes it might take an hour or so for the speaker to warm to his topic—even to get near his topic. Sometimes when the Indian speaker would finish, he would not drop his voice at the end of his sentence. The white waited for him to continue speaking, but only silence ensued. It was some time before the white realized it was now his turn. The phrase, "I have spoken," however, was a clear signal for the other to begin.

Communication problems also arose because of the Indian's holistic view of the world in which he lived. For the Indian, everything was strung together rather than being sharply separated. In life, there was no gap separating the dream world and the real world or, for that matter, yesterday and today. All were part of an undifferentiated and ever-constant flow. An Indian in telling about an event might move freely between what he saw and what he dreamed or even wished or expected. Facts always had their interpretations, which often were as real as the facts themselves, if not even more so.

Religion and the sacred permeated every moment of the Indian's existence, waking or sleeping. There was no sharp distinction between the natural and the supernatural for all were part of *Wakantakan*, or the great mystery. Every male had to acknowledge this, and it was his duty to fast, pray, and seek his vision which would be his guide for life.

For an individual or a people to succeed, things had to be religiously right. To help assure that, many different rituals were practiced. Indians did not appeal to Wakan or Manitou as a Christian might petition the heavenly father. The rituals were intended to put things in order to assure that one was in harmony with the universe of which man's life was but a single part. Harmony and order, the interrelations of all things, was the goal of the Native American:

> You see I am alive
> You see, I stand in good relation to the earth
> You see, I stand in good relation to the gods
> You see, I stand in good relation to all that is beautiful
> You see, I stand in good relation to you
> You see, I am alive, I am alive.[35]

Among the seven sacred rituals of the Lakota was *inipi*, the Sweat Lodge ceremony, a kind of purification which healed both body and spirit.[36] As Bunge points out, in Sioux the ceremony is literally called "by means of which they make life."[37] We recall that Captain William Clark became its advocate on his trek West.

The big medicine of the Sun Dance was outlawed in 1883 but

stayed alive in practice. By enduring the ritual, a brave became recognized as an elite warrior. Wooden sticks were driven through the pectoral muscles or back muscles; thongs were attached to these and the brave was suspended from a framework out-of-doors. (With some Mandans, the support was the roof of the lodge.) The hanging Indian swung around until the thongs would break through the skin and effect his release. He might tug against them or, if taken down, drag several buffalo skulls by the thongs along the ground until the skin parted. A common method among the Sioux was to tie the long end of the thongs to a sacred cottonwood pole, bending it back and forth to break the skin. It was a proud moment for the entire village when the ordeal was successfully completed.

Still another ritual was the "crying for a vision" that we have mentioned on several occasions. In it, the brave would seek for meaning in life by going out of the village to some desolate hill, cliff, or mountain and stay there until the Spirit moved him. His vision might be a clear and definite one or it might be vague. Upon return, he consulted the medicine man or the holy man (often the same person) to determine the meaning of his vision. Sometimes the brave could not get a vision and would have to go back and try again. He knew visions were not given to all, yet he accepted on good faith the claims of others to their visions.

Other rituals were *Yuwipi* or Healing ceremonies (a combination of prayer and medical help for the afflicted), and the Ghost Keeping ceremony (a special care for the dead, in which someone was appointed to show that concern). Some others were the Making Relatives ceremony, the Girl Becoming a Woman ritual, and the Sacred Ball game. Many are no longer in wide practice. Nevertheless, in today's pan-Indian Native American Church, many of these ceremonies, along with variations on their themes, have been given new vitality. To the other customs this church adds the Altar, the Water Drum, the Morning Water Woman, Walking with Peyote, and many more.

Indian eschatology—that aspect of religion concerned with last things such as death, immortality, and the afterworld—generally is quite vague. For most, the spirit world is much like the world of nature and beauty in which they presently live. In most other religions, heaven is other-worldly; the Indian heaven is worldly. A few, however, such as that of the Pawnee, are quite elaborate. All suggest a nether world, a world of spirits with certain animals acting as go-betweens for the Indians now alive and those elsewhere. One such messenger bird is the crow. Its blackness associates it with the other world and its ability to mimic the human voice puts it in a special class of animals, enabling it to communicate between the two worlds.

One of the holiest of religious objects is the sacred pipe. Although

Indians regularly smoked pipes (the French called them *calumets*), a special place was reserved for the *sacred* pipe, used when a symbol of the holy and the important was wanted. It can take on different forms for special occasions, its bowl being carved as a buffalo or some other animal, but the standard pipe is made with common symbols. One such symbol is four rings carved on the stem signifying the four winds; this version is called a "Four Winds Pipe."

The bowls of the sacred pipe usually were carved from Catlinite, or cinnabar. (The name *Catlinite* honored the artist George Catlin, who felt great affinity for the Mandan and other Missouri River tribes with whom he lived for several years while painting their history.) This cinnabar can be found in scattered sites across the West, but it is most frequently quarried at Pipestone National Monument in southwestern Minnesota. By federal law, only Indians are allowed to dig out the material, which is usually one layer below a limestone formation. Such sites were considered religious sanctuaries by the Indians and it was strange to see warring tribes working peaceably side by side in these pits.

Eastern *kinnikinic* or ground-up red willow bark served as tobacco for the sacred pipe. When it was placed in the pipe bowl, the pipe then was regarded as a holy and sacred object. Agreements made while smoking the pipe were not to be taken lightly; this was equivalent to whites swearing an oath on the Bible. According to their myth, the Sioux were given the sacred pipe by the Sacred White Buffalo Calf Woman. This story is perhaps the most important religious myth of the Sioux, tying together as it does the two sacred objects, the pipe and the buffalo.

As we discussed in an earlier chapter, myth is not a fairytale or falsehood (as the vulgar meaning has it) but a story with a message, a flexible vehicle that carries an important truth for man. Every culture has its myths or stories that help make life within that culture meaningful. What is important in myth (and myth is a part of all human life) is not so much the literal meaning of the story as the message it conveys for human life. We easily recognize the "dead" myths, for they no longer contribute to our living. The living myth governing our lives can be seen only by those outside of it. They *know* it; we *live* it. Myth is a part of tradition, as tradition is a part of culture, as culture is a part of life. As Jaroslav Pelikan, a scholar of the history of religion, put it, "*Traditionalism* is the dead faith of the living, but *tradition* is the living faith of the dead." Bearing in mind the living tradition, let us look at a few typical myths of the Indian.

The Sacred White Buffalo Calf Woman is a story about two Indian boys who were hunting. Suddenly, they saw a woman, who was very beautiful, coming to them. As she approached, one boy thought bad thoughts and the other cautioned him, urging respect. The beautiful woman turned the boy with bad thoughts into a bag of bones and told the other to go back to the village and tell the people what had happened and that she would visit them.

In anticipation of her coming, the villagers built a huge tipi lodge. In it she appeared with the pipe, instructing the people and the chief in its use. She presented it to Chief Standing Hollow Horn, promising that prayers used in conjunction with the pipe would be answered. She also instructed the Indians in the seven sacred rites mentioned above. As she left the village the people saw her turn into a white buffalo.

The albino buffalo thus became a sacred symbol, and when one was seen by Indians, it was approached with great awe and reverence. Whether or not the story was "true," by it the people understood that they would always be on good terms with the holy. The pipe has a line of keepers to watch over and preserve it. What purportedly is the original pipe is kept at Green Grass on the Cheyenne River Reservation in South Dakota.[38] Its keeper is a chief whose name is "Buffalo that walks on two legs" (Tátaṅka húṅuṅpa máni).

Another myth explains for Indians the existence of Devil's Tower in Northeast Wyoming, near the Bighorn Mountains in the Belle Fourche Valley. Devil's Tower is an outcropping of columnar basalt which measures about two miles around the base and slightly over eight hundred feet high. It is surrounded by broken bits of the columns, rock piles called talus. The tower stands alone in a valley of red dirt and high cliffs and can be seen for many miles.

Once there were seven Indian maidens who were playing in the area. A large grizzly bear came upon them and they ran away as fast as they could, but despite their efforts, the bear was gaining. Exhausted, the maidens stopped and awaited their fate. But then the ground on which they stood began to rise and they rose with it into the air. The bear, standing on its hind legs, clawed at the rising tower but the tower rose too fast for him. All the bear could do was to make claw marks (the columns) in the rocky sides. The girls were safe but were puzzled as to how they would get down off the high tower. Then the spirits took them up into the sky and today they are still there. They constitute the Seven Sisters constellation or, as it is known to western astronomers, the Pleiades.

This myth declares the goodness of the spirit world and also explains the unusual basalt formation. Such stories make the world a greater unity for the people who tell—and live—them.

Indian religion governed all life from the cradleboard to the grave. Studies in comparative religion find basic similarities between themes that seem to suggest that fundamental structures of the human mind are common to all mankind.[39] The witch woman is one theme found in the religion of the American Indian. It points to woman as the source of evil in the universe.

The Kiowa are a tribe whose numbers are small. They explain this fact by saying that they once lived in the bowels of the earth (another common theme). There, one brave saw a vine hanging down and, climbing it, reached the surface of the earth. He saw that this was a better place to live. He called down to the others, who climbed up one by one until it came to the turn of a fat woman. Halfway up, her weight broke the vine, leaving all the others stranded. And so woman was the cause of the Kiowa being such a small and powerless tribe. This story justifies woman's lower place on the social scale. Still another myth tells how death was brought into the world by a woman. Although these myths differ in details among a number of tribes, they are basically variations on a theme.

Sacred numbers are a theme also found in various cultures. For example, just as three is a sacred number in Christianity, so four is with the Plains Indians. In Christianity, there were three in the Holy Family and of course in the Trinity, Christ was lost in the temple for three days, at Peter's denial the cock crowed thrice, three died on the cross, Jesus died in three hours, and it would be three days before his return, to cite a few instances.

For the Indians, most things happened in groups of four, although seven also is a frequent number. Four sacred fire arrows were kept by the tribe (uncovered only once a year and reverently carried about like the *Torah*). The quest for a vision required four days of isolation, and the sacred four winds pipe acknowledged this number. Creation took place in four days, and in this, animals were given four chances to succeed at a task to help the Creator.

The Swiss psychiatrist Carl Jung, who had a deep interest in American Indian religion, noted these parallels between Christianity and Native American religion. The White Buffalo Calf Woman bears a striking resemblance to the Virgin Mary, and the figure of Christ on the cross shedding his blood for all somewhat parallels the Sun Dance ceremony. Strings of tobacco ties compare with the rosary or the prayer beads of the Orient. Countless other parallels suggest themselves. Jung developed a theory to account for this. He believed that four is a sacred number for Christianity as it is for the Indians. But for Christianity, the fourth number particularly applies in the inner world. In the case of the Trinity, Jung argued that completeness requires Mary, as a mother figure, to be its fourth member. (He was one of the few Protestants to applaud the Roman Catholic declaration of Mary's Assumption into Heaven.) He pointed also to the four Evangelists and the four horsemen of the Apocalypse.

Paul Steinmetz, a Jesuit priest, has applied Jung's theory in trying to reconcile Christianity with the religion of the Indians. Steinmetz lived twenty years with Indians at Pine Ridge, South Dakota, partaking of their rituals, sometimes leading them himself, to the bewilderment and protest of some and the encouragement of others. He gives an account of his experiences in a recent article.[40]

Jung's theory of archetypes maintains that basic to all humans are innate shared notions. These ideas do not originate in the unconscious of the individual but in the collective unconscious that we all share as human beings. Thus the basic archetypal figures, such as the "old wise man," "the child figure of innocence" and "the woman as witch," are latently present in all of us. This explains the structural similarities in myths of nearly all cultures. The White Buffalo Calf Woman is equivalent to the Mediterranean Earth Mother, the Virgin Mary, and the world-wide Madonna figure. Studies in comparative religion by scholars like Claude Lévi-Strauss and Mircea Eliade seem to show such structural similarities, although neither of the latter subscribes to Jung's archetypal theory.

Certainly, one need not look far for examples of such parallels.[41] The biblical story of the loaves and fishes has its counterpart in the Indian tale of a Buffalo Man whose identity is unknown but who later becomes known as the Man Who Called the Buffalo. The anthropologist George Grinnell tells this story: A village is starving and a mysterious stranger takes pity on the hungry. He orders the chief to make certain preparations. The "Buffalo Caller" disappears in the night and returns to offer a small piece of buffalo meat to a hungry person, who says that it never will be enough to satisfy his hunger. Upon eating it, however, there is always more left which can be given to others. Then the Buffalo Caller teaches the tribe how to call the buffalo for themselves. They no longer have to fear starvation, now being able to survive on their own.[42]

Other similarities of what is sacred can be found in the common themes of sacred mountains (Bear Butte, Mount Harney, Sinai, Everest, McKinley, and Fujiyama) and sacred rivers (the Ganges, Jordan, Nile, Yangtze, Amazon, and Missouri). Neither mountains nor rivers need be spectacular to be sacred, however. Rainy Mountain, sacred to the Kiowas, is little more than a bare round knoll on the edge of the Wichita Mountains in southwestern Oklahoma. But although Mount Scott nearby is taller and more rugged, Rainy Mountain may have been the first height seen by the tribe as they migrated from the flat plains to the north.

For Indians, the animals of this earth were like the biblical angels, for they served as messengers of the spirit world. (*Angel* in the biblical sense means "messenger.") Rituals, too, bear strong family resemblances as they mark the stages of life from birth through puberty, maturity, marriage, and illness to death. Whether we speak of sweatbaths or baptism, we are talking about purification rites. The same is true of Bar Mitzvah, Confirmation, and coming-of-age rites. Common human needs call for the institution of certain common beliefs and rituals. Of course, the religion of the Indians, like that of nearly all aboriginals, was animistic. Everything was alive in some sense; everything had a "power."

As Bunge says, there were no weeds in the world of the Indian. Everything existed for some purpose and worked toward some end. When one could not discern that purpose, the traditional concept of a Trickster god was brought into play. Sometimes Grandmother Spider, but more often God's dog, the coyote, was given responsibility for what was unfathomable to man.

For example, Coyote was told to distribute the stars in an orderly way. Instead, he playfully threw them up for fun, scattering them across the sky, and now man must work to put some semblance of order in them by inventing the constellations. Christianity may disclaim any Trickster aspect of God but when it faces the unexplainable, it may simply cite God's unfathomable will, in some ways a trickster counterpart. As the saying goes, "The Lord giveth; the Lord taketh away. Blessed be the Lord!"

To stay alive, then, the red man believed we must seek to share the power of the others. These include the trees, the rocks, the fish, the buffalo, and the deer. We can even gain power from our enemies in battle. Nonetheless, we must always respect the other in some way by making a token return. One might throw part of the fish back into the river or leave a piece of buffalo meat on the plains. Such respect for nature was a primary requirement incumbent on all. The generosity of nature might be withdrawn if obligations were neglected in this matter.

In such a world view, man is not seen as a superior being, nor is he steward of the world, having the power to do with it what he will. Many Indians regard the attempted exercise of such power, rooted as it is in Genesis, nothing short of arrogance. Together with ecologists, the American Indian can now point to environmental problems that have resulted from the desire to dominate nature. As Chief Sealth said, "If men spit upon the ground they spit upon themselves."

Reciprocity, then, is an important, indeed, a key concept for life on earth. The deer "people" or the beaver "people" need to be recognized as persons in their own right. In effect, we make a covenant with them, as God did with Abraham, and this covenant assures that if we always maintain respect for them, they will help us with food.

Religion was a major source of power, hence it was "big medicine." For this reason, the Indian was never exclusivist in religious matters. He had few qualms about assimilating the white man's religion, often mixing it with his own. For him, it was just one more source of power. In pragmatic fashion, he considered all religions true to the extent that they proved useful.

There is no clearer difference between the white and the red cultures than their attitudes toward land. For whites, the worth of land lay in its use. Essentially it was viewed as dirt; it belonged to him who would make it fructify. This was the philosophical basis of the white man's claim to land ownership, and it came into play as he encountered the untitled land of America. Conquest won it and land use established the basis for keeping it.

Having "free land" for the taking was something new for the settlers. In Europe lands had been owned by the nobles and the church. The first question raised on coming to the New World was, to whom did this land belong? The agrarian newcomers were not long in deciding that it belonged to those who worked it and made use of it. The philosophical foundations for this were laid by the philosopher John Locke.[43] Ownership of previously unowned land was acquired by "mixing with it the fruits of one's own labor." His position was based on his experience in a European agrarian economy, and his ideas proved heavily influential in America. Not only did he help write the first draft of the constitution for the Carolinas, but sections of the Declaration of Independence itself were drawn straight from Locke by Jefferson.

This utilitarian view of land prevailed and has been challenged only since the advent of conservationists and modern-day ecologists.[44] The utilitarian view remains pervasive. When people today enter the national forests of the United States, they see signs that say, "Land of Many Uses." This philosophy is national forest policy. "Use" of course means primarily *man's* use.

For the Indian, however, land was not simply dirt; it was earth. And in his animistic outlook, the earth was one's mother, as the sky or sun was the father who impregnated the earth to make all "people," animals and human beings alike. One could not own one's mother any more than one could own the sky, the sun, or the air.[45] This respect for the earth as mother made the Indians reluctant to take up farming with its metal plows. It also was why they removed the iron shoes from captured army horses; it was not right for man to scar his mother's breast.

In pre-industrial culture, land served as a source of identity. One was almost literally one with the land.[46] Apparently whites had forgotten their own biblical teaching that "Dust thou art, and unto dust shalt thou return." But for the Indian, to be on one's land was to stand in a holy place. This was especially true in the sacred Black Hills of the Sioux, where the white invaders carved monumental likenesses of their leaders on a mountain face.

Land, made up as it was in Indian belief of various people or "persons," essentially was a community of which man was but one integral part. To harm the land—that is, one's community—was to harm one's own people. As with the sacred, land was a kind of "feeling" for the Native American. To be forced to move from it was worse than was exile for the ancient Greeks, for it was to be removed from the sacred, the source of life and meaning.

The white man, viewing land as an object rather than a living subject, was interested in it only to the extent that it would produce yield, or an economic benefit; this was the judgment of an early advocate of the ecological movement, Aldo Leopold. Others were not so perceptive. Zebulon Pike could describe the West through which he travelled only as "a great American desert." Webster called it a "vast wasteland." Strangely, neither considered the fact that it was the source of life to thousands of Indians.

The Indians have been described as having a "thirst" for land; when one has a thirst, he drinks from a stream without harming it, wasting it, or using it up. The *Washichu* (white man), on the other hand, had a "hunger" for land.[47] Indians regarded them as "land eaters" and consumers. When the land was drained of its vitality and no longer yielded, they would abandon it, wearing out tract after tract. For the white entrepreneurs who went West, their sole thought was aggrandizement. Only after a struggle was Yellowstone established as "a park for all the people" rather than as a private place to produce an income from tourists.[48]

To be forced to move from the land was for the Indian literally to be dis-placed and therefore disoriented. When Indians who lived in the mountains were removed to the swamps of Florida, it was not only the climate that killed them but their loss of identity with the land from which they had received their nurture.

For the Indian, then, land was numinous and to it he looked for a sense of the spiritual. This was a major differentiation from the whites, who looked beyond the earth for their sense of the spiritual. One Indian spokesman has said, "We are very concerned about the white man destroying our surroundings. Our relationship with the land is as a sacred marriage created by the Great Spirit. This marriage must not be broken or our people cannot survive."[49]

Perhaps nowhere is this feel for the land better expressed or with a deeper sense of pathos than in the oft quoted reply of Chief Sealth

(Seattle) to President Franklin Pierce. The chief spoke in 1854 when
the United States wanted to purchase the land in the Northwest on
which the Suqualmish (Duwamish) resided.

The great chief sends word that he wishes to buy our land. . . . How can you
buy or sell the sky, the warmth of the land? The idea is strange to us. If we
do not own the freshness of the air and the sparkle of the water, how can
you buy them?

Every part of this earth is sacred to my people. . . . We are part of the earth
and it is part of us. The perfumed flowers are our sisters; the deer, the horse,
the great eagle, these are our brothers. The rocky crests, the juices in the
meadow, the body heat of the pony and man—all belong in the same family.
So when the Great Chief in Washington sends word that he wishes to buy
our land, he asks much of us.

If we sell you the land, you must remember that it is sacred and you must
teach your children that it is sacred. . . . You must teach your children that
the ground beneath their feet is the ashes of our grandfathers. So that they
will respect the land, tell your children that the land is rich with the lives of
our kin. Teach your children what we have taught our children, that the earth
is our mother.

Whatever befalls the earth, befalls the sons of the earth. If men spit upon the
ground, they spit upon themselves. This we know. The earth does not belong
to man; man belongs to the earth. This we know. All things are connected
like the blood which unites one family. All things are connected.

Whatever befalls the earth befalls the sons of the earth. Man did not weave
the web of life; he is merely a strand. Whatever he does to the web he does
to himself.[50]

Indian contact with whites generally was tentative, each culture
understandably suspicious of the other. Since the white man first
made contact several hundred years ago with the Plains Indians, there
seldom has been a mutual understanding. Black Elk, the Oglala Sioux
medicine man, at first thought all white men were sick, since they
had such an unhealthy color (hence the description "pale face").
Sometimes whites were known as "hair face," since many, especially
the early mountain men, were bearded. The white man was an eternal
puzzle to the red man. There is the Indian observation, perhaps apoc-
ryphal, "Whites make big fire, sit far away: Indians make small fire,
sit close." The Indians could never understand why whites killed off
the buffalo, which needed no husbandry and which ate the free
grasses, and then brought in their own cattle that had to be herded
and fed.

There were both little things and big things that the Indians did not understand about the whites. A little one was why the whites insisted that "grass grow upside down," which is how the Indians viewed the work of the sodbuster who turned over the grasses with his plow. A big thing and hatefully detested was the white man's punishment by hanging. Common Indian belief was that death by hanging did not permit the spirit to escape the body because of the choking action of the rope. One could do nothing worse to the Indian than to take away his possibilities for survival in the spirit world. Yet this exactly is what happened to thirty-eight Sioux who were hanged by the U.S. Army, the largest mass hanging in U.S. history.

In many ways the Indians compared whites to the honey bees, which were introduced to this continent from Europe: "They were industrious, they stung and they procreated quickly."

Accurate accounts of the casualties of whites and Indians during their various battles, fights, and skirmishes between the days of Columbus and 1890 are impossible to establish. For the most part, figures on each side have been grossly exaggerated, aided and abetted by popular literature, movies, and television. The problem is not solved by today's historical revisionists who seek to write from the point of view of the Indian. They tend merely to revert to the unfounded view of Rousseau's "Noble Savage," the "innocent child of nature."

Although the term *Indian wars* is often heard, particularly in the period of the 1860s and 1870s, there never was a full-blown war with Indians in general. Peaceful relations with some tribes was a constant. Skirmishes, fights, battles there were, but never an all-out war as we understand the term today.

A prominent scholar of the West estimates that the total of Indians killed by whites in the five or six major "massacres" in the West was somewhere between 615 and 1,171, with the lower figures representing the more likely truth. These include the well-known Custer fight at Washita, Chivington's Sand Creek Massacre, and the battle of Wounded Knee. Overall, "it seems possible that for the period 1789-1898 Indians killed some 7,000 soldiers and civilians. It is improbable that more than 4,000 Indians were killed during the same period."[51]

One of the reasons for the relatively low numbers killed on both sides is that Indians ordinarily did not fight as European armies did. Hit and run guerrilla tactics and individual raids were more the order of the day. In short, they often fought the whites in the way they fought other tribes they considered hostile. There were no great armies lined up against each other, each pounding the other until one was decimated or routed. To think otherwise is to misunderstand the West, its natives, its terrain, or its battles. Although any death is a tragedy, one must put such casualties into perspective. For example, in the United States there are fifty thousand deaths alone from auto accidents each year. In comparison, however odious it may be, the death toll from fights over a hundred-year period does not appear particularly severe. Yet one must remember that by way of percentages, a number of tribes were virtually wiped out. Therein lies the real tragedy.

Nor were wagon trains, such as the ones that carried freight over the Santa Fe Trail or the ones that transported emigrants on the Oregon and California Trails, the targets of wholesale depredation by Indians. Indeed, more deaths among these would-be pioneers were caused by wagon train carelessness and inexperience than by marauding Indians. "During the twenty peak years of emigrations prior to the Civil War, drownings and gunshots killed 350 overlanders, almost exactly the same number as were rubbed out by Indians."[52] Only rarely did the Santa Fe Trail see death by fighting, for it was a freighting rather than immigration route and its activities did not threaten to take over Indian land. Its central post, Bent's Fort, near present-day La Mar, Colorado, was never attacked.

As the white man pursued his course west, "treaties" (a bitter euphemism) were established and reservations were set aside for the red man. The history of treaties is a sad one. The Indian reservations that followed were a source for graft for the white man and an unnatural way of life for the free-roaming Indian. Often the most worthless areas were given for reservations. Mountain Indians often were sent to the arid plains and parched deserts; plains and desert Indians were sent to the swamplands of the southeast. Reservations produced an increasing dependency. Wards of the government, Indians long had no citizenship privileges, which were granted only in 1924. Indians could recreate the good old days only by shooting arrows into rationed cattle penned up for distribution at the agency. Such Indians were sometimes referred to by their own people as "apple Indians"— red on the outside, white on the inside. Sitting Bull, always a shrewd observer of the scene, remarked, "It is bad for young men to be fed by an agent. It makes them lazy and drunken. All agency Indians I have seen were worthless. They are neither red warriors nor white farmers. They are neither wolf nor dog."[53] Sitting Bull himself was killed at Standing Rock Agency by two Sioux "policemen."

As Père De Smet saw over a century and a half ago, the demise of the American Indian would be rapid and inexorable. George Catlin, who lived seven years with the Plains Indians in the 1830s, painting them in all their splendor, knew them as few whites ever did. He wrote, "The North American Indian in his native state is an honest, contemplative and religious being."[54] Yet he also wrote sadly, "The tribes of the red man of North America, as a nation of human beings, are on their wane; that (to use their own very beautiful figure), 'they are fast travelling to the shades of their fathers towards the setting sun.' "[55]

The love that Catlin had for the Indian was summed up in his creed:

I love a people who have always made me welcome to the best they had.

I love a people who are honest without laws, who have no jails and no poorhouses.

I love a people who keep the commandments without ever having read them or heard them preached from the pulpit.

I love a people who never swear, who never take the name of God in vain.

I love a people "who love their neighbors as they love themselves."

I love a people who worship God without a Bible, for I believe that God loves them also.

I love the people whose religion is all the same, and who are free from religious animosities.

I love the people who have never raised a hand against me, or stolen my property, where there was no law to punish for either.

I love the people who have never fought a battle with white men, except on their own ground.

I love and don't fear mankind where God has made and left them, for there they are children.

I love a people who live and keep what is their own without locks and keys.

I love all people who do the best they can. And oh, how I love a people who don't live for the love of money![56]

In a sense, the demise of the American Indian began the day the white man landed on these shores. The natives were not a technological people and they could not match the inventions and tools— and numbers—of this ever-expanding group of immigrants. Their old ways of life disrupted, Indians became increasingly dependent on whites for guns, utensils, canvas, food, and whiskey—an 1802 federal law barred providing liquor to Indians but it was impossible to enforce. Indians became addicted to all these and could not break away.

Because Indian culture was a world apart from the whites, the intermixing of the two was totally destructive to the Indian in nearly every way imaginable. They no longer could turn back to the old ways and the old days, however much they wanted to. It was not only their world but the world itself which had changed.

The tight and coordinated organization of the whites could not be bested or even matched by loose Indian confederations. The whites pushed on with a Messianic drive, and nothing could stand in the way of their sense of destiny. A thoroughly beaten people, the Indians' few victories, such as Little Bighorn, only served to hasten their downfall by arousing white pressures against them. Indians and whites have never really understood each other, even to this day. Indians became the excluded as no others have, and they remain at the bottom of the list of the poorest minorities in America. Truly they were and are the dispossessed.

U.S. government efforts on their behalf began with the establishment of the Bureau of Indian Affairs, a branch of the U.S. War Department, in 1824. The office was full of graft and corruption, a state of affairs that improved little with its transfer to the Department of the Interior, where it still is housed. President Grant in a "peace policy" attempted reform, utilizing the various churches and their good will and sacrifice.

After the Chivington Sand Creek Massacre, the Indians finally gained the right of "competent witness" so that they could testify in court, even against whites. Although Indians were granted citizenship in 1924, it was not until 1948 that Arizona and New Mexico permitted them to vote in non-Indian elections.

Suffering a near total loss of dignity, the Native American became almost fatalistically resigned. Whites were forward looking; to them the Indians seemed a mythic people, always looking over their shoulders. There could be no comfortable place for them in the American mainstream. Alienated as they go back and forth between reservation and urban centers, they have lost but are trying desperately to regain a sense of identity. Attempts to restore it seem artificial and so far have touched only a few.[57]

4. Gold and Silver
The Quest for El Dorado

Gold and silver may have been the first metals used by humankind, and from the earliest times they have figured in myth and history as symbols of beauty, wealth, and power. Gold was long the prerogative of rulers: it was among the kingly gifts brought to the manger by the three magi (one of the four hundred references to gold in the Bible). In our day, the precious metals are even more important for their roles in science and industry—gold and silver circuits are used in electronics, and the vehicle that landed on the moon was protected by a covering of gold foil—but that is another story.

Myth, as usual, grounds fiction in truth. Jason and the heroic crew of the ship *Argo* are the prototype of adventurous searchers for precious things. The truth is that gold was discovered in Phrygia and Jason sought it, as the Spanish sought it in the New World and the Forty-niners sought it in California. Instead of panning for gold, the Phrygians used lambs' wool, catching the shining grains and flakes in the lanolin-saturated fibers. The golden fleece was real.

The story of King Midas is a different kind of myth, warning of the dangers of avarice and pride. The god Bacchus granted the king's request that whatever he touched would turn to gold. When his food and drink, and even his daughter, turned to lifeless metal, Midas pleaded to be freed from his deadly golden touch. The god told the king to wash away the cursed gift in the river Pactolus. Again, a truth—gold is found in streams. The New World story of El Dorado contains a similar idea. Sixteenth-century Spanish explorers were tantalized by reports of El Dorado—the Gilded One—a king who would ceremonially cover himself with gold dust and dive into a lake. They rushed to discover the tribe that commanded such great wealth and the lake bottom that was covered with an age-old accumulation of gold. (The search for the lake still continues, and El Dorado has come to mean a mythical place where gold is as common as clay.)

Cortez heard such rumors in 1519, being told of naked natives wearing gold in their ears, lips, and noses. Indeed, the Aztecs did

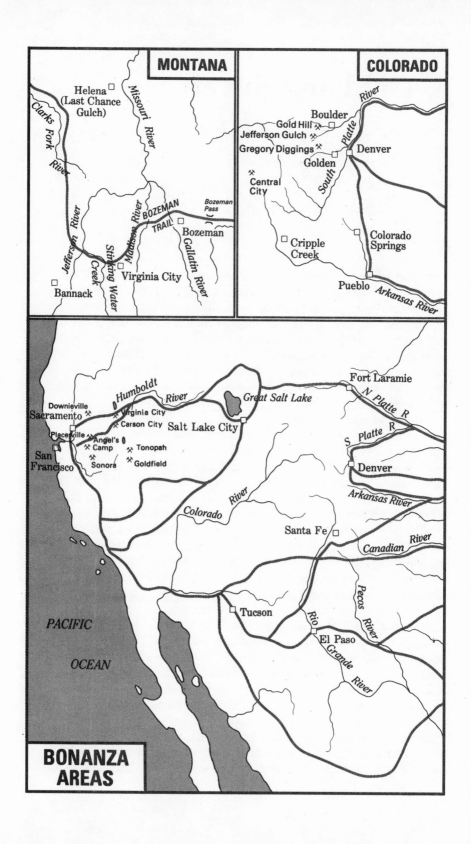

possess riches of this kind, and Cortez promptly defeated their king, Montezuma, at Tenochtitlan. In 1533, the conquistador Pizarro discovered that the Incas also were rich in gold. He captured their king, who "attempted to ransom himself by filling a room seventeen by twenty-two feet full of gold."[1] Far from satisfying Cortez and Pizarro, the capture of such treasure only gave them a voracious appetite for more. Convinced that there was still to be found a fabulous source of wealth, the Spanish continued the search. They found the mines that had supplied the Aztecs with silver and gold. They were at Zacatecas in central Mexico and in what is today northern New Mexico near Santa Fe. The unfortunate Indians were forced to continue working the mines for the benefit of Spain. At one time, nearly a fifth of the world's silver was shipped out of Mexico's port of Veracruz (founded by Cortez).

Hernando De Soto looked and lusted for gold along the gulf coast east of the Mississippi River. In 1528, Narváez also mounted an expedition, but died when a storm sank his ship. The four survivors (one a black man named Estevanico, probably a slave) travelled west along the Gulf coast trying to reach Mexico City. Alternately captured and traded by Indians, they too heard about fabulous gold somewhere in the area. Highly detailed, the stories told of Indians eating from gold plates and of cities with tall buildings and streets paved with gold. These cities were said to have hoards of silver and precious gems as well. Of such stuff dreams were made, but it was eight years before they could tell their tales of gold to the Mexico City officials. In due course, however, the reports of their leader, Cabeza de Vaca, set the adventurous Spanish afire with eagerness to search for these cities, which came to be known as the Seven Cities of Cibola.

An advance group sent from Mexico City to find the trail to this wealth was led by a Franciscan friar, Fray Marcos de Niza. Accompanying him were the four survivors of the Narváez tragedy and a sizable detachment of soldiers. They headed north toward the great Sonoran Desert, returning within the year. The enthusiastic Fray Marcos reported seeing one of the cities himself, estimating its population at an unheard of three hundred thousand. With such evidence, he felt it best to return immediately and report to his superiors. The absence of Estevanico from the returning party seemed to confirm the friar's story: he was rumored to have been killed while trying to seduce women from one of the cities of Cibola.

The great explorer-soldier Coronado made haste to set out for the cities to gather their gold for Spain. He mounted an expedition that included three hundred fifty soldiers and civilians, nearly a thousand Indians, and nearly fifteen hundred head of livestock. Such a large group was unable to travel at speed, so a portion of it was dispatched to move ahead. This group of one hundred quickly reached a village where Fray Marcos had indicated there was one. Instead of existing on the scale rapturously described by the priest, however, it was only a poor pueblo with others like it nearby. The inhabitants had no gold plates and ate only the traditional frijoles and maize that the Spanish had found elsewhere. The population was a mere hundred and fifty; but they proved formidable. The small group challenged the proud Spanish, and Coronado had to do battle, losing an unseemly number of men.

Cursing the "lying Fray Marcos," Coronado still pursued the chimera of the cities of gold. He led his men farther and farther north and east, penetrating the plains as far as the future Kansas City. Instead of finding gold there, he discovered only strange-looking "hump-back cows," the American bison. Bitterly disappointed, he returned to Mexico. He had nevertheless accomplished much, opening the Southwest to Spanish influence and making contact with the Pueblo Indians.

What was the truth of the fabled cities of gold? The rumor was most likely based on the limited placer mining by Indians in Alabama, northern Georgia, and North Carolina. Gold was not found in street-paving quantity but the area did produce twenty million dollars' worth of the metal between 1799 and 1829.

The year 1848 was relatively peaceful for Americans. The War with Mexico ended and California was added to the United States by the Treaty of Guadalupe Hidalgo. The treaty also gave the United States the northern parts of Arizona and New Mexico. (The lower parts of those states, including the best southern rail route to the Pacific, were obtained in the Gadsden Purchase in 1853.) Some members of the disbanded Mormon Battalion, which had been organized for the Mexican War, were wending their way back to Deseret while others explored the land of California where they were sent by the army. The trails to Santa Fe, Oregon, and California were already filling with wagon trains of people and commerce. Shortcuts were employed although, as the Donner party found out, sometimes they could prove to be final endings. When guide books were unreliable, there now was a well-rutted trail to follow.

The Indian Wars of the sixties and seventies still were over a decade away, although the troublesome Apaches in the Southwest were actively preying on those moving through their land. Few whites dared settle anywhere except in large established communities. The army had yet to build its many Southwest forts to protect the settlers and those who came seeking their fortunes. Adventurers and families unsatisfied by life in the placid Willamette Valley of Oregon wandered on down to try their luck in newly opened California.

One man, born in German-speaking Switzerland in 1803, felt that same dissatisfaction as he grew up. His name was John Augustus Sutter and he fled his beautiful but regimented native land. A would-be entrepreneur, he also fled his many creditors. At thirty-four, the spirit of the American adventure beckoned him to the great cities of the United States. He wandered around New York and St. Louis and even travelled to the Sandwich Islands (now Hawaii). He always loved wilderness—his creditors found it difficult to pursue him there—and he was attracted to the Sacramento Valley in central Mexican California, where the only inhabitants were Indians. An affable man and a great talker, Sutter has been called a con man, but if he was, he conned himself as well. He had a rich imagination; one of his great fantasies was that he could become in this new land a benevolent feudal baron like those he knew and admired in the old world. He often talked about his many (imagined) connections to old-world royalty and regaled eager listeners with stories from his travels. He was an impressive man and quickly ingratiated himself with the Mexican governor, who issued him a land grant of fifty thousand acres, on the condition that he become a Mexican citizen and help keep Indians, Americans, and foreigners out of California. Sutter accepted the conditions, although he didn't care much for the Spanish; he thought them too "Europeanish" in outlook and formalities: "My real object was to get away from the influence of the Spanish. . . . I had noticed very well that one's hat had to be taken off before the military guard, the flagstaff and the Church, I preferred a country where I could keep my hat on. In other words, I wanted to be my own Master."[2]

Now a landowner in the Sacramento Valley, he needed tools and materials with which to build a fort. He got both from the Russians, who had abandoned their own Fort Ross. (True to form, he never paid his benefactors.) His fort was to be worthy of his ambitions, measuring 330 feet by 220 feet with high adobe walls. His workers were Indians and Sandwich Islanders directed by white overlords. He finally had a kingdom which he called New Helvetia, after the Latin name for Switzerland. The post flourished from the start; "from 1841 to 1848 Sutter's Fort was a focal point for the increasing flow of covered wagons bringing in settlers from the States."[3]

His increasing power and wealth, together with his friendly relationships with the Americanos made the Mexicans look suspiciously at their supposed friend. Indeed, Sutter agreed with the expansionist aims of the United States. In 1845, not counting the Indians, there were only seven hundred non-Spanish in all California.[4] That was an unpromising setting for a man wishing to expand his business. Sutter was delighted when California joined the United States in 1848.

Promptly becoming an American citizen, Sutter saw that his building plans called for a fresh supply of timber. The nearby countryside had already been cleared for the fort. Accordingly, he contracted with a wandering Canadian named James Marshall, who drifted down from Oregon and Washington. Marshall, a skilled carpenter and all-around millwright, located a heavily wooded area forty miles away on a fork of the American River at the site of present-day Coloma.

Marshall's crew of workmen was an odd-lot bunch of Mormons, Indians, and a few non-Mormon Americans. They spent about a month in constructing a sawmill and millrace, opening and closing the water gates from time to time to deepen the channel. Marshall himself has left an account of what happened on January 24, 1848, a date that would prove to be historic.

I gave orders to have a ditch cut through the bar in the rear of the mill, and after quitting work in the evening to raise the gate and let the water run all night, as it would assist us very much in deepening the tailrace. . . . One morning in January—it was a clear cold morning: I shall never forget that morning—as I was taking my usual walk along the race after shutting off the water, my eye was caught with the glimpse of something shining in the bottom of the ditch. There was about a foot of water running then. I reached my hand down and picked it up; it made my heart thump, for I was certain it was gold. The piece was about half the size and of the shape of a pea. Then I saw another piece in the water.[5]

Marshall showed the nugget to his men, saying that the find might not be gold and asking them to keep it secret while he consulted with Sutter. Riding the forty miles back to New Helvetia, Marshall joined Sutter in testing the metal, applying nitric acid to it and so forth. Sutter even turned to an encyclopedia and checked the characteristics of gold. At last they were convinced. It was gold! Marshall urged Sutter to return with him immediately to the spot but Sutter declined because of the weather. The excited Marshall wanted to be near his find and hurried back in a driving rain.

As Marshall had done, Sutter asked his men to keep the news quiet, but in his heart he knew it would be impossible. Sutter was as much dismayed as pleased at the find, realizing that gold in any quantity would bring hordes of treasure seekers. (His forebodings were accurate. His enterprises were ruined by waves of trespassers, and twenty-five years later he retired to Pennsylvania bankrupt.)

Word did begin to spread immediately, from both Marshall's and Sutter's men, although the remoteness of the find kept the news from reaching the East until August 1848. Within two years, forty thousand people would descend on central California. For a time, however, the local populace had the opportunity to get rich without being crowded out by others. The locals included Indians, Mormons, Sandwich Islanders, and farmers from Washington and Oregon.

Sailors caught the news like a mighty wind in their sails. They ran before it, leaving their vessels as ghost ships in the harbor at San Francisco. By the middle of June, the great port city itself was a ghost town. It was not hyperbole but simple observation that "the farmers have thrown aside their plows, the lawyers their briefs, the doctors their pills, the priests their prayer books, and all are now digging gold."[6] Just as the dumbest farmers were said to grow the biggest potatoes, "the veriest greenhorn was as likely to uncover the richest mine on the gulch as was the wisest ex-professor of geology."[7]

The California strike was a true bonanza (Spanish for "fair weather"), not a *borrasca* (Spanish for "barren rock"). There was a rich mother lode one hundred and twenty miles long and six to eight miles wide, and it all lay at moderate elevations of two to three thousand feet. Virtually all the rivers touching the area—the Feather, the Stanislaus, and the American—showed flakes, grains, and nuggets of the Midas metal. From the Mexican settlement of Mariposa on the south to Downieville on the north, gold was there for the taking. It had waited there undiscovered until the interior was settled; the Spanish and the Mexicans had largely restricted themselves to missions along the coast.

Madness and anticipation filled the air everywhere. It affected all classes, well-born and workers alike—as the gold rush of 'forty-nine established its own brand of egalitarianism in a nation less than seventy-five years old. Miners and prospectors were the same no matter what their country of origin. They were a camaraderie of gamblers and courtiers of Lady Luck.

No one caught the new yellow fever like Americans, however, for gambling was as American as apple pie. The country began on a gamble, breaking away from a protective and powerful England. Gambling was the hallmark of the nation's capitalistic system. What were Astors, Rockefellers, Vanderbilts, and Gettys but successful gamblers? Gold was in the air and in the blood, seemingly put there as a challenge and crucible to form the American character.

Without question, "a deep relationship [exists] between the search for gold in America and the impact of that search on the American character."[8] As one who was at the scene put it, "Talent for business, literary and scientific acquirement, availed little or nothing in a country where strength of muscle was required to raise heavy rocks and dig deep pits. It was strength, absolute brute force, which was required to win the gold of the placers."[9] Never had the world seen such a gathering of nationalities and minorities and, although there were periods of contention, most got along as comrades in the quest for gold.

In California, shanty towns grew into important river ports— Stockton, Sacramento, Maryville, and others. If a gold strike showed color for as long as three months, a miniature town sprang up on the spot. A witness to this activity reported, "As soon as placers were discovered on the mountains, roads were opened; ranching and trading posts were established, and public houses opened at convenient distances on the road; so that in twelve months it was no longer necessary to carry blankets, even into the lower mines."[10] Such towns had their brothels, saloons, hoteliers, cooks, crooks, assayers, freighters, and even branch banks. Generally the people who ran these establishments did not dig the gold in the stream. They got gold, and plenty of it, by mining the miners, who when they struck it rich, threw their wealth around as if it were endless.

Incidently, the cooks and eating establishments were mainly Chinese, and Western America dined on their fare. When cooking chicken, the chefs never failed to open the gizzard, for rumor told of a gold nugget found in a gizzard and there always was the chance that it might happen again! The Chinese did not take to food and laundry work out of choice; being at the bottom of the social ladder, they often were not allowed to dig for gold unless whites had abandoned the area. Industrious workers, they were penny pinchers who loved to gamble. Bret Harte's poem "The Heathen Chinee" paints a colorful picture of this neglected immigrant group.

Inflation set in quickly, eggs costing nearly a dollar each, bunks— shared by other miners, sometimes forty to a floor—costing twenty dollars in gold dust a night.[11] Gold dust was the local currency, and it bought anything that money could buy. Price often was stated in "pinches of gold dust." Big-thumbed bartenders obviously were in demand. The inevitable spilling of a few grains on the floor was noted by eagle-eyed waitresses, who vied for the privilege of sweeping the floor after work.

Town names changed as quickly as their fortunes. Dry Diggings became Placerville and later Hangtown. Men's names changed in the same way. One scholar tracked an individual through his rise and fall:

Pat Quinn
C. Patrick Quinn
Colonel Patrick Quinn
Col. C.P. Quinn

Patrick Quinn
Pat Quinn
Old Quinn[12]

Early in the California Gold Rush, most gold taken was placer gold. (The "a" is short in placer, and is pronounced like the "a" in "placid.") It was accessible to all, and no bulky technology was needed to get it. Placer mining was long known and practiced in the Middle Ages. Americans by and large lacked the mining experience needed to get at gold hidden underground. Some would acquire the new skills by trial and error but most would learn from their European counterparts, who were about to descend on the gold fields en masse.

In the beginning, lack of skills was no impediment to getting rich. All one had to do was stake a claim, sometimes on a piece of federal land ten feet by ten, or one hundred by one hundred. Then, with a pickaxe, shovel, washpan, and a willingness to work hard in streams whose temperatures seldom exceeded forty degrees, one was in business.

Gold was easily recognized, for it usually retained its bright yellow color. An inert element, it did not combine chemically with other elements to produce compounds; it was found intact, mixed in with grains of sand or in veins of quartz. Often it was found with a heavy bluish sand that prospectors cursed for clogging up their sluices and cradles. Few realized that the hindrance was a rich mix of silver. Silver seldom was found in a pure state, usually occurring as silver chloride or silver sulfide.

Most of the miners found placer gold in flakes or grains along the river banks, in graveled and dried-up river beds, on sandbars, in river potholes, on the shelf of bedrock beneath the riverbed, and in cracks of rocks, boulders, and hillsides. Sometimes, as in Nome, Alaska, it even was found in sand washed up along the shore. Gold originates in the bowels of the earth and is brought to the surface by volcanic and geothermal activity. Earthquakes, avalanches, melting snows, and spring runoffs carry it ever farther from its source. The gold embedded in quartz veins is often separated by the grinding action of the elements and scattered in the sand and gravel. The presence of water near gold was helpful; placer mining used hydraulic pressure to wash gold-bearing ore from the hillsides and to separate the gold from the dirt and gravel accompanying it. Since gold was heavier than dirt or rock, it would fall to the bottom when swirled around with them in a current of water. Panning and sluicing were equally effective, for gold is nineteen times heavier than water and four times heavier than sand.

The technique of panning for gold was simple enough and, after a few tries, a gold seeker could do it almost by second nature. He would scoop up dirt and gravel from an inch or two of the bed of a running stream and, tilting the pan with its contents, add water to it. Then, with a flick of the wrist, he would slough off the water, dirt, and gravel, and hopefully examine the bottom of the pan for some shiny gold sand. Any flakes or grains would be removed to a pouch or other suitable container. Occasionally a gold nugget would be found, often in isolated spots apart from other diggings. One huge nugget, weighing 195 troy ounces, was found in Calaveras County in California. (The world's largest nugget was discovered in Australia. It weighed a whopping 472 pounds.)

In a likely stream, each panning might recover a few cents' worth of gold; often the precious residue would be worth considerably more. The average take of the placer miner in the beginning was about twenty dollars a day, varying with the miners' skills and locations. But intensive placer mining quickly denuded the streams and open hillsides of their scattered gold; soon the tedious labor of panning no longer was worth the effort. Hence, tramp miners quickly moved on to other diggings hoping to find the "glory hole." Like fishermen moving from hole to hole and lake to lake, they quickly changed their sites, not only from territory to territory but from country to country around the world. Canada, Alaska, Australia, and South Africa are only a few of the places where the precious metal was sought.

Besides the pan, simple tools such as knives or chisels were used. Gold was found in the crevices of rocks, deposited when rivers had overflowed their banks in times past. Digging it out was termed "crevice mining," and even Mark Twain indulged in it. (Twain once called a mine "a hole in the earth owned by a liar.")

Gold also was sometimes winnowed from other elements. The technique was much like tossing wheat or grain into the air so that the lighter fluff was blown away and the heavier elements fell down to be collected. Most early mining was done by individuals trying to make it on their own. This proved grossly inefficient. Miners soon learned to work together. Collectively, they produced a popular labor-saving device called a rocker, which resembled a cradle. Rocking worked on the same principle as panning. This new method was faster and more productive than the pan. One or two persons shovelled auriferous (gold bearing) dirt into a rocker while another agitated the stuff by rocking the cradle. Beneath the rocker's false bottom was another bottom made of cleats or riffles. Sometimes a perforated iron plate was used. Washed with water, the heavier gold would fall through its holes and, the dirt and gravel would travel on out the open front end of the rocker. The operation was made more effective when mercury (quicksilver) was put on the cleats or riffles; the mercury would cling to—almost grab—the grains of gold and hold them. It would do the same with silver. The amalgamation of mercury and precious metal later could be separated by heating, the mercury evaporating in steam or gathering in separate droplets of condensation.

The next improvement in gold technology was the "long tom." This device was a simple planked sluice about twenty feet long and eighteen inches deep. It too had riffles or cleats for retaining the bottom-seeking gold. Several of the units could be put together, and the overall length was limited only by the water supply and the men available to work it.

Still another form of extracting gold from the earth was "coyoting," a reference to the burrowing of the coyote for field mice, picas, coneys, and other rodents. The heavy gold, sinking through the sand and gravelly bottom of the riverbed, would keep pressing through the moist earth until it rested on bedrock, often fifteen to twenty feet below the river. Even dry streams had their substrata of gold. Miners would dig a large hole in the bed and tunnel out from the center, somewhat like the spokes of a wagon wheel. The auriferous soil would be brought up with a hand winch and put through the standard washing and sluicing operation.

The gold seekers were learning their skills on the job. As the *Calaveras Chronicle* observed, "The only occupation in which men appear to engage without the least preparation is mining."[13] Nonetheless, a "Scotsman remarked that the Americans showed a greater organizational ability than the other nationalities in the mines."[14] Certainly, the difficult and often unproductive labor had its attractions: "If nothing else, the participant in a gold or silver rush was a thoroughly free man who could make what he would of the opportunities before him."[15] This appealed to many and, indeed, reflected the very nature of the American enterprise. The gold seeker, like his earlier counterparts the mountain man and the fur trapper, was eager to make it on his own. Unfortunately, as their trades petered out, they all became hired hands because they were unable to accumulate the capital needed to build and develop their trades. In the future, companies would supplant individuals. But for now it was another moment in American history for the free and unfettered individual, and many sought to make the most of it.

Working together to get at the gold, individuals began to form their own companies and to make their own agreements, going as far as to issue stock for capital. In some ways this cooperation dimly foreshadowed the early federation or union movement. The entrance of foreign miners into the field, particularly the Cornish, gave impetus to the movement that was to become prominent later at the Nevada Comstock mine.

Rules now were drawn up between participants to make mining a more orderly operation. Work requirements were spelled out; a member might lose his rights in the diggings if he didn't work his part of the claim a certain number of days in the week. Illness, of course, provided an exception.[16] This was rough-hewn business management at the grass roots.

Mining groups might define the boundaries of the mining district in which they found themselves and all agree to abide by the same rules. Home government thereby was established and simple miner courts were instituted, based on parallels back East. When claims needed adjudication or criminals needed punishment, a jury was drawn from the miners' association and a defender and prosecutor were picked to try the case. Sometimes justice was summary, but given the situation, the procedure served its purpose fairly well. These were not vigilante groups, for everyone's identity was known and most members were elected or volunteers.[17] The immense variation of the local rules governing the mining district, usually recognized by the state or territory, made mining laws then and now a hodge-podge of entanglements. Even today they have yet to be straightened out and made consistent.

In the early days when gold was readily available on the surface, there were few attempts at hard-rock mining, which penetrated deep into the earth. Neither trained miners nor the needed venture capital and machinery were yet available. As the surface treasure was exhausted, however, deep mining was begun; it changed the character of mining and the type of men who did the work. In the transition from placer to vein mining, the first problem was a legal one. Adits or entrances to the deep vein were dug and shafts sunk to varying depths. The question was who owned the vein where it meandered through other claims. There was little problem when the vein surfaced, that is, where it showed its "apex." Yet often the vein had "dips, spurs, angles and variations"[18]—often surfacing several times in a given area, and at first there was no way to determine if this was the same vein or a different one.

Eventually Congress took on the task of straightening out matters by inaugurating the Apex Law of 1872, which declared that the claimant "must fix his surface boundaries in such a way as to embrace the apex of his vein. If he succeeded in doing so, the claimant could pursue his vein for an indefinite distance through the vertical downward extension of the side limits of his rectangular claim."[19] This clarification (perhaps typical of congressional law) produced utter confusion in the field. It seemed that litigation had become the new way to get rich.

Digging ore beneath the surface involved drilling, blasting, and toil that heretofore was known only to coal and tin miners. The problem was not merely to wrest gold from the earth (where generally it was mixed with quartz, itself a very hard substance). Once the mine had been established, additional carts, mules, and teamsters, were needed to deliver the ore to a crusher machine to break down the composite. Earliest of the crushing machines was the slow and laborious (for the beast that powered it, anyway) *arrastra*. This was "used for the free milling of gold or silver; a circular pit whose bottom was lined tightly with rock facing, over which heavy stones were dragged, usually by a horse- or mule-power, to grind ore."[20] A variation was the "chili mill," which used stone wheels for crushing. Later, stamp mills, simply called "stampers," were employed. These "crushed ore by means of a series of pestles, or stamps, raised and lowered by a camshaft."[21] They would strike the ore against a base of perforated iron, through which the pulverized rock would fall. This material was washed and run through mercury to get the amalgam of gold and mercury. Although the reason was not known at the time, many who worked near the mercury became ill, poisoned by the fumes of mercury fulminate. Later, cyanide was used, which exacerbated the unhealthiness of the miner's environment.

The mercury, in increasing demand because of the gold rush, was produced from cinnabar. Fortunately, California had a goodly supply and until 1881 produced as much as one-half of the world's mercury. Much of it came from the new Almaden mines owned by Mexico but which were taken over without recompense by the United States.

Although placer mining sometimes altered the course of rivers and streams and made ugly piles of gravel here and there, it was not seriously destructive of the environment. The next technological development in mining, called hydraulicking, however, was grossly destructive. In hydraulicking, hills and mountain sides were washed away by jets of water from high-pressure hoses. The practice created landslides and floods and choked the rivers with silt, which worked its way downstream. During flood times, the silt was dumped on lush farmlands, doing ruinous damage.

The powerful streams of water that uncovered new quartz and gold veins, making them accessible to pickaxes, left open gashes and resulted in continual erosion for years afterward. The eroded mountainsides became known as "slickers," bare of rocks, trees, or other vegetation. Water for the hoses was fed by adjacent streams or was sluiced to the hydraulicking spot from man-made reservoirs high in the mountains. The noise of the powerful hoses was deafening, as was the fall of materials in landslides, shattering the serenity and beauty of the wilderness. A high point of big mining irresponsibility, hydraulicking was eventually limited by legislation. Nonetheless, this rape of nature is still evident wherever such mining took place. Land honeycombed by shafts is scarred and ugly. (But for sheer appalling destruction of the countryside, nothing equals the great copper mines of Montana: not even towns were spared. Entire streets and their buildings have caved in as the undermined ground has collapsed. The state long was dominated by Anaconda Copper, which dictated nearly every aspect of life, virtually determining who would stay and who would leave.)

Permanent big companies with voracious appetites were at work now and demanded to be fed, whatever the cost—and it was considerable. These were not just transient individuals trying to make a small fortune in order to return home. Rather they sought absolute control over what they owned, and the public be damned.

Waves of immigrants engulfed California during the first year of the Sutter discovery. Miners and would-be miners converged on America's West Coast and spread out from there. Hawaiians, Australians, and Chinese came from the Pacific, most jammed in tramp steamers. In San Francisco alone, there were twenty-five thousand Chinese by 1852. South Americans worked their way up the West Coast, and Europeans crossed the Atlantic to get into the action, bringing new dimensions to the American scene. The Welsh, Cornish, and English brought technological knowledge gained in the tin and coal mines. Germans and French brought their engineering skills to bear. All pooled their resources in one vast school. The principles of mining, whether of gold, lead, zinc, copper, silver, or coal, were variations on a theme.

Those from Europe and the American East could follow the now established overland trails West. Others sailed around the Horn through the treacherous and shifting tides in the Magellan Straits. Some ships did not make it through the passage and their wreckage was cast up on the southern-most point of Tierra del Fuego, the land of fires.

Although passage by sea was long and tedious, taking from four to eight months to complete (many were treated to an out-of-the-way stop in the Sandwich Islands en route), at least passengers could stay on their ships until they reached San Francisco. Not so with those who chose to take the shortcut through the Isthmus of Panama. This route was supposed to take only five to seven weeks and to cost about four hundred dollars. As the numbers streaming West grew, however, getting passage on the west side of the isthmus became a problem. When ships' captains found out how much the market would bear, they scalped tickets mercilessly. Waiting for cheaper fares, travellers' grubstakes would get lower and lower. Not only that, malaria was rampant, debilitating those who were delayed. The jungles, sleazy hotels, inflated prices, and the waiting and waiting and waiting for a ship made the dangers of the Horn almost attractive. Only the vision of gold at the end of the journey sustained them.

Disillusionment awaited them in San Francisco. There they were greeted by inflated prices on all necessities and realized that the best mining spots already had been picked clean, with only the tailings remaining. Amazingly, however, although these latter-day argonauts momentarily harbored doubts, they were not daunted, for optimism was the virtue common to all miners. The California experience was unique and those who participated in it revelled in sharing its glory and excitement.

In less than a decade after the discovery of gold, placer mining was no longer productive in the mother lode country, and there the glory of gold tarnished. Prospectors, known as sourdoughs, took their mules or donkeys farther and farther out, looking for new gold sources, hoping to find just one more bonanza. Rumors from their excursions filtered back and others followed them as children followed the Pied Piper of Hamlin. The pioneering prospectors made their way to such diverse places as Washington, Oregon, Nevada, Idaho, Montana, Arizona, and Canada—all within a decade and a half. Word came of a Canadian strike on the Fraser River in British Columbia and, in spring 1858, miners vacated the state of California. They were back by fall: "The Fraser River . . . proved to be 10 per cent truth and 90 per cent humbug."[22] But no matter where the miners deployed, and regardless of their failure or success, they kept a sense of humor and a common outlook. One story was told of a pack train of ten mules that arrived at an outpost, nine carrying whiskey and one carrying flour. Remarked one miner, "How come they sent so much flour?" Another story was told of the burial of a miner. As the preacher gave the eulogy and read the Good Book, his comrades lowered the coffin into the ground. Suddenly, one miner looked at the dirt shovelled out from the grave, and saw color. "Amen, and God rest his soul," he shouted, overriding the preacher. They quickly set the coffin to one side and started digging feverishly!

Such was the California experience, a rewarding one all in all. From "1851 to 1855 [the United States] contributed nearly 45 per cent of the world's output of gold."[23] The most productive year was 1852 when 81 million dollars in gold was produced. By 1860, this output was reduced to 44 million. During this general period, the highest wage averaged twenty dollars a day.[24] "At least a quarter of a million men came to California during the five years that constituted the gold rush proper, and . . . these men dug more than $200 million in gold. Nothing in any way so rich had ever before been encountered in any part of the world."[25]

Truly "the California Gold Rush was a national experience rarely matched in American history—in the nineteenth century only the Civil War surpassed its import."[26] As Frederick Jackson Turner later declared, the frontier was shaping the American spirit and telescoping history in the process. "Within . . . [a] twenty-five year span, California gold mining passed through successive stages of development that in other countries and in other industries would have required generations."[27] In so doing, the miner replaced the mountain man in opening up the wilderness, but unlike the trapper, he carried civilization with him.

Those in California who saw the gold running out drifted elsewhere to find their fortune. Many moved eastward to the Washoe Mountains in western Nevada Territory. Around 1859 in the Carson River and Mt. Davidson area in present-day Nevada, miners discovered the outcroppings of what seemed to be two quartz veins containing both gold and silver. Unbeknown to the discoverers, these were not two separate veins, but both part of the same. The first discovered was in the area called Gold Canyon; the other, in Six Mile Canyon. Subsequent digging proved them to be part of a big motherlode, a true bonanza, like that found earlier in California. Five miles long and nearly a mile in width, this lode eventually produced three hundred million dollars' worth of gold and silver. It was the famous Comstock lode.

The area had been known for years to miners who did some placer mining here and there. Two brothers, Hosea and Ethan Allen Grosch, worked the area as early as 1853, but it took until 1856 before they knew they had stumbled upon a mighty silver treasure in the area known as Gold Hill. They traced different veins of silver in 1857 and filed claims to their discoveries. That year, however, Hosea hurt himself with a pick and died shortly afterward of gangrene poisoning. Ethan told his father that he would give him Hosea's claim and went to California to do so. Unfortunately, he was caught up and lost in a snowstorm on the way, and though he struggled back to civilization with a companion, he died less than two weeks later. His companion, whose foot was amputated as a result of frostbite, knew only a few rumors about the claim and did not pursue them.

Other miners who worked the area never recognized the silver content of the materials, however, since, unlike gold, silver is difficult to distinguish from its carriers. It was a wise and wizened miner from Virginia, James Finny, affectionately known as "Old Virginny," who worked the area and recognized the significance of the ore. The time was 1859. Finny could not convince others of the lucky strike until two different miners hit the vein elsewhere in June of that year. Their mine became known as the Ophir, after a mythical biblical city of riches.

These two developers of the Ophir mine were surprised when another man visited them and accused them of jumping his claim, established long ago. The intruder's name was Henry Comstock, and he had indeed been in the area for several years, although he had a reputation for being more of a talker than a worker. He told the two that the claim they were working belonged to Ethan Grosch, who had given him a share in it to reside there and keep others from intruding. The story was never verified, but Comstock did for a time live in a cabin built by the Grosch brothers. Subsequently, the two miners and Comstock compromised and agreed to split the claim between themselves and another, a friend of Comstock.

Working the project together, they found that their mix of gold and silver ore assayed at an astounding $3,876 a ton. The silver eventually was to predominate, and miners poured in from everywhere as word got out about the new find. For the first year or so, individual miners could work the diggings, needing only basic tools, but soon it became clear that the only way the real riches could be tapped was through capital investment and development, with extensive use of expensive machinery.

The call for venture capital went out and it was answered by a number of wealthy men, one of whose name would become as famous as the mine itself. He was George Hearst, father of the newspaper magnate William Randolph Hearst. The elder Hearst made the original family fortune through investments in the Comstock and other mining properties.

Miners from the coast were working their way to Nevada over the High Sierras by way of Placerville. They arrived at Placerville in droves, making the once rich mining town rich again as a supply depot. Widened roads were constructed to the mine site, and soon the population in Nevada was numerous enough to people a city near the Comstock. Called Virginia City, it has been said to honor "Old Virginny" Finny (not so). In March 1861, the Territory of Nevada was created, including Virginia City within its bounds. The man appointed secretary of the territory was Mark Twain's brother, Orin Clemens. For a time, Mark Twain served as the popular and witty editor of the Virginia City newspaper.

The mines were being developed rapidly, and miners who formerly worked alone for what they could find now worked for wages under the direction of others. The wages were good, however, for the mine was a rich one. How rich, Comstock never dreamed, for he sold out his share for a paltry eleven thousand dollars or so. If he had held it, it would eventually have brought him some eighty million dollars.[28] It is ironic that both Comstock and Marshall, who discovered the California gold, died penniless—Comstock even a suicide.

Miners at the Comstock often supplemented their wages by the practice of "highgrading," or stealing ore from the mines. The ore was so rich that even a small amount paid handsomely. During the fifty years of the gold boom, it was estimated that "hard rock miners walked off with a fortune estimated conservatively at four million ounces—166 tons—of gold worth a staggering $80 million."[29] Virtually every mine was highgraded, and both management and employees knew it. Indeed, most miners felt that highgrading was their right, since work was hard and injury was a constant danger. Mine owners, however, saw the lifting of gold ore by the miners as simple theft. Over the years they bent every effort to eliminate highgrading and, by and large, succeeded.

The Comstock was not an easy mine to work. The increasing depths of the shafts made new and difficult demands on the miners and on machinery and mining techniques. Fortunately, many of the Comstock miners were Cornish with generations of mining experience behind them.[30] They also brought with them useful machinery, such as the powerful long-handled pump, like those that serviced their farm wells back home. They also brought their wives and families and their entire culture. Later, they sent for many relatives, latecomers who became known as "Cousin Jacks." They were in the forefront of the union movement, much of whose momentum began with the Cornish at the Comstock.

In the mines they had their own special guardians, called "tommyknockers." These elflike creatures, the miners believed, were always on the spot to warn of impending disaster. The tommyknockers would forbid the mines to flood or cave in until the men were safely outside. The Cornish made effigies of the sprites to stand guard in the mine. One miner declared after narrowly escaping death from a chute clearing blast, "I was sure that I owed my life to the tommyknockers, those unseen, wee, small folks who came over with the Irish and the Cousin Jacks, to tap on the rocks and warn mining stiffs, when there is some serious underground danger, as they had warned me when I had spit the fuse."[31]

Because silver ore was so soft, a cave-in was a constant worry at the Comstock. The usual method of shoring up the shafts with timber supports was little help, and the mine owners sent to California for a young German engineer who had solved other problems there. His name was Phillip Diedesheimer, and he invented a type of jiggered squares or structured cube frames of timbers. These shored up the mines much like building blocks, each resting partly upon the other, giving support from floor to ceiling. The squares became a standard piece of mine engineering and were used extensively where safety was a consideration. The invention was known in the trade as Diedesheimer square-sets.[32]

This problem solved, another immediately appeared. As the shafts went deeper and deeper, some to 2,600 feet, the air grew hotter, often exceeding 120 degrees. The stale air at that depth was barely breathable and so denuded of oxygen that the candles burned only with a flickering blue glow instead of a bright orange. The miners could work only fifteen minutes out of every hour in that intense heat. Ice was continuously transported to them in the shafts, and each miner used about ninety-five pounds of the ice-water mix during a shift. Even with the use of fans, ventilation was extremely poor.

Fires were commonplace in the large amount of timber in the mines. Explosions from black powder (later, dynamite and blasting caps) crippled many. The tamping of the powder and the crimping of the blasting caps were moments of great hazard. Moreover, the numerous blastings over a period of time produced severe hearing impairment. Flooding was frequent as new tunnels were dug. Further, men were often scalded by sudden steaming as hot water springs broke through the walls. Hernias were common and many miners wore the popular bulb belt to hold them in, especially the muckers, men who loaded and pushed the ore carts out of the mine. Their usual quota was sixteen cars loaded and pushed out in each eight-hour shift.

Those who chiselled and drilled their way through hard rock, sometimes granite, gave the world the memorable phrase "Deep Enough!" It came to mean not only the hole drilled but, in effect, "That's as far as I go," or, "I've had it for now," or, "I've reached my limit—any more and you can shove it!"

Often, ore was taken from great heights and cast into chutes that carried it to a lower level, where eventually it grew into tailings, a huge build-up of discarded rocks at the base of a hill. These tailings can be seen nearly everywhere in mining country and often have a sulfurish yellow cast to them. From time to time, the chutes would become blocked by two or more wedged boulders. Unblocking them was extremely dangerous, for the miners had to get in among them much like loggers breaking up a jam.[33]

Although drilling rock to insert blasting powder appeared easy, it was in fact highly skilled and dangerous work. It took two forms: "single jacking" and "double jacking." In the single jacking, a miner took a sharpened steel drill and hit it with a four-pound sledgehammer. After each blow, the drill was turned and twisted to receive the new blow. The twisting and the pounding had to be in unison to be effective, so timing and the rhythm of the stroke were crucial if one wanted to produce the deepest hole in the shortest amount of time—and this is what the bosses demanded.

In double jacking, two men were involved, one holding and twisting the drill, the other hitting it with a heavier, nine-pound sledgehammer. The men switched roles each minute, and each needed strong faith in the other's skill. The team action helped produce the solidarity that made its way into the union movement, for one miner's life often depended on the other. Single jacking was done in shafts not wide enough to accommodate double jacking. Single drillers often worked in a cramped position, usually on their knees.

Miners were proud of their skills and liked to compete in contests of drilling. Some competitions, to ensure fairness, had a heavyweight and a lightweight division. The contestants and bystanders made bets, and considerable money changed hands at these affairs. The usual contest was to drill as deep a hole as possible into granite during fifteen minutes. Eighty-five strokes a minute was the desiratum, the men switching positions every sixty seconds in perfect harmony, without a stroke being missed. Forty to forty-five inches of depth would likely place a man in the winner's circle.

Eventually, heavy compressed-air drills replaced much of the hand work. However, miners were unhappy with these labor-saving devices, for they brought efficiency at the expense of the miners' health. The new drills produced a fine dust that entered the miners' lungs, causing silicosis. This was not only disabling but often life-threatening. The new drills were dubbed "widow makers."

If ventilation in the mines was bad, sanitation was no better, for the mines were usually "90 by 90," a reference to prevailing heat and humidity. Everywhere the dank smell of rotting timbers and black powder smoke combined with the stench of urine and human excrement. Toilet cars were few and far between as they didn't carry payloads of ore.[34]

One man proposed a solution to the poor conditions at the deep Comstock. A German engineer named Adolf Sutro suggested to the owners that a separate air and ore track tunnel be constructed to provide drainage and needed ventilation. With the tunnel built on a gravity slant, loaded ore cars could be run downhill. Sutro proposed a five-mile tunnel, the biggest one in the West.

The mine owners balked, seeing no need to make the miners' life easier. The workers were producing quite satisfactorily and they saw no reason to take on an added expense. After all, there was no shortage of miners. The owners were particularly upset by Sutro's demand that he be given a percentage of the profits for each ore car to emerge from the tunnel.

Sutro, however, was persistent. He next went to the San Francisco silver kings, who would realize profits of over three hundred million dollars within twenty years. Unpersuasive there, he went to Congress and then even travelled to England to get money for the project. Still unsuccessful, he returned to this country and finally won his backers. The tunnel appeared very promising in its beginning stages, and more money flowed into the project, which was financed by stock purchases. Unfortunately, the tunnel was so long in being built that while it was under construction the mine's silver resources came near to being exhausted. Realizing this, Sutro sold his shares for a handsome profit and then completed the tunnel. A thirteen-year project, it served only a declining business. A millionaire by now, Sutro turned to politics and became the mayor of San Francisco.

The economic depression of 1857 pushed many people West, but there was little work to be found in Nevada Territory mines now. Near the end of the nineteenth century, however, gold and silver again were struck at Tonapah, just south of Carson City. A few years later, another big find was made at the Jumbo mine at Goldfield. But labor problems plagued the Goldfield mine, and the unrest carried over to other mining areas. Meanwhile, the western Coeur d'Alene country of Idaho became a major producer of silver, zinc, and lead and exported over one billion dollars' worth of the metals within a sixty-year period.[35]

Moving northeast out of the Comstock country and east of Coeur d'Alene, miners found themselves in Montana Territory in the early 1860s. There at Alder Gulch, Bannack, Virginia City, and Last Chance Gulch, they found another genuine bonanza. By the end of 1863, ten thousand miners were working the area's streams and ten million dollars in gold dust had been shipped from there. The capital of the territory at first was Bannack, but, Virginia City was founded to house incoming miners, and in turn became the new capital. It is now a ghost town about fifty miles northwest of Yellowstone National Park and is preserved as an interesting national historical site. Finally, Last Chance Gulch, a hundred miles north, struck it rich, renamed itself as Helena, and became the permanent capital.

Virginia City won fame for its solution to the problem of frontier lawlessness. Organized thieves plagued the area, seeking gold without working for it. To protect themselves, the miners and the merchants organized one of the most effective vigilante organizations in the West. The law thereabouts was so corrupt that the sheriff, Henry Plummer, was head of the gang of thieves. The vigilantes struck quickly, and within a few weeks there were "twenty-two men dead . . . and dozens of others scared out of the country because they saw the handwriting on the wall."[36]

Much criticism may be levelled against vigilante action, but sometimes, given the lawless conditions and the inability of the government to function as a protector, it may have been necessary. What happened in Virginia City had its counterpart earlier in San Francisco for several months in 1851 and again in 1856, when vigilantes there gave a number of criminals "suspended sentences." Commenting on the action at the time, the *Alta California* wrote, "Lynch Law is not the best law that might be, but it is better than none, and so far as the benefit is derived, we know no other here."[37]

The good news and bad news about Virginia City travelled fast. The criminals departed with the bad news of the vigilantes, and tenderfoot Easterners arrived upon hearing the good news of the strike. Foreigners from as far as Australia made haste to get in on the new find. It was now apparent that gold fields did not last; this might be the final opportunity to get rich. How to get to Virginia City was the most immediate problem. The railroad did not yet run west of the Missouri River, and the Civil War still was afire. Gold seekers could follow the Oregon Trail on their own as far as Julesberg in northeastern Colorado or Ft. Laramie in southeastern Wyoming, but from those points there was no marked trail to the gold fields.

Two entrepreneurs saw the possibility of making money by opening up a trail north. They were John Bozeman, who had left his family in Georgia to go West, and John Jacobs, who was married to an Indian woman and was knowledgeable in the ways of the mountains. Jacobs vanished quickly in the mists of history, but Bozeman's name lived on as their route to the gold fields of Virginia City became known as the Bozeman Trail.

The trail led north directly along the eastern edge of the mighty and beautiful Bighorn mountain range. Sixty miles into Montana, it moved directly west to the gold fields. Today, Interstate Highway 25 and Interstate 90 parallel the trail through Wyoming and Montana.[38] The Bozeman carried its first organized travellers between 1863 and 1865, and the route itself was relatively easy for man and beast. Unfortunately, it ran directly through the Powder River country, a favorite hunting ground of the fierce Sioux. Two Oglala Sioux chiefs, Red Cloud and Crazy Horse, would have something to say about Bozeman's intrusion.

Another trail was carved out along the west side of the Bighorns by the famed mountain man Jim Bridger. His route was the safer of the two because of its remoteness from Indian hunting grounds, but the passage was longer and tougher on cattle. So, by and large, it was the Bozeman that saw the most traffic and the greatest amount of bloodshed in battles with the Indians.

By the time easterners arrived, the Montana fields were placered out and hydraulicking was in use. Another technique became popular here—the method of dredging. In this process, a lowland area would be artificially flooded and made into a pond. A floating dredge would pick up the auriferous ground with its rotating chain of buckets on a large wheel. The muck was then dumped on riffles where the heavier gold would be deposited while the lighter gravel was shunted off to the side. It became a much-used way of getting gold after other methods were exhausted, but it is difficult to say which more greatly violated the land, hydraulicking or dredging. Each produced permanent ugly scars and tailings.

Between 1849 and 1869, then, not only had El Dorado been found but Silverado was there right next to it, and the Silver Kings built San Francisco into one of the most cosmopolitan towns in the world. The *nouveau riche* were having a field day, but wildness was turning inexorably toward civilization. An English observer discerned great changes since the time when Yerba Buena (San Francisco) had been "a canvas city; given up to dissipation . . . [to now being] a substantially built city; equally have the mines changed, and the 'vagabond' population stands forth in the shape of engineers, excavators, mechanics, and cunning inventors, and, better still, organised bands of labourers, who, under the guidance of these, first bring profit to themselves and benefit to the country generally."[39]

Prospectors made new discoveries not only in gold and silver but, equally important, in copper as well. The age of electricity was coming, and copper to conduct its power would hurry it along. But that is yet another story. Gold and silver were found in Utah and in Arizona. In Arizona, a prospector named Ed Schieffelen searched in what appeared to be barren desert; scoffers told him that the only thing he would find would be his tombstone. In a way, he proved them right, for he struck it rich and the town of Tombstone came into being, a testimonial to his persistence. Eventually, eighty million dollars' worth of silver would be excavated.

The finds of gold and silver kept appearing, some in California, others in Alaska and in the Klondike country, where Ketchikan, Dawson City, and Chilkoot Pass became bywords of their time. Colorado and South Dakota also were still to be reckoned with in the search for gold. Indeed, Colorado produced its own gold and silver kings and its own San Francisco, only their city was located not on the ocean but on the frontal range of the Rockies and its name was Denver. It is to that part of the gold rush that we now turn.

Gold, having been discovered and exploited in the far West, was now firmly associated in popular thinking with that locale. However, as early as 1849, the year of Sutter's find, some Cherokee Indians paused on their way to California to pan for gold in the Platte River. They were not far from the confluence of the two forks of the river—the north fork flowing from the vicinity of Ft. Laramie, the south from the Colorado Rockies and Pike's Peak. Other members of the party were shown the gold but considered the find insignificant, and the group moved on. Nonetheless, this wisp of a find was enough to start rumors about gold along the Platte.

The first substantial discovery was in 1858 along Cherry Creek, a tributary of the South Platte near present-day Denver. Color also was spotted at nearby Auraria, and the rush was on. Although Pike's Peak was sixty-five miles south, the rallying call for the rush became "Pike's Peak or Bust." An economically depressed East heeded the message, and fifty thousand men and their families picked up and headed west. Most were disappointed and soon went home with a different message on their wagon canvas. This time it read, "Busted by God!"[40] Gold was there but hard to find. Placer spottings were just frequent enough to tease and poor enough to discourage all but the most persistent miners. The tenacious usually were single men, for married men with families could not afford to stick it out. In the first ten years of mining, 1858-1867, the territory produced only twenty-five million dollars in gold and silver, a mere 5 percent of the half billion dollars produced by California in its first decade of discovery.[41]

The itinerant New York journalist Horace Greeley went to see the diggings for himself, making famous the slogan "Go West, Young Man, Go West"—go west and grow with the country. Enthusiastic at first, perhaps because he was shown a mine that had been salted (jokers had filled a shotgun with gold dust and sprayed the inside walls with it), he soon changed his views. He began to play down the gold strike in his news dispatches, emphasizing to his readers that the rewards didn't warrant the hardships of the trip west.

Nevertheless, miners scoured the Denver area and westward, ranging through passes with altitudes of six to nine thousand feet. They stumbled on deposits of gold and occasionally silver, but quickly the finds petered out. In 1859, in an area through which ran a stream called Clear Creek, their luck changed.

The north branch of the creek penetrated an area called Gregory

Gulch, and gold was found there in quantity. The reaction was frenzied. The towns of Blackhawk and Central City sprang up to accommodate the treasure hunters. After Clear Creek, the first major strike
in Colorado was found around present-day Idaho Springs, also in
1859, and other strikes were made a short distance west at present-
day Georgetown and its sister city of Silver Plume. (An old-time nar-
row-gauge railway still winds across switchback after switchback,
giving tourists a chance to see what the area looked like in its heyday.)

Other miners moved southwest of Denver, and about seventy-
five miles into the valley called South Pass, they struck the precious
metals again at slightly over nine thousand feet. The town built on
the spot was called Fairplay, expressing more a wish than a reality.
The Spanish had visited the location to gather salt from the valley. If
they had looked harder they might have discovered their El Dorado.
Fairplay is still there today, incorporating within itself the ghost town
of South Pass City. Mining tools, ore carts, machinery, and all the
paraphernalia that went into improvising a town are displayed on the
site.

Just west of Fairplay, what is now the town of Leadville made an
entrance into history in April 1860. Gold was struck nearby at a site
called Oro, but known to the locals as California Gulch. Five thousand
miners descended to work its placers, and within three years the gold
was gone. The city, however, remained, and its greater days were
still to come. One of its later shopkeepers and its postmaster was a
man named H.A.W. Tabor. Originally from Vermont, he and his wife
Augusta tried homesteading in the West but quit when Tabor was
caught up in the Pike's Peak rush. After prospecting unsuccessfully
for over a decade, he was fairly settled down by 1878. Few visited
Leadville, since its gold had been worked out, but occasionally some
optimistic souls would come around to rework the tailings, like dogs
looking for scraps. Two such men entered Tabor's store, offering part
ownership in any paying claim they might make in return for a grubstake in supplies. Tabor obliged, as he was wont to do, for despite
his recent sedentary life, his heart still was with the miners. He had
been disappointed in his own search for a glory hole but perhaps he
could share in the dreams of others.

Within a short time, his debtors discovered a rich vein of quartz
and silver and the kind of blackish sand found around the old Comstock, which proved to be a sign of rich silver carbonate. They named
the mine "Little Pittsburg" and Tabor's grubstake investment of between seventeen and sixty-four dollars turned into profits of one-half
million; he later sold his part of the claim for one million dollars.[42]
The mining was tough at that altitude—over ten thousand feet—and

miners had to become acclimated before they could do any kind of day's work, but the tribulations were well worth while.

With his own profits earned from Little Pittsburg, Tabor seemed to be blessed with the Midas touch; he bought other mines and parlayed his winnings. His luck was such that when some con men sold him a worthless mine they had salted with gold dust, a few feet of further digging uncovered another bonanza and added to his wealth.

The silver boom of Colorado was under way, occurring in many cases on sites where gold had petered out. Leadville, a hundred miles southwest of Denver, became a great city, and it was Horace Tabor who put it on the map as each investment brought him bigger profits and the town more fame. Unfortunately, his wife Augusta, who had pinched pennies for many years as keeper of a boarding house, did not change her old ways. Manipulating both civil and ecclesiastical law, Tabor put her aside and married a Roman Catholic divorcee, who in her own way was to become as famous as he. She was the vivacious Elizabeth McCourt Doe, better known as Baby Doe. Unlike Augusta, she knew how to spend money. A woman of lavish tastes, she bought sets of stagecoaches and horses whose colors and decorations matched what she was wearing on any given day. Tabor loved her spendthrift ways. Tabor did his part by building two opera houses, one in Leadville and one in Denver. The Leadville building was called "at the time . . . the most magnificent structure between St. Louis and San Francisco."[43] Built in a record hundred days at a nearly equal cost in thousands of dollars, it seated eight hundred patrons. All supplies used in its construction were transported by wagon and mules over Mosquito Pass, thirteen thousand feet in elevation, for the railroad would not reach Leadville until June 1880. (When the railroad came, President Grant was on board and graced the opera house with his presence. Now the pass is used for donkey races to and from Leadville.)

The opera house nearly missed its grand opening in 1879. Two days before, vigilante action broke out in the town, which was still very much wild and woolly. Thirty-five vigilantes broke into the jail, seized two prisoners, and, after a trial by "Judge Lynch," summarily hanged them from a construction beam only a block from the opera. A note attached to one of the bodies read, "Notice to all Lot Thieves, Bunko Steerers, Foot Pads, Highwaymen with their Pals and Sympathizers, and all other classes of Criminals. This is only the Commencement, and This Shall be Your Fate . . . [Signed] The Seven Hundred."[44]

The Tabor Opera House still exists and plays summer melodramas for the tourists. Visitors are surprised to learn that one of the early performers there was Oscar Wilde, who lectured on "The Practical Applications of the Aesthetic Theory of Exterior and Interior Decoration, with Observations on Dress and Personal Ornament." Thus Tabor brought culture to the West.

With money came power and influence, and Tabor served as lieutenant governor of the newly created state of Colorado. His marriage to Baby Doe was attended even by Chester Arthur, the president of the United States, while Tabor served an interim appointment as senator.

Tabor's luck had been remarkable but it proved finite. Silver dropped drastically in price after the repeal in 1883 of the Sherman Silver Act. Tabor died a pauper in 1899. On his deathbed, he told Baby Doe that, whatever else she sold, she should hang on to the Matchless Mine, for he believed it would yield riches once again. She did keep it, living there in a shack during the hard mountain winters and the hail-driven summers. When she emerged to get groceries and other bare necessities, she always told the merchants to charge them to her account, as she had in her days of wealth. Out of compassion and remembrance of her spendthrift days, the merchants played the game as though nothing had changed. She followed this pattern until 1935; then seventy-three, she was found frozen to death at the Matchless shack. So ended the era of Leadville and the Colorado silver bonanza.

The 1860s and the 1870s witnessed the drama of the Indian Wars. Conflict seemed inevitable, with an increasing number of settlers making their way West. Instead of passing through, many were staying in the Great Plains. The journey had become easier as the railroads brought more people and more commerce. Gold was the magnet for some. As prospectors flocked to the latest celebrated strike, others looked for it in places previously untried or off limits to whites. A prime example of forbidden territory was the Black Hills country of Dakota, the sacred hills of the Sioux and other plains warriors.

Protected from white encroachment by the Ft. Laramie Treaty of 1868, rumors of gold there resulted in increasing pressure on those who would uphold the treaty. A piece of paper seemed an intolerable obstacle to gold-obsessed people who could sense riches on the other side. Gold had been discovered in the Black Hills as early as 1833 but miners were chary of entering its sacred precincts, where the Sioux looked with jaundiced eyes on all who trespassed. Many trespassers were never heard from again.

In the area surrounding the Black Hills, the army was given the unenviable job of keeping both whites and Indians at bay. If ever a group found itself in the middle, the army was it. Pressure was building on the government to violate the treaty; a newspaper in Yankton editorialized: "What should be done with these Indian dogs in our manger? They will not dig the gold or let others do it. . . . They are too lazy and too much like mere animals to cultivate the fertile soil, mine the coal, develop the salt mines, bore the petroleum wells, or wash the gold."[45]

Indian ire and white resentment were rising; clearly something had to be done and done quickly. To quell the avarice of the whites, General Crook, whom all sides respected, told the would-be miners that the government was in the act of negotiating with the Indians concerning entry into the Black Hills. Indeed, to placate the Indians, two important chiefs were included in the negotiations; one was Spotted Tail and the other the enigmatic and warlike Red Cloud. Spotted Tail seemed willing to sell out, saying to the government, "As long as we live on this earth we will expect pay. We want to leave the amount with the President at interest forever. . . . I want to live on the interest of my money."[46] But Red Cloud, true to form, wanted nothing to do with treaty revisions.

With settlers and potential miners clamoring for action, a way was found for the army legitimately to reconnoiter the area under the exploratory rights allowed by the treaty.[47] The whites were delighted when the man chosen to head the expedition was the Boy General of Civil War fame, George Armstrong Custer. Accompanying the crack outfit was President Grant's own son, Frederick; George Bird Grinnell, the well-known anthropologist; and one of Custer's many nephews. Although the army objected to what seemed the increasingly political tilt of the mission, the group was burdened with a wide variety of non-army personnel. These included photographers, engineers, medics, topographers, surveyors, scientists, and two private miners. The array was impressive with its thousand soldiers and teamsters and a wagon train nearly two miles long. Pictures were taken as it wound through Castle Creek Valley. The landscape today shows virtually no change.

The entourage ran into an occasional native in the Sacred Hills, but no Indians were found in force. When Indians were encountered, they were presented with gifts and assured that the mission was a purely exploratory one.

Near Harney Peak, the highest point in South Dakota, miners found some color but nothing in quantity. Nonetheless, when the message reached Ft. Laramie that a trace of color had been noted, rumors spread wildly about a "rich find" of gold in the Indian lands. Dakota papers were not to be deterred by truth and ran banner headlines about the discovery of gold in the Black Hills. One enterprising local insurance company offered life insurance policies to miners going into that dangerous area.[48]

Whites now threatened to go invade the hills and protect themselves in any way necessary. The army strongly forbade such action; in August 1874, Sheridan wrote General Terry, "Should companies now organizing . . . trespass on the Sioux reservation, you are hereby directed to use the force at your command to burn their wagon trains, destroy the outfits and arrest the leaders, confining them to the nearest military post!"[49]

But when the chips were down, the white soldiers would not shoot their own people, and whites stormed the Black Hills en masse. At least they had no easy entrance. The way into the major gold fields was circuitous and tortuous, as teamsters and stagecoach drivers quickly learned. It ran through canyon after canyon; those who travelled it did so at considerable peril, and not only from Indians.

A major fount of the gold was found in the vicinity of present-day Deadwood and Lead (pronounced "leed," as the quartz was the lead or pointer to the gold lode). There, the Homestake mine opened in April 1876, only two months before the death of Custer at the Little Bighorn. Soon George Hearst, the California magnate of Comstock fame, bought into the mine and developed it. It is now the largest gold producer in the United States. (Mine officials regulate the work on the gold vein and know exactly where it leads and how many years it will take to exhaust it.) By 1924, fully 90 percent of the gold from the Black Hills emanated from the Homestake.

Deadwood is known today as much for the list of outlaws and gamblers who followed the wealth dug up by the miners as for the mine itself. Wild Bill Hickok, who was shot in the back there by Jack McCall, was the man who held the famed Deadman's Hand of aces and eights. Calamity Jane worked odd jobs around the place, often dressing as a man and serving as a teamster. Both Wild Bill and Calamity Jane are buried in the nearby Boot Hill cemetery by Mt. Moriah. Deadwood, which seems an apt name for the town in view of its legends, originally referred to its trees killed by smelter poisons.

A final bonanza came before the turn of the century. It was found through the enterprise of a cowboy. While working the range of his boss, Robert Womack did occasional prospecting on the side, mostly in out-of-the-way places where cattle had strayed. He got some gold from panning and, encouraged, buttonholed nearly everyone he met looking for a grubstake to develop the areas that looked promising. One was a piece of land above nine thousand feet high west of Colorado Springs and Pikes Peak. The place later would be known as Cripple Creek because of injuries to cattle crossing the rock-strewn stream. Womack got his grubstake and, by showing some gold from his promising claim, sold it for a quick profit of about five hundred dollars. The claim eventually would give up more than five million dollars of gold. Like many others who struck it rich, Womack died penniless.

The area of the actual gold find was a scant six square miles and overlooked an extinct volcano, Mt. Pisgah. The gold was found in 1891, and by 1896 twenty-five thousand people made Cripple Creek their home. That same year saw twenty-five million dollars in gold removed from the area, making it a world competitor in gold production. In its heyday, the town had "41 assay offices, 91 lawyers, 46 brokerage houses, 88 doctors and dentists, 14 newspapers, 70 saloons and 1 coroner."[50]

The number of brothels is not known, but a very gaudy Victorian one is preserved in the ghost town of Cripple Creek today. Mine shafts can still be seen descending into the earth from the front lawns of some preserved houses. Cripple Creek suffered the usual fires that plagued other wooden towns and twice was burned to the ground and rebuilt.

The town was the scene of two strikes, the first in 1894 and the second nearly a decade later. The first strike was a small affair, occurring when the company tried unsuccessfully to reduce daily wages from $3.00 to $2.50. The second, however, was a major confrontation that proved to be a test of how strong the union movement had become during the previous four decades. During that time, the Western Federation of Miners had urged its members to belong to rifle clubs in case of labor troubles; owners were quick to label them the Federation of Murderers. In August 1903, the union called thirty-four hundred miners out on strike over various grievances, both in Cripple Creek and at the places where the owners shipped the ore. The company brought in nonunion men to work the mines and the state militia to protect the "scabs" from the wrath of the federation. Well equipped, the militia tried to intimidate the union with Gatling guns, bayonets, and loaded firearms. They were paid by company owners, so close was the relationship between state and capitalist. The company and its allies in state government hoped to break the back of the union movement.

Protesting, the miners blew up a shack, killing a superintendent and another company man. Martial law was declared and unionists were beaten, rounded up, jailed, or put in pens, but the strike went on. In June 1904, thirteen scabs were dynamited to kingdom come by the miners.[51] This was too much, and the miners now felt the full force of the overwhelming power that confronted them. The union was broken, but its cause was taken up by unions everywhere, particularly in the copper mines.[52]

The gold era was short-lived, like the fur era that preceded it. To the workers, mines were not simply holes in the ground but personal things, as the names they gave their mines indicated. Those names have stories to tell—"Emma," "Lucky Cuss," "Independence," "Molly Brown," "Matchless," "Rough and Ready" and "Vulture." The gold rushes helped to fill the American West with adventurous people. The promises and disappointments of the search for gold shaped America and the people who answered its call.

5. The Missionaries
For God and Country

The opening of the New World was accomplished by a procession of explorers, entrepreneurs—and missionaries. Indeed, the explorers in many cases were themselves missionaries. In the seventeenth century, Louis Hennepin, a Franciscan, and Jacques Marquette, a Jesuit, explored the Great Lakes and Mississippi Valley. As the eighteenth century arrived, the Jesuit Eusebio Francisco Kino was at work in the American Southwest and the Franciscans Juínpero Serra, Silvestre Escalente, and Francisco Dominguez were not far behind.

The early religious explorers moved through the tribes, preaching their gospel and mapping the land for those who would follow. Later, particularly in the West, permanent mission centers were established where the Christian life (and European ways) could be observed and assimilated by those living nearby and others who came to view the strange new settlements. In the rich and fertile Willamette Valley of Oregon, Protestant missionaries set up farming communities next to their churches to shape the Indian into a facsimile of a white farmer. They taught white values and white skills in order to prepare the red man to adopt the white man's religion.

Although the cultural values of the missionaries were inevitably present in all that they taught, not all of the ministers attempted overtly to separate the Indians from their traditional ways. In the High Plains and Northwest, Roman Catholic missionaries did not try to change hunters and nomads into farmers. Indeed, the new Indian Christians carried on many of their old religious rites as before. Native American rituals became combined with Roman Catholic ones to form new hybrids with new meanings.

The Roman policy of adaptation had ample precedent. After Constantine, Western christendom long baptized not only converts but much of their native culture as well. Pagan festivals were turned into Christian holidays. Greek and Roman rites of spring were incorporated in the celebration of Easter. A pagan symbol, the wedding ring, was blessed and used in the marriage ceremony of the church. When

Protestant reformers appeared, however, they rejected such cultural accommodations. They emphasized purity and conversion, insisting that the new life in Christ meant a clear break with old ways. This approach proved to have limited appeal to the tradition-minded red man in the American West. The tolerance of Roman Catholic missionaries seemed less threatening to Native Americans, who showed a heavy preference for the colorful ceremonies of Catholicism.

In any event, many missionaries saw the natives as predisposed to Christianity. Indian ideas about a "happy hunting ground" in the hereafter seemed close to the Christian idea of heaven. While not all Indians in fact believed in life after death, most looked with favor on the teaching that all persons are equal in the eyes of God. Living as they did in a universe of spirits, the Indians were quite ready to accept one more great spirit, especially one whose white followers manifested such impressive power.

The lasting impact of the missionaries on Indian cultures, however, was not limited to their religious teachings and their European ways. Intentionally or not, the missionaries became evangelists for the wonders of life in the West. Their journals and diaries, published back East, inflamed readers' imaginations and helped inspire the waves of immigration that would overwhelm the Native Americans in their own lands. Enthusiasm for a new start in the Northwest was called Oregon Fever, and it was spread most effectively by the wives of ministers. The letters written to friends and family by these women described the practical, everyday side of life in the new land. The women—and men—who read their accounts could easily picture themselves taking part in such domestic adventures. Even the difficulties and disasters sounded romantic as the writers stressed the joy they felt in doing God's work.

Another source of publicity for prospects in the new land was the missionary newspapers. Most prominent was one run by the Protestant Board of Missions. *The Christian Advocate and Journal*, a Methodist publication full of stories portraying the eagerness of the natives for the word of God, almost singlehandedly sent a tidal wave of missionaries and migrants West.

A less accessible collection of information was nevertheless influential—the *History of Jesuit Relations*, which gathered the reports of the far-ranging "blackrobes" to their superiors. It recorded the culture, religious progress, and languages of the natives as well as the topography of their lands. A great many of the reports from America were contributed by the Belgian Pierre Jean De Smet, who travelled more than 125 thousand miles on his missionary journeys and wrote in six languages. For immigrant trains, he drew maps and gave accurate details about what lay ahead. By such help, he even earned the gratitude of Brigham Young of the Latter-Day Saints. As one of the few men trusted by both whites and Indians, he took part in many treaty meetings, and his writings are a major source of information about government-Indian relations.

Missionaries have long been among the most proficient linguists in the world. Their desire to preach the gospel to pagans has prompted them to learn even languages spoken by only a handful of people and to translate the Bible for different cultures. (The problems that arise can be appreciated by considering how to translate the "daily bread" of the "Our Father" for Eskimos, who never taste bread but depend on blubber.)

The missionary work of translation has not been all in one direction. Native tongues have been given forms that allow them to be used in communication with outsiders. The wife of a missionary invented a basic alphabet for the Nez Percé, who had no previous written language. This was quite a feat, for Lewis and Clark had found the sounds of that language, which they called Chappunish, unintelligible and unreproduceable. Thus missionaries have served as bridge builders between cultures.

The ministrations of missionaries in the American West went far beyond purely spiritual matters. With or without medical training, they were called on to provide medical care to Indians and travellers alike. Their missions served as inns and halfway houses for wayfarers, as did the monasteries of old. They offered hospitality that, in the wilderness, is a necessity of life.

In barren areas of the world, hospitality often has been regarded as a great and natural virtue, for without it many travellers surely would die. Even the fierce Bedouins in northern Africa permit entrance into their camp during the day when the coffee pot is boiling. There, the stranger (a word often synonymous with enemy) may have his needs taken care of. (But when the coffee pot is taken off the fire and darkness sets in, woe to the stranger who attempts entrance.) It is said in Moslem religion that the one thing Allah asks of those seeking entrance to the kingdom after death is, "Were you hospitable?"

Although Native Americans often sought to incorporate elements of the white missionaries' religion and were influenced by their ways, the very different mores and cultural values frequently became a cause of conflict. One Indian agent appointed by the government to the Utes moralized against their gambling on horseraces. When his admonitions had no effect, he plowed up their racetrack while the men were away on a hunt. When the Utes returned, they killed him.

Gambling and whiskey drinking among the Indians were vigorously condemned and forbidden by ministers who came out of America's Puritan heritage. Even Indian dances and rituals were regarded as taboo by Protestant missionaries who in their stern view of life equally condemned social festivities and popish pomp.

The frequent displays of nakedness by the braves and the casual baring of breasts by the women also shocked the ministers and their wives, although the wives often were less prudish than the men. Indians who treated their own wives cruelly or who had many wives were roundly excoriated by missionaries of nearly all varieties. The Mormons, however, were not bothered by polygamy, as they practiced it themselves.

In general, Roman Catholic missionaries took a benign attitude toward the Indian way of life. Dancing, moderate drinking, and gambling never were condemned as such. Roman Catholics did all of these themselves. Then too, elaborate ceremonies were a part of Catholic worship, so Indian ones could hardly be prohibited. But while the Roman outlook was more accommodating of man's physical nature, on some issues strict lines were drawn. In the case of a polygamous Indian man, the priest might tell him to pick his favorite and stay with her only. Which wife to choose was up to the Indian.

In one matter of physical excess, none of the missionaries could condemn but only stand back and marvel. Uniformly, whites were amazed at how much the Indian could put away when food was available. As some drinkers are said to have a hollow leg, Indians were said to have hollow stomachs. This was a matter of necessity: life for the red man was feast or famine. Especially among the nomadic hunting tribes, they never knew where the next meal would come from.

Perhaps the most potent appeal of the white man's religion to the Indians lay in how it converged with their "belief in a personally acquirable magic."[1] Spiritual strength was no mere metaphor with them: they believed that one could gain or lose power. With power, the Indian considered himself or his cause invincible; without it, nothing could be achieved. This belief was the basis for the missionary's first successes because religion for the Native American meant a personal power. Those who had it and could wield it would be superior individuals, just as tribes that had it would be superior tribes. They would have prowess over others for, in their terms, religion was "big medicine."

At first, most whites misunderstood what the Indian meant by "medicine." They thought it referred to those herbs and substances that promoted bodily healing. Pierre Jean De Smet, however, explained to his Jesuit superiors the proper meaning of medicine as conceived by the red man. Firstly, signifying power, it could be won or lost and referred to "anything that they cannot understand, whether supernatural, natural or mechanical. A watch, an organ, a steamboat, or anything in fact, the comprehension of which exceeded their capacity to understand is called Wahkon. God is called Wahkon-tonga, Tonga meaning great or large."[2] Perhaps the term *mystery* or better yet *mysterious*, conveys some of this notion. Thus God was not so much the "Great Spirit" as the "Great Mysterious."

The religion of the whites was seen as "big medicine," and the Indians, perceiving the power wielded by the whites, attributed this to their religion. This conclusion followed naturally since the Indians derived their power from their religion. To harness such white power was a worthy aim. Yet it wasn't power because it was religion. Rather it was religion because it was power.

As an example, De Smet tells of striking a friction match to light his pipe while talking with a chief. The chief was struck with awe. Noting his amazement, De Smet gave some matches to the chief. Years later, the two crossed paths again and the Indian gave the priest a heartfelt welcome. The chief said, "It is to thee, Blackgown, that I owe all my glory in the victories I have gained over my enemies."[3] Just as the priest was feeling flattered at his religious influence on the chief, the chief opened his totem sac and showed the matches De Smet had given him. Not one had been used! The very carrying of them into battle gave him "big medicine" or power. The priest might have commented in Latin, "*Post hoc, ergo propter hoc*"—after this, therefore because of this.

Although white religion early penetrated the Southwest and coastal California, it was late in reaching the Northwest. The most religious things most Indians in those areas knew were blasphemies, learned from mountain men or sailors who touched the Pacific shores. We recall the mixed emotions of Lewis and Clark upon hearing them. On the one hand they didn't like the taking of the Lord's name in vain; on the other, recognizing the language of sailors, they were glad for evidence that they were nearing the coast.

Before the missionaries came, many Northwest Indians had acquired as totems various crosses and medals from trading with Spanish sailors coming into the Juan de Fuca straits that led into Puget Sound. (Interestingly, Juan de Fuca was not a Spaniard but a Greek who had changed his name to avoid trouble with his shipmates. Further, he never saw or entered the straits that bear his name because, as they often are, these portals were enshrouded by fog when he was there. He nevertheless deduced the presence of the straits and he was right.) Russian landings on the continent also contributed a scattering of religious articles and icons to the Indians' collections.

Long before either white traders or missionaries reached the

Northwest, missions for Indians had been established in the West up to the eastern side of the Rocky Mountains. Among the most active of missionary groups were the Methodists, a branch of separated Anglicans promoted by Francis Asbury. Quakers, Baptists, Presbyterians, and Roman Catholics were other groups involved. The road to Fort Kearney in south-central Nebraska was well-populated with such missions. Indeed, they were popular stops and trading posts with those heading Westward. The Fort Kearney road was to become the first long leg of the Oregon and Mormon trails.

As we have seen, the missionaries promoted not only civilization but also settlement. The historian Ray Billington called them publicists and propagandists for Eastern emigration, especially to Oregon: "They publicized their adopted lands so effectively that by 1840 not a farmer or shopkeeper in the Mississippi Valley but carried in his mind a golden—and largely false—picture of the Willamette and Sacramento valleys."[4] De Voto notes the same phenomenon but with a more jaundiced eye: "There were only two agencies for the extension of civilization on a large scale, armies and missions, and in the light of history the primitives who drew the armies were much better off."[5] What is true is that towns did evolve from missions as often as they evolved from forts. Tucson, San Diego, San Juan de Capistrano, and Los Angeles all grew up around missions, as Detroit, Pittsburgh, and Chicago developed from forts.

Although the mountain men had been in and out of the Oregon country before the missionaries, by and large they were not the carriers of religion, even though a few were deeply religious in their private lives. Jedediah Smith, remember, carried a Bible with him on his fifteen thousand miles of wilderness wandering.

Concerning religion, the mountain man probably was more influenced by the Indian than the other way around. The mountain men were eager to attain the knowledge and skills of the Indian in order to survive and flourish, and with their learning they came to imitate and often adopt the whole Indian belief system. Jim Bridger, for example, held an especial regard for Indian belief in omens.

Many mountain men also assimilated many Indian views by way of their Indian wives. Several armchair observers in the East ridiculed the mountain man for considering all sorts of portents before acting, but then, these observers never faced a capricious and deadly nature as the mountain man did daily. The critics might have been queried concerning their attitudes toward walking under ladders, breaking mirrors, or getting up on the wrong side of the bed. It justly has been observed that one man's religion is another man's superstition.

The role of the mountain men in the missionary movement was primarily that of guide, for without their help the men of the cloth could not have reached their destinations. Yet no more incongruous company could be imagined than mountain men and missionaries bound together for months on end, moving to Oregon land. The contrasts between them were highlighted at the boisterous rendezvous. Nonetheless, often each earned the other's respect. An outstanding example was the admiration between Pierre Jean De Smet and Tom Fitzpatrick, known to the Indians as "Old Brokenhand" or "White Hair." Indeed, De Smet knew and admired the skills of many of the mountain men, including Bridger, Smith, Carson, and others, and perhaps in his own way he was almost one of them. Certainly, his superior, upon reading his reports, wondered aloud whether De Smet was more adventurer than priest and seriously thought of removing him from his "mountain man-like" wandering.

The stern-minded Protestants were less appreciative of the mountain man and his shenanigans. At the 1837 Green River rendezvous, a stopover before continuing on the Oregon Trail, one missionary reported:

A man by the name of Dr. Newell [a mountain man] won a woman on a wager. On hearing that his old Flathead wife was coming . . . he said he must get rid of the woman. Accordingly, he went and sold her to her previous owner for One Hundred Dollars.   A second individual, they tell me, lost his wife on a wager. A few days after, he won a horse and bought his wife back again. The buying and selling of Indian women is a common occurrence at this Rendezvous, especially among those having a white face. The principal White trader [probably Fontenelle, a well-known mountain man] . . . had taken three wives. He tells the Indians to take as many as they can—thus setting at defiance every principle of right, justice and humanity and law of God and man.[6]

Protestant missionaries especially chided their guides for pushing the group forward on the Sabbath. The mountain men usually persisted in doing so, knowing that delay would risk the possibility of bad weather, adding more hardship to what already was being endured. Their politest reply to the ministers was something like, "Praying's your business, getting to Oregon's mine!"

In some ways, the missionaries and mountain men exhibited striking parallels. The different groups of missionaries were as competitive among themselves as were the different fur companies. All were single-minded and willing to endure any obstacle, even death itself, to achieve their goals. The goal for the mountain men was furs and for the missionaries it was souls. Yet, in times of mutual danger, they could join in unity.

The competition between Protestant and Roman Catholic missionaries was of a different order. Protestants regarded the United States as a Protestant country. Certainly the public school system reflected the predominantly Protestant communities it served. Protestant prayers opened the school day, and the King James Bible was used, sometimes as a reader. Although John Carroll, the first Roman Catholic bishop in America, was a friend of Benjamin Franklin and an ardent patriot, charges of foreign allegiance clung to his church. In any event, the quiet American Catholic Church centered in its Maryland ghetto was overwhelmed in the mid-nineteenth century by waves of Irish and Italian immigrants. Their numbers and exotic ways alarmed the Protestants and increased suspicions about the papists.

Nevertheless, the religious liberty for which John Carroll had labored awaited his coreligionists when they arrived. However hostile their Protestant neighbors, they could establish their churches and even set up their own school systems. A minority, they sided with other minorities, especially the Jews, to form political coalitions. Both Roman Catholics and Jews were concentrated in the cities; as one scholar noted, "In America as a whole, the Catholic church of the nineteenth century was urban, immigrant and an intruder."[7] Mainstream Protestantism continued to celebrate the life of rural and small-town America.

Although some farming towns on the prairies were virtually German Catholic villages transplanted from Europe, the movement West was essentially Protestant. More individualistic and not dependent on a priesthood for their rites, the Protestant pioneers outran their churches, depending on a rough Kantian morality to regulate their relationships before the preachers arrived. Roman Catholics and Jews were the Johnny-come-latelies.

For a better understanding of the missionary movement in the Pacific Northwest and its influence on America's sense of itself, let us look at the development of the region and some of the principal characters who played a part. For years, the Oregon country was dominated by various fur trading companies whose interests were almost exclusively pecuniary. For example, in 1825 the Hudson's Bay Company (English) set up major headquarters at Fort Vancouver on the north side of the Columbia River, opposite present-day Portland. The Astorians (American) were headquartered near the mouth of the Columbia in 1811, and the Northwest Company (Canadian, merged with Hudson's Bay in 1821) was present even earlier on the Snake River and the Lower Columbia. In addition, other splinter groups and free trappers worked the disputed territory, going in and out at will.

At Hudson's Bay, the officials tended to be English Anglicans or Scottish Presbyterians, and their workers were Roman Catholics. Some of the workers were French Catholics, but nearly a third serving largely as guides were transplanted Eastern Iroquois who had been influenced by the Jesuits. Eastern Delawares and Hurons working for Hudson's Bay had a similar background. The Northwesters included a similar mix of ethnic and religious groups. Americans operating in Oregon, however, were mostly Protestant, although they also employed many French Catholics.

Since religion is an integral part of Indian life, the Eastern Indians had an avid audience as they described their experience of Roman Catholicism to their counterparts in the Northwest. The Iroquois gave glowing accounts of the pomp, costumes, songs, and rituals of the Mass and sacraments, all activities appealing to Indian taste. The admired white emissaries of this new religion were referred to as "blackrobes." Later the term came to be used for any Roman Catholic priest.

Higher-ups in the trading companies, coming as they did from non-Catholic and even anti-Catholic backgrounds, were especially wary of Jesuits, who were known for their efforts to reclaim England for the Pope. They approved the suppression of the order in 1773 and feared its revival in 1814. The only problem was that their Roman Catholic employees had to be accommodated. They didn't require Mass every Sunday, but they did want Christian marriages and burials and celebration of the major feasts of the church.

From time to time, Hudson's Bay posts were visited by a company inspector to determine how well they were being run. In 1825, George Simpson, a high-level official, noted that many of the employees (Indians and part-Indians mostly) exhibited a great interest in the white man's religion. Their request for instruction moved Simpson to recommend that the company help establish missions in its area. The idea appealed to the businessmen, who may have felt that religious employees might do a better job or at least take part in fewer brawls and killings. Hudson's Bay already had given help to a mission school in their Red River country near Winnipeg. Like those at Red River, missionaries for the new Oregon effort could come in via Montreal, solidifying the British presence in the disputed area around Fort Vancouver.

To show that he was serious and to gain the good will of the Indian employees, Simpson encouraged two young boys to seek schooling in white man's ways, sending them to the Red River post. Their names were Spokane Garry and Kootenai Pelly, their first names designating their tribal affiliations.

Kootenai Pelly died at the school, but Spokane Garry learned basic English and wrote a letter to his tribe, which was delivered personally by Simpson. After two years of education, Spokane Garry returned to his tribe. He had a Bible and knew something of its contents; he was able to read a bit of it to his fellow Indians. He also had learned the rudiments of farming skills, also viewed as "medicine." With his white man skills, Spokane Garry had acquired power or "big medicine," and his people lorded it over other tribes. Spokanes, formerly low in the regard of their neighbors, immediately won great prestige, and other tribes were lowered accordingly now. The Nez Percé felt particularly humiliated and shortly acted to obtain "medicine" for their people.

The Nez Percés, who had been good to Lewis and Clark, decided to call in a debt from the red-headed explorer, who had been appointed Superintendent for Indian Affairs in the West. Hence they gathered a small group to go to him and petition for their very own missionaries. They hoped that success in their venture would restore their former high status as a people.

In 1831, the American Fur Company mountain man, Lucien Fontenelle, was setting off down the Missouri bound for St. Louis. The Nez Percés asked to go with him, and the mountain man obliged because, after all, favors beget favors. Among the various versions of this trip, the best seems to be that of Francis Haines who did years of careful research on the Nez Percé.[8]

In Haines's account, four Nez Percés made up the original group going to St. Louis to petition for missionaries. Their leader was Chief Black Eagle. On their way, they came to a camp of Flathead Indians (whom Lewis and Clark knew as Salish) and explained their intentions. Flatheads and Nez Percés got along well, and the Flatheads decided to send along some of their own emissaries to get in on a good thing.

Meanwhile, an older Nez Percé had second thoughts about the long trip and dropped out of the group. He was replaced belatedly by another Nez Percé, either No-horns-on-his-head or Rabbit-skin-leggings. One of them already was with the party, and the other now joined, since both went to St. Louis. The three Flatheads in the group were led by Man-of-the-morning. The trip to St. Louis was nearly two thousand miles, and it gave the Indians plenty of time to think over what they were doing. By the time the entourage reached Council Bluffs (named for a meeting place between Lewis and Clark and the Indians on their way West), two Flatheads and one Nez Percé had turned back. Their departure left four to continue the journey.

Early in October the reconstituted group arrived at St. Louis, a burgeoning frontier town. An overjoyed Clark, his hair now more gray than red, greeted them warmly, as they had done for his men a quarter of a century before. As Superintendent of Indian Affairs, he was eager to do all in his power for his Indian friends.

Unfortunately, Clark could not discover what his visitors wanted:

no one in the area could translate the Indian tongues. After initial greetings, sign language proved futile. It was insufficiently developed to communicate abstract religious ideas. It was a pristine irony to travel hundreds of miles only to be unable to communicate. The whites gained a vague idea of what the Indians desired—something to do with *Wakan*, the holy and mysterious—and so they consulted the bishop of St. Louis, a Vincentian named Rosati.

Bishop Rosati seems to have got some inkling of what the Indians wanted, but he couldn't accommodate them, being short of priests himself. He conveyed this last disappointing idea to the Indians. During the negotiations Black Eagle died, a month after his arrival in St. Louis; less than three weeks later Man-of-the-morning also died. It was in death that they came closest to their desire to be close to Christianity, as both were buried in a Roman Catholic cemetery in that river city.

By December, the remaining two emissaries headed back home on the steamer *Yellow Stone*, the first steamship to get up river as far as Fort Union (near today's northern borders of Montana and North Dakota). On the way they stopped briefly at a Sioux encampment and were feasted by the Sioux, who provided them with proper Sioux garments for the occasion. Because of this stop, we now know what the two looked like, for it happened that the New York artist George Catlin was at the camp. He painted separate portraits of No-horns-on-his-head and Rabbit-skin-leggings, both made in 1832, which are among his finest works, and it is indicative of white understanding of Indian culture that the two were immortalized in costumes unrelated to the experience of either man.

Shortly after arriving at Fort Union, a trading post from the days of Manuel Lisa at the confluence of the Missouri and Yellowstone rivers, No-horns-on-his-head succumbed to disease, and it was Catlin who conveyed this information. Post records indicate a long history of fatal maladies affecting civilians, Indians, and soldiers alike. This crossroads post was a meeting place between two worlds and was to become the northernmost center for the spread of smallpox. The last of the delegation, Rabbit-skin-leggings, was killed less than a year later by the Blackfeet, hereditary enemies of nearly every tribe they bordered.

Reflecting on the entire saga, Haines says: "Thus the mission brought toil, privation, and death to all its members and ended, seemingly, in complete failure. Yet, in five years, the missionary zeal inspired by the story of those Indians had planted stations on the Willamette, the Walla Walla and the Clearwater Rivers, to be followed shortly by others in the Bitterroot Valley and at Spokane Falls."[9]

The tribal disappointment at the failure to secure the white man's

Christian religion was great, amounting to another disgrace. Yet this was not their only setback, for several more times the Nez Percé and the Flatheads failed to get missionaries when lesser tribes were successful in doing so. It took four pilgrimages over a ten-year period to get the service of a blackrobe from St. Louis.[10]

The incident became the talk of the Catholic city of St. Louis. Religionists of all stripes took up the cause but they interpreted it in their own ways. From a public relations viewpoint (and missionaries were not beyond this sort of thing), the plea of the Indian messengers was a heaven-sent opportunity. Jesuits noted that the Indians had asked for "blackrobes" and the claim continues that the delegation exclusively sought the ministrations of the Society of Jesus. Haines, however, points out regarding the Indians: "They were not divinely inspired toward Christianity, nor were they seeking for a higher moral standard. They wanted better 'medicine' to increase their prestige and power. They did not seek reading and writing as tools but as magic formulas to aid their 'medicine.' Hence it is absurd to argue whether they really asked for the white man's 'Book of Heaven.' They were looking for new incantations to use upon this earth, not information on a possible world to come."[11] It was a heart-rending story nevertheless. Known popularly as "The Macedonian Cry" or "The Indian's Lament," it was widely publicized and the story spread East like wildfire.

William Walker, an Eastern Indian who had been white-educated, got the details of the story from Clark and then wrote about it in a letter to an Eastern friend. Deeply moved, Walker's friend embellished the story and sent it to the Methodist *Christian Advocate and Journal*, along with some imaginative drawings of his own. Adding to the effect, many Easterners took literally the notion that Flatheads were flat-headed, or deformed, and the cause of the Western missions was established. What began as a spark became a roaring flame. Contributions to missions among their own Eastern Indian constituents was lagging for lack of visible progress. But to Eastern Christians the thought of Western Indian missions was fresh and exciting, and it pulled at the strings of their purses as well as hearts.

The battle for the West would be fought not by soldiers but by missionaries and immigrants. Senator Thomas Hart Benton of Missouri, who had pushed for settling the West as early as 1818, welcomed and utilized this new momentum.

In 1828, there was formed an American Society for Encouraging Settlement of Oregon Territory. Behind the movement was a sometime educator and full-time entrepreneur, Hall Jackson Kelley. An effective promoter, Kelley interested others in his plans to establish a small colony of farmers in that distant and still relatively unknown

Oregon land. He pushed his cause with reams of literature and end-less meetings. Glowing reports of the rich soil that produced great crops several times a year had many farmers interested in moving there, lock, stock, and barrel. Kelley had never been there himself, but no matter; he was a great promoter and people believed him. The Rockies themselves had been surmounted since Bill Sublette had hauled his wagons over South Pass, a bare level plain seven thousand feet in elevation. "Even the *American Biblical Repository* rejoiced (later) in the knowledge that there was an easy road to Oregon 'excavated by the finger of God.' "[12]

Despite the hoopla, however, the farmers failed to part with their hard-earned money, and plans for the colony fell through. Un-daunted, Kelly decided to investigate the Oregon land for himself. Guided by the noted mountain man Ewing Young with whom Kit Carson "greened," Kelly got to the promised land in 1832-1833.

Vancouver's chief factor, Hudson's Bay's tough but kindly John McLoughlin, discouraged Kelly's plans for colonization. Quite ob-viously they would interfere with the fur trade. Although its demise was already in sight, McLoughlin was not eager to encourage colo-nization from the United States, which would strengthen the claims of the fledgling nation to the disputed land.

Despite Kelly's personal failure, his enthusiasm caught fire with another Bostonian. The cause was taken up by a real, god-fearing, successful Yankee trader named Nathaniel Wyeth, whose success in the ice business only spurred him on to new endeavors.

Catching the Oregon fever, Wyeth mounted a two-pronged ex-pedition to Oregon land. First, he sent a ship all the way around the treacherous Horn. Its destination was the delta of the Columbia River. The voyage had three purposes. One was to bring supplies; another was to catch, pickle, and bring back salmon, which were plentiful in those waters; and the last was to take back the furs Wyeth hoped to gather on his way overland to meet the ship.

In this second prong of the expedition, Wyeth and a group of men made their way West, trapping as they went. The plan was a sound one and worthy of any capitalist penny-pinching Yankee, but Wyeth was plagued with bad luck and ineptitude. His company stopped at the 1832 rendezvous at Pierre's Hole, just west of the mighty Tetons, where a number of his men deserted him. Perhaps they had lost confidence in his abilities, but it is likely that many freeloaders simply had seen Wyeth's trip as their ticket to the West. Probably they never intended to honor their contracts. Wyeth and the remainder of his men went on to Vancouver.

Bad news awaited him there, also. His ship had been delayed considerably because it had been struck by lightning and needed repairs. It would arrive too late to fish, after the end of the salmon season. With John McLoughlin's help, however, Wyeth started back East. On his way, Wyeth stopped at the 1833 rendezvous at Green River and there he felt his luck had finally turned, for he won a contract to supply trappers at the 1834 rendezvous at Ham's Fork. His bad luck was shared with the Nez Percés and Flatheads, for they expected their long-awaited missionary at the 1833 rendezvous. But the missionary appointed by Bishop Rosati died while making preparations for the journey. Again, the Indians came back empty handed, discouraged, and embarrassed, but still hoping.

At the 1833 rendezvous, Wyeth picked up two Indian lads, a Nez Percé and a Flathead whose father was white. He brought them back to Boston with him, hoping he would learn their tongue and they his. The exchange of languages would be useful in future adventures West. Not daunted by the events of the past year, he planned carefully for the new expedition, having his supply contract in hand. At the prices brought by supplies in the mountains, he was sure to make a profit this time.

Although the peak of missionary activity was still a dozen years away, it was gathering impetus at this time. The most organized and active group was the Methodists. Their zeal was exemplified by Jason Lee, who never lost his fascination with the story of the Indian delegation to Clark. Upon hearing of Wyeth, Lee arranged to meet him, and the two got along famously. Lee begged to accompany the Yankee on his 1834 trek West. With his own interest in spreading Christianity, Wyeth not only agreed but even offered the use of the two Indian lads over whom he had charge. He also helped Lee raise funds for the missionary work, employing the two boys as crusaders. They mounted a successful campaign for money to send missionaries to the Nez Percés and Flatheads. The boys played their parts well and enjoyed the publicity. De Voto says that one actually was deformed, generating much sympathy. Forty thousand dollars was raised for the missions.

The Methodist Mission Board was delighted but authorized Lee to use only three thousand of the amount. Lee invited his slightly younger nephew, Daniel Lee, and two additional workers to accompany him. They all prepared to go West and spread the Word of the Lord. Wyeth and his group eventually arrived at the 1834 rendezvous site at Ham's Fork. Again Wyeth had sent a ship around the Horn to meet him in Oregon land.

At the rendezvous, Wyeth found he had been double crossed; his contract with the trappers was not honored. Forgetting his desire for profit, he decided to seek revenge. He set up his own trading post known as Fort Hall, just inside present-day central Idaho's east border, intending to ruin the fur trade of those who had betrayed him. One method he pursued was to undercut prevailing supply prices.

At Fort Hall, Jason Lee preached his first sermon, attended by trappers and Indians. Also present were two naturalists, Thomas Nutthall and John Townsend, who reported that all during the sermon, the listeners never moved and "were as stone."

Wyeth and Lee continued to Vancouver to meet Wyeth's second ship, the *May Dacre*, which was carrying their goods. There they learned that the vessel had been damaged by storms and would be delayed several months in reaching the Columbia. A discouraged Wyeth sold Fort Hall to the Hudson's Bay Company, returned East, and abandoned all thoughts of Western adventure. Lee remained and became a beckoning symbol for missionaries to come.

He consulted McLoughlin about establishing missions for the Flatheads, but the Hudson's Bay man persuaded him instead to set up operations near present-day Salem on the Willamette River. Following this advice, Lee preached Methodism to the Chinooks and French Canadians instead of to the Nez Percés and Flatheads. This first mission settlement in Oregon had among its pupils the two Indian boys who had gone East with Wyeth.

Lee kept extensive records which help us appreciate his many activities. He also wrote letters to the mission board, which was unhappy that he had not gone to the Flatheads as previously agreed. In his defense, he cited McLoughlin's advice and the advantages of his present location. Being near the ocean meant easier access to supplies and more varied congregations. Had he serviced the Flatheads, he argued, nearly all of his energies would have been spent in getting around to the scattered groups, leaving little time to preach. Although he didn't mention it, his present post also put him out of reach of the notorious Blackfeet. Neither did Lee question McLoughlin's motives, which may have been to keep him south of the Columbia, so that any colonizing would be on lands likely to become America's in any event.

A single-minded man, Lee devoted his considerable energies to preaching and teaching. Nevertheless, he found himself also engaged in countless hours of household work, prompting him to write the mission board in 1836 to ask for women. "A greater favour could not be best bestowed upon this country, than to send to it pious, industrious, intelligent females."[13] In 1838, he took two Chinooks and returned East to garner more funding and to gather more people to return West with him. Along the way, he was gratified to meet several missionary couples headed for Oregon land. It was evident that his pioneering efforts were bearing fruit. Stopping at the Popo Agie rendezvous, Lee also met a competitor of sorts, John Augustus Sutter, who would produce not Oregon fever, but California fever.

Lee was very successful in obtaining funds and people. Fifty-one would-be colonists joined him on the ship *Lausanne* to sail around the Horn and spread Christianity and American influence in the Northwest.

The secular aspect of Lee's work, however, was not appreciated by the Methodist Mission Board, and in 1843 it withdrew its support of his services. Only after his death in 1845 was his work seriously recognized as the pioneering effort that called others to the Pacific Northwest.

Now that the ground was broken, the missionary movement gained momentum. In 1835, Samuel Parker and Dr. Marcus Whitman set out to see for themselves the opportunities offered by the mission fields of Oregon. Many thought that Parker, a Presbyterian minister of fifty-seven years, was too old to travel the Oregon Trail. Whitman, a medical doctor from New York, was a Presbyterian church elder. Educated in New York, he had practiced for four years in Canada. The two attended the 1835 rendezvous, where Parker meditated on the beauty of the great West: "The Trois Tetons were in full view . . . but only three of them are so high as to be seen at a great distance. . . . Here I spend much time in looking over the widely extended and varied scenery, sometimes filled with emotions of the sublime, in beholding the towering mountains. . . . After some hours occupied in this excursion, I descended to the encampment, much gratified with what I had seen of the works of God."[14]

Parker, a great note taker and writer, was the one who recorded the famous duel between Kit Carson and the bully Shunar at this rendezvous. And it was here that Dr. Whitman, before a vast arena of spectators, removed a Blackfoot arrowhead from the back of Jim Bridger. The Indians especially admired this medical feat. It gave Whitman entrée to their culture—and led, twelve years later, to his death at their hands.

Nez Percés were at this rendezvous, still looking for their missionary from Missouri and still doomed to disappointment. Seeing their zeal for religion, Parker asked Whitman to return East with the American Fur Company caravan to publicize the Nez Percé desire for religion. Whitman objected to the elder Parker's going on alone but to no avail. Parker said he would do all the surveying and documenting needed to present a full report at the 1836 rendezvous the following year.

Whitman set out in the dead of winter, taking with him two Indian lads he named Richard and John. His appearance in the East proved highly encouraging to Oregon enthusiasts, since it proved that even in bad seasons, travel could be carried out. Whitman enrolled the boys in a New York school. While they learned English, he tried to gain a working knowledge of their language.

Parker, who was perhaps more interested in theology and Oregon settlement than in missionary work, did not return to the next rendezvous. He returned East by boat, never to go back. He sent letters to the gathering, and these were given to Whitman when he arrived.

Meanwhile, things were proceeding quickly in the mission field. The American Board of Commissioners for Foreign Missions, following Lee's advice, began to recruit married couples for the work. Whitman obliged by marrying Narcissa Prentiss, and the two went West together. She was a particularly striking young blonde woman who created excitement wherever she went.

Accompanying the Whitmans was another missionary couple, Henry and Elizabeth Spalding, and a single missionary, William Gray. They were an oddly assorted group. Whitman and Spalding had known each other previously, even before Spalding married Elizabeth Hart, for Spalding was a rejected suitor of Narcissa Prentiss. While Elizabeth lacked the blonde beauty of Narcissa, she proved to be more adept at coping with her duties and getting along with the Indians.

The contrast between Whitman and Spalding was severe. Whitman, a no-nonsense type of person, made decisions quickly and unilaterally and then stuck with them. Spalding was abrasive and puritanical. One of life's losers, he had few friends even among the mission board members. Spalding bore the stigma of illegitimacy and was not even raised by his own mother. At seventeen, he left his caretakers to enroll in a Cincinnati theological seminary, graduating at twenty-two. His life in the seminary was a constant struggle, for he was poor and had to work at part-time jobs. In 1833, he married Elizabeth, but she also was impoverished, subsisting by taking in boarders. Yet they shared a passion for the missionary life and appealed to the mission board for appointment to the Chocktaws. Refused, Spalding offered to serve any Indian group and was assigned to the Osages. To prepare himself, he studied medicine and so came to know Whitman. When Whitman made plans to go West, Spalding petitioned to go along, and his request was granted.

Spalding carried an unusually strong anti-Roman Catholic and anti-British bias, both of which would work against him. He saw popery in every shadow. Francis Haines describes him as a "kind and obliging, a true though not very humble Christian."[15] He acknowledges Spalding's hot temper but notes his strength and endurance. On the whole, Spalding would prove troublesome, not only to his companions but to the Indians he sought to convert.

William Gray, the unmarried missionary, was a man with many ambitions but unable to carry out a single one. Unsuccessful in academe and medical school, he turned to cabinet making. Tiring of that, he sought fulfillment in the western mission field. A lonely man, he may have envied Spalding for winning a wife like Elizabeth. He certainly admired her as much as Spalding admired Narcissa. Gray wrote of Elizabeth: "While she had coarse features, she also had a serious turn of mind and was quick in languages. She knew the skills necessary for women in general, and did well all things needed for her station in life. . . . With the native women, Mrs. Spalding appeared easy and cheerful and had their unbounded confidence and respect. She was remarkable for her firmness and decision of character in whatever she and her husband undertook. She never appeared alarmed or excited at any difficult dispute or alarms common to the Indian life around her."[16]

Such was the entourage that went to the 1836 rendezvous at Green River and joined the boisterous celebration. The white women were instant celebrities at the gathering. Indians, told of the whites' custom of kissing to show affection, smothered the two. It must have been quite an experience for such conservative women—and also for their husbands.

Indians crowded around Narcissa especially, never having seen a white woman and one whose hair color, like Captain Clark's, was so different from their own. The mountain men also took to Narcissa, who, unlike Elizabeth, walked around and conversed with them as if she were part of their group. But while Narcissa soaked up admiration, Elizabeth was industriously learning Shahaptian, the language of the Nez Percé and the Yakima. So adept was she that by the time they reached the Clearwater River country, on the way to Fort Vancouver, she was practically fluent. Her skill would prove useful in her work at the missions, for one of the responsibilities of the women was to teach school.

At any rate, the women made history; they were the first white females to cross South Pass and the first to reach the Pacific on the Oregon Trail. In addition, their babies, Narcissa's in March 1837 and Elizabeth's some months later, were the first white children born in that land. (The Whitman child was accidentally drowned in infancy.)

Although the mountain men enjoyed the presence of the women at the rendezvous, they worried that the two would hinder them on the arduous trail ahead. Quietly, the train of mountain men left the rendezvous, hoping to leave the missionary group behind. When they realized what had happened, the missionaries hurriedly packed their belongings and rushed to catch up. Unfortunately, in their haste, they had to discard some of their provisions. This occasioned considerable regret, particularly later when the supplies were badly needed. Nevertheless, the trappers' protection was essential to the journey. The party arrived in Vancouver in September.

In Oregon, the missionaries met McLoughlin, the giant of a man and medical doctor whom De Voto would aptly call the "emperor of the North." As always he was the epitome of courtesy and generosity to the missionaries, lending them seeds, tools, and clothing, and helping them to get started in any way he could.

Jason Lee, whose mission was on the Willamette River, had written to suggest that the new missions be established at Lapwai, at the junction of the Clearwater and Snake rivers near present-day Lewiston. This was hundreds of miles east and slightly north of his own mission, in an area inhabited primarily by the Nez Percés. Thus the Nez Percés would get their "big medicine" at last. Unfortunately, Spalding and Whitman were quarrelling. Misunderstandings and various grievances had started on the trip West and now broke into the open. These worsened over the next six years.

After consultation with McLoughlin, the Spaldings went to the Nez Percé land and the Whitmans went a bit south to the Cayuse country at Waiilatpu on the Walla Walla River. Whitman was warned by the Hudson's Bay people that the Cayuse were not to be trusted but, typically, Whitman made up his mind and would not change it.

Neither mission was directly on the Oregon Trail. The Whitmans' place was about twenty-five miles off the trail and the Spaldings' considerably farther. Nonetheless, when the overlanders ran into problems, especially medical ones, they didn't mind a detour, even as far as Waiilatpu.

Anxious to win the white man's medicine, the Indians swallowed the indignity of labor and worked hard to help set up the missions. At Lapwai, hundreds of Indians helped build necessary shelters and sheds. In the meantime, the Spaldings lived in a tipi. Anxious to begin the mission work even while getting settled, Elizabeth started her school and, as its popularity grew, it came to enroll several hundred Indians. Haines's commentary highlights her achievements: "Imagine a woman with a multitude of household duties, living in a tipi with none of her accustomed conveniences, producing by hand sufficient lessons for a school of two hundred students."[17]

Later, Elizabeth developed an alphabet for the language of the Nez Percés and translated the "Our Father" so they could say the prayer in their own tongue.[18] The Indians were fascinated with learning how to print; all they had known previously was the use of pictographs (drawings) or petroglyphs (rock carvings). The men went back to their tipis with great pride, carrying with them the results of that day's work. No kindergartner ever was so pleased and so proud of his accomplishments. Three years later, the missionaries received a printing press, a gift from Hawaiian missionaries to further efforts to increase literacy among the American Indians. Passages from the Bible were the material most frequently printed.

As farm parents know, schooling is a mixed blessing, for it diverts attention and labor from life-sustaining activities. If the red men and children were to spend days in school, they would have to be fed. Consequently, Spalding, like other missionaries, set up projects to cultivate the land, using Indian labor. The demeaning work was not popular, but the Indians put up with it, for their desire to acquire "big medicine" was very strong.

Fences were built, land was plowed, and soil was hoed to be maximally productive. The hoe became a very precious instrument and at one time over one hundred and fifty were in use. So highly prized was it that its value in trade was one Indian horse. Times were changing from the days when beaver "plew" or skin was the common currency.

A carpentry shop, a smithy, and a grist mill were built. The mill meant that breadstuffs could be produced. These were much in demand by the overlanders, who hadn't tasted the white's "staff of life" for many a month. For a while, things went well for Spalding but, unfortunately, his personality interfered with his work and troubles began to multiply.

He was vehement in his opposition to all things Catholic, continually railing against Latin rituals and popery. Once he visited an Indian woman who had just buried her young child. (The Christian burial was a change in traditional practice; formerly the corpse would have been placed in a tree.) Upon seeing a cross that the woman had placed on the grave, Spalding became furious and kicked it away, berating the woman for using the papist symbol.

He also ranted against Indian medicine men, who rightly viewed the whites as their competitors. Spalding declared to the Indians that the medicine man's power came from the devil, while he had his from God. Their patients, he proclaimed, would be damned; his would be saved.

To assert his influence and convert the Indian to white Protestant cultural values, Spalding forbade the Indians to go on the warpath or to the buffalo grounds. He also objected to their ceremonial dances, to their gaudily decorated war horses, and to their gambling. Spalding broke up some of the Indians' games by hurling the cards into the fire; more than once he whipped those who violated his puritanical edicts.[19] He hardly ingratiated himself by constantly haranguing the undisciplined young braves, who had been raised with typical Indian permissiveness. The youths certainly were not wild by their people's standards.

Before long, Spalding's "righteous anger" began to inspire Indian mischief. The braves tried to provoke Spalding, and their every success encouraged them to continue. They burned the fences they had put up and the shingles on the roofs as well, but Spalding continued his intemperance. He once administered seventy lashes to an Indian wife of a white smithy because she left her husband. This was a common Indian custom when the squaw was dissatisfied with her domestic situation. In retaliation, the Indians stopped Spalding from running his mill. When the Indians saw that this drove away white traders from whom they profited, however, they allowed the mill to operate.

Spalding bitterly complained in a letter to the mission board:

I have had a gun cocked and presented to my head for fifteen or twenty minutes while four of the principal men stood with as much indifference as if a dog was to be shot down and when the proper moment arrived I arose and walked off, the muzzle of the gun brushing my cheek. At one time, probably five hundred people were collected threatening to go to my home tie and whip my wife and for no other reason than because she had sent to the chief of the place requesting him to send away two of his men who had just presented themselves before the school naked and painted with the most horrible figures and continued their indecent gestures until Mrs. Spalding was obliged to leave the house.[20]

Nonetheless, Elizabeth loved her work and tolerated these various annoyances. She writes of playing with an Indian child who was infested with fleas, knowing that she was sure to share the infestation as a result.

News of Spalding's problems with the Indians and his quarrel with Whitman gradually leaked back to the mission board, which became increasingly dissatisfied with Spalding's work. Those who complained most bitterly about Spalding were his own white workers and Indian laborers. The board was about to recall Spalding in 1842, but the move did not go beyond a paper draft because of a personal and passionate plea made to the board by Whitman.

Marcus Whitman had established his mission in the heart of Cayuse country at Waiilatpu. It was probably no accident that Spalding's situation east of the Columbia River and Whitman's south of the Columbia near Walla Walla in present-day Washington did not appear to threaten British claims to the northern part of Oregon land. McLoughlin, who had advised them, was convinced that the Columbia River, a natural dividing line, would eventually become the legal line of demarcation between the United States and British interests. The extension of the U.S. border to the forty-ninth parallel was a major victory over British expectations.

Whitman got along well with McLoughlin, the Indians, and most overlanders headed for the Willamette Valley. Spalding, however, was a continuing problem, but fortunately the two met infrequently. Like the Spaldings, Whitman and his wife also set up mills, carpentry shops, and storage buildings to sustain their community and carry on their work. Understandably, much of the physician's time was taken up by medical matters. At first, Whitman was deeply appreciated by the Indians, in view of the surgical skills he had demonstrated in removing the arrow from Bridger. The demand for his services in that sparsely populated and remote area frequently drew him away from the mission post. This placed a great deal of the burden on Narcissa, who was not as adept at handling mission affairs as was Elizabeth Spalding.

Indeed, Narcissa Whitman sometimes seemed as lacking in appreciation of customs different from her own as was Henry Spalding. She gave offense on a number of occasions, as when she refused to accept a set of the paws of "God's dog," the coyote, from Chief Tilokaikt of the Cayuse on the occasion of the birth of her child at the mission. The chief was offended, and in Indian culture when the chief is offended the entire tribe is offended.

As Whitman's work developed, it changed from helping Indians almost exclusively to giving more care and attention to arriving whites who, in the next five years, grew from a trickle to a flood on the Oregon Trail. His mission became less formally religious and more basically humanitarian. He took on the care of children of trappers. The mountain men Joe Meek and Jim Bridger both had daughters at Whitman's school. (Also living at the school was the Spalding child.) Whitman boarded orphans from the wagon trains whose parents died en route. Women who became pregnant on the Oregon Trail or who arrived nearing term were deeply thankful to find an experienced doctor in the wilderness. But not all callers were god-fearing and trustworthy: overlanders sometimes looted the mission, taking food and supplies. This could happen only when the doctor was away, but that was frequently.

When wagon trains arrived too late to continue on to the Willamette Valley and had to winter near his mission, Whitman put the men to work building sheds, drying foods, and improving the property, and fed them in return. He was an angel of mercy. Indians, whose diet seemed to give them considerable bowel problems, called upon him frequently. Lung diseases also were common in Indians, a situation that Whitman attributed to their going barefoot in rain and snowy weather. The doctor also performed bloodletting, a practice common in that time among Indians and whites.

In his ministrations, Whitman was following the example of John McLoughlin, who was no-nonsense in business and ready to help in time of need. His long presence in the Pacific Northwest largely pacified the various warring tribes and eased the way for the white man's arrival. With help from his own Hudson's Bay men as well as Indians, he aided in recovery of stolen goods from white trappers and gave sanctuary to those in difficulty. To the new arrivals, he extended as much as thirty-one thousand dollars in credit to help them set up their farms and stores. For this he was excoriated by Hudson's Bay officials from England for abetting colonization against the interests of Britain. Eventually, the Hudson's Bay Company pressed him to resign his post, despite the success of his dynasty, which had raked in huge profits for the company. Finally, he settled in the American section of Oregon, becoming both a U.S. citizen and, to the chagrin of the Protestant missionaries, a Roman Catholic. (Evidently he had resolved his long bias against the Latin church.) There can be no question of the value of his legacy to Americans. His fairness in treatment of the Indians won for the Hudson's Bay Company in that area a deep respect. He also assuaged the strong anti-British feelings that Americans brought with them, a legacy of the War of 1812.

In the mid-1830s, the U.S. government began to appreciate the potential of the missions to strengthen its interests in the Oregon dispute. In 1836, President Jackson sent a man to investigate the situation in Oregon and help in whatever way he could to encourage the American presence. Jackson was unhappy that U.S. citizens in the area were dependent on the British Hudson's Bay Company; he believed that sturdy Americans should and could fend for themselves. Jackson's representative assessed the needs of the emigrants and, in 1837, gathered a group of whites and Indians to journey to California and bring back to Oregon a herd of over six hundred cattle. The difficulties under which the mission was carried out were awesome. Getting through Mexican customs was only slightly less daunting than surmounting the rugged mountain passes afterward.

The jaunt also was the occasion of an injustice that had bitter consequences. In Mexican California an Indian member of the herders was killed by a white man. The Indians wanted the murderer punished but the complication of Mexican-American jurisdiction allowed him to go free. Perhaps the incident was not important in itself, but added to other causes of resentment it eventually caused the downfall of the Protestant missions in the late 1840s.

Among the increasing number of missionaries and emigrants was

William Gray—again. He had come West with the Whitmans and Spaldings in 1836, returned home to get a bride, and was back in 1838. He too proved cantankerous with the Indians. On one occasion when Indians stole his carefully nurtured watermelons that were ready for harvesting, he dosed the remaining melons with a strong emetic. As a result of Gray's trick, Indians believed even more strongly in the white man's ability to regulate health and sickness.

The year 1838 brought four more missionary couples to the half-way rendezvous at the Popo Agie River in Wyoming, at the base of the massive Wind River mountains. Leading them was the noted mountain man Andrew Drips. The Swiss John Sutter, a decade before his gold rush fame, also was present and impressed the wife of one of the missionaries, a Mrs. Smith, with his continental courtesies amidst the rude surroundings. The pioneer Methodist missionary Jason Lee was there as well, returning East with two Indian boys.

The year 1839 saw more of this religious movement West, and 1840 began the floodtide of emigration. After Joel Walker, a relative of the mountain man Joseph Walker, had led a group of emigrants and missionaries to the Northwest, the Oregon Trail was the scene of steady traffic.

Although the well-organized Protestants had a head start in the Oregon mission movement, Roman Catholics were coming into the field. They were to add to an already confused mix of religions whose diversity would have a number of important repercussions.

In 1834, McLoughlin, genuinely concerned for his French and part-Indian workers, most of whom were nominally Roman Catholic, petitioned his Hudson's Bay Company superiors to help obtain some Roman Catholic missionaries for Oregon land. Further, he corresponded with Bishop Josephy Norbert Provencher at the Red River settlement. Provencher was unable to oblige because of the shortage of workers in his vineyard. The bishop was convinced of the need, however, and started plans that would prepare the way for a priest. In 1835, he sent catechisms to McLoughlin, although he knew that virtually none of the Hudson's Bay Company workers could read. "Yet the Bishop surely thought that books were to be a part of the basic supplies of a mission and that book learning would be the natural by-product of the missioner's religious instruction."[21]

Provencher did not let the grass grow under his feet. Searching the East, he was able to enlist an experienced missionary who already had done considerable religious work with the Indians in New Brunswick. His name was François Norbert Blanchet (1795-1883). Blanchet came to Red River, bringing with him another priest. The new man enabled the bishop to release one of his own staff for mission work—Modeste Demers (1807-1871). Demers and Blanchet travelled together to Oregon land, where they worked with tribes of the North and South Cascades and the area's French and "Prairie French" (Indians with French fathers). Both priests were Jesuits and carried with them the strengths and weaknesses of that religious order.

The Society of Jesus had been founded in 1534 by Ignatius Loyola, a Spanish military man who was recovering from battle wounds. The order was established on military lines; it maintained exceptional discipline and sought only the very brightest and most determined young men for its membership. It required of its members a special vow of obedience to the Pope. So binding was this vow, Ignatius wrote, that if the Pope says something is white that actually is black, a Jesuit must believe it is white. Their critics (many belonging to rival orders) regarded them as military martinets. Loyola's primary concerns were missions and education, but the success of his followers in reconverting Protestants across southern Europe from France to Poland gave them the reputation of counter reformers *par excellence*. The order pursued the interests of the Pope and the church so effectively and single-mindedly that they were accused of twisting every situation to their own advantage (the term "Jesuitical morality" still is in use). Many countries banned the order after 1759, and it was dissolved by the Pope between 1773 and 1814 (surviving in Prussia and Russia, whose rulers refused to publish the papal orders). The revived order seemed somehow less threatening, and it continues today.

The trip to Oregon land by Blanchet and Demers with some Hudson's Bay personnel who were delivering supplies to Vancouver was a rugged one. They crossed mountains and portaged rivers and finally arrived at the dalles on the Columbia River. The Jesuits, teachers from the start, knew that the best way to influence people was to train them in your school, and Demers and Blanchet accordingly brought teaching materials with them. As they established themselves, they sent for more materials, which proved to be a great attraction to Indians. Demers settled around Cowlitz, located on the Cowlitz River about fifty miles north of Vancouver, where a chapel already had been built in anticipation of his arrival. Blanchet stationed himself at St. Paul du Wallamet, situated north of modern-day Corvallis.

Missionary priests were instructed to learn the native languages immediately, and most were highly successful in doing so. Instruction was in French while the priests mastered Chinook. Chinook was almost the *lingua franca* of the area, and with it a minister could preach to different tribes, either individually in their own lands or together at special events. Chinook was a patois of fractured French and English, but few American Protestants ever mastered it.

For several years French was the dominant language among the whites in Oregon land but, as emigration swelled from the United States, English replaced it as the leading tongue. The Oregon land was a puzzle, because "the Catholic mission was in French, under British sovereignty, while the Protestant missions were English-language based and American in origin and allegiance."[22]

The Hudson's Bay Company helped Blanchet and Demers in 1838 by shipping books, church needs, and various teaching materials. But the cargo was lost when the ship was wrecked on the bar at the treacherous Columbia inlet; some of the items had come around the Horn from as far as Montreal. They included readers, spellers, devotional literature, and various articles used in religious service. Such items later proved particularly important in winning the Indian to Roman Catholicism, for they provided color in a bleak wilderness that had known only the stern black and white world of Protestants. "At Cowlitz and St. Paul du Wallamet, 'the mission sessions consisted of the celebration of the Mass, in itself a liturgical drama and thereby an audio-visual aid to the instructional program, followed by the recitations of prayers, lessons on the Apostle's Creed, and the singing of hymns and plain chant, repeated daily for three weeks.' "[23]

This was a far cry from the Protestant service, which had only Bible reading and preaching of white mores and morals. The Roman Catholics offered the excitement of bell ringing at the Mass, incense burning, lit candles, chanting (always a favorite of the Indians), genuflections, and secret signs, such as the sign of the cross and two fingers used by the priest in holding the host. In addition, the Mass was said in Latin (like a secret language) and the celebrants wore multicolored vestments, emphasizing red, an exciting color for warriors. Much of the ceremony seemed magical to the Indians—just what they were looking for in their quest for "big medicine." The priests adapted their terms to Indian experience by calling the sacraments the "seven medicines" and the Mass "the Great Prayer." The psychology of visual and auditory reenforcement was complete. (Later priests-missionaries to Oregon land wore large crucifixes which equally impressed the natives.) There followed all the accouterments of religion—rosaries, crosses, medals, and holy water. Marketing never knew better days.

Often the teaching aids employed by the priests made the difference between keeping or not keeping a convert. Among the most popular aids were two unusual ones designed specifically for the Indians. Both were said to be invented by Blanchet, an exceptionally resourceful man.[24] The first was known as a Sahale stick, which means "stick sent from heaven." It was a large stick on which were carved various Christian symbols and events. Thirty-three notches, for example, indicated the years Christ lived on earth, and three notches showed his years of public ministry. Events such as Creation, the fall of Adam and Eve, the Great Flood, and the Crucifixion also were depicted. Some of the sticks evolved to become square-sided totem poles with carvings and paintings of the Christian message. One of these is preserved in the archdiocesan archives in Vancouver, Washington.

Carving the Sahale sticks was time-consuming work, but their effectiveness made them worth the effort. They were presented to chiefs, who were instructed in their use so that they could become catechists to their tribes. This pattern was highly successful. Many Protestants distributed gifts equally to all. Their egalitarianism violated Indian custom in bypassing the authority of the chiefs, who occupied the office through which gifts should flow.

Probably the most curious and successful of the pedagogical devices was Blanchet's "Catholic Ladder," which recalled Jacob's Ladder of the Old Testament. It was a painting that depicted the history of the world from Creation to the Second Coming. As on the Sahale stick, the major events could be detailed and, with each, a study lesson was given. And as with the Sahale stick, each chief was given his own; it became almost a personal flag. Each was a bright banner that could be put on a post beside a lodge to announce the chief's importance as convert and catechist. One of the early Catholic Ladders at Vancouver was approximately six feet high and slightly over a foot wide.

Blanchet himself wrote, "The Catholic Ladder was very useful in imparting instruction, as many of the neophytes did not understand French sufficiently to be instructed in that language. It also was exposed in the church on Sundays and fully explained to the congregation who listened with the most respectful attention."[25] Demand for the ladders grew so rapidly that a cottage industry was developed to produce them. Eventually copies had to be reproduced in Montreal and even Paris to be sent back to the missionaries.

One banner had been given to an Indian chief who was proud of his possession although he was not a convert. Indeed, he was ready to welcome a Protestant minister, a Reverend Mr. Walker, and to help him set up a mission with the Clackamas. To greet the minister, the chief raised the banner in his camp as a gesture of Christian welcome. Upon seeing it, Walker became infuriated and tore it from the pole. Insulted, the Clackamas rejected the Protestant mission, and the entire tribe turned to Rome.

Walker evidently learned his lesson. He was one of the first Protestants to construct a ladder—a Protestant Ladder.[26] He outclassed the Catholic version by expanding to dimensions of ten feet by thirty inches. There was a major difference, however, between Catholic and

Protestant ladders. The Protestant one did not so much depict an account of the Christian message as emphasize the evils of Romanism. The Pope was depicted in hell and Luther was shown pointing to heaven. This negative approach never succeeded as did the more positive Roman Catholic one. There were no standardized ladders for either group; many variations appeared in size and content.

As this clash indicates, strong animosity was beginning to arise between the Protestant and Roman Catholic missionaries. Rumors of Jesuit corruption were circulated, slander was spread about priests and nuns, and even books supposedly documenting priestly immorality came upon the scene. As they had elsewhere, spiritual differences became political and then abusively personal. Protestants accused Roman Catholics of mere showmanship with their trinkets and ceremonies. Protestants were especially critical of the effective teaching devices of the Jesuits. Responding to these charges, Blanchet said:

This objection is dictated by only the most notorious bad faith. They [the Protestant ministers] know that the ceremonies of the Catholic Church make a favorable impression on the minds of the savages from which it flows, cannot offer them this allurement from the fact comes this sall [sic]; it is not the ceremonies that save. They distribute Bibles in profusion, but that ridiculous means of conversion for the inhabitants of the forest does not bear fruit to suit the ministers, especially if they are forced to seek a comparison with the Catholic missions.[27]

Elsewhere Blanchet caustically declared, "The Protestants civilized the Indians so rapidly that the aborigines died under the treatment."[28]

Often, Roman Catholic missions and Protestant ones were set up side by side, as at Nisqually and Clackama (near Oregon City on the Clackama River). Others were widely separated, as were the Roman Catholic mission of Yakima and the Methodist at Dalles.

Most missionaries were strong willed, regardless of religious affiliation. Bil Gilbert tells of Asahel Munger, a Methodist who was "determined to work a miracle for the edification of the savages. Acting on this passion, he nailed his hand to a fireplace mantle. So impaled, he roasted to death on the mission hearth."[29]

In 1840, one of the most remarkable of the missionaries, one who has entered this narrative before, entered the land where he eventually was to be better known than any other. He had a lake named after him as well as a "fire canoe"—one of the most widely travelled steamboats on all the Western rivers.[30] He was Pierre Jean De Smet, S.J.

Born in Belgium in 1801, De Smet had a Flemish background. De Smet eventually travelled 125,000 miles in his missionary work, making sixteen trips between Europe and America. He died in 1873 after spending thirty-two years in the missions. A public figure, he knew most of the top Indian chiefs and army officials and was even given the rank of major. A man of remarkable physical strength, he was, as his superiors complained, as much a mountain man as a missionary! To the Indians he was as much a public relations expert for their cause as a spiritual father. His campaigns for funding and for winning people to support his work were successful. Even Kit Carson praised him. "I can say of him that if ever there was a man that wished to be good, he is one. He never feared danger and when danger required his presence among the savages and if good works on this earth are rewarded hereafter, I am confident that his share of glory and happiness in the next life will be great."[31]

We have been following the vigil of the Nez Percés and Flatheads as they kept watch for the missionary long promised by Bishop Rosati in St. Louis. De Smet was the one eventually sent, and he was worth the wait. The year 1840 found him on his way to the Green River rendezvous to begin his mission to the Flatheads. Coming from the tiny country of Belgium, he must have been amazed at the vastness of the West; the Oregon land alone was larger than Germany, France, Italy, and Spain combined. The priest also was astonished at the variety of mores and morals among the different tribes. He wrote to his superiors that "Theft, among the Assiniboins, is only disgraceful when it is discovered; then shame and infamy are attached rather to the awkwardness of the thief, for having taken his measures so ill. . . . In theft, falsehood and adultery, the Assiniboins differ from the Indians of the Rocky Mountains, especially the Flatheads and the Pend d'Oreilles, who detest these vices. It may be observed that the Assiniboins have been in relations with the whites during a succession of years."[32]

De Smet arrived at the mountain men rendezvous in June 1840, joining a huge gathering that included several missionary couples and the Joel Walker family. In July, the Belgian Jesuit celebrated the first Mass in the present state of Wyoming. Moving on to Pierre's Hole, De Smet was welcomed by some "1600 Flatheads, Nez Percé and Pend d'Oreilles [who were] awaiting the 'Black Robe.' "[33] From there he travelled to Montana, saying a first Mass there and moving around its western borders near Three Forks, which had been visited thirty-five years before by Lewis and Clark.

Like Captain William Clark, De Smet felt at ease among the Indians and had not only tolerance but great respect for their culture and way of life. He, too, got along famously with them; in one of his letters, he describes eating dog with his charges. "I found the meat really delicate, and I can vouch that it is preferable to suckling pig, which it nearly resembles in taste."[34]

In late August, De Smet left the Flatheads and returned to St. Louis for supplies and consultation with his superiors. Floating down the Yellowstone and Missouri rivers, he stopped along the way to acquaint himself with the Crow, Mandan, and Sioux, who were delighted with his visit. After reporting on his exploratory trip, De Smet was appointed Superior of the Rocky Mountain missions. He thus embarked on his life work, founding, administering, and raising funds for missions.

In April 1841 he returned to the West, this time accompanied by another priest and two Jesuit brothers (laymen), who were skilled craftsmen. Coming along later were another priest, Nicholas Point, S.J., and another carpenter-brother. (Point was a painter and recorded many scenes encountered on their journeys.) The men brought with them four large-wheeled Red River carts similar to those used by European farmers in Canada.

The mountain man Tom Fitzpatrick guided the group through Utah and Idaho (where De Smet said another first Mass) while going to the Bitterroot Valley of Montana where the Flatheads lived. There, St. Mary's and St. Ignace's missions were established. Few whites frequented these areas until the discovery of gold. Mostly the land was populated by Blackfeet, Flatheads, and Pend d'Oreilles.

Throughout his travels in the West, De Smet was a careful and thoughtful observer. Indeed, the changing history of the American West could be read through his letters: "These plains, naturally so rich and verdant, seem to invite the husbandman to run the furrow, and promise an ample reward to the slightest toil. Heavy forests await the woodsman, and rocks the stone cutter. The sound of the axe and hammer will echo in this wilderness. . . . This great territory will hold an immense population, destined to form several great and flourishing States. But then what will become of the Indians . . . who have possessed it from time immemorial? This is, indeed, a thorny question awakening gloomy ideas in the observer's mind."[35] De Smet's solution was to school the Indians and make them citizens. Yet he was fully aware of the effects of missionaries, writing: "Catholicity, by the very force of her missions, contributes to the civilization of nations."[36]

A man of thoroughly humane qualities, De Smet was immensely popular among both Indians and whites. He was a conciliator who lived in one culture but admired others as well. He tells of Indians eating skunk and lightly dismisses it with a *de gustibus non est dis-*

putandum (there is no disputing matters of taste). He was saddened when he visited the Mandan, Arickara, and Minetaree Indians: "I could not discern a single man at all advanced in years whose body was not mutilated, or who possessed his full number of fingers."[37]

Instead of Protestant stiffness, De Smet was relaxed in dealing with his charges. Explaining the Ten Commandments to the Oglala Sioux, he notes, "When I arrived at the sixth and seventh [Thou shalt not commit adultery, and Thou shalt not steal], a general whispering and embarrassed laughter took place among my barbarous auditory."[38] He did keep busy: "Among the Rapahos, I baptized 305 little ones; the Sheyennes, 253, and among the Brules and Osage Sioux, 280; in the camp of the Painted Bear, 56. The number of the half bloods that I baptized in the plain of the Great Council and on the River Platte, is 6. In the different forts on the Missouri, I baptized, during the months of June and July last, 392 children. Total number of baptisms, 1586. A great number died shortly after, in consequence of diseases which reigned in the Indian camps."[39]

De Smet was present as a mediator at the Treaty of Fort Laramie in 1851. His description of his journey there gives a vivid picture of life at that time: "We numbered thirty-two persons; the greater part were Assiniboins, Minataries, and Crows, who were repairing to the great Indian council to be held in the vicinity of Fort Laramie, and by the same route that we had chose, and which was scarcely less than 800 miles in length. Two four-wheeled wagons and two carts for transporting our provisions and baggage, composed our whole convoy. The four vehicles were in all probability the first that had ever crossed this unoccupied waste."[40]

He gives us a vivid glimpse of the Indians who took part: "The great chiefs were, for the first time in their lives, pantalooned; each was arrayed in a general's uniform, a gilt sword hanging at his side. Their long, coarse hair floated above their military costume and the whole was crowned by the burlesque solemnity of their painted faces."[41] De Smet also left invaluable detailed accounts of buffalo hunts and Indian ceremonies.

Philosophically, he mused that "The Indians who refuse to submit or accept the definitive arrangement, alone favorable to them, would resume the wandering life of the plains, and close their sad existence as the bison and other animals on which they live, vanish."[42]

De Smet recorded vast numbers of conversions, so many that he might be suspected of taking on any willing person as a convert, but this was not the case. For twenty years, De Smet refused baptism to Pananapapi of the Yankton Sioux; in 1844, the chief reiterated his pleas and prepared his tribe until his petition was accepted.[43] De Smet wished to convert Sitting Bull but was unsuccessful. However, the chief did accept a crucifix from De Smet. (The Western writer Stanley Vestal owned the prized possession.)

De Smet also participated in the famous 1868 Treaty of Fort Laramie (actually negotiated near Fort Rice). Disappointed by previous broken promises, many tribes failed to show up, and De Smet personally went to them, urging them to come. He was so respected by the Sioux that he and one other white were able to get signatures of some Indians who did not attend. As one historian declares, "Only De Smet could ride through 350 miles of hostile territory into the war camp of the confederated Sioux nations and against all probability, contrive a peace for the government."[44] Indeed, the Sioux claimed that only two whites ever spoke the truth to them—De Smet and General Harney.

Missionary work in Oregon land was at the peak of its success in 1845, but from then on troubles set in. Competition accelerated between missionaries of different faiths and between them and Indian medicine men. Increasing numbers of white settlers began to erode the good relations with the native inhabitants established by the able personnel of the Hudson's Bay Company.

Then, too, the attitudes of some missionaries were jarring even to their fellow countrymen. On a September Sunday in 1840, for example, the Joel Walker family arrived at a Methodist mission in the Willamette Valley. Hungry, they asked for dinner. The missionary retorted that it would be sacrilegious to serve a meal on the Sabbath. Instead, he invited them to share in the mission's spiritual food of prayer.

[On another occasion in 1845, some] emigrants were aghast when the Methodist missionaries at the Dalles refused to assist in the rescue operations (of emigrants who had been) imprudently led into the unmapped Oregon interior. Fortunately, [the long-time mountain man, Joe Meek] then encountered a fellow mountaineer, Moses Harris, who agreed to help. Securing relief provisions from area Indians, Harris and several other men located the suffering emigrants and guided them back to the safety of the main trail. Meek's difficulties in securing aid at the mission were not unique. Already the previous year several overlanders caustically noted that the Dalles missionaries evidenced distressingly little concern with their plight.[45]

Emigration was bringing not only the trappings of white culture but various physical ills as well. These included measles, dysentery, smallpox, scarlet fever, cholera, and typhoid. Indians, extremely susceptible to the new infections, tended to treat them as they did most ills; they would steam themselves in the sweat lodge and then plunge into a nearby icy stream. The sweat lodge, however, was not a good treatment for those who were already feverish, and the sudden chill afterward could be deadly. Many who survived were weakened.

Measles and some other common contagious diseases often proved fatal to Indians, who had built up no immunity to them. When the Indians saw their own die while whites recovered, they could only surmise that the whites had stronger medicine which was being deliberately withheld from them. But sickness was rampant, as even the self-sacrificing Elizabeth Spalding was taken seriously ill and couldn't carry on her work for a time.

In 1842, word reached the Methodist Mission Board of the internecine warfare among its missionaries. This, together with the gradual draining of finances, moved the board to consider withdrawing its support from the Willamette area.

Some of the arriving whites disliked the missions and fomented trouble. Why, they asked weren't Indians receiving rent for the land used by missionaries? Shouldn't the missions pay for water rights and other things? When Indians raised these issues, the missionaries were shocked, feeling that their services more than compensated for their use of land and water. Nothing was resolved and the Indians became increasingly resentful. The situation deteriorated so that Indian attendance at Spalding's school dropped to zero. He was finally forced to earn his living more as a trader than as a man of the cloth.

Tom Hill, the Indian crusader, had an especial hatred for Spalding, and the passion was mutual. Hill knew whites well, as he had been a hunter for mountain men such as Carson and Meek. He also fought for Frémont in California. His every experience with whites seemed to embitter him more. The final straw came in 1846. Hill and two hundred Cayuse went to California to get goods for the whites in Oregon. On the trip, thirty Indians died of measles; Hill believed they had been poisoned by whites and denied effective white medicine. Hill's hatred was fanned to a white heat. Continuing quarrels with the white settlers combined with the onset of an unusually severe winter turned the Indians into a powder keg about to ignite. The explosion came at Waiilatpu, Whitman's Cayuse mission.

The Indians were convinced of white chicanery as they saw more of their own people die of measles. They asked Whitman for effective medicine but still the deaths persisted. Finally, a party led by Chief Tilokaikt broke into the Whitman mission on November 29 and tomahawked the doctor three times, leaving his body a bloody mess. Narcissa Whitman was shot; when she ran upstairs, she was pursued, dragged out of the house, and shot several times more, fatally. Twelve others were massacred, among them Joe Meek's daughter. Jim Bridger's young daughter escaped injury but died a year later. Of the seventy-two persons at the mission only eleven escaped. The Cayuses took five men, eight women, and thirty-four children captives. A number of women were raped.

While the murderers were still milling around, the Jesuit priest Brouillet rode in from the nearby Umatilla mission. He was horrified by what he saw, but the Indians told him that he should be grateful to them for putting his competitor out of business. As quickly as he could, he quietly sent out news of the slaughter, and his warning prevented more deaths.

Now the Indians were out to get Hill's enemy, Spalding. Unknown to them, he had been at the mission earlier. Brouillet's warning enabled him to avoid danger. Elizabeth also was informed and, with her wards, obtained refuge with some friendly chiefs. Fortunately, there was no duplication of Waiilatpu at Lapwai. Now came the problem of what to do about the Indians.

The provisional legislature, previously established by whites, voted to assemble five hundred volunteers to rescue the prisoners and punish the Indians. Simultaneously, a three-man peace commission was appointed to try to restore calm. The respected Joel Palmer, who had brought his people there in 1840, headed this unit. Yet it was the long-experienced Hudson's Bay people who carried the day. John McLoughlin sent one of his best men, Peter Skene Ogden, an experienced trapper and fur brigade leader, to negotiate for the captives' release. McLoughlin's purpose was both humanitarian and self-interest, as hostilities would harm the already weakened fur trade. The imposing power of Hudson's Bay made Ogden's position a strong one. For five hundred dollars in trade goods—blankets, shirts, tobacco, guns, ammunition, and the like—the captives were returned approximately a month after the massacre.[46]

Meanwhile, volunteer troops, headed by an aggressive and punitive Colonel Gilliam, engaged in killing available but innocent Indians. (Gilliam accidentally shot himself and died.) Various skirmishes between the two sides created more trouble than was caused by the massacre itself. The troops disbanded in June 1848 without satisfying their thirst for revenge. They realized that their actions were worsening relations between whites and Indians.

Mysteriously, the ringleader of the massacre, Chief Tilokaikt, and several others involved in the bloody affair surrendered to whites in 1850, nearly four years after the event. Unforgiving Oregonians tried them all for murder, and they were duly hanged on June 3 of that year. Before they went to the scaffold, Spalding offered them Presbyterian consolations to ease their death. He was rebuffed, the Indians choosing instead last rites from a priest. It was a supreme moment of irony for Spalding.

The aftermath of the mission massacre went far beyond the actual damage done.

The legacy of the Cayuse skirmishes proved more significant in the Northwest than the war itself. Gilliam's uncompromising course exposed to all the north-western tribes a side of the white man they had not observed in the firm but reasonable agents of the Hudson's Bay Company. Worse yet, frustrated at repeated failures to run down Whitman's murderers, Oregon officials de-clared Cayuse lands forfeit, thus seeming to confirm the fear of the perpe-trators of the massacre that all those white-topped wagons bore people bent upon seizing their lands. If further notice were needed, the Oregon Donation Land Law enacted by Congress in 1850 opened all lands to homesteading without regard to Indian title. In future troubles the distrust of Bostons planted in Indian minds by the Cayuse affair figured importantly.[47]

Missionary work continued on the Great Plains, but always amidst a sea of troubles. Lay women and nuns augmented the work of mini-sters and priests. Quakers became involved when President Grant's Quaker policy dictated that Indian agents be selected by religious denomination. This was inspired largely by squabbling among various religious factions and the incredible corruption at Indian agencies. As a result of the policy, Roman Catholics lost eighty thousand of their Indian converts, transferred to other ministries. They only retained eight of their previous thirty-five missions but did receive govern-mental monies for their schools. Yet despite the changes, missionaries continued to be active.

A Swiss Benedictine priest, Martin Marty, worked feverishly with the Sioux after their victory at the Custer battle when the Indians feared the white man's wrath might result in their extermination. Marty's work eventually resulted in the conversion of nearly a fourth of the tribe, and he came to be known as the "Apostle of the Sioux." At the hanging of the thirty-eight Sioux convicted in the Great Sioux Uprising in Minnesota, thirty-two of the Indians were given last rites by Augustin Ravolt, a Roman Catholic priest from Quebec.

It became increasingly difficult for the Indian to practice his own religious rites; in 1883 Henry Teller, U.S. commissioner of Indian affairs, listed Indian offenses that he declared must be eradicated. These included feasts, dances (such as the Sun Dance, which gave such powerful medicine), polygamy, wife purchases, and all practices of the red medicine man.[48]

While the missionaries meant well and in many cases did well, the Indians themselves remained puzzled. They never really achieved the power promised by the white man's "big medicine," at least not in the form they expected. All in all, the white men and their religion left the Indian confused. One reason was that what whites practiced and what they taught often were separated by a yawning gap.

In our pluralistic culture, we often fail to appreciate the role of religion among close-knit peoples. There, it is no private matter but a vital thread in the warp and woof of the community. To take away such a people's religion and replace it with another is to tear at the very fabric of the culture. In many ways, this was the experience of the American Indian with the white man's Christianity. As Emil Durkheim argued, with the loss of traditional common values, a culture becomes fragmented and unstable.

Many saw what was happening to the Indian and sought to rescue the old culture by repairing the damage that had been done. Yet, the damage was so great that restoration was all but impossible. The Indian's world was gone, as surely as the world of European peasantry was lost to the white emigrants. Nonetheless, we must note one fascinating attempt to preserve the value of the Indian. It is the inspiring story of the Oglala medicine—holy—man Black Elk (1863-1950). A close relative of another medicine man, Crazy Horse, Black Elk had a vision in his youth. He was given the task of restoring the purity of Sioux culture and thereby healing his fragmented tribe. The tribe was under severe pressure from within and without, especially after the Custer affair, in which Black Elk himself had participated as a boy.

The sense of harmony with nature, so important to all Indians, had been lost and Black Elk sought to recover this in order to achieve purity, unity, and a sense of identity once again. Highly revered by fellow Indians of all tribes, Black Elk lived a life of prayer and fasting. In his twenties he travelled widely in this country and even accompanied the Buffalo Bill Wild West Show to Europe. He began to see that his vision was not meant only for his own people but for white culture as well. Despite the great material well-being of whites, they, too, were in need of purification. He saw in the Wounded Knee experience the paucity of natural values in both Indian and white cultures.

John Niehardt, a sympathetic scholar, visited Black Elk and put down for posterity Black Elk's vision in the work *Black Elk Speaks*. "This book is impressive on two levels: as a rare view of the inside of the mind and life of a culture now gone; and second, as a moving plea for harmony among the brotherhood of man and between man and the universe."[49]

The work was made more accessible in 1953 in the book *The Sacred Pipe*, an account given by Black Elk to the anthropologist Joseph E. Brown. The book is a moving one that tells the story of the Sioux religious culture, its practices and mysteries. It enables both red men and white to appreciate and strive for a greater unity in mankind. It points toward a universal culture, a goal which Western civilization has often glimpsed but so far has never approached.

6. Trails West

Santa Fe, Oregon, and Mormon

The early exploration and settlement of the West took place largely along the great rivers that stretched across the region. The Spanish in the Southwest and the Verendryes on the northern plains had made notable forays on foot, but Lewis and Clark were able to carry out their vast commission efficiently by using the waterways. With keelboat at first and then only *bateaux* they hauled their Corps of Discovery up the Missouri and Yellowstone and down the Columbia, taking in a number of tributaries along the way.[1]

The mountain men, in their single-minded pursuit of the beaver, also kept close to the rivers. Not until the rendezvous system was inaugurated in 1825 did appreciable numbers of people journey west by land. By the time the rendezvous system ended in 1840, the mountain men had discovered South Pass and so opened the way for streams of emigrants to seek their fortunes in the promised lands of California and Oregon. The day of the great overland trek had arrived.

It may be wondered why the early settlers undertook the arduous journey across the continent, passing unaware through what was to become the breadbasket of the country—the fertile plains of Nebraska, Kansas, and Oklahoma. The answer can be expressed in the words of Will Rogers: "So many things we know ain't so."

The pioneers who carved their farms out of the forests between the Appalachians and the Mississippi did not look upon the trees only as obstacles to be overcome. To them, the timber was a guarantee of the richness of the land. It was an article of faith that where trees grew, crops would grow. The treeless plains seemed an uncultivable desert. For decades, this misconception forestalled settlement on the prairies.

Exploration and enterprise in what was to be the American West, then, began with mapping the headwaters of the great rivers, discovering where they went and how far they were navigable. In this task, the army played an important role.

In 1806, Lieutenant Zebulon Montgomery Pike was sent by General Wilkenson to trace the headwaters of the Mississippi. Pike located these at Leech Lake in Minnesota—wrongly. Later explorers determined that the river arose near Itasca. Pike was then sent to trace the Arkansas and Red rivers to their sources in order to establish the exact southern and southwestern borders of the Louisiana Purchase. In this mission, Pike also was unsuccessful, but he can hardly be blamed for stopping short of his goals. The Arkansas River flows twelve hundred miles from its source in the mountains near Leadville, Colorado, over ten thousand feet above sea level. The Red River, which serves for part of its length as the border between Oklahoma and Texas, is over a thousand miles long. Pike's efforts did, however, add considerably to knowledge of the area that he explored.

After visiting the famous Royal Gorge of the Arkansas River, with its thousand-foot cliffs, Pike headed south, making his way in and out of Mexican territory. On one dip into Mexico, he was arrested by Spanish soldiers and taken to Santa Fe, the provincial capital that even then was nearly two centuries old. From there he was taken to Chihuahua, where his papers and maps were confiscated. Before he was released in Louisiana, Pike observed Mexico's urgent need for trade goods and noted the exorbitant prices they brought. Back in the United States, he spread the word about the immense possibilities for commerce with Mexico, publishing his views in 1810 in his *Journal of Western Exploration*, which was translated into several European languages.

Pike thus was one of the first to promote trade routes across the American Southwest. Nevertheless, he is probably best remembered for giving his name to Pike's Peak, a fourteen thousand foot mountain north of present-day Pueblo, Colorado, where he established a fort. Pike himself considered the "fourteener" peak unclimbable. Now cars and tramways take thousands of visitors to its top each day, and the poem *America the Beautiful* was written there.

Another explorer of the Mississippi was Major Stephen H. Long, who established Fort Snelling along its northern reaches. Such forts protected traders and travellers, as well as making a show of power to the Indians. Many of them would become the sites of great cities.

Like Pike, Long searched for the source of the Red River and, like Pike, he was unsuccessful. He did manage to trace the Platte, which empties into the Missouri near present-day Omaha. Leaving the Platte, he also visited the awesome Royal Gorge of the mighty Arkansas River and went on to found Fort Smith on that waterway. Long's major claim to fame, however, was the judgment he carried back to civilization, declaring that the lands he had passed through were nothing more than a "great American desert." He thus gave rise to the view expressed by Daniel Webster in his famous wasteland speech: "What do we want with this vast, worthless area—this region of savages and wild beasts, of deserts, of shifting sands and whirlwinds of dust and prairie dogs? To what use do we hope to put this great desert and all these endless mountain ranges?"[2] But despite Webster's eloquence, the advocacy of Thomas Hart Benton, the pro-Western senator from Missouri, would prevail.

As the rivers of the West were explored and mapped, technology was appearing that would turn them into highways of commerce. Within twenty-five years of Robert Fulton's 1807 demonstration of steam power on the Hudson, steamboats proliferated on waterways all over the country. They were a great improvement on the keelboat, which had to be towed, rowed, or sailed, and soon they were proving their usefulness in carrying people and goods.

From early on, paddle-wheel steamboats plied the waters of the Missouri, called for good reason the "Big Muddy." In 1832 structural modifications allowed such vessels to penetrate even the debris-strewn waters of the Upper Missouri as far as its confluence with the Yellowstone at Fort Union. The first steamer to do so was named the *Yellow Stone* and was owned by John Jacob Astor.[3] A double-decked sidewheeler, the craft was 120 feet long, with a beam of 200 feet and a hold 6 feet deep. A number of famous passengers made that first trip, the artist George Catlin among them. The location of Fort Union proved practical for fur traders, and later the army, recognizing the strategic importance of the site, built its own Fort Buford nearby. Sitting Bull would later surrender there.

Boats, unlike wagons, could accommodate huge and heavy loads—from two to four hundred tons in water no deeper than six feet. Boats were major carriers of commerce in their time and maintained their dominance until the coming of the railroads.[4] Their feats were sometimes legendary. As late as 1876, Captain Grant Marsh, acknowledged as the greatest of the riverboat pilots, scraped his craft, the *Far West*, all the way to the delta of the Little Bighorn River to pick up soldiers wounded in the Custer battle. He carried them back to Bismarck in record time.

The red man called the steamboats "big canoes." The boats were both admired and feared—each carried at least one small cannon, and the crew knew how to use it. One steamboat, which we met in an earlier chapter, was decorated to be impressive: a serpent's head was painted on its bow and a vent in its mouth puffed steam as it pushed upstream.

As Captain Marsh showed, steamers could travel long distances up river. Major Stephen H. Long travelled to Council Bluffs in 1818 in a craft that drew only nineteen inches. Some vessels operating far upstream had only a twelve to fourteen inch draft; some pilots bragged that they could navigate on a heavy dew.

Still, the steamboat's advantages were only one side of the coin. The shallow draft also meant that strong winds could blow a boat around like a leaf on the water. Without a daggerboard or similar device, the boat easily could be pushed sideways into a protruding bank, where it might be poked to death by jutting trees.

Steam power was slower in coming to the overland trails of the West. The first transcontinental railroad would not be built until after the Civil War. Until that time, particularly in the high mountains and the dry Southwest, foot and animal traffic remained the rule and created their own legends.

The unexplored West was a network of trails, many crossing and crisscrossing several times. "Trails to grass and water were most numerous on the plains, corresponding somewhat to the salt lick trails of Kentucky."[5] To find water, newcomers learned from Indians to follow the mustang or the deer, animals that had to drink daily, or to look for cottonwood trees, which consume fifty gallons of water a day.

In seeking water and grass, the animals followed a path of least resistance. Over the years, their hooves made a clear trail in the ground. Indians used many of these tracks and also produced their own cutoffs. Trails thus already existed in the West; like the rivers, they only required mapping.

The first major trail used by white entrepreneurs was established in response to the possibilities of trade with Mexico. The father of the Santa Fe Trail (which would lead to Taos and Chihuahua as well) was Samuel Becknell, who set off in 1821 from Missouri to trade with the Indians. He had advertised for credit and found Missouri merchants who were glad to extend it. With goods carried on pack animals, Becknell and four other men proceeded toward the Great Bend of the Arkansas River, a well-known trading center between Indian tribes and between Indians and whites.

When Becknell's party arrived, however, they found that the Indians had little or no goods left. Becknell could do nothing but head ever farther west toward La Junta (near the future site of Bent's Fort). Unsuccessful there, he travelled through Raton Pass, the gateway from Colorado to Mexico. Once in Mexico, he ran into Mexican soldiers. Instead of arresting him as they had Pike, they welcomed his party, joyfully telling him of Mexico's newly won independence from Spain. They urged him to bring his goods to Santa Fe, where the people were in great need of supplies as a result of Spain's blockade of Mexican ports.

The Americanos and the Mexicans each had what the other wanted. What could be a better bartering situation? The Mexicans had fine mules, furs, chinaware, and, most of all, abundant silver in various forms, much in Mexican dollars. Becknell had textiles, cutlery, tools, notions, and various sought-after items. Quickly selling everything, he returned to Missouri with a 1,500 percent profit.

Heady with success, Becknell set out the next year not with pack mules but with three wagons loaded with trading goods. Since at that time wagons could not negotiate his original route over Raton Pass, he pioneered a variation on his earlier trek, later to be known as the Cimarron Cutoff. The shortcut lessened the trip by nearly a hundred miles and saved approximately ten days of travel. However, it was risky, for it cut through the land named by Spanish explorers *Llano Estacado*—the staked plains. As we have seen, the scarcity of water in this region made it extremely hazardous to cross, both for men and for animals. Travellers who ran dry on the route sometimes could kill buffalo and drink the water from the animals' stomachs. Some slit the ears of their mules and drank the blood to quench their thirst in the almost constant summer heat of 110 to 120 degrees.

The staked plains were also Comanche country. Seeing the trade caravans becoming more and more regular, the Indians increased their attacks. Several of Becknell's own men were captured by Comanches in one fracas. Fortunately, Auguste Choteau, experienced in trade with the Osage Indians, secured their release. Future trading parties were well aware of the twin dangers of scarce water and hostile Indians. The increased harassment by Pawnee, Kiowa, Comanche, Cheyenne, and Arapaho led traders to band together for protection. Eventually some hard lobbying led to increased government protection by the army.

Yet Indians and heat were not the only hazards. In the early days of the trade, a Baird-Chambers wagon train bound for Santa Fe was caught in a blizzard that killed their pack animals. They buried their cargo in huge caches that they dug on the bank of the Arkansas. They then stayed the winter at Ark Island near present-day Dodge City. In spring, they walked to Taos, brought back more pack animals, dug up their caches, and went on to Santa Fe, where they sold their goods for high profit. The area where the party was stranded is still known as "The Caches," and for years after, the depressions left by the caches remained visible in the ground.

That same year, 1823, a group of Americans headed by Stephen Cooper made a significant trade in Santa Fe. They brought back "four hundred mules, jennies and Spanish jacks that sired the first Missouri mules."[6] The mules may well have been the most valuable cargo to come out of Mexico, as the animals were in heavy demand by the increasing westward migrations. Mexicans long had been known for breeding the finest mules anywhere. Indeed, what came to be known as the "Missouri mule" really was a Mexican animal, and soon they were trailing to Missouri by the thousands.

No present-day truck or tractor has had its merits and demerits more thoroughly discussed than did the animals that provided the power in the nineteenth century. Debate raged on the comparative virtues of the mule, ox, and horse for Western travel.[7] Most teamsters voted for the horse. It could be controlled easily and, if fed properly, served its rider well. The horse, however, was not made to pull heavy freight over long distances. For such heavy hauling, oxen and mules were used. Besides, few Indians raided for mules and none for oxen, but the horse was passionately coveted by the Plains Indian. What the car is to the average American today the horse was to the Plains Indian.

Some old timers valued the mule because it could, they said, smell an Indian a mile away; they claimed that it was as good a scout as any human. Unfortunately, few farriers knew how to shoe mules or oxen properly, so many of the draft animals developed sore feet and became useless. Mules stood the fierce heat of the plains better than oxen, but the oxen fared better in dirt, sand, and mud.

Cost also was a factor in deciding between an ox and a mule. A mule cost about seventy-five dollars, while an ox could be purchased for twenty-five. Oxen only needed a wooden yoke where mules required expensive leather harnesses, but both had to warm up in order to pull with maximum strength. For that reason, trips were planned so that excessive hard and uphill terrain would be tackled only after several hours on the trail. If food ran out, roast ox tasted better than mule meat, although in emergencies both were eaten. So were horses, for that matter, although the briny taste was not popular with Americans.

Before wagons were used on the trail, mules served as pack animals, and sorry was the party that had no Mexican attendants to service its animals. Ornery and contentious (that is to say, intelligent and self-centered), the mules often inflated their bellies with air as they were loaded, only to exhale once the packs were strapped on. The result was loosened loads that required repacking. The most effective method of relaxing the high-kicking mules was to blindfold them. Loading on the packs had to be carefully done; mistakes would allow the cargo to lurch at just the wrong moment. On a cliff path, this could mean the loss of the mule and cargo.

When used as pack animals or draft animals, mules were led by what the Mexicans called a *madrina*, a mare with a bell around her neck that tinkled with each step. At the sound of the bell, the other mules gathered by her side. Often in a large caravan there were several *madrinas* and each mule went to its own special bell mare, somehow distinguishing the different sounds of various bells.

The Santa Fe Trail could be entered from any number of Missouri border towns, such as Franklin, Independence, and Westport (present-day Kansas City). Unofficially, Independence was the principal starting point. Senator Thomas Hart Benton, always eager to promote Western commerce, introduced legislation in Congress to improve and make safe the eight hundred miles of road to Santa Fe. Some of the bills appropriated money to survey the trail and make it a more passable road. Others sought money to back the provisions of the Indian treaties and guarantee the safety of traders passing through the red man's lands. Such treaties quieted the Pawnee, Kansas, and Osage Indians. No negotiations were held with the most hostile, the Kiowa and Comanche; they were regarded as Mexico's problem, as they dwelt on its side of the Arkansas.

Benton also encouraged the building of army posts along the trail. Fort Leavenworth was established at the eastern terminus and, as the years went by, other forts were strung out along the trail.

In the early years of trail travel, however, merchants had to provide for their own protection. On May 16, 1824, three years after Becknell had opened the trail, a party of independent merchants set out for Santa Fe in a show of collective strength. Their caravan consisted of "eighty one men, one hundred and fifty six horses and mules."[8] With such potent force and firepower, they arrived without incident in Santa Fe on July 28. Their 35,000 dollars' worth of goods brought a handsome profit of 155,000 dollars, leading more and larger caravans to take the route to riches. They gathered at a spot later known as Council Grove. An oasis on the arid Kansas plains, it was there, in 1825, that the government and the Osage Indians agreed to terms permitting safe passage for the traders. The treaty, which gave eight hundred dollars to the Osage as well as other guarantees, was concluded under a giant oak tree, whose stump remains a monument today. More or less, this treaty signified "the official birthplace of the Santa Fe Trail."[9]

Early traders to Santa Fe were dismayed when the Mexicans imposed a tax of five hundred dollars on each wagonload of goods, although, in truth, it was not a tax so much as an open bribe and could be paid simply by raising prices on the merchandise. To spark business, the traders, when still two hundred miles out, would send runners ahead to Santa Fe announcing their impending arrival. The citizens would respond by making hasty arrangements for fiestas to accompany the wheeling and dealing about to take place. When they arrived, the American merchants would set up booths, rent shops, or trade right out of their wagons. In later times, the trade extended to Taos and to Chihuahua.

The early wagons were rather small. Spurred in part by the tax burden, the ingenious merchants soon introduced to the trail the huge Conestoga wagons first used in Pennsylvania. (The word "stogie" was coined for the cigar smoked by its teamster.) The wagons could carry a load of five thousand pounds but needed a large number of animals to pull them. Since the tax was five hundred dollars per wagon, large or small, the larger Conestoga improved profits for the traders. On the return trip, usually to St. Louis, the wagons carried only a thousand pounds of Mexican merchandise to ease the burden of the worn-out draft animals.

The wagons were cumbersome but sturdy and well suited to the trail to Santa Fe, as the land was relatively smooth and flat. On the Cimarron Cutoff, only one major but easy pass had to be negotiated, the Glorietta Pass near Santa Fe. Where the earlier and smaller wagons were pulled by six or eight mules, the Conestoga required ten to twelve and sometimes twenty animals per wagon. The pace was a steady fifteen miles or so a day. With oxen in yolked pairs, men called "swampers" threw small stones at the animals to encourage them to keep moving; but with mules, the driver had to crack his whip constantly just over the ears to urge them on. Many teamsters were very precise, never touching the ears of the mules while coming within inches of doing so. A "cracker" was attached to the end of the whip, and during the long drive, a number of crackers were worn out.

With animals in heavy demand for the Santa Fe Trail, the market in mules and oxen grew each year, and by 1859 the freighting firm of Russell, Majors, and Waddell had some six thousand teamsters for ready hire and forty-five thousand oxen available. Located near Leavenworth, the company served both the Santa Fe and the later Oregon and California adventurers. This was the same firm that funded the ill-fated Pony Express, which operated for only eighteen months. The firm lost over a hundred thousand dollars in that venture. Majors's home in Kansas City now is a historical site.

Eventually, Senator Benton's influence led to the establishment of various forts along the trail, some of which would be used as bases in the war with Mexico. Among these were Fort Zarah, Fort Dodge, Fort Larned, and Fort Union. Fort Larned is preserved today, as are the ruins of Fort Union near Las Vegas, New Mexico, but Fort Zarah is now only an off-highway picnic site without toilets or water.

Senator Benton, the chief lobbyist for Western expansion, even talked President Jackson into providing army escorts at points along the trail. Unfortunately, the escorts were foot soldiers and they served mostly to slow down the wagons, proving more a bane than a boon.

After some months, the government recognized that to be effective, cavalry troops were needed. In any event, no troops were allowed to cross the Arkansas River into Mexican territory—and the greatest danger from Indians was precisely on the south side of the Arkansas. On occasion, however, the Mexicans themselves provided escort from Santa Fe to the Arkansas, for which the traders were grateful.

On one occasion, caravaners were able to help Mexicans in return. One hundred Mexicans were hunting buffalo when they were attacked by Indians, who were angry at the plunder of their food supply. The Mexicans ran out of ammunition and fled to the American caravans for protection. Together the Mexicans and Americans warded off the charges of the red man, but neither side could defeat the other. The caravan then sent to Taos for help and were reinforced by forty hawk-eyed mountain men, Kit Carson among them. That settled the problem for the traders and buffalo hunters.

Highways follow the Santa Fe Trail fairly closely today. Beginning at Council Grove, the low-rolling land in several hundred miles becomes almost perfectly flat. Cottonwoods still tell of hidden creeks, and scudding clouds interrupt the otherwise near constant sunshine. Mirages are common along the trail, as is the phenomenon known as "phantom rain," where clouds may be seen pouring out water that drifts in smoky sheets toward the earth only to evaporate before touching the ground.

Wagons were affected by the low humidity. Even the best kiln-dried woods shrank and the iron tires came loose on the wheels. The wheels were often placed in a river or creek overnight to swell them back to normal dimensions.

Major rivers such as the Arkansas, the Red, and the Canadian had to be forded, although in summer they usually were not deep. Wagons crossed rivers diagonally, letting the current help push them to the other bank. Shifting sand and quicksand were problems; to solve them, matted willows were placed on the river bottom when possible. Hurrying across the mats, the wagons seldom became mired.

The trail was broad, so wagons often travelled three and four abreast rather than in single file. (Some of their deep ruts are preserved near Fort Larned.) Travelling side by side enabled the teamsters to "jaw" with each other on the long journey and laugh at each other's appearance, for they blackened their eyes with charcoal to reduce glare from the bright sun.

At various points along the trail, drivers looked for landmarks that identified the right path and indicated how far they had come. The Great Bend of the Arkansas was one such marker; later Fort Zarah was another. Not many miles west is Pawnee Rock, which thrusts out of the ground like Courthouse Rock on the Oregon Trail. Although conspicuous on the flat plains, the landmark is relatively low. Today, cars can be driven to its top, which has picnic facilities.

The crossing where the muddy Pawnee joined the Arkansas River was the site on which Fort Larned was built. The Caches, near where Fort Dodge would be established, was another mark of progress. At this point, caravans without wagons had to decide whether to take the dangerous Cimarron Cutoff or to go through the safer but tortuous Raton Pass. A number of years passed before the mountain man Uncle Dick Wooten built his toll road at Raton Pass to provide an easier and much safer route for wagon traffic. Until that time, most took the cutoff. (The two routes converged near Watrous, New Mexico.) Other markers were Wagon Mound, a large rock formation on a butte of land; Rabbit Ears Pass; and later Fort Union, established in 1851. Finally, passing the port of entry at Las Vegas and going through Glorietta Pass, the wagons made their way to Santa Fe.

Some chose to take a delayed cutoff near Choteau's Island, a bit farther west than the usual cutoff point near Ft. Dodge. This placed them near what was to become the largest trading post between St. Louis and Santa Fe—Bent's Fort. Established in 1833, the trading post-fort stayed in business until 1849. Its story is important to the Santa Fe Trail; the list of workers, proprietors, and people who were there or used its services reads like a Who's Who of the early West.[10]

The history of Bent's Fort begins with a man named Ceran St. Vrain and two Bent brothers, Charles and William. All three were Missourians who had joined in the Northwest beaver fur trade during its waning days. They found that the price of pelts was only half of what it had been and was falling. Exploring new avenues of opportunity, Charles Bent captained a wagon train to Santa Fe, taking along his brother William. In Santa Fe, they shrewdly observed the scarcity of goods, as had Pike before them. The town was the last stop on El Camino Real, the highway from Mexico City, and supplies somehow didn't make it that far. The paucity of merchandise made the Santa Feans eager to purchase nearly anything a trader had to offer, and they did not lack the wherewithal to pay for their purchases. With such an opportunity staring them in the face, Ceran St. Vrain and Charles Bent immediately set about establishing Bent, St. Vrain, and Company to take advantage of the situation. At this time, Ceran and Charles Bent were about thirty years old, while William was only twenty. William became a partner shortly afterward and two other Bent brothers, George and Robert, also got involved in the enterprise.

Although young and short, William had a way with the Indians; they affectionately named him "Little White Man." Marrying into the

Cheyennes, William took for his wife Owl Lady, the daughter of a medicine chief, Grey Thunder. Over a period of time he married two other Indian women. William was fair in his trading and furthered his cause by helping tribes that had been enemies to become, if not friends, at least less bellicose with each other. The Kiowa were allied with the Comanche, for example, against the Cheyenne and the Arapaho. William's bringing these sets of tribes together was a remarkable achievement.

At first, William set up a stockade fort for trading on the northern bank of the Arkansas in a buffalo-hunting area claimed by the Southern Cheyenne. Charles noted its business success and suggested that William build a more permanent structure nearby. Work began almost immediately as William brought in hundreds of workers from Taos. The site was about twelve miles north of the confluence of the Purgatoire and Arkansas rivers. The building-fort, made entirely of adobe, was ready for business in 1833. Set in the vicinity of La Junta and La Mar, Colorado, it was a favorable crossing spot for the various tribes.

Originally named Fort William, mountain men referred to it as Bent's Big Lodge, but eventually all came to call it simply Bent's Fort. West of the fort, the twin Spanish Peaks were visible, a marker indicating the turnoff point for Raton Pass. The fort was rectangular; it had two gun towers, a platform along its inner walls, and a fur press in its center arena. Rooms held various trading supplies, such as powder and lead, buffalo and beaver hides, whiskey, blankets, and tools of various sorts. An inside corral also was built and, to prevent theft of the stock in it, cacti were planted along its upper walls. Even though the fort was less than half a mile from the river, a giant cistern was dug within its grounds to assure a measure of independence in case of siege. The fort never was attacked, however, both because of its strength and because its proprietors maintained friendly relations with the Indians.

This Castle of the Plains even had a billiards room. Other separate rooms included Bent's own quarters, a dining room, a cook's room, a kitchen, a blacksmith shop, a carpentry shop, and various storage areas. The fort also had an insulated ice room, filled by ice blocks cut from the nearby Arkansas River in winter, so it enjoyed most of the civilized conveniences of St. Louis in its isolated and arid setting.

On one occasion, Charles became ill, probably from diphtheria, which produces a mucus membrane that blocks the throat. He was in danger of death when William called upon his Indian father-in-law, the medicine chief, for help. The Indian quickly fashioned a small cactus ball on a string, greased it, and had Charles swallow the lump as far as he was able. He then jerked out the ball, bringing with it the life-threatening mucus plug. Charles's life was saved, although undoubtedly he had a sore throat for some time after.

The location of the fort, the most important trade center between St. Louis and Santa Fe, made it a favorite of the mountain men. It was popular, too, with traders who rested their animals there for the long pull up Raton Pass. Kit Carson worked for the Bents as a busy buffalo hunter, for the employees and guests needed a thousand pounds of meat each day. Old Bill Williams, Uncle Dick Wooten, Tom Fitzpatrick, Ewing Young, and other mountain men also frequented the trading post.

Since the beaver trade was producing few profits, traders looked for other items to barter and found them in buffalo hides. The Bents bought the hides for twenty-five cents and sold them in St. Louis for two dollars. Meanwhile, St. Vrain moved his residence to Mexico and built up trade connections. With another Bent brother, he set up an additional trading post, appropriately named Fort St. Vrain. Charles Bent also furthered the trading business by ingratiating himself with Mexican officials and by marrying a woman from Taos.

War with Mexico, declared in 1846, brought General Stephen Watts Kearny to Bent's Fort, which became a military base for the duration. Kearny went from there to annex all the land north and east of the Rio Grande, and William served as Kearny's guide.

At this time, James Magoffin, an American businessman and diplomat knowledgeable in Mexican affairs, stopped at the fort, carrying secret messages to Mexican officials from President Polk. With him was his younger brother, Samuel, and Samuel's nineteen-year-old pregnant wife, Susan Magoffin. She was the first woman to travel the trail to Santa Fe, and in her journal she gives an entertaining description of the fort and its carryings-on.[11] Unfortunately, the baby she delivered at the fort died, but Susan continued to write and to provide a rich account of travel on the trail. Her round trip, with its stopover in Mexico, was completed in fifteen months.

General Kearny went on to Santa Fe, where he bribed the officials and took over the government in a bloodless coup. He installed Charles Bent as governor, which seemed an ideal appointment, for Bent was well-known. Yet, Bent, "a strong willed person with a sarcastic tongue, had enemies. His running feud with the Martinez family of Taos and his trade relations with the enemies of the Taos Indians combined with resentment of the conquerors and fear of land seizure was to produce the Taos rebellion of January 1847, in which Bent was killed and scalped."[12] Twenty other Americans were slaughtered in the uprising. Kit Carson's wife, living with the Bent family in Santa Fe, escaped harm.

Affairs went from bad to worse for Bent's Fort. Whites no longer felt safe with their Indian friends, and Indians resumed intertribal feuds, causing trade to deteriorate. Soldiers coming and going at the fort ruined the grasses, used up wood supplies, and polluted the water. Furthermore, the government didn't pay all of its bills to the fort. At this time, the Cheyennes lost half their tribe to cholera, probably spread by the influx of civilization. In 1849, the fort was abandoned and blown up—apparently by William. The circumstances are disputed. William set up another installation nearby called "Bent's New Fort" but the halcyon days were over. In our own time, the old fort has been excavated and rebuilt according to its original specifications. It is one of the major restorations of the National Park Service.

The Santa Fe Trail saw few "Forty-niners" during the California Gold Rush in 1849-1850, nor was it much used by emigrants. The trail was principally a route for commerce. Josiah Gregg wrote the outstanding chronicle of its adventures.[13]

Over a period of time, the trail became safer and trade between Mexico and the United States increased. Army protection became permanent and, in 1850, regular mail and passenger coach service was inaugurated between Independence and Santa Fe. "By 1855, the Santa Fe trade alone amounted to five million dollars. In 1865 three thousand merchant wagons rolled westward over the trail. . . . In 1866 the number of merchandise wagons increased to more than five thousand."[14]

The trail did not long survive the coming of the railroad. In 1872, the tracks reached the Cimarron Cutoff, and the cowboy town of Dodge City with its famous "Boot Hill" grew up at the end of the line. On February 9, 1880, the first train puffed through the Raton Pass tunnel and on to Santa Fe. For all practical purposes, that year marked the demise of the storied Santa Fe Trail. Information and artifacts from its heyday may be seen at the Santa Fe Trail Museum a few miles west of the restored Fort Larned. At present, Congress is being asked to establish the entire trail as a national historic site. Certainly the trail played a large role in the development of the West.

As the Santa Fe Trail primarily served commerce, the Oregon Trail served emigrants. It was opened by mountain men who explored the rivers and passes in that high country in their quest for furs. Missionaries followed, and then the would-be settlers and fortune hunters.

From the East, travellers seeking the Oregon Trail took the rivers to the jumping off places, which included Independence, Westport, St. Joseph, and Council Bluffs. Restless Missourians could just go west from where they were, hooking up with the established trail somewhere along the line. But large-scale migration had to wait until it was proved that wagons could make the trip to California and the Northwest. Despite the constant traffic of single and hardy adventurers, the trail would be remembered for the passage of entire families, including babies and grandparents. The feasibility of wagon travel took some time to establish, but as early as 1836, Sublette, Jackson, and Smith brought wagons to the Green River rendezvous. Narcissus Whitman commented in a letter: "We are really a moving village—The Fur Com. has seven wagons and one cart, drawn by six mules each, heavily loaded. . . . We have two wagons."[15]

The fur men found that with wagons, twenty-two men and fifty-two mules could transport what it took forty-five men and ninety mules to do by backpack. Dr. Marcus Whitman, at that 1836 gathering, had two wagons that he intended to take all the way to Oregon, but he had to abandon them along the Snake River with less than half of the journey completed.

Four years later, in 1840, a couple of mountain men and their wives reassembled the remains of the Whitman wagons and, crossing the Blue Mountains, took them on to Oregon. The next year, 1841, wagons made it all the way in a single trip with the Bidwell-Bartelson group, guided by that redoubtable mountain man Tom Fitzpatrick. That settled the question, and Secretary of War John Henry Eaton officially announced that wagons could be taken to Oregon.[16]

The road over South Pass, which missionaries said had been "imprinted by the finger of God," now began to see increasing emigration. In 1843, 875 took to the trail. The settlement of the boundaries of the Oregon land in 1846 gave additional impetus to travel and, in 1852, 15,000 followed the tortuous winding trail to the Northwest. Oregon fever (later combined with California fever) was sweeping the country.

When a New York journalist, writing for the *Democratic Review*, coined the phrase "manifest destiny," he gave a name to an attitude that was already widespread. Many were eager to fill the continent with American spirit and enterprise. And, as the historian Frederick Jackson Turner has observed, the West gave distinctive character to that spirit. The farther west the pioneers went, the more they shed their European heritage and established a new identity. The West was both the inspiration and shaper of the American mission to the world.

The people who took to the Oregon trail were people of substance, both financial and moral. They were not social marginals but mostly were middle-class, literate people. The anti-British bias of the time led some to compare themselves to those who had made the Boer trek in South Africa shortly before—although the Boers had marched to maintain racial exclusivity and the Americans were trekking to a land that, until then, had enjoyed some of the most inclusive racial relationships in the Western world.

The Oregon-bound pioneers needed a grubstake of at least five hundred dollars; it was known that travellers could not live off the land on the way. Mountain men and missionaries were clear on that point. Among their provisions, the Oregon travellers carried the torch of patriotism, and it never burned more brightly than when they celebrated Independence Day, the Fourth of July, on the trail. One of their motivations for making the trek was to save Oregonland from the British, who had claims on it, claims rooted in the presence of the Hudson's Bay Company, which had trapped in and administered the region for years.

The emigrants accepted none of the claims of the despised British and were propelled by a messianic fervor, regarding themselves as God's chosen people. Like the Hebrews of the Old Testament, they firmly believed they could not fail in their endeavors; and they combined optimism, enthusiasm, and romanticism as they marched along the trail.

Not all went to build a new Jerusalem; motivations were varied. Some went for their health, to escape the increasing disease of the cities. Free and fertile land attracted others; some fled high taxation. The West also was proving to be Jefferson's "escape valve" for overpopulation in the East. The area was getting so crowded that often one settler could see another neighbor's land! In families struck by Oregon fever, the man often exhibited the infection more strongly than the woman, for she was asked to leave behind all her relationships, heirlooms, and household luxuries. Many women also feared the suffering they would endure on the trail if they were or became pregnant. Dying in childbirth was always an ominous possibility at home, and the danger was exacerbated on the trail, away from all medical help and civilized support. Many women were nevertheless enthusiastic, and their journals record their delight with the raw and vital beauty of the West. Some, however, could not adapt to the trip and persuaded their families to turn back. Many others had nothing to go back to, for they had sold their farms and houses. This alone kept them headed to Oregon, even though they might have preferred to return east.

One of the most bizarre stories of the zeal to go West was that of a young man, Willie Keil of Bethel, Missouri. When the youth died in 1855 four days before his trip was to begin, his father took the body to Oregon with him in a specially prepared coffin.[17] Rumor spread of this hearse crossing the prairies, and many Indian groups insisted on seeing the body, listening to German hymns sung on those occasions by the members of the train.

Staying power was the virtue most required of those who took to the trail, for the two thousand miles from Independence to the Willamette Valley made it the longest one in history. Their route would take travellers through dry, choking alkali plains and across flooding rivers that threatened death by drowning when the top-heavy wagons overturned.

In the early days of migration west, wagon trains included perhaps twenty-five to thirty families, but later, trains with two hundred wagons were common. Each train elected its own captain, and larger trains divided into smaller units with a number of captains. Rules were drawn up and signed by all, and serious violations were cause for expulsion. As isolation in the wilderness meant almost certain death, most squabbles on the trail were minor. If important decisions affecting the entire group had to be made, the captain would call a general council for a vote; if at any time the group was dissatisfied with its captain, a new election would be held. Despite such exercises in democracy, the technical problem of taking the group through the wilderness was the job of the guide, almost always an experienced mountain man. Such employment kept mountain men in business after the beaver fur trade ran its course. Later many of these same guides would serve the army in its explorations of the West. Among the more prominent were Jim Bridger, Kit Carson, and Tom Fitz-patrick.

The wagons used by the emigrants were relatively small compared with the great Conestoga freighters used on the Santa Fe route. No draft animal could pull such monsters two thousand miles through mountains and streams. The typical wagon box designed for the Oregon trail measured ten by four by two feet, although some were slightly larger. The weight of the empty wagon was a thousand pounds, and it could carry a thousand to fifteen hundred pounds of cargo, the amount depending on how many animals were used to pull it. Six to eight horses could pull such wagons in the East, but on the trail horses were replaced by three yoke (pairs) of oxen or a team of six mules. As four animals could pull the regular load comfortably, the extra two acted as backup. A fresh team might be rotated with a spent one, or on occasion all six might pull to reduce the strain. The health of the animals was all-important. The byword on the trail was to look first to the well-being of the teams. Despite constant repetition of this admonition, many overloaded their wagons and strained the animals. Then the only recourse was to discard excess baggage, leaving the trail strewn with sundry items. The Indians long wondered over found objects such as dress forms, rocking chairs, butter churns, and bricabrac shelves.

The wagon box was scoop bottomed, which helped prevent its

contents from spilling out, especially when climbing a hill. Caulked, the wagon box could be floated across a river. With blocks between the axle and wagon box to raise the bed by eighteen inches, the wagon could make it across shallower streams without wetting the goods inside. The latter practice carried great peril, however, for the raised wagons, already top-heavy, became even more prone to overturn and dump their cargo into the stream.[18] Boulders along the trail also made the wagon an easy mark for tipping. Even on level land, the wagons seldom were in balance, with the tool box on one side, and sometimes (but not often, for the weight was prohibitive) a forty-gallon water barrel on the other. Milk buckets usually hung on the undercarriage, churning their contents into butter by day's end. Tar and grease buckets also swung from the wagon.

Sharp turns with the wagons were impossible, as the front wheels and axles were fixed to the carriage. Indeed, few of the vehicles had brakes and very few had springs, so the ride was a rough and a dangerous one, especially in the high country. To ease steep descents, a log or extra wagon tongue was dragged from the rear axle.

To withstand the considerable wear and tear, wagons were well crafted from kiln-dried hardwoods. Commonly employed was "elm or Osage orange for hubs, oak or hickory for spokes, ash or beech for felloes, ash for framework, hickory for tongues and hounds."[19] Because such woods were not available on the trail, extra supplies were taken along. Yet, despite their kiln-dried construction, once the wagons hit the arid plains, the parts shrank and required constant adjustments and repairs.

One remedy was to knock wedges into place to hold the iron tire on the wheel. As on the Conestoga, wheels would sometimes be taken off and soaked in a stream to expand the wood. The iron rims then were expanded by being fired and slipped onto the frame. When local materials had to be used, the chief replacement was cottonwood, which soaked up water like a sponge and just as quickly shrank in the low humidity.

If the front wagon axle had little steering, the rear one had no differential and consequently, in making turns, the outside rear wheel travelled at the same rate as the inner one while covering more ground. This made a very hard pull on the wheel horse, mule, or oxen, for it bore the brunt of making the turn. The wheel on the outside of the turn mostly would skid until it caught up with the other wheel, making for uneven wear.

Pulling heavy loads uphill sometimes necessitated double and triple teaming. When the hill was very steep, a large pulley wheel would be placed at the top of the hill and the draft animals put on the downside. Long lines, usually chains, were attached to the wagon.

This saved the animals' energy, for then they could pull with gravity rather than against it. In crossing wide streams that were deep in the main channel but shallow near the bank, as many as ten to twenty teams were used. The purpose was to have many of the animals' feet on the stream bottom, pulling, while the animals in deep water floated. To accomplish this, yoked oxen on the far side of the stream would be backed into the water as far as they could go while keeping their footing on the stream bed. Then they were hooked up to the team coming from the other side. This was like two adults, with a child in the middle, lifting it over a puddle of water by its arms.[20]

Oxen could travel at the rate of about two miles an hour on a level plain, so the emigrants advanced about fifteen miles each day, some days making as much as twenty miles, other times only ten. Wheels had to be lubricated constantly, otherwise they would screech like a dry-axled Mexican carreta (two-wheeled ox cart). Lubrication prolonged the life of the much-needed wagon. The emigrants were glad to find, at some points along their route, thick lumps of oil on the ground. They greased their wagons and moved on, unaware of the rich oil domes over which they passed.

Milk cows often accompanied the families, and many wagons had cattle trailing behind. The owners usually were at the rear of the wagon train, for they had to travel more slowly. Ordinarily one herder attended thirty cattle, and a number of single men worked their way to Oregon by serving as cattledrovers. Some emigrants brought their dogs, but dogs mostly proved a nuisance, snipping at the heels of cattle, barking at coyotes in the night, and running off the trail to places unknown. Generally, only the trained watchdogs were worth their keep.

The grubstake with which each party started was fairly standard. Each adult required:
   150 pounds of flour
   5 pounds of baking soda
   40 pounds of bacon (packed in bran to prevent meltdown)
   10 pounds of jerky
   30-40 pounds of dried fruit
   40 pounds of sugar
   40 pounds of coffee
Also needed were various amounts of rice, yeast, vinegar, and molasses. The coffee was an important priority, for pioneers drank it often and drank it strong. "Tain't no such thing as strong coffee," they would say, "only weak men!" A Dutch oven was standard equipment, and various tools and household needs such as sewing kits were taken. Tables and chairs were too heavy and bulky to carry; they easily could be constructed at their destination. The three-legged stool

was a necessity, however. It was small, weighed little, and held its sitter securely on an uneven surface, something a four-legged chair could not guarantee. Each family also had its own medicine chest with its favorite remedies. A must was laudanum, an opium derivative. It alleviated the runs and it also gave the user a sense of dreamy well-being. It was surely used on the sly to ease coping with trail hardships.

The time for starting the long trek depended largely on the general weather conditions. Some parties left in March, bringing extra grass and grain to keep their animals until the prairie grasses bloomed. This made for extra weight in the beginning but gave a head start on the six-month journey. A late spring, however, might mean that the animals would use up the stores of grain before they could live off the land. As a departure month, April was less a gamble but it brought the specter of rain and delay on muddy trails. Most emigrants, particularly the later ones, had some idea of what to expect when they took the Oregon Trail. Nevertheless, it was hard to separate fact from fiction and rumor from truth. Tales of Indian depredations tended to be exaggerated, as were idyllic accounts of conditions in Oregon. And if missionaries described the Oregon Trail as carved by the finger of God, some of those who took the route decided that it must have been a stern and Puritan deity!

Soon, increasing traffic on the trail produced a demand for guidebooks. One of the first was an entirely unreliable publicity piece put out in 1831 by Hall Jackson Kelley. Kelley's pamphlet was based on an earlier attempt to encourage migration by fur trader Joshua Pilcher, who had a cause to promote. More helpful, although a bit glowing and over optimistic, was Lansford W. Hastings's *An Emigrant Guide to Oregon and California*, published in 1845. This book showed great imagination, as parties discovered when they followed its suggestions on shortcuts. In 1859, army Captain Randolph B. Marcy published his reliable classic *The Prairie Traveler*. Other useful works were *The Emigrant's Guide* by Joseph Ware and the published writings of frontier personalities like Captain John Frémont (also optimistic!) and Pierre Jean De Smet. As late as 1864, only five years before the railroad was completed, J.L. Campbell published his *Emigrant's Overland Guide.*

Many told, as did Marcy, the distances between various landmarks, how many days it would take to travel between points, and what to avoid on the trail. They told how to estimate the width of a river by triangulation and gave hints on health and avoiding polluted water. Some guidebooks included instructions on cooking at high altitudes and gave weather information, such as that for every thousand feet of altitude the temperature dropped approximately three degrees. Further, they noted, in the dry West a hundred inches of snow produced the equivalent of an inch of rain, whereas in the East only ten inches of snow would melt down into an inch of moisture. Guidebooks also dealt with psychological barriers, preparing travellers for "seeing the elephant," that is, facing hardship so great that they would want to give up.

The helpful works told how to lower a wagon down a steep hill by using a tree as a snubbing post, or how to dismantle vehicles and lower them over cliffs. Descriptions of poisonous snakes and their habitat, as well as how to treat snakebite, always drew interest, even though most snakes fled from traffic on the trail, as did other animals. Pioneers were advised that the bite of a "sidewinder" (rattlesnake) seldom was fatal to a healthy adult. The pioneers read this literature almost as religiously as they read their Bibles. Indeed, travellers virtually memorized both books, and this helped ease the monotony of the trail.

Daily life on the level parts of the trail was fairly routine; the high country brought more variety and problems. But when buffalo were spotted, everything stopped. No one could resist the excitement of a buffalo chase and the promise of badly needed fresh meat.

A typical day on the Oregon Trail would begin with the camp awaking at 4 A.M.[21] Sentinels would rekindle fires for warmth and cooking, and animals that had been let out to feed the previous night were brought together outside the camp. Some were loose, others staked, and still others hobbled by ropes tied between two legs or by a dragging weight. Only animals whose behavior had shown they couldn't be trusted were hobbled. Many animals, scared by wolves that gnawed at their trailing leather thongs, always kept close to the protection of the camp.

By 5 A.M., the draft animals were being yoked or harnessed, breakfast was eaten, and all campers took care of their toilets. Women, to have a modicum of privacy on the bushless and treeless plains, went some distance from camp and made a circle by holding up one another's long flowing skirts. They took turns entering the improvised enclosure to take care of business. The camp disassembled by 7 A.M. and the day's march began. Those late in getting their things together found themselves at the rear of the train. A few such dust-eating experiences encouraged promptness. Except for such stragglers, democracy prevailed; each wagon took its turn in the lead and fell back a spot on successive days.

During the day, women knitted in the wagons or strolled alongside; the men walked or rode their horses. Scouts went out ahead and to the sides, looking for dangers. "Injuns" might lie hidden in some deep draw or gully. Small children played in their wagons, digging out niches for themselves among the clutter there; older ones walked alongside, playing games and sailing buffalo chips like organic Frisbees. By nightfall the youngsters had pockets full of collectibles, which they were likely to throw out the next day to make room for others. Sometimes the children stood precariously on the tongue of the moving wagon, steadying themselves with hands resting on the back of the oxen. This was dangerous, and occasionally a child fell and was maimed or killed, run over by the heavy grinding wheels. Most youngsters, however, considered the trip to be a lark, freed as they were from most of the old farm chores.

By 11 A.M., the wagons halted for "nooning." The draft animals, rather than the people, needed the rest. During such breaks, women prepared food for lunch and supper, washed clothes or dishes, and did their mending. Some managed to bake bread. Many complained about sore backs, for they had to bend constantly to cook or to wash in the stream. They had little time for socializing, so busy were they with never-ending chores.

After the nooning, the train started up again around 2 P.M. and continued until nearly 10 P.M. In the West, any moon at all during the night gives a bluish light sufficient for chores to be done. If Indians were suspected in the area, animals would be crowded into a wagon square or circle and each wagon chained to others. Guards were posted; they sat rather than stood so they would not be silhouetted. Shotguns were preferred to rifles by those on night duty, since in the near darkness such weapons were much more effective against raiding parties. Frequently, guards fell asleep after a long day on the trail; if caught in this dangerous lapse of duty, punishment varied from being forced to travel at the rear of the train to temporary exile from it. Yet despite the constant vigilance, an occasional horse would be stolen by a "sneaking redskin."

On the generally dry trail, people mostly slept under their wagons. The occasional rain proved both a blessing and a curse. The blessing was in the cool relief from the baking temperatures and the soft water prized for washing women's hair. The curse was that some prairie storms could be fierce, with violent winds, thunder, and lightning. Often St. Elmo's fire (a kind of static electricity) glowed on the horns of the cattle, sometimes spooking the beasts and leading to a stampede. Storms also could cause rivers to rise, delaying a crossing by two or three days. The rule of thumb when near a river was always to cross before bedding down, lest the water rise during the night. During a storm, prairie winds unbroken by trees would shake and rattle the wagons. On occasion, the storms would bring hailstones the size of eggs whitening the prairie and causing animals to flinch with pain when hit. Later prairie homesteaders would joke that the wind was so strong it blew down a barb wire fence.

Water was often scarce when the trail veered from the winding river. One trick used in dry areas was to swish a blanket through the heavy morning dew and then to wring out its precious contents into containers. Another was to dig shallow wells in dry stream beds, using a barrel to line the temporary well.

The pioneers generally were healthy people. In the days before antibiotic medicines, those who survived childhood diseases and accidents were hardy. Nonetheless, they had their troubles with illness. The "relax" disease, dysentery, was rampant. One cause was waters heavily impregnated with alkali. Lack of proper sanitation was another major factor. Not only was the condition physically weakening but it also could lead to sore buttocks, making a hard wagon seat or saddle an instrument of torture. Infection sometimes resulted, and boils might follow. Large blisters had to be painfully lanced. In his book *The Oregon Trail*, Francis Parkman gives a graphic and autobiographical description of this condition. Opiates provided some relief, at the risk of addiction. Fortunately, the dry climate and the flowing rivers meant that mosquitos and flies were seldom a problem.

As the wagon trains approached and entered the mountains, high altitude sickness was common, but most travellers became acclimated in time. Those with unsuspected respiratory and heart problems, however, were plagued by chest pains, shortness of breath, heart palpitation, headaches, faintness, dizziness, and nausea.

Unquestionably, the illness that was most feared on the trail was the gastrointestinal disease of cholera. Some became ill with it in the morning and died by noon; others lingered for as long as a few days. The bacterial disease, whose cause was then unknown, produced quick and complete dehydration, sending its victims into shock. We now know that it was transmitted orally, justifying the old medical warning against "fingers to feces." Conditions on the trail were ripe for such contagions, because with water scarce, dishes often were scraped clean only by sand, and hands remained unwashed after toilet. To the pioneers, cholera seemed an arbitrary and ominous danger because it would spread in one wagon but not in another. Knowing that it is caused almost exclusively by poor personal hygiene has removed the mystery.

Drownings were frequent; it is surprising how many who took the trail did not know how to swim. Gunshot wounds also were common, for most of the men who had never carried weapons before now prided themselves on being armed and ready for "Injuns." Sticking a pistol in their belt, they often discharged their guns accidentally. The gunslinger would be shot in the foot or in an even more embarrassing place.

Those who died—the young, the old, and the in between—were

nearly always buried on the trail. Sometimes their burial places were marked by a cross, but more often the train and cattle ran over the spot, obliterating the grave. Despite the grief at leaving behind an unmarked grave, the practice was done out of harsh necessity. Otherwise wolves would dig down to eat the corpse, or Indians would rob the grave of its belongings.

Once into the Oregon land, people who were ill or injured, as well as women who had become pregnant or had delivered on the trail could stop for examination at Dr. Whitman's mission at Wai-ilatpu, near Fort Walla Walla, established in 1836. Although it entailed a two-day ride off the trail, few missed the opportunity, and the stopover also provided a chance to restock the family medicine cabinet.

There were relatively few depredations by Indians on the Oregon Trail, and the larger trains mostly passed unscathed. The most common confrontations consisted of the red men standing near the trail begging for handouts of tobacco, food, and trinkets. This sight presented a sharp contrast to the Eastern and Rousseauean image of the noble savage and child of nature. Told to pay no attention, many women nonetheless pitied the beggars and slipped food to them, ignoring the views expressed in Captain Marcy's guidebook:

The Indians of the Plains, notwithstanding the encomiums that have been heaped upon their brethren who formerly occupied the Eastern States for their gratitude, have not, so far as I have observed, the most distant conception of that sentiment. You may confer numberless benefits upon them for years, and the more that is done for them, the more they expect. They do not seem to comprehend the motive which dictates an act of benevolence or charity, and they invariably attribute it to fear or the expectation of reward. When they make a present, it is with a view of getting more than its equivalent in return.[22]

Despite the many battles with Indians depicted in movies and books, during the peak years of 1840 through 1860, when a quarter-million people traversed the "Big Medicine Path," as the Indians called the Oregon Trail, only 362 emigrants were killed by Indians, and about 425 Indians were killed by whites.[23]

Hazards for the animals were considerably greater. Once the trains had passed the point where the North Platte River forked away from the mainstream, oxen began to drop, leaving their bones all along the way. The oxen were worked to death as they were driven through the soft, clinging sandy soil dragging their heavy loads. The sight of pile after pile of bones is recorded in many journals. Those that survived had to be watched carefully at water holes, for in some of them loco weed grew on the bottom. Uninformed herders, seeing the oxen with their heads in the water, would think that the animals were only drinking when they were eating the poisonous, leguminous plant. The inevitable consequence was a bloated belly and death.

Although the traditional epithet for oxen was "lowly," the travelling pioneers thought them most worthy, and many a woman wrote in her journal of her affection for this huge *bos mutus*. The burden on oxen was somewhat relieved by the practice of trading them for fresh ones at special stops along the way; the new owners would feed and rest the animals, profitably trading them to the next train several weeks later.

As Western travel increased, the government responded to pressure for greater protection by buying more forts from early traders or by building new ones at key points along the trail. These isolated posts offered respite from the rigors of the trek and an opportunity to pick up needed supplies or to consult with an occasional army doctor. As Captain Marcy's guidebook asserted, "It is our army that unites the chasm between the culture of civilization in the aspect of science, art, and social refinement, and the powerful simplicity of nature."[24]

One of the first (1848) and also most important forts was Fort Kearney, located on the Platte, 325 miles west of Independence. In its early days the fort consisted mostly of sod huts. Another was Fort Laramie, on the Laramie River at its intersection with the North Platte. Established as a fur trader's post in 1834, it was sold to the army in 1849. Abandoned in 1890, it has been restored as a national historic site. Visitors can tour the old officer housing, supply shops, kitchens, and recreational rooms, and see frontier life demonstrated by National Park Service personnel dressed in period costume. At last report, supplies of army hardtack from the 1860s were still available for sampling. Fort Laramie was as far west as Francis Parkman travelled before turning off to the south. (Despite his fame as author of *The Oregon Trail*, he never saw the most rugged part.)

Fort Hall, just inside present-day southeastern Idaho, also served as a rest area. It was started by Nathaniel Wyeth, the Boston ice merchant, who hoped to draw business from nearby rendezvous, whose promoters had broken a contract with him. He had few supplies to sell, however, and subsequently sold out to the Hudson's Bay Company. Farther on, Fort Boise was little more than a mark on the map.

The long trail brought out both the best and the worst in people. Some grew so angry at others that they separated from the train and went to California rather than Oregon. The prime example of trail dissension was the ill-fated Donner party, whose eighty-nine members headed for California in the summer of 1846. Their tragedy, enacted near beautiful Lake Tahoe, is worth recapitulating for it taught a valuable lesson to all who took to the trails.

The Donner party was engaged in constant bickering almost from the very start. One member, John Reed, even was found guilty of killing another and for his punishment was exiled from the party which included his wife and children. Once the train reached Fort Bridger they found themselves already behind schedule and gambled on gaining time by taking the Hastings Cutoff, a largely imaginary trail, written about by the author of the guide book that bears his name. At this particular time, Hastings was away leading another group and left word that he would mark the trail ahead and they should have no qualms in following it. Meeting more and more delays, the Donner group sent a party ahead to California, instructing it to return with more supplies. This group did get there and sent back supplies as well as two Indian guides to help lead the others. Not until late in the season, October 23, did the main train reach the foothills of the mighty Sierras, on the other side of which was their destination, the sunny Sacramento Valley. To get there, they had only to cross a high pass, now named Donner Pass. Normally the pass receives over thirty-one feet of snow a season, and as they attempted to reach it, an early storm overtook them, making them snowbound. They were still locked in the vastness of the mountains on December 16 with supplies nearly exhausted. Desperate, a party of fifteen volunteers left for help. They floundered through the pass to reach assistance but not before their own supplies ran out, forcing them to resort to cannibalism. The bodies eaten were those of four members who died. The two Indian guides refused to eat human flesh and themselves were killed and eaten.

Rescuers finally reached the main party on February 19, 1847, only to find the emigrants' ranks decimated as they, too, engaged in cannibalism. Later, those rescued explained how they shuffled around the meat of the bodies in order not to know if they were eating their own relatives. Of the original group of eighty-nine emigrants, only forty-five survived.

Fortunately, the Oregon trail saw no such disaster, but it too lacked road signs, and many wandered from its course seeking shortcuts. Most wagon trains, however, used natural landmarks to follow the trail, and each time an expected landmark came into view, a loud cheer went up from members of the wagon train, for each one was a sign of progress toward the distant goal.

Those who set out on the trail at Independence knew it was a hundred miles to the Kansas River ferry, manned by Delaware and Shawnee Indians. These Indians had learned the white man's needs and also that it was profitable to have a monopoly on supplying them. Later, Columbia River Indians too went into the ferry business as the pioneers took the river route to Portland.

At first, the Oregon Trail followed the well-worn Santa Fe route. Then, from the ferry, the trail headed northwest 150 miles to reach Fort Kearney and the broad and sometimes mighty Platte, a strange and braided river which often had to be crossed several times a day. (Present-day Interstate 80 follows the Platte and the old trail.) From this point the river and its north fork were followed 300 miles to Fort Laramie, passing on the way Chimney Rock, Courthouse Rock, and Scott's Bluff, the latter supposedly named after a trapper, Hiram Scott, who had died nearby. Each formation was distinctive, its silhouette projecting into the plains skyline. Wagon ruts from the trail still can be seen today in the area, a few miles past Fort Laramie in southeastern Wyoming near the Nebraska border. Register Cliff also is nearby, where emigrant after emigrant carved his or her name for posterity on its soft stone.

Midway between Fort Kearney and Fort Laramie, the true West began, a dry and arid land where mirages of all types were common. "Some pioneers observed ships skimming across the sands under full sail. Others reported mirages of large herds of buffalo and antelope. [One saw] a mirage railroad track elevated on pilings and also marveled at the flocks of water birds with brilliant plumage that he glimpsed beside a silvery lake in the same vision. . . . Sometimes, western travelers encountered a phantom army."[25]

As the pioneers entered the dry country, the terrain almost immediately became hilly and rough. Although the real mountains still lay ahead, travellers began to have an inkling of what was to come.

Approximately ten days' travel out of Fort Laramie brought the pioneers to Independence Rock, another monument on which many carved their names and time of passing. From there, they followed the Sweetwater River toward the continental divide at South Pass, still a hundred miles and eight to ten days away. When they sighted Plume Rocks, they knew they were near the pass. This marker was the only indication that the divide at seventy-five hundred feet had been reached, as the rise at South Pass was gradual. At last the travellers were on the western slopes where the rivers flowed toward the Pacific, and they eagerly turned southwest toward Fort Bridger, where supplies could be replenished and oxen could be shoed by the mountain man-blacksmith Jim Bridger.

Their next destination was northwest along the Bear River toward

Soda Springs and just beyond, Fort Hall. The fort, near present-day Pocatello, was situated on the thousand-mile Snake River, which has its source in the mountains of Yellowstone Park and empties into the river of destination, the mighty Columbia.

In the early days of the Oregon Trail, as we have seen, Fort Hall offered the wayfarers little more than a few trading goods and some half-accurate conversation about the way ahead. Oregon was still nearly eight hundred miles and eighty-five days away. The next major stop was Fort Boise, a Hudson's Bay post built on the point where the Boise River joined the Snake. From there, the trail led over the Blue Mountains to the dalles and then on to the Willamette Valley to Oregon City and points south.

At the Raft River crossing fifty miles downstream from Fort Hall, the pioneers came to a point just about equidistant from Oregon and California. This was the last place where one could choose between destinations without backtracking. California or Oregon? The decision was a tough one and not only wagon trains split over it; families did so as well, with close relatives going in different directions. Most chose Oregon, although the toughest part of the trek was still ahead. Instead of high plains and low mountains, they would be passing between "fourteeners" (peaks fourteen thousand feet high) and negotiating deep canyons and raging rivers. The pioneers' immediate goal was the great Columbia River.

Once there, they faced another choice, whether to raft down that mighty current directly to their Willamette Valley destination or to take the rough overland trail. Whichever route was selected, travellers were sure to wish they had chosen the other, for both were treacherous. Rafts with their cargo of top-heavy wagons frequently turned over, and Indian helpers regularly defied death in trying to assist the pioneers. Once the Barrow Road was built south of Mount Hood, considerably easing overland travel, only a few rafted.

When they had reached the mouth of the Willamette, the would-be settlers were graciously received at Fort Vancouver by the chief factor of that Hudson's Bay Company post, Dr. John McLoughlin. He was as large in spirit as he was of body, and he presided over the nearly self-sufficient post with its farms, seeds, cattle, and tools, all well supplied by Hudson's Bay Company ships. Gratefully, the emigrants drew heavily on these stores, as McLoughlin offered generous credit terms.

Having reached their destination at such great cost, the hardy pioneers might be expected to stay there, their restless spirits satiated with travel. Nevertheless, when news arrived of the California gold rush at Sutter's Fort in 1848-1849, many brand-new Oregonians left everything and went to seek their fortunes in gold in California rather than in land in Oregon. Such was the American spirit.

The Santa Fe and Oregon trails were overland routes travelled by streams of people for diverse purposes. But one trail that changed the course of Western development marked the passage of one group with a single goal. It was the Mormon Trail, blazed by leaders of the Church of Jesus Christ of Latter-Day Saints as they sought to find a refuge from persecution and establish a homeland to be called Deseret. "No history of the American West can ignore the Mormons [and their] handcart migration . . . because whatever special religious significance it may have had for its people, it symbolizes for all of interested mankind the energy, the determination, the perseverance of those religiously inspired people who endured fourteen hundred miles of desert and mountain, heat and snow, disease and hardship."[26]

The church was founded by Joseph Smith, born in Vermont in 1805. He claimed a series of visions as a teenager in Palmyra, New York, and in his early twenties he produced *The Book of Mormon*, which he presented as his translation of ancient records revealed to him by an angel. Smith taught, against the prevailing Calvinism, that mankind was perfectible; and he dreamed, in concert with the many nineteenth-century utopian movements, of establishing a theocratic community separate from the corrupt secular world.

In 1830 he published his book and began his church with six members. A fiery and charismatic speaker, Smith soon attracted many followers—and a great deal of opposition. In the first of their many uprootings, the Latter-Day Saints moved to Kirtland, Ohio, where their exclusive claims and increasing numbers, as well as the hard times that followed the panic of 1837, made the newcomers unwelcome. They fled to establish a new Zion in northern Missouri, where the governor soon called them public enemies and declared that Mormons should be "exterminated or driven from the State, if necessary, for the public good."[27]

Smith next led his followers to Illinois, where they founded the town of Nauvoo. State officials proved accommodating, and Smith himself held several political offices. The city soon became the largest in the state, with a population of fifteen thousand, and in its center a huge temple was constructed. The Mormons flourished—until internal conflict arose. When Smith published a new revelation advocating polygamy for church members, his followers split into warring factions. In the ensuing turmoil and violence, Smith and his brother Hyrum were jailed in nearby Carthage, where, in 1844, they were dragged out and murdered by a mob.

While one group of church dissidents migrated to Michigan, others sought a new leader to take Smith's place. The choice fell on Brigham Young, a plain man of forty-three whose lack of formal education did not detract from his great practical ability. Young drew his troubled people together during the fall of 1846 and, in February 1847, he moved them across the frozen Mississippi into Iowa, to a temporary site named Camp Israel. There they made plans to resettle "somewhere west."

What Young planned at the time has been much debated. It is known that he had read Frémont's works and was familiar with Hastings's travel guide. Whether or not he had a specific destination in mind, he knew that there was an isolated area beyond Colorado and south of Wyoming. In any event, his planning for the trek was masterly.

While waiting for spring and travelling weather, Young organized his people. They would move in small platoon-like groups, each with its own leader. These leaders were subject to higher leaders, with ultimate authority resting in Young. Because the people had to sell their farms and property for a pittance, they would have to work for wages along the way. As they travelled, they hired out as itinerant laborers, plowing, splitting wood, and running ferries.

Most helpful was their encounter with General Kearny, who was heading west to settle political problems in California. Needing more troops, Kearny recruited the famous Mormon Battalion from the displaced saints. Kearny paid the Mormons fifty thousand dollars in advance salaries and clothing allowances; the money was put into the general fund. The enlistment meant a severe loss of manpower, so that women had to fulfill many traditionally male tasks, but the arrangement got the Mormons through the crisis.

On April 9, 1847, Young and 148 persons set out in seventy-three wagons to establish base camps along the route for the use of the following main party. Calling themselves a Pioneer Band, the mostly male members of the group were individually chosen for their particular skills. Together, they formed the nucleus of a community.

In the beginning, the group suffered some organizational lapses and the fellowship was marred by much petty stealing. Soon, however, Young ironed out his problems and became as effective as any leader of a migration in history. Tight and detailed schedules ruled everything. At 5:00 A.M. a bugle call awakened the party to prayers, followed by breakfast and camp-breaking. At 8:30 P.M. the march was stopped. After supper, all bedded down at an appointed time.

Because of the precision of the operation, the band progressed twenty miles a day, five to eight miles more than most caravans. By June, they were at the Missouri River and established winter quarters on the Nebraska side. By fall, twelve thousand of Young's followers would gather there. The site, appropriately named Mormon Crossing, is now a state camp ground.

The trek was planned in an orderly step-by-step way. Following in the wake of the advance party, some members were designated to establish small farms to provide food and shelter for later travellers. Groups moved from one sanctuary to the next, all the way to the "gathering place," the promised land beyond the Rockies.

The Mormons got along well with the Indians, helping the red men through the winter with food and shelter. In turn, Mormons were given rights to set up their camps on Indian-controlled land. Further, where many whites considered the Native American merely a population destined to be displaced, like the inhabitants of the original land of Canaan, the Mormons considered the Indians to be a lost tribe of Israel, the Lamanites. There was a place for the Indian in the Mormon world, and many Indians converted to the faith of "these peculiar people," as Mormons called themselves.

To avoid problems with the "Gentiles," that is, non-Mormons, the followers of Young travelled the north side of the Platte, pioneering that route instead of taking the Oregon Trail on the south side of the river. The Mormon group included New England and Midwestern farmers, as well as English immigrants recruited by Young when he visited industrial slums there. Unlike the Oregon-bound, many of Young's followers were socially marginal people, and to them Young was another Moses, leading them to Zion and the New Jerusalem.

Along the way they met Pierre De Smet, the Jesuit missionary, who treated Young kindly and gave him advice. Young was grateful, and a tribute to the Roman Catholic priest appears on a monument in Salt Lake City, the City of the Saints. De Smet's views on the Mormons changed over time, however. At first he praised them, writing in 1851 of "the success of the Mormons, who in less than five years have changed the face of a frightful desert, and live with great abundance."[28] In 1854, however, he was comparing them to the anti-Christian and militaristic Mohammedans while noting that "the sect of the Mormons is making extraordinary progress in the United States."[29] Finally, in 1858 he told his editor, "This fantastical sect will finally repose only outside of all other jurisdiction. It will master and subject all, unless it is mastered and expelled in season."[30]

Leaving the Platte, the Mormons followed the Oregon Trail to Fort Bridger, taking the Hastings Cutoff from there. At the fort, Bridger strongly advised them not to cross the towering Wasatch and Uinta ranges for, even if they managed the feat, they would only find alkaline plains and the Great Salt Lake beyond, an infertile place if ever there was one. As a parting shot, the mountain man "offered Brigham Young a thousand dollars for the first bushel of corn grown there."[31] A real enmity had sprung up between the two, eventually to climax in the burning of Bridger's post by the Danites, a band of Mormon avenging angels.

Heading toward the Green River, Young met the Mormon elder Samuel Brennan, who was returning east after taking 269 Mormons by boat to California. He, too, advised Young to change the course and instead to set his sights on California, but Young would not hear of it.

On July 12, the advance band of Mormons were nearing their goal, but Young was flat on his back with "mountain fever" and was being carried on a stretcher. Rather than delay, Young directed an advance group of twenty-three wagons to struggle ahead. This group made its way through Echo and Emigration canyons, emerging ten days later to view their Deseret, their Land of the Honeybee. Soon after, Young reached the spot and, according to legend, rose from his stretcher to declare, "This is the place!" This historic date was July 24, 1847, and the Mormon leader's four-month journey was at its end.

Although the land before them at first was parched and cracked, a sudden and unusual rain made it bloom. The event was regarded as a miracle, and the group, following what they saw as "God's example," adopted irrigation as the means to sustain that bloom with their own crops. Planting flourished, and by the fall of that year, over eighteen hundred saints were in the land. His base established, Young returned east to help and encourage others to follow. On the way, he met fifteen hundred more converts trailing thirty-five hundred head of cattle. Young saw that his work was successful and would be permanent.

The theocratic state that Young established and called Deseret was a kind of collective and cooperative. He followed the rule of "From each according to his ability; to each according to his need." He shunned individualism, believing that it worked against the common good. His religious center firmly established, Brigham Young set up a Perpetual Emigration Fund to assist others to come to Deseret, and he sent missionaries out all over the world to make converts to the cause. Sixteen thousand Europeans heeded that call and came in the years 1849 to 1855. For a time, prosperity was the rule, especially when Forty-niners stopped in to replenish their supplies. The prospectors, however, felt that the goods were sold at immorally high prices, and enmities once again began to develop between the Mormons and the outside world.

On another occasion, divine providence again seemed to come to the aid of the Mormons. A swarm of crickets or grasshoppers descended on their crops, ravishing everything in sight. But at the height of the plague, thousands of seagulls flew in to devour the crickets. Despite this intervention, however, the remaining crops didn't succeed.

A new crisis arose as the rising numbers of emigrants threatened to deplete the Emigration Fund. Young struck upon a novel idea to get his followers to Utah, an idea that led to the famous "Handcart Companies" that went West between 1856 and 1860. The first companies started from Iowa City and faced a thirteen hundred mile trip. The brigades were organized meticulously, each brigade of from one to three hundred persons broken down into groups of ten. Each group of ten was given handcarts, one wagon for general supplies, one yoke of oxen, two milk cows, and one tent.

The handcarts were made exclusively of wood to save expense, although a few had iron tires. Six to seven feet long and four to five feet wide, they only weighed about sixty pounds and could carry over four hundred pounds of cargo, mostly food and personal belongings. Built like Chinese rickshaws, the carts had two poles extending forward from the body, joined by a curved bar against which two men leaned to push the vehicle forward. Sometimes one man pushed in front while the other pushed from the rear.

Only a religious vision could inspire such an effort, and American determination could not be better exemplified than by these human draft animals pursuing their daily goal. To keep up their spirits, they sang songs like this:

> Who cares to go with the wagons?
> Not we who are free and strong!
> Our faith and arms, with a right good will
> Shall pull our carts along.[32]

Despite the courage and overall success of the handcart companies, there were many deaths. On one occasion, a party that had started late got caught in the snows near South Pass and Devil's Gate in Wyoming. Rescue teams were sent from Salt Lake, but they arrived only to find two hundred handcarters frozen to death.

Brigham Young made many contributions to history, but the handcart brigade was unique. "Nearly 3,000 people were members of handcart companies, employing 653 carts and 40 supply wagons. The total loss of life in this venture was about 250."[33] The Mormon experience reflected the spirit of a people who, although oppressed and persecuted, nonetheless had the gumption—and the organizational skills—to grind out a better life for themselves. In part, their character was created by the demands of the American West, just as they reciprocally helped to produce that West. The Mormon Trail became a strand in the legend that shapes our sense of ourselves.,

7. The Military in the West
Glory, Shame, and Pathos

As more and more white Americans pushed westward, Indian resentment of them increased. Game on which the red man depended was killed or scattered, new diseases appeared that decimated the tribes, and the Indians' already hard lot was turning impossible. Later, when treaties were made and broken and white authorities insisted that Indians stay on reservations that were often located in areas and climates far removed from their ancestral homelands, the red man rebelled. His responses were various and unpredictable but frequently took the form of hit and run guerrilla actions against whites. An occasional clash or uprising here, a few more there, and soon fights between whites and Indians became almost customary. In the 1860s and 1870s, a rash of arguments, grievances, and misunderstandings erupted in bloodshed on the frontier and became known as the Indian Wars of the West.

These encounters were not wars in any traditional sense. Mostly they were skirmishes, small pitched battles, quick-strike maneuvers. Many were called massacres, but the word was too charged emotionally, and its application tended to depend on whose side was involved. The word was most accurately used to describe a number of fights in which most of the losses—and some were considerable—were confined to one side.

The simplest way to describe the conflicts between the white and red man is to call them "fights." In fact, the army itself was so confused about what to term these fights that occurred over a period of forty years that its Indian Campaign badges were not issued until 1905, in the twentieth century!

Some of the fights were so small that they produced no casualties. But the Indian did not necessarily fight to kill; collecting coups was a valid enough reason for action. Many fights were almost inconsequential to the larger picture; they mattered only to those killed and those who mourned the dead. Although the fights sometimes were between civilians and Indians, such as the second Battle of Adobe Walls, most were frays between Indians and the army or territorial militia.

Some sort of frame is needed to bring into relationship these individual yet connected events. We will take a close look at the U.S. Army in the West and at some of its notable encounters with the Native American. There are countless stories of glory and shame, heroism and suffering on both sides of these encounters. Some of the stories have entered our national legend, others are little known. All are important to an understanding of our history and the proud and bitter legacy that has come down to us today.

With the establishment of the major trails West—especially the Santa Fe Trail to the Southwest and the Oregon Trail to the Northwest, the army was called upon to protect the whites who travelled and to help keep the peace for those who settled. Often, a show of force was sufficient to do the job; at other times, drastic and deadly action was needed. The thousands of square miles under the army protectorate were completely disproportionate to its relatively few men and matériel. In 1864, for instance, the army in the West had only five thousand officers and men, a figure that rose by 1870 to about thirty-seven thousand. Fluctuations occurred from time to time, and perhaps the overall average number of men in the field before 1890 was twenty-five thousand officers and men. Who were the men who made up these abstract numbers? Why were they there and what was their life like?

Before the Civil War, soldiers mostly were army regulars. Would-be privates signed up for the princely sum of thirteen dollars per month, of which one dollar was withheld until the end of the enlistment period. An additional twenty-five cents was withheld every two weeks as a compulsory contribution to the Soldier's Home. Soldiers also were charged for equipment lost or broken through abuse or carelessness.

After the Civil War, advancement in rank was virtually impossible because the war had produced so many brevets (higher, but temporary ranks) that any opening was immediately filled. When death or retirement opened up another slot, a surplus of brevets rushed to fill it. Retirement pay was given for the highest rank attained rather than for the rank at the time of retirement, so for many, a few more years of service, even at a lower paying rank, were worthwhile.

Even with deductions, take-home pay was generally sufficient for soldiers to get by on. Foreigners made up a heavy percentage of enlistments; at times, more than a third of the enlisted men were foreign. They joined for various reasons. Some wanted to learn English and get paid while doing so; others wanted to see the country; still others had been soldiers in their own lands and that was what they knew. Some enlistees were drifters who used the army as free passage West; once there, they deserted for the gold fields, absconding with good equipment to boot. For them, the army was little more than a grubstake.

Desertion was a continuing and major problem. For example, during the year ending October 1, 1867, some seven hundred of the famed Seventh Cavalry took "French leave"[1] and, in 1871 fully a third deserted. Even severe punishment did not seem a deterrent. In earlier days, deserters were branded with a "D" on their left flank, marking them for life. Later, this cruel practice was halted, as was flogging, but leg irons were used and left their own scars, rawing the ankles that wore them. Another excruciating punishment was the hanging of a man by his thumbs. Custer reinstituted the rule that those caught in the act of desertion be shot, and this order was carried out at least once within his company. (Yet, when some deserters were wounded, Custer publicly denied them medical attention but privately permitted it.) Confinement to the guardhouse could be the worst punishment of all during summer in the high plains or the desert southwest. Fort Union, now a preserved ruin in northeastern New Mexico, must have offered such a hell of heat. The return of deserters was encouraged by a bounty of fifty dollars paid to civilians who turned them in to the authorities.

Life in the army of the West was a tough and grinding existence. At some posts, the men suffered abuses at the hands of arbitrary commanders. The abuses documented in Richard Dana's *Two Years before the Mast* could have been duplicated in army life as well.

Combat duty was not equally distributed. Most units actually saw little action, but some were almost constantly in combat. Before it could fight Indians, however, the army had to find them, and that was no easy task for white soldiers from the East or South. To assist the troops, Indians were employed as scouts and trackers. The saying was, "It takes an Indian to track an Indian." Because of the many different branches within the same tribe of Indians, scouts seldom considered such employment to be disloyal. Indeed, Sitting Bull was killed, apparently with no regret, by scouts from among his own people. The officers Frank and Luther North even had their own special detachment of Pawnees who made excellent soldier scouts.

Often, Indian scouts did not fight and were not expected to. Their job was to lead the army to its foe and their reward was the spoils of war. Some soldiers who were frankly mercenaries also fought for spoils, and Custer himself brought home a tipi and horses from his battle at the Washita. Indian scouts sometimes engaged in fighting, however, and fought bravely and well. On occasion they practically saved the day for the white soldiers, as did the Crow scouts with General Crook in the Battle of the Rosebud.

The camps or forts to which soldiers were assigned varied mostly in the degree of boredom they engendered. Some were stockaded, although most were not. Few Indians would attack a strong post manned by professional soldiers with ready cannon. Still, on rare occasions, Indians did attack a fort.

The earliest soldiers in the West were infantry or dragoons (mounted infantry). Later, they were joined by cavalry units.

The typical day in the life of a cavalry man was: reveille, 5:30; breakfast and stables, 6; sick call and fatigue, 7:30; boots and saddles for morning parade (mounted and in full dress), 8; adjutant's call, 8:20; guard mounting and drill, 10:15; recall, 11:45; dinner at noon; squad drill for recruits, 1:15-2:15; troop drill (dismounted), 2:30-3:30; stables, 4-5:15: retreat and evening dress parade, sunset. Then after officers' and N.C.O. school several evenings a week, they called it a day with tattoo at nine.[2]

As this schedule shows, routine characterized life on the post. As one soldier put it, "We use the shovel more than the sabre"; one nickname for the forts was "government workhouses."[3] When soldiers weren't drilling and training, they were busy building roads, escorting wagon trains or payroll wagons, and accompanying visiting dignitaries.[4]

A rigid social wall divided enlisted men from officers, except for an occasional clandestine affair between enlisted men and lonely officers' wives.

Stationed in remote areas with nowhere to go but the desert or dusty plains, soldiers turned to alcohol for temporary solace. Excess drinking was rampant, with all its consequences. Gambling also was a common pastime and led to a large number of sore losers who then became troublemakers. Physical disease was a constant danger, involving not only uncomfortable ills like the "bloody flux" and boils but those such as cholera and smallpox that resulted in swift and certain death. The Fort Buford cemetery record has some interesting entries.

1866. Grave 89. George Hallman—Private. Died of acute dysentery.
1867. Grave 90. Adan Dybb—Private. Died of chronic bronchitis.
1867. Grave 91. Cornelius Coughlin—Private. Killed by Indians.
No grave no. Roach—Citizen. Killed [with a black man named Tom] by Indians. [The teamsters] were beaten to death with whiffle trees taken from

one of their own wagons. Twenty-one arrows were sticking in each corpse, both were scalped.
1876. No grave no. Charles McAllister—Suicide.[5]

Other causes of death listed were dropsy, brain inflammation, palsy, consumption, and accidental shooting. Among soldiers in the West 8 percent of the deaths were attributed to suicide.[6]

The monotony of the soldiers' lives was broken up by ball playing, boxing, horseshoe pitching, and hunting. Contests of all kinds were strongly encouraged by post commanders. Companies even competed to see which could grow the biggest watermelon or squash. Any activity brought some relief from the tedium.

The occasional visiting dignitaries were especially welcome because they promised to disrupt the culinary routine as well as the daily grind. Even an inspector general could embarrass the cook into serving something better than the usual fare. Mountain men frequented the posts, and soldiers looked forward to their stories, observations, and yarns, treating them like travelling entertainers.

The Western tours of artists like George Catlin and Karl Bodmer were remembered for years. Their work seemed almost magic to many—not least to the Indians. One red man who sat for Catlin worried about being painted with his eyes open, fearing that he would never be able to sleep again! A frequent and welcome visitor was the Jesuit missionary Pierre De Smet; one unusual caller was the English nobleman Sir George Gore.

There were always a number of civilians at the forts. Some were wayfarers stopping over for supplies; others were resident contractors engaged for such services as teamster work, haycutting, or supplying wood.

Unscheduled but frequent diversions were contributed by Indians, who would raid the horse herds near the fort or harass the units out gathering hay or wood. Renegade whites also caused trouble. When they would hijack a paywagon, troops would enthusiastically set out to pursue them. These chases were not usually dangerous and offered a welcome diversion. In fact, many forts functioned more like sheriff's offices than battle commands. They represented stability in a land of constant change.

The army was assigned a great many tasks in addition to keeping the peace and fighting Indians. It surveyed and mapped the terrain. It safeguarded the railroads and telegraph lines and made many reconnaissances like Custer's foray into the Black Hills. When Yellowstone National Park was established in 1872, the army took over its administration, protecting the animals from poachers, fighting fires, and escorting tourists.

Serving in the West were four companies of black soldiers—two infantry and two cavalry units—all with white commanders. The troops were known as "brunets"; the Indians called them "buffalo soldiers" because their kinky hair resembled buffalo hair.

The most famous army fort on the high plains was Fort Laramie. The diet there was a near-constant round of bacon, beans, and beef. The byword of the cavalry was "forty miles a day on beans and hay."[7] The menu varied only when a hunter brought in a pronghorn or buffalo or perhaps a brace of tasty rabbits. Later, professional hunters like Buffalo Bill were hired to secure such provisions regularly. Soldiers could also buy a few special treats from the post sutler.

Hardtack was a standby, although it was often riddled with worms. "Meat's meat!" was the saying, as the men gulped down their crackers. One lot of hardtack biscuits first issued in the West in 1867 was found to be dated 1861. (As we have noted, the reconstructed Fort Laramie still had a supply of nineteenth-century hardtack for tourists to sample when this book was written.)

After the Civil War, such outdated army surplus—clothing and weapons as well as food—flooded Western posts. Even after newer weapons had reached the Indians, budget-minded Eastern bureaucrats were insisting that the army use up its old guns before being issued more recent models. This policy resulted in unnecessary deaths.

That was not the only misunderstanding between those who directed the army from the East and those who ran it in the West. The East believed that the troops could live off the land, not appreciating the difference between the favorable climate and soil in the East and the arid desert of the West.

There was also conflict between the army and Eastern civilians, especially those influenced by the philosophical-theological movement of American transcendentalism. Sympathizing with the mythic and romantic Rousseauian concept of the noble savage, the Easterners constantly criticized the army's dealing with the Indians. The army took the more empirical view of those liable to attack and looked upon the Indian as an aggressive and brutal enemy. Nevertheless, many soldiers perceived that the red man was seeking to protect his people and homeland, both of which were being destroyed by whites. It was not hard, in moments of reflection, to imagine how it would be to walk in his moccasins.

United States Indian policy was long plagued by conflicts of authority. The Bureau of Indian Affairs was created as early as 1832, the year in which the Blackhawk War ended. It was placed first in the War Department and then, in 1849, in the Department of the Interior. Differences of viewpoint and philosophy between the bureau

and the departments and between the Eastern headquarters and the
Western commands made for exasperation and chaos on many occasions.

In this chapter, we will focus on the four decades between 1850
and 1890, the time of most frequent Indian-army encounters. The year
1890 marked the official close of the frontier. Confrontations were
most common from 1869 to 1875, the period when "there were some
200 pitched battles between the Army and the Indians."[8] From the
end of the Civil War to the last fight between soldiers and Indians at
Leech Lake, Minnesota, in 1898, there were 938 fights.[9]

These cold statistics might seem to indicate, as one writer dryly
observed, that a soldier could expect to be in one fight during a five-
year enlistment.[10] Further, killing Indians was expensive business. It
was estimated that in 1866, approximately sixty thousand dollars was
spent in killing one Native American.[11] Then, as now, peace was less
costly than war! While the numbers of deaths in the West are not
overwhelming in comparison with casualties on the scale of the Second World War, it is poignantly true that an individual death is always
final. Events and policies that lead to the deaths of irreplaceable persons acquire thereby a somber aspect that must pervade any discussion of them.

The vast migrations to Oregon and the Mormon Deseret in Utah
made 1850 a much travelled year. Inevitably, the Indians reacted with
alarm to so many emigrants passing through their lands. To minimize
friction, a conference was called in southeast Wyoming. Convening
at Fort Laramie on September 15, 1851, the meeting worked out an
agreement that was variously known as the Fort Laramie Treaty, Fitzpatrick's Treaty, or the Treaty of Horse Creek. Bringing in thousands
of Indians from far and wide, Thomas Fitzpatrick himself was a drawing card, for he had been a long-time mountain man known for fairness in his trade with the Indians. Generous gifts to be distributed
also encouraged attendance. Old Brokenhand—three fingers had
been blown off by an exploding weapon—served as Indian commissioner.

It was no easy matter to prevent hereditary enemies from seeking
revenge upon each other at the affair. Among the whites present were
a veritable Who's Who of the West. Jim Bridger was there, as was
Pierre De Smet and Chief Washakie of the Snakes.

The purpose of the conference was to make peace not only between Indian and white but between warring factions of the Indians
as well. To help calm relations between Indians the treaty tried to
establish borders between the vast tracts of land used by each tribe.
To ease the passage of settlers, the treaty provided grants to the In-

dians of fifty thousand dollars a year, to be paid in annuities. If safe passage along the Oregon Trail was guaranteed by the Indians, these grants would continue for fifty years. Many of those attending signed the document on September 17, 1851. Everyone understood that Indians who violated the terms of the treaty would be subject to loss of annuities.

There was one hitch at the end of the conference. The wagons carrying the goods to be distributed had not arrived. Some Indians suspected trickery, but fortunately the wagons did show up three days later, on September 20, and the promised goods were distributed the next day. With the treaty signed and goods given out, a number of chiefs were invited to go to Washington to meet the Great White Father who had provided such a largess. President Fillmore presented medals to the Indian leaders, and they returned to the plains impressed with the white man's power and their own importance.

When the treaty came before the Senate, however, the upper house "reduced the annuity period to fifteen years but increased the amount of goods to seventy thousand dollars."[12] This amended version was never agreed to by the Indians.

Peace was short-lived. Three years later, in the summer of 1854, four thousand Indians were gathered around Fort Laramie, awaiting their annuity handouts. What happened proved to be the first major conflict of the army with the Teton (western branch) Sioux, and it caused a blood feud that lasted for decades. Details of the story are still disputed but the essentials are clear.

On August 17, 1854, a Mormon wagon train was approaching Fort Laramie when a cow owned by one of the pioneers fell behind, from either lameness or fatigue. The Indians claimed that it wandered into a nearby Miniconjou Sioux camp where it was promptly slaughtered and eaten. A man named High Forehead acted as butcher.

The Mormons presented a slightly different version[13] in reporting the incident to the Fort Laramie commander, Lieutenant Hugh B. Fleming. Out of West Point only two years, Fleming had about seventy-five men under his command. He had had troubles with the Miniconjou a year earlier (perhaps his own fault) and he responded with determination to do something about the "thievery." On the day the Mormons had reported their loss, a Sioux chief, Conquering Bear, came in to discuss the incident himself. He was concerned that he might not get his annuities because one of his tribe had violated the treaty. Indicating his desire to follow the letter of the law, Conquering Bear offered to bring the cow killer to the fort. Apparently this was unacceptable to Fleming, who wanted to arrest the cow killer with full ceremony. He ordered Lieutenant John L. Grattan, one year out of West Point, to take a detail of twenty-seven privates and one interpreter to the camp to make the arrest. By this time, High Forehead had fled to the camp of the nearby Brulés.

Grattan took along two cannon, which he cautiously loaded along the way. Negotiations were started as the party marched. Conquering Bear reported the flight of the culprit and indicated that if High Forehead didn't want to give himself up, he could not be made to do so. Accordingly, the chief offered horses to Grattan to make up for the dead cow, but was refused. Conquering Bear then appealed to Grattan's sympathy, telling him how a member of a previous emigrant train had taken pot shots at his people, wounding an Indian child. A stubborn Grattan only saw his authority being challenged. It did not help that negotiations and demands were being carried on through an interpreter, Lucine Auguste. Auguste not only had a reputation for hating the Miniconjou but also was pretty well drunk at this time. Those who understood the language said he called the Indians foul names and almost challenged them to take on the soldiers.

Grattan became impatient and marched his men and cannon directly to the middle of the Brulé camp. There he was said to have pointed the cannon at the tent of High Forehead and, when the fugitive did not appear, had his men level their rifles at the Indians, apparently in an attempted bluff. Someone, from which side is not known, fired a shot and all hell broke loose. The cannon fired, drawing swarms of Indians into the fray, while the soldiers broke and ran to get out of the camp. The enraged Indians jumped the soldiers, killing and later mutilating them. Only one wounded soldier managed to make his way back to the fort, but he died a few days later. Thirty men were killed over one disputed cow—and the matter was not over yet.

The furious Indians went on to raid a nearby fur company post, taking the annuities stored there. Lieutenant Fleming, anticipating an attack upon the fort itself, drew his forty men together to defend it. The Indians, however, dispersed with goods in hand and hatred for whites in their hearts. The Indians began to carry out sporadic raids in vengeance, as hostilities resumed once more on the high plains.

In a final ironic twist, the Indian commissioner, who was away from the fort at the time, later ruled that the army had no jurisdiction in the affair of the cow. It was a clear instance of the inability of the Bureau of Indian Affairs and the army to work together. The army became resentful, for it seemed to be damned if it did, and damned if it didn't. The army was put into many such no-win situations and slowly built up its own list of grievances.

To maintain the white man's authority, General William Selby Harney was ordered to mount a punitive expedition against the Indians. The situation was to seesaw in this manner for the next several decades.

The Tennessee-born Harney, for whom the highest peak in the Black Hills is named, was recalled from a vacation in Europe to take charge of operations in the West. Marching his nearly six hundred troops out of Fort Leavenworth, he set out to demonstrate to the Sioux that they could not trifle with the U.S. government. He went after the Brulé village that had sheltered High Forehead and located it in southwestern Nebraska in the Blue Water Creek Valley. It was known as Little Thunder's village, and there on September 3, 1855, "the troops killed 80 warriors, wounded five, and captured 70 women and children."[14] (Some historians put the Indian dead at 136, but the lower figure probably is more accurate. In reporting battles, each side tends to exaggerate the other's casualties.) This action also is known as the Battle of Ash Hollow. Tourists on Highway 26 in west central Nebraska pass the site as they go from Ogallala to Yellowstone National Park. Few who see the historical marker can imagine the stench of death that once rose from that beautiful valley. Harney, a no-nonsense soldier, pursued the Sioux until they were willing to have a conference and repledge themselves to the provisions of the 1851 treaty made at Fort Laramie. On this front, relative peace prevailed for almost a decade.

Earlier, I referred to the Minnesota Uprising of 1862 as an example of problems between Indians and whites in the early 1860s. A closer look at this tragedy will help us to understand the battles that followed.

In the late eighteenth century, the Sioux had been crowded out of the woodlands of Wisconsin by the Chippewa and other tribes and forced to make their way on the barren plains. Those who lived in eastern Minnesota were known as the Santee Sioux. Like the other Sioux, when the horse appeared they became expert riders and ruled the plains. But once again, they were crowded out of their land, this time by the whites who were moving into their territory. Most of the Minnesota settlers were Scandinavians and Germans. Finding the new countryside similar to the land they had left, they established centers such as New Ulm in south central Minnesota.

The bloody affair of the Minnesota uprising was precipitated, like so many others, by corruption and incompetence within the Indian agencies. The summer of 1862, presaging an unusually harsh winter to come, was short and cool, and food was scarce. In July, the Indian agency had food but would not distribute it because the supplier had not yet received payment from the East. The hungry Indians pleaded that they needed their annuities and needed them right then, despite government red tape. Desperate, they went to another agency to state their case at a council and were rebuffed once more. Indeed, the unsympathetic agent, Andrew Myrick, suggested that they eat grass and their own excrement to tide them over. The Indians erupted in rage, plundering agencies, forts, and villages and taking a number of women captive. Four to eight hundred whites were slaughtered, many being horribly mutilated. (A plausible estimate of white dead was 644.) The trader Myrick was found dead, his mouth stuffed with grass. The worst massacre west of the Mississippi River now terrorized whites over a twelve thousand square mile area; thirty thousand settlers fled their homes and farms. General Henry H. Sibley (inventor of the famous army tent stove) and General Alfred Sully were sent with troops to drive the Sioux from southern Minnesota. The Battle of Wood Lake was decisive, and many white captives were returned. In punishment, well over two hundred Indians were condemned to be hanged in a public square in Mankato, Minnesota. The sentences of many were commuted by President Lincoln, however, and thirty-eight were hanged on the day after Christmas, 1862, in the largest mass execution in U.S. history.[15] Death by hanging was abhorrent to Indians, for many of them believed that it prevented the spirit of the warrior from leaving his body.

Two years later in Colorado Territory, another massacre occurred when whites went on a rampage. Known as the Sand Creek Massacre, it was carried out by a group of hundred-day territorial volunteers led by a former Methodist minister. His name was John M. Chivington and he had preached from the Good Book all the way from his birthplace in Ohio to Colorado. There he continued preaching to miners, set up a Sunday School, and helped to build the community.

Several years before the massacre, Chivington, who was well-liked by influential people, was asked by the governor to serve as a chaplain in a Colorado militia unit being set up to aid the Union army. To the governor's surprise, Chivington boasted that he was a fighting man and asked for a commission instead. His request honored, the fighting parson distinguished himself against Texas Confederate sympathizers at the Battle of Glorietta Pass in New Mexico. The victory was the beginning of the end for Confederates in the West. Chivington next fought Indians, and the thrill of it seems to have gotten into his blood. He was indeed a fighting man.

On June 4, 1864, the sleepy town of Denver witnessed a horror that unnerved the citizenry and turned their fear and anger on the Indians. On that day, four mutilated bodies of whites were brought into the city and placed on public exhibition. They were the corpses of a family—J. Hungate, who ranched thirty miles southeast of Denver, his wife, and their two daughters. One girl was four years old, the other an infant. Feelings already had been running high against the Cheyenne and Arapaho, who were refusing to give up their hunting grounds for life on a reservation. A clamor for revenge rent the air, directed not only at those who had killed the ranchers but at all restive red men.

Advertising for hundred-day volunteers, Chivington easily signed up over seven hundred men. Many were rowdy adventurers but the colonel hoped to put their enthusiasm to good use. Their endurance was tested first. When the hundred-day enlistments were nearly up, Chivington and his volunteers had yet to find any Cheyenne and Arapaho to punish. Chivington was worried that his troops might go home with their mission unaccomplished. But in late November 1864, they tracked to an Indian village forty miles northeast of Fort Lyon. There, a group of Indians headed by Black Kettle and White Antelope were camped on Sand Creek. Those in the Indian encampment had recently taken part in a Denver conference with the governor and the army. There they had agreed to be peaceful and to turn over any bad Indians to Fort Lyon. They also had agreed to return some prisoners they held, as well as stolen stock. Because of these agreements, they believed they were under the protection of Major Wynkoop and his troops at Fort Lyon.

Their sense of security was shattered on November 29 when Chivington and his men charged down upon the sleeping village. The volunteers were told to take no prisoners, not even women and children. At first sign of the attack, Black Kettle ran up an American flag by his tipi to show his loyalty, and then he hoisted a white flag as well to show that he would not fight. Chivington's party was not deterred; the troops fired their cannons into the village and charged, shooting their rifles and revolvers. Many warriors hastily tried to defend the village but were quickly scattered. Some women and children ran into ravines, trying to hide under the brush. Black Kettle himself escaped, but White Antelope was killed.

The attack went on all day, and some of the volunteers began to have second thoughts about participating in an affair that clearly had got out of hand. Some accounts report that about 300 Indians were killed, among them 225 women and children. Other figures place the number of dead at 123, of whom 98 were women and children.[16] During the hearings on the massacre, an interpreter who was with the troops described the scene: "They were scalped, their brains knocked out; the men used their knives, ripped open women, clubbed little children, knocked them in the head with their guns, beat their brains out, mutilated their bodies in every sense of the word."[17]

Virtually every dead Indian was scalped by the whites, who displayed their grisly trophies publicly in Denver. The avenging assault increasingly lost its lustre as more and more details of brutality leaked out. An investigation uncovered more sordid details, and finally Chivington resigned from the militia to escape a court martial and possible punishment.

This is the story that has entered history and legend. Its simple outline of good and evil owes much to the relegation of certain facts to the footnotes or appendices. In the first place, Chivington, the apparent opportunist and villain, had political enemies. His disgrace ended his political aspirations for Congress and set back his advocacy of immediate statehood for Colorado. (In the end, Colorado statehood came in 1876.) Nor was Chivington the sole instigator of the retaliatory campaign. From the Denver conference between Black Kettle and the civil and army authorities, General Samuel R. Curtis had sent word to Chivington: "I shall require the bad Indians delivered up; restoration of equal numbers of stock; also hostages to secure. I want no peace till the Indians suffer more."[18] Further, Black Kettle "did not move his band to Fort Lyon, as both Governor Evans and Colonel Chivington had demanded. No arms were surrendered, no hostages given, no bad Indians delivered up, no stock restored."[19] (But some historians say that the Indians surrendered half of their arms.) Moreover, a large number of scalps were found in Black Kettle's village, some of them recently taken. In the aftermath, Major Wynkoop of Fort Lyon was relieved of command by General Curtis on the ground that the Major had disobeyed orders.

In any event, the story of Sand Creek, minus its shades of gray, electrified the nation, especially the distant humanitarian Easterners. Although the massacre had been carried out by hundred-day volunteers, all soldiers in the West came to be viewed as brutalizers and Indian-haters. (This was unfair, as we have seen, because many military men had witnessed first hand the treatment of agency Indians and sympathized with their right to justice.)

The Sand Creek action inflamed Indian feelings over a wide area, and again they went on the warpath. Julesberg in northeast Colorado was sacked twice, farmhouses were raided, cattle killed, and travellers harassed. Once more the pendulum of action and reaction went into play.

In 1865, General Connor set out to chastise the red man in northeast Wyoming's Powder River country—which increasingly became the leading Indian-army battleground. His force of three thousand men raided various Indian villages, and his special unit, Major North's Pawnee Scouts, singlehandedly found and killed a band of twenty-four Cheyenne. Connor's late summer and early fall campaign was successful, but then the biting cold of the plains set in, presaging a hard winter. Connor was forced to return to his base and sit out the winter. The cost of his short campaign was approximately twenty million dollars.

The West was becoming expensive just as the federal government was becoming budget conscious. At the close of the Civil War, the militia and conscripted Yankees in the West wanted out, and the army had to replace them with regulars. To keep costs down, the military was ordered to concentrate on defense and peace-keeping and avoid offensive campaigns. Emissaries again were sent to the Indians to urge treaties. Unfortunately, the budget-cutting and peace-making efforts ran counter to the facts. With heavy postwar traffic West, white and Indian conflict increased and the army was inevitably involved.

The discovery of gold created new problems. Driven by reliable reports and rumors alike, large numbers of treasure seekers hurried from one part of the West to another, anxious to make their fortunes. Gold was found in Idaho in the early 1860s, and new and richer discoveries followed at Alder's Gulch, Bannack, and Virginia City in Montana Territory. Shortly thereafter, news of gold in the sacred Black Hills of present-day South Dakota caused whites to clamor for admission to Indian land. Tensions between whites and Indians were building to a climax. A few chiefs saw that, despite occasional victories, Indian defeat was inevitable. Others, however, looked only as far as the next battle.

Gold fever sent prospectors searching for new diggings when deposits began to be exhausted in California. Some travelled to the Fraser River country in British Columbia and later went on north to the Klondike. The search took some to the mountains north and west of Wyoming. There, in Montana Territory on the eastern side of the continental divide, vast wealth was uncovered, easily accessible to pan and pick. The year was 1863 and the place was Alder's Gulch. Placer miners flocked there by the thousands, all hoping for that "flash in the pan." By the end of the year, ten thousand miners were working the streams and ten million dollars in gold dust had been shipped from the spot. There were any number of glory holes.

To house and supply the throngs, the town of Virginia City was founded. The rapid development in Montana demanded improved trails. The most travelled one was the Bozeman Trail which, as we have seen, ran squarely through the favorite hunting ground of the Sioux.

Clearly new negotiations with the Indians were needed to ensure safe passage for the whites flocking north. In 1865, a number of Indians made concessions to that end and, in 1866, an attempt was made to reach universal agreement. Runners were sent out from Fort Laramie inviting all concerned Indians to another council at the fort. It was hoped that the "bad faces"—those who didn't agree to the previous concession—would come as well. The council began on June 1, 1866, but the great Chief Red Cloud, the most important of the "bad faces," refused to come. Coinciding with the opening of the council, there arrived from the East a large army headed by Colonel Henry Carrington, an engineering expert. He brought "a train of 226 mule teams . . . loaded with equipment and supplies, including a saw mill, mowing machines, shingle and brick machines, blacksmith and harness-making equipment, axes, saws and tools of all kinds. There were rocking chairs, churns, quantities of canned fruit, turkeys, chickens, pigs and cows."—and a thirty-piece brass band.[20] His mission was to strengthen existing forts and to build new ones along the Bozeman to protect its patrons.

Meanwhile, Red Cloud changed his mind and came, more as an observer than a participant. What he observed he did not like. He felt that Carrington's force once again argued the duplicity of the white man who, while giving gifts and forcing concessions through a treaty, was planning to put down the Indian whether or not the treaty was signed. Both Red Cloud and Man Afraid Of His Horses refused to sign. Margaret Carrington, wife of the colonel, reported that before leaving with warriors loyal to him, Red Cloud complained publicly: "Great father sends us presents and wants new road, but white chief goes with soldiers to *steal* road before Indians say yes or no!"[21]

Colonel Carrington began to have some inkling of what to expect as he carried out his mission. He was not encouraged to find that the fort, which was supposed to supply him with a hundred thousand rounds of ammunition, had less than a thousand rounds itself.[22] While reporting this shortage, Margaret Carrington also said that she personally had seen barrels of gunpowder being carried away by Indians. Trouble, if not already at the boil, clearly was brewing. Yet despite this, "2,000 of the Sioux accepted the treaty and remained at peace, while 4,000 or more took part in Red Cloud's War."[23]

Ironically, observed Mrs. Carrington, the Indians who didn't sign the treaty were the ones who controlled the territory where her husband's forces were to go. Worse, some Indians had declared that before many moons had passed, there would be no shod horses on the Bozeman Trail. Thus began one of the most fascinating and poignant chapters in the history of the army in the West.

Guided by Jim Bridger, Carrington's outfit left Fort Laramie on September 17 to carry out its mission of protecting the Bozeman Trail. (Mrs. Carrington became an admirer of Bridger's talents; she got to know him well over the next six months and was amazed at his rich experiences in the West and his "headful of maps and trails and ideas.")[24]

Travelling, the party passed on their left the nearly mile-high Laramie Peak, its beauty silhouetted against the western sky. It took them eleven days to reach Fort Reno (formerly named Fort Connor), situated on the Powder River a hundred and eighty miles northwest of Fort Laramie. Looking back over the journey, Carrington saw that another fort was needed on the way from Fort Laramie to Fort Reno; anyone caught between the two was over five days from help. His suggestion became reality later; the new installation was named Fort Fetterman, founded in 1867 approximately eighty miles northwest of Fort Laramie.

Carrington's troops stayed at Fort Reno for a week and a half, strengthening the place with men and matériel. Temperatures as high as 113 degrees, however, gave them reason to move on to the shade of the Bighorn mountains, where two new forts were to be established. Before they set out, Carrington's men received another portent of things to come. Under their very noses, a group of Indians stole the sutler's mules and horses. A detachment of troops rode out quickly after the thieves but could not catch them; the soldiers declared that "they just seemed to disappear into thin air." The troops brought back a lone Indian pony laden with treaty goods. Heavily burdened, the pony evidently had been unable to keep up with the stolen herd.

On reaching the Bighorns, Carrington chose a site for a major new fort, to be named Fort Phil Kearny (not to be confused with Fort Kearney in Nebraska). Seventy miles north of it, where the Bozeman Trail crossed the Bighorn River, another but lesser fort was built and named C.F. Smith.

The site of Fort Phil Kearny is preserved by the National Park Service, although it has not been rebuilt. Its idyllic setting belies its bloody history. Four miles from the Bighorns, a short distance northwest of Lake De Smet, the outpost was built on a plain near Big Piney Creek, which ran into the Powder River. From a military point of view, it was a very strategic location. The Bozeman Trail passed only a few miles away and from two nearby promontories, Pilot Hill and Sullivant Hills, lookouts could see as far as eleven miles. At any sign of danger pickets could signal by mirror to travellers passing through the area. From the fort, they also could see Lodge Trail Ridge some miles to the southwest.

Plans for the building of Fort Phil Kearny had been drawn up during the previous winter at Fort Kearney in Nebraska, and Colonel Carrington, a methodical man, went right to work. (A conservative soldier and trained engineer, he could read the scriptures in Greek and Hebrew.) An immense amount of wood was needed, as the stockaded fort was to enclose many buildings that would house men and equipment. The fort proper was to measure 600 by 800 feet; adjacent would be a 200 by 600 foot rectangle that would include stables and quarters for teamsters and others who might find their way there. The colonel set up a forty-five horsepower sawmill whose parts he brought along on his trek west. Later, two steam mills were built to facilitate the work. A logging camp was set up at Piney Island, about seven miles away, where woodcutters, heavily escorted by troops, cut logs to be hauled to the fort. A haycutting area was designated, and block houses were built there for refuge in case of Indian attack. Fortunately, the heat of the summer days turned into the cool of mountain nights.

There even was "color" in the nearby streams. Only a few days after the arrival of the troops, some men deserted, heading for the Montana gold fields. They had used the army for free transportation west. A detachment of troops gave chase but was halted by a number of Indians who ordered them to go back to their post and tell the commander to abandon the fort. Nevertheless, the fort was completed in October 1866, its flagpole raised on the thirty-first of that month. A flagpole stands in that same location today.

Well-built and well-fortified, the fort lacked only the manpower needed for the action ahead. The brass recognized this but had trouble doing anything about it. General William B. Hazen visited the installation shortly after its completion and complimented the commander, promising more troops shortly. The promised troops were continually delayed, however, although eventually some strength was added. Both cavalry and infantry manned the fort.

From the start, the fort knew no peace. Sniping by Indians took place nearly every day. Indians continually were seen stalking the fort, noting its daily routines and probing possible weaknesses. No one inside felt safe, and any party leaving the stockade for any reason was heavily guarded.

To assess the dangers, Carrington conferred with Indians who appeared friendly. However doubtful their information, their counsel was rewarded with papers certifying them as good Indians. Carrington also took the precaution of sending the mountain man Jim Bridger to parley with some friendly Crows. Bridger brought back the information that the Sioux and the Cheyenne were smoking the war pipe, agreeing to stick together in any ensuing fights. Bridger advised the colonel that the Indians were steadfastly and intensely opposed to the forts along the trail, and suggested that it might be prudent to abandon them. Carrington knew that Bridger was no coward, but he was not free to follow Bridger's sage advice. In spite of the impending conflict, Bridger stayed at the fort and continued to perform useful services.

Sporadic skirmishes began and the battles in the area over the next two years came to be known as Red Cloud's War. He had big medicine and thus a considerable following among the Sioux.

Starting the war early and in earnest, a Sioux war party killed two men of Carrington's command and wounded three others on July 17. Shortly thereafter, six men of a trading party camping near the fort also were killed and horribly mutilated. Margaret Carrington reported twenty such incidents from July to September, as the burning fuse neared the powder keg in the Powder River basin. A later historian estimated that between "August 1 and December 31, the Sioux killed one hundred and fifty-four persons at or near Fort Phil Kearny." Perhaps twenty more were wounded and seven hundred head of livestock captured.[25]

The worst of the encounters with Red Cloud's men shocked the nation with the number of dead and mutilated. December 21, 1866, began normally under a cold but sunny sky. Woodcutters were working as usual seven miles from the fort when a lookout signalled an attack by Indians. This almost routine occurrence was met with routine response. Troops were alerted to ride out and scare the Indians away.

Carrington appointed a command led by a very reliable officer, Major James W. Powell. When word about the assignment reached Captain William J. Fetterman (Brevet Lt. Colonel), however, he demanded that he be allowed to lead the unit instead. He and Lieutenant James Grummond were known to the fort as fireeaters and were chomping at the bit to see action. They had made no secret of their view that Carrington was overly cautious in his approach to fighting the Sioux.

Carrington acquiesced to the request, and Fetterman and Grummond were assigned seventy-eight men to their command, twenty-eight cavalry and forty-eight infantry. Several others also volunteered to go along. Captain Frederick Brown, who was about to return to Fort Laramie, said that he wanted to get one scalp, preferably Red Cloud's, before he left the theater. Two civilian traders with repeating rifles also wanted in on the action, making a total of eighty-one men who took to the field. The additional firepower of the last two was welcomed, especially as the troops had only single-shot muzzle loaders. One of the traders had a nineteen-year-old wife at the fort but he told her to have no concern for his safety. Previous shows of force had met no serious opposition.

Having given command to an acknowledged zealot, Carrington took precautions. He inspected the troops, approving most as fit for combat, eliminating a few and replacing them with others. Making sure that he had many witnesses, he gave explicit orders to Fetterman.

Fetterman often had boasted, "Give me eighty men and I will ride through the whole Sioux nation." Carrington emphasized that the only purpose of the outing was to protect the woodcutters. He gave the orders not once but twice in front of the house where Lieutenant Grummond lived with his pregnant wife, Frances: "Relieve it [the wood train] and report to me. Do not engage or pursue Indians at its expense. Under no circumstances pursue over the ridge, that is, Lodge Trail Ridge."[26]

Carrington obviously was concerned that Indians might try to decoy troops into an ambush. As the company was about to leave the gates of the fort, he had his orders repeated once again within earshot of soldiers nearby.[27] Fetterman and his party had been admonished at least three times and quite possibly four times.

As the command passed out of sight, Carrington realized that, in his determination to discourage its leaders from exceeding their commission, he had failed to send a medical detail with the troops. He quickly assigned Surgeon C.M. Hines and two orderlies to ride directly to the woodcutters. If Fetterman had been there and left, Hines was to follow and catch up with him.

Shortly, the pickets at Pilot Hill signalled that the woodcutters no longer were being menaced by the Indians. It appeared that the Indians had finished their fun for the day or had retired at the sight of the troops.

Yet something unusual was happening. Lookouts and, indeed, even the men at the fort could see a small number of Indians on Lodge Trail Ridge, the boundary Fetterman had been forbidden to cross. A howitzer was fired at the ridge several times, and to the surprise of everyone, about thirty Indians ran from nearby shrubbery.

Meanwhile, Surgeon Hines, not finding Fetterman with the woodcutters, followed the troops' trail up to the ridge and there was flabbergasted to see a valley swarming with Indians and no sign of Fetterman and his troops. Hines hastened back to the fort with his alarming report. About the same time, near noon, the sound of gunfire was heard beyond the ridge, strongly suggesting engagement between troops and Indians. Within fifteen minutes, Carrington had a relief column on the way, headed by Captain Tenador Ten Eyck. The forty-man unit, like Fetterman's, was composed equally of infantry and cavalry. Wanting to stay on high ground in case of trouble, Ten Eyck took a longer route to get to Fetterman's probable location. Under the circumstances, it seemed prudent to circle around two extra miles. Just before one o'clock, Ten Eyck reached the ridge summit as the gunfire ceased. Fetterman's troopers were not to be seen; instead Ten Eyck saw hundreds of Indians milling around in the valley below, daring him and his men to pursue them. Keeping his high ground, he sent a runner to report to Carrington.

While this was happening, the wood detail had returned to the fort. With the eighty men of Fetterman outside along with the forty men commanded by Ten Eyck, the fort was virtually empty of fighting men. Prisoners were released and they, together with the woodcutters and other civilians, were given guns to shore up defenses. Sensing extreme urgency, Carrington then sent another forty men to back up Ten Eyck's force.

As Ten Eyck waited for new orders, the Indians left the valley. Seeing no further danger, Ten Eyck cautiously edged his way down the ridge. The grass was practically shoulder high in places and, at first, he saw nothing alarming. But soon he saw a sight that was to haunt him the rest of his days. In a small circle among boulders lay the bodies of Fetterman and all of his command. Their mutilations were so severe that their description in the official report was withheld for two decades. The bodies lay in piles, pierced by so many arrows that a soldier said they looked like porcupine quills. One corpse alone held forty shafts. One later count estimated that forty thousand arrows had been used in the fight. This figure cannot be accurate; four thousand is more likely. Both Grummond and Fetterman had powder burns by their temples, indicating that at the final moment both had committed suicide. The two traders apparently had made good use of their repeaters, for over a hundred shell casings were scattered about their bodies.

So shocking was the scene that the hardened soldiers began to vomit. Ten Eyck collected forty-nine bodies, including Fetterman's, and returned with them to the fort. The others had to be left until morning. The massacre site is marked today by a monument next to Highway 14, about ten miles north of the fort.

The next day, many soldiers were understandably hesitant to return to the scene, but Carrington insisted that the rest of the bodies be brought back, and led the detachment himself. The nervous were reassured when Jim Bridger served as the scout for this foray. If any Indians were still around, Bridger would know it.

In his firmness and courage, Carrington had no illusions about the continuing danger. While his forces were away, the fort would be virtually defenseless. With visions of yesterday's debacle seared in his memory, the colonel ordered the powder magazine emptied and all explosives placed in the center of the fort. If an Indian attack should threaten to overwhelm the defenses, the officers were to gather the women and children and blow them up rather than subject them to capture and torture by the Indians. Despite their opportunity, however, the Indians did not return to make their victory complete. Without further incident, Carrington returned with the remaining bodies, including Lieutenant Grummond's. Tearfully, the colonel and his wife consoled the young, pregnant widow.

The next day brought sudden snow and then sub-zero cold. In a way, the blanket of white covering the bloody battlefield was welcome, but soon the snow drifted up to the top of the stockade, offering a path over the wall. A ten-foot trench was quickly dug next to the wall, a moat in the snow, but almost as quickly, it filled up with new drifts. The fort could only redouble its alertness and take its chances. Despite the snow, the more than eighty bodies remained to be buried. The garrison managed to dig a grave fifty feet long and seven feet deep. A mass burial took place on the day after Christmas.

The desperate precautions taken by Colonel Carrington on the day following the massacre showed how precarious he considered his situation to be. Outside help was imperative, but the nearest military posts—Fort C.F. Smith, seventy miles to the north, and Fort Reno to the east—had been under the same kind of siege as Fort Phil Kearny. At Fort C.F. Smith, "no party entered or left between November 30, 1866, and June 8, 1867."[28] Carrington even lacked ammunition after the Fetterman affair; there was "not a single full cartridge box in the garrison."[29]

The only available help was at Fort Laramie, 236 miles away. A horseman might cut nearly fifty miles off the ride if he could reach Horseshoe Station, a mere 190 miles distant. From there, a message could be sent to Fort Laramie by telegraph. The mission would be difficult in itself, and it would be opposed by every means at Red Cloud's command. Carrington called for volunteers, and three or four men responded. Apparently, they set out separately, hoping that one would get through. One of them did, in a ride that should make him remembered as the Paul Revere of the West. Born of Portuguese ancestry in the Azores, he was John Phillips, better known as "Portugee." He was a civilian and a partner to the two traders who had lost their lives with Fetterman.

Offered the best horse in the fort, probably the colonel's, Phillips set out in sub-zero cold on December 22, 1866. The long nights of winter helped to cover his first dash. Riding from dusk to dawn, he reached Fort Reno, sixty miles along the way, and found that, as suspected, the commander there could give no help. He rode on, through a raging blizzard, travelling more boldly as he left Red Cloud's territory farther behind. He made his way to the telegraph at Horseshoe Station. There a message was wired to Fort Laramie, but it was not acknowledged. Worried that the message had not gotten through because of the storm damage to the wires, Phillips went on to Fort Laramie. He arrived at night on Christmas, in the middle of a holiday party. A relief column was organized immediately and the troops set out in thirty-below cold to make the journey.

Phillips's horse died a few days later, probably from a lung hemorrhage. Exhausted himself, Portugee Phillips rested and recovered. Eventually he took up farming nearby. For his reward, the government gave him a grant of three hundred dollars. His troubles, however, were not over. His ranch was harassed and his cattle stolen by Indians, bitter over his saving the fort. Thirty-three years later, in recognition of his losses and their causes, his widow was given an additional five thousand dollars.[30]

In the aftermath of the disaster, Carrington was called in the dead of winter to a military hearing on the matter in Washington, D.C. Traveling with him were fifteen women and children as well as his aides. The temperature was forty below and some of the party suffered frostbite injuries that required amputations.

The hearing, and subsequent ones that included an investigation by a committee of the U.S. Senate, exonerated Carrington. The congressional panel concluded sympathetically:

The difficulty "in a nutshell" was that the commanding officer of the district was furnished no more troops or supplies for this state of war than had been provided and furnished him for a state of profound peace. In regions where all was peace, as at Laramie in November, twelve companies were stationed, while in regions where all was war, as at Phil Kearny, there were only five companies allowed.[31]

When Carrington left Fort Kearny, he was replaced by Colonel Henry W. Wessells and additional troops who were supplied with "Springfield rifles, Civil War muzzleloaders converted into breechloaders [which] could be reloaded very quickly."[32] Both the manpower and the additional firepower would soon be needed. Word of the improved weaponry did not reach the Indians, who thought the foe still poorly equipped.

On August 1, 1867, it was Fort C.F. Smith's turn to do battle. A powerful attack was launched against their haycutters by nearly a thousand Cheyennes in league with Red Cloud's Sioux. The Indians were repulsed by troops and cutters who barricaded themselves behind logs and used their new Allin-altered Springfields to good effect, killing or wounding thirty-eight warriors. The devastating defeat, known in history as the Hayfield Fight, was embarrassing for the Cheyenne and Sioux and especially for Red Cloud.

The very next day, August 2, Fort Kearny once again faced Indian wrath when the fort's wood train was attacked. The train and its guards were led by Major Powell, the officer supplanted by Captain Fetterman in his bid for glory. Receiving warning from the pickets that Indians were gathering to attack, the major set up a carefully planned defense. Twelve wagon boxes were taken off their under-carriages and placed in an oval pattern, forming a barricade with six wagon boxes on each side. Two wagons blocked the ends of the oval, but these could be moved quickly for entrance or exit. The sides of the wagon boxes had holes drilled in them to serve as rifle slots. Heavily armed with the new modified rifles and well equipped with sidearms and ammunition, the men inside the barricade awaited the charge.

Powell put the best sharpshooters at the loopholes. Other sol-diers, not so proficient, were put to loading weapons and keeping ready-to-use rifles at the side of each sharpshooter. Each marksman had three loaded rifles at his side at all times; when he fired one, it immediately was given to a loader and replaced with another loaded rifle. The succession of rifle fire was so quick that the Indians could not comprehend how such a volume of fire could come from so few men. It was their introduction to the Allin-altered Springfields, which needed no ramrod or powder; spent cartridges were simply ejected from the chamber and a fresh one put in.

As the mounted Indians charged, the soldiers held their fire until the warriors were only fifty yards away. Then they put up a wall of fire so severe that the Indian charge was split right down the middle. As the red men rode past the barricade, the marksmen continued to fire into their backs. More charges came, and then the Indians attacked on foot, approaching as close to the barricade as possible. Many al-most reached the oval before being shot.

Indian bodies began to pile up next to the barricade until, finally, after four hours and six charges, and army reinforcements with a mountain howitzer, the Indians concluded that their medicine was bad that day and left. After cleaning up and reassembling the wagons, the jubilant party returned to the fort, eight hours after the first warn-ing of danger. More than one member of the group mentioned some-thing about having avenged Fetterman. The lowest estimate of Indian losses was from one soldier who counted sixty bodies, but other guesses went much higher, to over a thousand. Whatever the Indian losses, when the soldiers returned to the spot the next day not a body was to be seen. The site of the Wagon Box Fight is now marked by a monument near U.S. Highway 87, a few miles northwest of where the fort was situated. It is one of three associated with Fort Phil Kearny. The Fetterman marker is another, and the third commemo-rates the feat of Portugee Phillips.

Red Cloud's prestige suffered irreparably from the two days of defeat and loss in the Hayfield fight at Fort C.F. Smith and the Wagon Box fight at Fort Phil Kearny. His medicine was shown to be powerless and his authority failed. Still, he would have one more moment of triumph before his eclipse by Chief Crazy Horse. A peace of sorts settled down on the Bozeman, bought at high cost on both sides.

In 1868, a new treaty was drawn up at Fort Laramie. In it, the Black Hills were ceded to the Indians in exchange for their promise not to interfere with the building of the transcontinental railroad farther south. Making his last hurrah, Red Cloud insisted that the Bozeman Trail be closed permanently. The government acquiesced and ordered that Forts C.F. Smith, Phil Kearny, and Reno be abandoned. In August, soldiers bid farewell to the Bozeman. As those leaving Fort Phil Kearny looked back, they could see it burning to the ground—Red Cloud's work. All the victories in the area had been pyrrhic. Even Red Cloud seemed resigned to the ultimate domination of the invaders. He lived on until 1909, travelling in the East over a half dozen times and becoming a bit of a celebrity in the white man's world.

While the nation focused its attention on the northern plains, hostilities were coming to a boil on the central and southern plains. In 1867, General Winfield Hancock, worried about the Cheyenne threat to Kansas, tried to bulldoze the tribe into making new concessions at a conference held at Fort Larned. Angered, the Indians bolted the conference and scattered over the plains.

Chaos prevailed. White hunters were decimating the buffalo herds while Cheyenne, Arapaho, Kiowa, and Comanche were freely raiding homesteaders. The situation was approaching a crisis. Another council was called in fall 1867 and produced the Treaty of Medicine Lodge, named after the nearby hamlet in southern Kansas. This treaty "marked a fundamental turning point in the history of United States Indian policy. . . . It sought to remove [the Plains Indians] from the path of white settlement and to establish a system for civilizing the tribes."[33] Reservations were designated for different tribes, who were expected to respect each other's borders. The treaty, in practice, brought virtually no change in the Indian way of life.

In March 1868, General of the Army William Tecumseh Sherman, with little Phil Sheridan, replaced Hancock, a move that portended a larger role for cavalry in the West. Sheridan took over the Department of the Missouri amidst increasing pressure for him to do something about the "Indian problem." Both Sherman and Sheridan were quite willing to pursue the scorched earth strategy that had been successful in the Civil War, but their immediate task was to get Indians back onto the reservations and to stop their incessant raiding. To achieve this goal, they planned to mount an unheard of winter campaign. Indian strength was known to be weakest in that season. Many returned to their reservations to live on handouts until spring, when the grass would be good and the hunting worthwhile. In winter, hungry Indian ponies could barely stand, much less be ridden; but army horses, living on oats carried by the cavalry stayed strong and fresh.

To start the campaign, Sheridan quickly called in his favorite cavalry officer from Civil War days, George Armstrong Custer, known to his friends as "Autie."[34] Custer had been out West since fall 1866, assigned to the Seventh Cavalry, but it was Sheridan who gave him his first major challenge. In Sheridan's area, 124 settlers had been killed by Indians, and Custer was instructed to track down the perpetrators. He did so in the controversial Battle of the Washita. Although praised and damned for his actions, Custer's orders were quite direct. He was "to proceed [to the] Washita River, the supposed winter site of the hostile tribes, to destroy their village and ponies; to kill all warriors, and bring back all women and children."[35]

Proceeding through a foot of snow, Custer found the village. Unknown to him, its chief was Black Kettle, the Black Kettle of Sand Creek, who was said by some to be a friend of the *Washichu* (whites). Custer later recorded his strategy: "The general plan was to employ the hours between then (about 2 A.M.) and daylight to completely surround the village and at daybreak, or as soon as it was barely light enough for the purpose, to attack the Indians from all sides."[36]

At the appointed hour, the band blared out the Garry Owen (Gaelic for Owen's Garden) and Custer charged. Braves were killed, along with some children and squaws. The village was completely razed, nine hundred animals slaughtered, and nearly a thousand buffalo robes burned. Custer brought back a prize tipi as a memento. He later answered criticism of his military action:

Before engaging in the fight orders had been given to prevent the killing of any but the fighting strength of the village; but in a struggle of this character it is impossible at all times to discriminate, particularly when, in a hand-to-hand conflict such as the troops were then engaged in, the squaws are as dangerous adversaries as the warriors, while Indian boys between ten and fifteen years of age were found as expert and determined in the use of the pistol and bow and arrow as the older warriors.[37]

The victory was no sooner won than scouts reported finding a whole string of hostile villages along the nearby river. Custer, fearing for the safety of his supply train, hurried back to defend it. This meant leaving eighteen troopers under Major Joel W. Elliot to fend for themselves as they pursued fleeing warriors. Elliot and his troopers later were found dead, their horribly mutilated bodies frozen in the snow.

Custer, the man of controversy, was encircled by controversy again. Although remains of killed farmers were found in the village and an Indian woman had been seen to disembowel a white boy prisoner before he could be rescued, protests poured in against Custer's action. To his other names, such as Yellow Hair and Son of the Morning Star, a new one was added. It was "Squaw Killer," despite his having brought back fifty captured women and children.

Sherman congratulated Custer, and Sheridan was delighted with the victory. Still, Custer had found considerable foodstuff at Washita, given to the Indians by General Hazen. Sheridan complained, "I am ordered to fight these Indians, and General Hazen is permitted to feed them."[38] Many settlers in the West shared his resentment. An editorial in the Yankton *Press and Dakotan* commented, "This abominable compact with the marauding bands that regularly make war on the whites in the summer and live on government bounty all winter is now pleaded as a barrier to the improvement and development of one of the richest and most fertile sections in America.[39]

A contemporary author said of the battle, "This was Custer's one significant victory on the plains; it enraged and disheartened not only the Southern Cheyennes but several other tribes."[40] One of Custer's officers, Frederick Benteen, used the public press to severely criticize Custer's action at the Washita.[41]

Another remarkable encounter between Indians and whites occurred toward the end of summer 1868. To combat the wave of depredations against homesteaders, Sheridan sent Colonel John Forsyth and fifty hard-bitten frontiersmen to track down the marauding Indians. The volunteers departed from Fort Wallace, Kansas, and made their way to the Arickaree River, a branch of the Republican, near the east central Colorado border near Wray.[42] The troops took refuge on an island in the center of the river when Indians led by the Cheyenne Roman Nose launched a surprise attack. The volunteers held off charge after charge with their repeating rifles. Colonel Forsyth was severely wounded and Lieutenant Frederick W. Beecher was killed. Roman Nose also was killed; he was said to have gone into battle reluctantly against bad sign without purifying himself. During the long siege, the troops had to dig for water and eat the rotting flesh of their horses.

On the first night, two scouts—nineteen-year-old Jack Stilwell and veteran Henry Trudeau—volunteered to run the gauntlet of hundreds of Indians to get back to Fort Wallace for help, 125 miles away. Sometimes hiding in buffalo wadis, sometimes dashing at full gallop, they made it. However, help arrived before they had gone halfway, for on the second night two more scouts were sent out. They stumbled onto a company of black troops led by Colonel Louis H. Carpenter. They came to the rescue of the beleaguered islanders, who had held off the Cheyennes for nine days. Forsyth's loss was six killed and seventeen wounded; Indian losses were counted officially at thirty-two, although Indian sources put the number of dead at seventy-five.

The increasing number of white settlers clamored for the red man to be put in his place, namely, on the reservation. Custer conducted various forays as he familiarized himself with the West. A highly decorated general of the Civil War, Custer also was a hard-working author; he thrilled the East with accounts of his experiences in the West, writing for the *Galaxy* while he roamed the valleys of the Yellowstone and Powder rivers.

In 1874, when gold was discovered in the Black Hills, Custer was sent to reconnoiter and keep order in the face of a frantic influx of miners. Far from being in collusion with the trespassers, as some supposed, the army tried strenuously to stop the trespassing. Sheridan wrote to General Alfred Terry in August 1874, "Should companies now organizing . . . trespass on the Sioux reservation, you are hereby directed to use the force at your command to burn their wagon trains, destroy the outfits and arrest the leaders, confining them to the nearest military post!"[43]

Meanwhile political troubles abounded. Ulysses Simpson Grant was president and his administration was riddled with corruption. His secretary of war, William Worth Belknap, had been impeached, and Grant's own brother, Orvil, apparently was involved in graft with Indian agencies. The situation regarding the Indian reservations grew so bad that Grant initiated his own Quaker policy, letting religious groups run the agencies.

Custer took an active interest in these affairs and described for his vast readership the abuses heaped upon the Indian and the army. He supported the charges of corruption against Grant's brother in testimony before Congress, and Grant never forgave him.

The Indian Wars were coming to a climax. Everyone, including the Indians, felt it. The likely outcome was very clear, as Sheridan made his plans and the army prepared to administer its *coup de grace* to the Indian problem. While Custer was still in Washington, Sheridan asked him to take part in the final struggle. Custer left Washington without permission, and Grant, still bitter at the boy general, called him back and refused to let him return to the plains and his Seventh Cavalry. Despite repeated requests, Custer could not even get audience with Grant to plead his case. Finally, in desperation, he wrote the president whom he had maligned in congressional testimony, "I appeal to you as a soldier to spare me the humiliation of seeing my regiment march to meet the enemy and I do not share its dangers."[44] The press was on Custer's side: "There is a degree of gallantry and manly pride in General Custer that we can but admire. He was a gallant solider when in the field; honest in all his acts, and yet his opponents can but give him credit for military honor; and yet when he tells the truth [because he is a Democrat] the Chief Executive of our Government attempts to disgrace him."[45]

Grant relented and Custer returned to his troops. The rest is history. Custer set out from Fort Abraham Lincoln with seven hundred troopers of the Seventh Cavalry and proceeded to his death at the Little Bighorn on June 25, 1876. Custer had divided his group into three battalions, two of them headed by Reno and Benteen. With Custer were 220 to 230 men, among them his brother Tom and a nephew. Custer's last words were to an Italian orderly, John Martini, who knew little English. Custer's adjutant, fearing that Martini would confuse the message, scribbled it on a piece of paper for Martini to carry. The words read, "Benteen: Come on. Big village. Be quick. Bring packs. W.W. Cooke. P.S. Bring packs."[46]

What exactly happened at that battle by the Little Bighorn River, no one knows in detail. Everyone in Custer's battalion was killed. Indians told conflicting stories, probably out of fear of retribution. Almost immediately, however, identifying stakes were placed at each spot on the battlefield where a trooper was killed, so some reconstruction of the battle was made. Custer was buried temporarily at the site now called Custer Hill; later his body was interred at West Point. Today, there is a movement afoot to bring the body back to the battlefield.

First official news of the defeat was carried by the steamer *Far West*, which had been moored near the mouth of the Little Bighorn River. Piloted by Grant Marsh, the most famous of the Western steamboat men, it made the run of over seven hundred miles carrying fifty-two wounded to Bismarck in fifty-four hours.[47] Rumors of the disaster had spread by "moccasin telegraph"; the more graphic accounts that followed caused a sensation around the world. Over a thousand imaginative paintings of Custer's Last Stand have been made; at one time nearly every bar in the country had one to inspire its patrons. A St. Louis beer company sponsored hundreds of them. One painting by Edward Paxton, which shows a sea of faces surrounding Custer, took ten years to paint. It now hangs in the Whitney Museum in Cody, Wyoming. In addition to the paintings, over three hundred books and forty-one movies have retold the story.

In August 1983, the battlefield now located on the Crow Indian

Reservation in Southeast Montana was swept by a fire that cleared the land. In all probability, the blaze was started by disgruntled Indians as part of a protest campaign. A group of archaeologists and amateur artifact seekers seized the opportunity to comb the grounds under ranger supervision. Top scientists from IBM set up a computer grid of the field, and ballistic specialists, together with forensic experts, were given materials from the excavation. Investigations uncovered some hitherto unknown facts. Where the soldiers used single shot .45/70 Springfield carbines, the two to four thousand Indians had Winchester and sixteen-shot Henry repeating rifles. Evidence suggests that instead of the usual swarming attack, the Indians held back and used their superior firepower, a tactic that was a rarity for the red man. Military authors now argue that Custer did not blunder but was a victim of circumstances.[48] In short, his luck ran out.

The Little Bighorn proved once again that the Indian could win a battle and still lose. From this time on, the Plains Wars effectively were over. Unrest continued and further effort would be needed to get Indians back on the reservations. There were the episodes of Chief Joseph and the Nez Percé in 1877 and of the Cheyennes, led by Little Wolf and Dull Knife, at Fort Robinson, Nebraska.

Yet there would be one last Indian swan song, one final closing of the curtain, and it would involve those greatest warriors of the Plains, the Sioux.

The gods must retain their threefold task: they must exorcise the terrors of nature, they must reconcile men to the cruelty of Fate, particularly as it is shown in death, and they must compensate them for the suffering and privations which a civilized life in common has imposed upon them.

—Sigmund Freud[49]

The year was 1890, the year that the United States government declared the closing of the frontier. The month was December, and its twenty-ninth day marked the end of the Indian wars. The occasion was the massacre at Wounded Knee—the time when the red man's religion got in the white man's way. It was the moment when the United States, premised on religious freedom, prohibited Indian worship. It was the era of the Ghost Dance Religion with its Ghost Shirt Dance.

Traditional religions had come from the East, and the whites had brought their own brands with them to the New World. But in the second half of the nineteenth century, a new religion arose in the West, in the Territory of Nevada. Around 1870, a Paiute or Paviotso Indian named Tavibo (meaning "from the East" or "white man's father") grafted aspects of Christianity onto Indian belief and ritual. If it was not a new religion, it was a new form of religion, and almost immediately a new fervor spread among the Indians. Rituals connected with the religion involved the taking of peyote, a non-addictive hallucinatory narcotic.

Tavibo claimed to have had several visions when he went up into nearby sacred mountains. He was told to announce that the Second Coming of Jesus was at hand. All who wished to be saved from their state of misery were to perform a special ritual dance, one that assimilated aspects of other Indian circle dances. The dance, which evoked visions of dead ancestors, was called by outsiders a ghost dance, and the religion, the Ghost Dance Religion. The faith quickly spread to California and the Northwest tribes, as well as to a few in the Southwest. The millennium was slow in coming, however, and gradually the observance declined.

Two decades later, however, new life was breathed into the religion by another Paiute who was named Wovoka (meaning "Cutter"). He seemed an unlikely charismatic leader, at least to the white man, but among Indians he often was identified with the Christ. Born in 1856, he learned of Tavibo's ideas as a youth, adopting and adapting them. He never travelled outside of the small Mason Valley area, near present day Reno, Nevada, and lived on the Walker River Reservation just south of Pyramid Lake. When his father died he went to stay with a very religious white family headed by David Wilson, where he was known to many as Jack Wilson. After a time he went back to his people and took an ancestral name, Big Rumbling Belly. Rather tall, a hard worker, he always was a man of peace. He, too, had a number of visions and preached these to his tribe. An important one occurred when he was sick with a high fever, probably in January 1889 during a major eclipse of the sun.[50] Wovoka said: "When the sun died, I went up to heaven and saw God and all the people who had died long ago. God told me to come back and tell my people they must be good and love one another, and not fight or steal or lie. He gave me this dance to give to my people."[51]

Wovoka never claimed to be the Messiah but believed that he, like John the Baptist, was a prophet who announced the coming of the Messiah. In his ecstasies, God granted him many special powers, such as controlling snow and rain; indeed, Wovoka, offered to sell his services to the territory. God revealed to him that he, Wovoka, would govern the West, President Benjamin Harrison would govern the East, and God himself would govern the world as a whole. During his trances, his spirit was said to leave his body and go to the nether world. There, he talked and hunted with old friends and relatives who had died but now were in a state of bliss.

His message from God was that the Messiah would come soon to put all things right for the Indian. The Indian would again be favored because God had designated the red men as his chosen people. The names the Indians called themselves—the People, the Chosen Ones—reflected this truth. The Jews and the Gentiles had proved unworthy of that role. There would be apocalyptic signs when the Messiah was about to arrive.

One sign would be a great shaking of the earth. There also would be a huge dust storm or flood or both. Translated into different tribal tongues, often only by sign language, the theme underwent many variations. One flood story had Indians fleeing to the mountains while all whites drowned in the valley. Other versions had the whites choking on mud or falling into deep holes in the earth or being smothered by dust. The Indians would be able to walk on top of the dust. A less cataclysmic view was that all humans would fall asleep but after four days Indians would awaken to a world free of whites, but one that would retain white accouterments for Indian use. Some visions even had the good whites and Indians living together in heaven on earth. If the Indian failed to believe, some said that he would attain only one foot in height in the new world, turn into a stick, and be cast into a fire.

When all this came to pass, the plains again would be full of game and the buffalo would come out of their caves once more.[52] The dead would rise to be reunited with their living relatives, and no one would age beyond forty years. The belief was widespread that the Christ would appear in Spring 1890, when the star pansies would be blooming. Other versions extended the coming to the Fourth of July of the same year, but the event certainly was at hand.

The Ghost Religion might not have become so popular without the impressive powers of Wovoka as a medicine man. As with all medicine men, magical tricks played a considerable role in his ministrations. Indians were convinced that Wovoka was invisible to whites. He claimed the power to turn himself into a cloud, and witnesses confirmed the feat. More warlike Indians testified that he vomited up boxcars of ammunition.

A Cheyenne delegate, sent to investigate the new religion and assess its worth for his tribe, said that when Wovoka spoke at the same time to people of various tribes, all heard his message in their own tongues. (Whites who knew Wovoka scoffed at that. To their knowledge he spoke only Paiute and a smattering of English.)

Wovoka was said to have tattoo marks on his wrists, and these were interpreted by some followers as the marks of Christ's crucifixion. To those who sought him out, he gave sacred grass and some red ocher paint. The paint was to be applied only by the medicine man of the suppliant's tribe. Its purpose was to clarify any vision seen by the dancer in his trance; it was also helpful in warding off illness. Those who came to him for his message became apostles, spreading the good news.

Wovoka had a hypnotic effect on his followers. Other prophets were known to use hypnosis to produce fulfillments of their prophecies. Wovoka told one group of delegates that they would encounter a buffalo herd on the way back to their people, scarce as buffalo were at the time. He instructed them to kill one animal for food and to leave the head, tail, and hooves on the ground where it was slain. To their surprise, the group did spot a herd, and after killing a buffalo they followed their instructions to the letter. Once again going on their way, they looked back and saw the disjointed parts come together, stand up, and run back to the herd. They could not be shaken in their story, for they had the buffalo meat to prove it.

The ethnographer James Mooney recalls William James's distinction between tough-minded and tender-minded attitudes toward such magical claims. He points to a tender-minded Arapaho and a tough-minded Cheyenne who had visited with Wovoka. After Wovoka had told them of the spirit world that he had visited and that others could visit also, the medicine man passed a feather over the black sombrero held upside down on his lap. He asked both men to stare into the inverted black crown. The two walked away saying nothing, but on the journey home, the Cheyenne asked the Arapaho what he saw while peering into the sombrero. The Arapaho said that he saw the spirit world and some of his relatives there. The Cheyenne said he saw only the inside of the sombrero! But the Cheyenne did not deny the Arapaho's experience, for visions are not given to all.

Indeed, it seemed to many Indians that one way or another, their world was ending. They had nothing to lose and everything to gain by believing in Wovoka. Inveterate gamblers that they were, they went with the chance to win.

Every religion eventually is expressed in some kind of ritual, often a re-enactment to make the past at one with the present. For example, the Catholic Eucharist dramatically represents the climax of Jesus' ministry. In the Ghost Religion, the ritual was the dance. A ritual often intends to make new, in the sense of re-newal, and this is what was sought in the dance. To the Indian, renewal was an essential part of nature; he saw himself as part of nature rather than apart from nature, where the white Christian attempted to renounce the world and the flesh. Giving voice to the Indian view, one Arapaho told an army captain, "This earth too old, grass too old, trees too old, our lives too old. Then all new again."[53]

Wovoka taught the dance to visitors who in turn taught others when they went back to their tribes. Within two years, 1888 and 1889, the religion had become the center of sacred attention among many groups.

To prepare for the dance, which essentially was a peace dance and not a scalp dance as some newspapers charged, the warrior purified himself by fasting for twenty-four hours and then engaging in a series of sweat baths. All members of the dance held hands to close the hoop, and they danced counterclockwise around a sacred tree or pole in the center of their circle. Women and children were allowed to participate, another indication that it was no war dance. The dance continued for four successive nights and then on the fifth day it stopped. Occasional breaks were taken, but essentially it was a marathon dance of endurance. Often the dancers were driven into a frenzy by the drumbeat. The drumbeat accompanied and energized Indian ceremony.

The medicine man encouraged the dancers to give themselves over to trances and shouted out what they might see in their visions. There is no question that some had genuine cataleptic fits but others feigned them. The medicine man worked his powers of suggestion to the fullest and, like the Shakers, people began falling to the ground, dazed and often totally unconscious. In the trance state, the spirit of the person was supposed to leave the body and journey to the nether world where it saw strange and wondrous things. Dancers were told that if they died of exhaustion, they would be taken up immediately into the spirit world. Once those who fell had awakened, they were encouraged to compose a song to tell of their vision. Some were songs of joy and portents of things to come; others told of their present condition. Here are several examples:

> Our father, the Whirlwind, Our father, the Whirlwind,
> Now wears the headdress of crow feathers,
> Now wears the headdress of crow feathers.

> My children, my children,
> Look! The earth is about to move.
> Look! The earth is about to move.
> My father tells me so.
> My father tells me so.

> The crow is circling above me,
> The crow is circling above me,
> The crow having come for me,
> The crow having come for me.

> Father, have pity on me
> Father, have pity on me,

> I am crying for thirst,
> I am crying for thirst,
> All is gone—I have nothing to eat.
> All is gone—I have nothing to eat.[54]

The frequent reference in the songs to the crow has deep meaning, as the crow represents death and the nether world. Its mission was to fly between this world and that one and to carry messages from one to the other.

Almost immediately, the religion with its good news won converts by the thousands. It offered hope to a people being pushed to the margins. It was to the Indian "prostrate under the heel of the white conqueror . . . doubly significant, because it held out a hope to him of freedom from oppression—divine help in his extremity."[55] Among the tribes adopting the religion were not only the Sioux, but the Paiute, Shoshoni, Crow, Assiniboin, Cheyenne, Arapaho and a few Comanche. Navajos avoided it because of their aversion to ghosts.

Although originally there was no special garment connected with the vision of Wovoka, a "ghost shirt" came to be a prominent part of the religion. The ghost shirt gave the message greater appeal, for it was said to offer the wearer immunity from the white man's bullets. It signalled the beginning of a change from a dance of peace to a call for resistance. The Sioux would follow the movement in the latter direction.

The shirt, a later addition to the movement, was a garment of unbleached muslin or rough white cotton. Originally worn as an outer garment, the shirt became an undergarment offering protection. (It recalls the scapular popular in Roman Catholicism before the second Vatican Council.) The shirt was a symbol of the Indian's differences from the white man. Nothing of white origin could be worn on it; no metal and no thread other than sinew was permitted. The shirt was decorated only with Indian symbols, such as the crescent moon, the stars and sun, and the crow.[56]

The shirt symbolized to the Indian a return to his roots, to a state where he was pure and independent of the whites. On one occasion when an Indian wearing the shirt was shot at, he escaped all bullets. To a mythic people, that instance was proof that the garment made its wearer invincible.

The origin of the shirt may owe something to the white endowment robe used in Mormon baptisms. Many Indian converts were baptized in such a shirt and believed it to confer big medicine on its wearer. James Mooney concluded, "it is sufficiently evident that the Mormons took an active interest in the religious ferment then existing among the neighboring tribes and helped to give shape to the doctrine which crystallized some years later in the Ghost Dance."[57] Durkheim's view of religion as a powerful unifying factor in society seems to work here.

The years 1889 and 1890 were bad ones for the Plains Indian, especially the Sioux. Although they numbered thirty thousand, their reservation was cut in half. Crop failures owing to two years of drought put them near starvation. And Pine Ridge Agency, which served about six thousand Sioux, had its beef ration cut by a million pounds.

Religious fervor and physical deprivation vie for the title of chief cause of the ensuing upheaval. Both contributed to the Indians' growing agitation and anxiety. The opportunity to mobilize them was not missed by Short Bull, Kicking Bear, Hump, and a few other devotees and high priests of the new religion. They urged more and more dancing to speed the Second Coming of Christ. Even the mighty but enigmatic medicine men Red Cloud of the Oglalas and Sitting Bull of the Uncpapas accepted the validity of the religion. Indeed, Sitting Bull made plans to leave his Standing Rock Agency to travel nearly two hundred miles to Pine Ridge to await Christ's Coming, which was expected imminently or at least within the first six months of the new year. He applied for a pass to leave his reservation, but the authorities refused. Regardless, the Uncpapa chief made up his mind and let his view be known.

As Indians gathered at Pine Ridge in south central South Dakota, the air was charged with expectation. An inexperienced agent repeatedly called for troops to quell what he thought would be an outbreak of hostilities, but experienced agents at other reservations downplayed the threat and prepared to ride out the Ghost Dance storm.

Yet there were reasons for the whites to be concerned. Many Indians, confident of their glory days to come, started harassing and raiding whites. Rapid City residents became alarmed, assuaged only by the gathering troops that began to concentrate there, in case of an actual outbreak of hostilities. Occasionally, Indians would waylay whites, forcing them to look directly into the sun, insisting that the whites verify for themselves the Messiah which the red men claimed they saw there. Whites prudently acquiesced to effect their release, giving further support to Indian bystanders.

Militant Indians now made depredations on nearby peaceful Indian camps, angry that they were not giving support to the cause. Hundreds of ghost dancers now gathered on a Badland mesa called the Stronghold to await the impending Coming. Most were drawn from four tribes—the Brulés, Sansarcs, Miniconjous, and Oglalas—and with their lodges, they formed a sacred circle on the plateau, posting lookouts for possible approaching troops. As the unrest increased, the dance was singled out as a cause, rather than as the symptom it was. Some agents tried to prohibit it, but that only made it a forbidden fruit that seemed even more attractive. The dance went on, becoming a challenge to the white authorities. In 1889, Sitting Bull, talking to a schoolteacher said:

Our religion seems foolish to you, but so does yours to me. The Baptists and Methodists and Presbyterians and the Catholics all have a different God. Why cannot we have one of our own? Why does the agent seek to take away our religion? My race is dying. Our God will soon die with us. If this new religion is not true then what matters? I do not know what to believe. If I could dream like the others and visit the spirit world myself, then it would be easy to believe, but the trance does not come to me. It passes me by. I help others to see their dead, but I am not aided.[58]

As the situation worsened, the army decided to take all leaders of the movement into custody, even those who gave it only tacit encouragement. Thirty-eight names were on the list, including Hump, Kicking Bear, Short Bull, and Sitting Bull. Finally responding to the agent's plea, troops moved into Pine Ridge on November 19, 1890. Among them were elements of Custer's Seventh Cavalry, officers and men who had fought under Reno and Benteen at the Little Bighorn. Who can say what feelings still lay in their hearts? Colonel Forsyth, whose forces had been besieged at Beecher's Island, also was there. Indeed, as senior officer he was in charge.

With the coming of the troops, near panic broke out among the Indians, and many of the Pine Ridge Reservation fled to the Badlands, on the northern edge of the area. These are desolate, barren, and eroded hills, which Custer once said looked like hell with the fires burned out.

At Standing Rock Agency, Sitting Bull's domain, the authorities decided to arrest the fifty-six year old chief. He had been peaceful since his return from self-imposed Canadian exile but still was considered a thorn in the side of whites. He was always there and his presence was irritating. At first, Buffalo Bill Cody was called in to do the job. The showman-scout had employed the chief in his Wild West show and was a friend. On November 28, 1890, Cody arrived at Fort Yates bearing gifts for the chief; one of them was Sitting Bull's favorite horse and another was a wagonload of candies, for the chief had a sweet tooth. The authorities had second thoughts, however, and decided against using Buffalo Bill as an emissary, choosing instead the Sioux Indian agency police. If things went wrong, the Indians would get the blame and not the whites. The arrest was scheduled for the twentieth of December but was moved up to the fifteenth because of well-founded rumors that Sitting Bull was preparing to go to Pine Ridge and with the others to await the end of the world for the white man, and shortly thereafter the Coming of the Indian Messiah.

The Indian police who were to arrest Sitting Bull were given whiskey by officers to ward off the cold of the early December morning. They went to his cabin and awakened him before dawn on December 15, 1889. Taken naked from his blankets, he agreed to go peacefully and started dressing. He was slow in doing so, however, and the police hurried him out the door. The fracas became noisy and others gathered around the cabin to find out what the affair was about. Sitting Bull was embarrassed, half dressed as he was, and young members of the tribe, seeing his willingness to go with the police, taunted him. They said he no longer was a warrior since he accepted his fate so benignly. The great chief, seeing himself maligned, now refused to accompany the police. A scuffle broke out and Lieutenant Bullhead, one of the Sioux police, was shot in his side. Immediately, he and Red Tomahawk, another policeman, shot Sitting Bull, killing him instantly. In addition to Sitting Bull, eight warriors were killed, as were six of the reservation police.

Eyewitnesses reported that with the noise of the shooting, Sitting Bull's gray circus horse went into an act for which he had been trained in the Wild West show. It immediately sat on its haunches, raising one hoof as a salute to the audience there. Upon seeing this macabre act, some of the Indians were convinced that the spirit of their chief had entered into his horse. With great haste now, Sitting Bull's body was taken back to police headquarters and buried in quicklime.

Many members of Sitting Bull's tribe now fled the reservation and joined Big Foot, a Miniconjou Sioux chief, who also was on the wanted list. Big Foot and his people were on their way to try to obtain more food and annuities from authorities when they were accosted by the soldiers. Big Foot waved a surrender flag and indicated he would go peaceably with the troops to Pine Ridge. Asked why he had harbored Sitting Bull's men, the chief replied that he could not abandon his brothers. They camped at Wounded Knee, just fifteen miles northeast of the Pine Ridge Agency. Other Indians gravitated to the area as troops now began to encircle all the Indians in the vicinity into a human roundup and surrender.

What happened is now history. The troops under Colonel Forsyth who had pitched their tents at Wounded Knee began a search of Bigfoot's people for weapons or anything that might be used for weapons, such as knives, sharp pointed utensils, and axes. The troops, in addition to their regular arms, had four Hotchkiss guns at their disposal. These were rapid-firing cannons which could deliver both shell and shot.

The Indians voluntarily gave up some weapons, but a number were spirited away. Big Foot insisted all weapons were turned in, but as the soldiers searched the tipis and other places, more weapons were discovered. Angrily, officers openly called Big Foot a liar and "bad face." While the soldiers and Indians were arguing, a young brave named Yellow Bird, who was wearing a ghost shirt, harangued both the soldiers and his own brother Indians. Reminding the two sides of the immunity to white men's bullets by the believers of the Ghost Dance religion, he began silently to go through the gyrations of the dance in front of all. Commanded by the colonel's representative to cease the provocation, he continued the dance nevertheless. The soldiers were about to seize him when Big Foot explained that the lad would stop dancing if allowed back into the sacred circle of his people. Brought into the hoop, Yellow Bird sat down and remained silent. For a moment, the tension seemed relieved until a mute Indian, said to be an adopted son of Sitting Bull, began to saunter to the pile of discarded guns to deposit his own rifle there. Somehow it discharged, whether accidentally or deliberately is not known, and later some claimed it wounded a nearby soldier. Now all hell broke out where a people were waiting for heaven. In unbridled fury, troopers' rifles spit out death, and soon the steady fire of the Hotchkiss guns took their deadly toll.

Indians were running helter-skelter looking for cover. Some went to their tipis—others to a nearby ravine where many women and children took refuge. But the soldiers' guns spared no one, and the Indians who were on the spot were killed, while a search and destroy party went after fugitives. Of the approximate three hundred and fifty of Big Foot's people, one hundred and fifty-three were killed—men, women, and children—and fifty more were wounded. Starting in mid-morning on December 29, 1890, the affair was completed by mid-afternoon. Known as the Battle, or more properly, the Massacre at Wounded Knee, the confrontation also extinguished the lives of thirty-one soldiers, some killed in the crossfire of their own forces.

A number of the Indian bodies were claimed by those who were not shot. The rest of the Indian corpses were thrown into a large pit and buried on January 1, the first day of the new year, 1891—but not before many were stripped by the soldiers of their ghost shirts. These were grisly reminders of a tragic episode, for the shirt had conferred no immunity. The white shirt now served as a different symbol, for it marked the end of the Indian wars.

With this failure and disappointment, the Ghost Shirt religion lost its meaning and power. Practiced a bit longer by the Pawnees, it then became, for the most part, a children's dance. A few among the Sioux still accept it today, but no longer is it big medicine. Wovoka himself lived on until 1932, a largely forgotten prophet. The last Sioux survivor of Wounded Knee died in 1955 at the age of ninety-one.

> The crow is making a road,
> He is making a road,
> He has finished it,
> He has finished it.
> His children,
> His children—
> Then he collected them,
> Then he collected them [on the far side.]
> —Arapaho Ghost Dance Song

8. Settlement in the Interior
Land, Sodbusters, and Cowboys

The interior West—the areas of present-day Kansas, Oklahoma, Nebraska, the Dakotas, and Montana—were leapfrogged over in the early movement westward. California and Oregon were the centers of attention, offering farms or riches or both. Few saw any opportunity in the intervening territory. It appeared on maps as the "great American desert." Yet the land was there, waiting to play its part in the expansionism that dominated the outlook of the government. The West was a population escape valve for the overpopulated East, and Americans were still on the move.

The public demand for free land began as early as 1841 and brought about the passage of the Pre-Emption Law of 1842. This act "gave anyone who had cultivated the land the right to buy 160 acres [a quarter section] at the minimum price."[1] It was in force until 1891, the official closing of the frontier.

In 1854, a plan favored by Senator Thomas Hart Benton, the chief sponsor of the Westward cause, was embodied in the Graduation Act. "It provided that lands not sold should be reduced in price over a period of 30 years."[2] This law was replaced by the momentous Homestead Act of 1862, signed into law by President Lincoln in the middle of the Civil War. The Homestead Act authorized "any citizen or intended citizen [age 21 or over] to select any surveyed land up to 160 acres and to gain title to it after five years' residence, making prescribed improvements, and paying a modest fee for the service of the register and the receiver."[3]

It also provided that, after a six-month stay, if the resident wished to borrow on the land for its improvement, the "homestead entry" could become a "pre-emption entry." This allowed the resident to purchase the land at $1.25 per acre, receiving full title later.

Westerners still weren't satisfied, correctly arguing that 160 acres of what Webster called "vast, worthless land" could not support them as did the rich bottomlands of the East. The East, by way of the

Congress, agreed and in 1873 passed the Timber Culture Act. It speci-
fied that a resident could obtain an additional 160 acres by planting
a fourth of the land in trees within a four-year period. Although a
great help to the farmer, the act did little for the forestation of the
barren lands.

Various other land acts, catering more to special interests, were
passed in 1877 and 1878. As a result of all these acts of Congress,
over one -and -a -half -million land grant applications were approved.

The Westward movement was stanched during the Civil War, but
immediately at its close the floodgates burst and a new group of
people streamed in that direction. They were the homesteaders, a
remarkable people who cut their own niche in American history. Some
were farmers who had worn out their land. Others were Union soldiers, whose service exempted them from the five-year residence requirement. Some were freed slaves seizing an opportunity they had
never dreamed possible. All looked for independence and security in
the interior West. The scene was set for the building of a vast empire.
Its chief architect and, to some extent, its director, was the railroad
dynasty.

Land grants proved to be a mighty motivation for moving the
nation, and few took such advantage of them as the railroads did.
The vast spaces of the United States had to be united somehow. River
boats began the process, as we have seen, but they could not tie
together the Atlantic and Pacific coasts. With the invention of a practical steam locomotive in 1801 and the rapid improvement of its successors, iron rails began to overtake the competition of water and
road. In the late 1850s, the railroad began its advance west of the
Mississippi toward the Missouri River. A track right across the continent began to seem feasible.

The government already had a policy of land grants to the states
for schools, buildings, canals, and waterways; in nearly all cases a
generous right of way went with the grant. Empire builders felt that
it was time to do the same for the railroads. Such grants would speed
construction of a transcontinental link that would have great political
significance and offer huge marketing benefits as well.

Further, some citizens of distant and disconnected California were
having thoughts of separation and empire of their own. That rich land
had to be held for the burgeoning and re-United States. The Civil
War was over and some of its best engineers, as, for example, General
Grenville Dodge, came out of the theater of war to lead the national
effort to connect the eastern and western coasts by rail.

Congress approved the first land grant to a railroad in 1850,
awarding a right of way to the Illinois Central. As the practice de-

veloped, the railroads received right-of-way land in a checkerboard fashion, one section on one side of track and another on the opposite side. These checkerboard squares of land would have immense value, for they were the sites on which towns would be founded. The Grangers, an organized farm movement, and the Populist political party opposed this giveaway, but to no avail. In the end, along with monumental corruption and scandal, the government got what it wanted and the railroads got what they wanted.

Once construction was under way, the railroads pushed the contractors to build with all possible speed, paying bonuses for early completion. This prompted a contest between the lines, and on April 28, 1869, ten miles of track was laid in one day by the Union Pacific. As one newspaper put it, an anvil chorus was played coast to coast with the sledgehammers pounding in spikes at three strokes to a spike, ten spikes to a rail, and four hundred rails to a mile. Often temporary materials were used in the frenzied rush. Some trestles were built on snowbanks, with permanent foundations inserted when spring arrived. Finally, on May 14, 1869, at obscure Promontory Point in northern Utah, the Union Pacific's locomotive *Jupiter* met the Central Pacific's *119*. With due ceremony, officials drove in the famous Golden Spike to unite the two lines. Inscribed on the spike was the sentiment: "May God continue the unity of our Country as this Railroad united the two great Oceans of the World."[4]

The workers, largely Irish, who brought the tracks west, and those, mostly Chinese coolies, who brought their tracks east, joined hands in celebration. The only one who was unhappy, it seemed, was Brigham Young, who had lobbied unsuccessfully to bring the railroad through Salt Lake City. It would be some time before a spur would be built to serve the City of the Saints. Perhaps Young's request was turned down because of resentment that lingered from the Mormon War of 1857-1858, when Deseret (now Utah) tried to obtain further autonomy and loosen its allegiance to the Union.

Thus, the railroad was there, the free land was there, and all that was needed was people. Passengers and mail could never put the railroad in the financial black, of course. But people would mean homes, shops, and enterprise. People would need freight services, and it was freight in the form of machinery, grain, and household goods that would make the railway barons wealthy. A productive population would take time to build, but the profits were sure to come. Whatever was bought or sold outside the immediate community had to travel by rail. The railroad had the monopoly on shipping. Whatever else might be said of the railroad barons, they were men of far vision.

The railroad magnates did not wish to wait any longer than necessary, however. They advertised far and wide for people to come West, both in the eastern United States and in Europe. Publicity was distributed as far away as Scandinavia, Russia, Germany, and England. The railroads even changed the name of Edmonton in the Dakota territory to Bismarck to appeal to Germans who admired their "Iron Chancellor." The railroads offered free transportation and sometimes free land to encourage people to settle in the West. For whatever reason, people came in droves from everywhere, and the former Indian hunting grounds were transformed into white settlements.

The railroads flourished. They sold land, established towns, and even offered buffalo hunting trips. The hunters didn't have to get off the train: shooting out the window into a dense herd was sure to kill some beast. No wonder Indian resentment focussed on this monster of white man's technology, which the red man called "many wagons, no horse."

Certainly the railroads were taming the country. Travelling west no longer took skills or fortitude. Journeys that formerly required weeks of hardship now were made in days of sedentary comfort. A different class of characters appeared on the frontier. One railroad, the Santa Fe line, introduced the Harvey Girls in its dining cars and railroad restaurants. These waitresses, many from the affluent strata of society, put a considerable check on the rough and tumble of the former West.

Of the many people attracted by the railroad, one group changed the land itself. The sodbusters, or homesteaders, came not as adventurers or exploiters, as did those who came before. Rather they came as permanent fixtures: as builders, as farmers who loved the land, nourished it, and made it fructify. Yet they were every bit as determined as those who passed over the land seeking a quick fortune.[5]

The sodbusters faced their own brand of hardship (and plenty of it), equal to any encountered by mountain men, Indian fighters, or the goldseekers. In their domain, "the winds blew continuously, myriads of insects gnawed growing crops into failure, of necessity houses were small and crudely furnished, and there was biting loneliness which all but unsettled and defeated newcomers. Money was scarce and the settler had to 'make do' with whatever materials were immediately at hand."[6]

For the most part, when sodbusters headed west, they came lock, stock, and barrel, in family groups.[7] No strangers to hardship and adversity, they had a single burning desire that led them to confront fearsome trials of soul and body—the quest for their own land, and that in great quantity. As the capitalist always desires more and more profit, the pioneers were infected with lust for land. They wanted it so badly they could taste it, and often, in the prairie dust storms, they did.

In their search, they came west by railroad or wagon or both. Often they followed friends or relatives who had come before and told them of choice locations nearby for filing. The local land office listed what was available, and the pioneer could stake a claim to 160 acres on the spot. Any children of twenty-one years or over could file in their own right, adding to the family farm. (It was not unknown for fathers to bring in nearly grown adolescents to file. If any consciences were uneasy, a slip of paper bearing the figure "21" could be put in the shoe of the youth. Thus prepared, when a registrar would ask the adolescent "Are you over twenty-one?" the youth honestly could reply "Yes." There were few birth certificates or other kinds of formal identification in those days, so the word of the lad was generally taken.)

Not all instances of truth-bending were so well intentioned. Unscrupulous companies hired drifters to file claims, which they then controlled and could sell for huge profits. People who filed had to swear that they would establish residence on the land. The real farmers did; many of the realty companies did not. One subterfuge was to build a small cabin; sometimes it was provided with wheels to ease moving it from section to section. Some hired claimants built an "Alice-in-Wonderland structure, twelve by fourteen—inches—not feet, then went to the nearest land office and swore that a dwelling stood upon their land."[8]

For the conscientious homesteaders, the first house often was a simple dugout, perhaps in a river bank or on a nearby hillside, vulnerable to flash floods. Life on the plains might begin in a more permanent structure made from the hard prairie sod and known as the sod house.

To build this sturdy and fireproof dwelling, strips of sod were cut from the earth in widths of sixteen to twenty inches, their length depending on how much weight the builder could lift. These were laid in staggered rows, so that no two joints coincided. Often a rough cottonwood-frame roof topped the structure and additional sod was placed upon it. Some houses were built into the side of a hill if one was available, saving the labor of making an additional wall. When this was done, however, cattle sometimes strayed onto the roof, eating away at the grass and, on occasion, crashing through to the amazement and consternation of the inhabitants—and the beast.

Early houses had a simple single room measuring about twelve by sixteen feet, with windows of greased paper or parchment letting in an eerie light. The chimney was constructed of mud, sod, or stones. The floor was usually pounded dirt, although some were planked. A trench was dug for cooking. Some kind of stove was a necessity, especially for heating. In larger homes, the stove was the center of activity. There the man would mend harnesses, the woman sew or read, and the children tend to chores or play.

Fuel was a major problem in the treeless plains. Although cottonwood was found by some creeks, it gave little heat when burned. A useful and handy fuel was buffalo or cow chips. They were light and compact and, even when gathered in a driving rain, would ignite quickly once they were broken up a bit. This fuel, rich in nitrogen, gave good heat. Mesquite roots also were used; they burned long and evenly and, unlike buffalo and cow chips, gave off a fragrant odor.

Hay, which was plentiful, was burned, as was grass, but these fuels were not efficient, blazing up explosively and disappearing quickly. Several versions of hayburners were introduced to the plains, but to keep one going, it was said, took two men and a boy.

The sod house was warm and relatively cozy in winter and cool in summer, despite the blizzards of January and the blazing sun of July. But it had its disadvantages. Dirt was known to fall from the ceiling-roof, often on the table during a meal. To prevent this, a canopy was made from canvas or muslin and hung directly below the ceiling. There were stories of rattlesnakes working their way through the sod roof, dropping into the canopy, and rattling away in the dead of night. Much rain would weaken the roof, and cave-ins were common. Although many householders slept on the raked dirt floor, some did have beds and, to prevent "night critters" from climbing into the bed to share the blankets, the bed legs were placed in small cans containing coal oil or skunk oil. If a bed was a part of the furniture, it usually would be taken outside during the daytime to give more room for chores.

Sometimes entire towns of sod houses were built next to each other for protection. One sod settlement was located a short distance from Fort Kearney on the Platte River. They were known generically as "dobey towns." Preserved sod dwellings can be seen at Fort Kearney, in the South Dakota Badlands, and by the Santa Fe Trail Museum near Fort Larned. Although sod houses lasted about seven years, their occupants had usually built something more substantial long before that time.

Fires were the dread of prairie dwellers. It was the custom to climb on the roof each night and search in all directions for any wisps of flame. The expression "spread like a prairie fire" had real meaning for the sodbuster. To protect themselves, pioneers usually plowed a fire break or two some distance from the house. To control or put out a fire when it occurred, they would build a backfire or drag the fire out with a frame behind their teams.

Work on the prairie was never-ending, and every man and woman had to be a Jack- or Jill-of-all-trades. Women made soap by filtering water through wood ash to produce potash; the product's quality was determined by its ability to support an egg. The potash was mixed with animal fats and leftovers and poured into a mold. The result was an effective, if harsh, cleansing agent. Potash also was used to scrub plank floors, if the sod house had one.

Candles were made by twisting string in fats and letting the mixture harden. A variation used a mixture of sand and skunk oil into which was thrust a stick with string twisted around it.

Serviceable starch was produced from water that potatoes had been boiled in. Brooms were made from corn stalks. In these and similar things, the pioneers were self-sufficient, but store-bought items such as buttons were scarce and precious. Great care was taken when washing clothes by rubbing or pounding not to break the irreplaceable buttons. Nevertheless, over time, buttons gave way to twigs or strings on clothing. Flour sacks were a major resource. They became dish cloths, towels, handkerchiefs, or blouses. They even served as lingerie, featuring a fashionable xxx label.

Every family or couple needed a garden, but raising one was no mean task, since wild animals competed with humans for the produce. If a few sheep were kept, the wool was carded and spun to make "homespun" cloth. When flax was available, the wool was combined with the hemp to produce the famous linsey-woolsey. All this was usually accounted as women's work.

Water would be carried by yoke and bucket if the stream was near, or by barrels loaded on an ox wagon if far away. Sometimes the water source was miles distant. Rain barrels were a must and could save considerable hauling.

When homesteaders could afford improvements, wells were dug by hand or sometimes by professional well diggers who toured the prairies with their equipment in search of business. They charged approximately twenty cents a foot for a hole six inches in diameter, and water could be anywhere from three to three hundred feet below the surface. The problem was that one never knew how far down one would have to dig to strike water. In seeking a likely site, many swore by the old forked divining rod—and many still do so today.

Windmills sometimes were used to bring up water from the deep wells. At first, the huge Dutch type were built, serving both to raise water and to turn a grist mill. Later, windmills more appropriate to the West were invented, and every house had one or more standing on their towers turning into the wind.

The ever useful ox or horse or mule was used to plow the tough sod to get at the precious soil beneath. The man or woman behind the plow constantly had to step around the clods produced by the plowing, thus giving rise to the epithet "clodhopper." The sod was so tough that three yoke of oxen might be needed to drag one plow. Later, John Deere's invention of the self-cleaning steel plow saved considerable toil, as it cut through the tough sod more effectively without dulling the blade. Prairie farming inspired other work-saving devices, such as the reaper-binder machine, introduced around 1870.

As more and more people homesteaded, communities were created and small towns grew up to serve the needs of nearby farms. This pool of people practiced all kinds of mutual aid, from barn-raising to quilting bees. All occasions for socializing were cherished, particularly after weeks and months of isolation on the prairies. Even those with "Methodist feet" (those whose religion frowned on dancing) enjoyed these gatherings—and often joined right in every festivity.

As more and more towns grew up on the prairies, carnivals and circuses and medicine shows toured them, providing a respite from daily drudgery. Local and county fairs featured plowing contests, shooting and running matches, horse races, and other events to help men forget the hardness of life on the prairie. Women's competition revolved around baking and cooking. Exhibitions of vegetables and fruit preserved in jars were a favorite. Ball games were played, and sometimes there would be something unusual, like a hot-air balloon ride that people would remember for years.

Many games were devised to help young single people to meet. Young women might make a man's tie from the same fabric as their gingham or calico dress. The ties would be put in a barrel and the blindfolded men would pick one. Those whose ties and dresses matched would be dates for the evening.

The women especially were grateful for these social changes of pace, for many never saw other women for months on end. Extreme loneliness, sometimes severe depression, were problems. Those unhappy in their marriages (for men could become dour and abusive) or overwhelmed with their work, had few places to turn. Every chance to socialize and compare experiences was valued. In summer, the heat could be a shimmering 110 degrees, sometimes with no wind. The unremitting sun leathered men's skin into a tough parchment. Crowsfeet wrinkles surrounded constantly squinted eyes. Women usually protected themselves with long sleeves, long skirts, and sun bonnets. In winter, there were blizzards. According to Everette Dick,

"The blizzard was a storm peculiar only to the open plains. It was less a snowstorm than an ice-dust windstorm which drove a smother of pulverized ice into the air from the ground and carried with it a veritable cloud of icy particles which beat with such stinging cold that neither man nor beast could stand to face it."[9]

During such storms, settlers placed guide ropes between their house and outbuildings to avoid the danger of wandering off into the blinding snow to freeze. In the spring and summer there was the threat of hail, nature's effort to humble the work of man. Often piling knee-deep, marble-size hailstones could crash through crops, pulverizing them to dust. Larger hailstones could cripple or kill. Other storm clouds (sometimes the same ones) brought twisters roaring out of the southwest sounding like a locomotive. Their funnels of dirt and death cut improbable swathes through one's family's land while leaving a neighbor's untouched. Small wonder that most prairie houses had slanted trap doors nearby leading to a storm cellar. The cool cellars often served also to store the jars of canned food.

The only way to live with such unnatural natural phenomena was to joke about them. One newspaper was reassuring: "Those of us who have lost their domestic animals and fowl need not be alarmed as the chances are that such stock will be blown back by the next wind."[10] Farmers told one another, "The only thing between us and the North Pole is a bob-wire fence, and that blew down two years ago."

If wind, hail, and drought were not enough, occasional insect plagues seemed to come out of nowhere. The year 1874 was particularly bad, with grasshoppers taking over and eating everything in sight. The beating staccato of wings and the crunching of insect jaws went on day and night. Fields were knee-deep, and farmers had to tie their pants cuffs to their ankles to keep grasshoppers from crawling up their legs. The plague was so bad that "Minnesota established a bounty of fifty cents a bushel . . . but the bounty was in the form of state script, and so many grasshoppers were turned in for collection that Minnesota went bankrupt."[11] Railroads were forced to hire men to shovel the pests off the tracks. With the engine's wheels running over endless grasshoppers, the rails became so slippery that no traction could be obtained.

Homesteaders in the paths of cattlemen driving their steers to market had mixed blessings. The cattlemen were none too respectful of nesters' land and often ruined some crops in passage. Considerable free fertilizer was left behind, however, and drovers customarily gave newborn calves and crippled steers to the farmer. These slowed down the drive and wouldn't make it to market anyway.

The pioneer farmers put away substantial quantities of food. They had to, in order to do their strenuous work. The daily fare consisted of saltpork or bacon, beans, corn bread, and corn, but hominy grits were part of the regimen as well. Some canned food, such as sardines and oysters, was available, as well as occasional canned fruits. But these were expensive, and mostly the farmers ate their own preserves—for instance, tomatoes preserved in brine. Hunting provided some variety in diet, as sage hen, quail, and rabbit were plentiful. Occasionally a deer, antelope, or even bear might be taken. By the time of the farmer, the buffalo already were long gone from those parts. The health of the pioneers was basically good, for in their isolation, contagious diseases affected only a few.

By and large, Indians were no threat to the homesteaders.[12] Mostly they came on occasional unannounced visits looking for handouts. They might steal a horse or two if the possibility presented itself. Some Indians who lived on wooded land even profited from the whites, charging them a small fee for gathering and cutting wood.

Those whose land was far from the railroad faced the problem of getting their crops to market. Neighbors would hitch as many as ten yoke of oxen to pull grain-laden wagons in tandem up to a hundred miles. These problems lessened as new rail spurs were built, but the farmer had no control over the cost of shipping goods to market. The railroads set prices and did not hesitate to squeeze and milk the farmer dry.

Progressive farmers were always experimenting and looking for better crops. Some raised new hybrids or brought in Russian wheat from Siberia, strong enough to withstand the Dakota winters. Dry farming also was introduced, and the government manuals describing its techniques wound up dog-eared with use.

Sheep were raised in some of the colder prairie states, as well as in Texas, New Mexico, Arizona, Wyoming, and Montana. Many of the herds were tended by Basques brought in from northern Spain and the Pyrenees. These isolated people with their strange and difficult language retained their own variation of wagon which served as their home in all kinds of weather. It more closely resembled a gypsy wagon than a Conestoga. With their trained dogs and horses, they attended their charges, leading them to the highlands in summer and the lowlands in winter. Hard workers, they kept mostly to themselves—and still do to this day.[13]

Cattlemen, as is well known, saw sheep ranchers as a natural enemy, as they thought sheep were eating at the roots of the grass they coveted for their livestock. The cattlemen engaged in "rimrocking" (throwing sheep over cliffs) and, for a long while there were various range wars and depredations. Bitterness eventually gave way to tolerance, however, as mistaken notions of sheep grazing were corrected.

Indeed, the West was becoming civilized, and the violent rule of the gun was giving way to a peaceful rule of law. Europeans arrived, not only as sportsmen and adventurers but also as investors. They brought new breeds of sheep and cattle that would change the face of the West. The frontier learned some lessons from the entrepreneurial East, yet it retained its own distinctive identity. For the world at large, that identity is tied up with the image of the cowboy.

> The West is a place for fantasies because it is remote in time and space. . . . The West is a place to be experienced and interpreted by each person who encounters it.[14]

Without question, the archetypal image of the cowboy is the most romantic and longest lasting mythic image to come out of America. The myth, although grounded in reality, probably began with the pulp magazines popular in the 1870s. There, the cowboy image was bigger than life and typified virility, action, excitement, freedom, loyalty, egalitarianism, independence, quiet determination, and competence.

Others have contributed to the portrayal of the archetypal cowboy. Among them was the Ivy League novelist Owen Wister in his book *The Virginian*. Wister was a friend of Theodore Roosevelt and Frederic Remington, both of whom also contributed strongly to the iconography of the West. Zane Grey caught the same spirit in his many novels, such as *Under the Tonto Rim* and *Riders of the Purple Sage*. The fifty-four books written by this son of an Ohio dentist have sold seventeen million copies and have been translated into twenty languages. In our own day, Louis L'Amour has upheld this tradition, and Jack Schaefer has added to it with his *Shane* and *Monte Walsh*.

The world's love affair with the American cowboy blossomed in the nineteenth century and has been going on ever since. Queen Victoria had Buffalo Bill give a command performance of his renowned Wild West Show, which also was a hit with Kaiser Wilhelm. Annie Oakley—the Little Shadow Catcher, as Indians called her—is said to have shot a cigarette out of the Kaiser's mouth. Today, both England and Germany have dude ranches, and West Berlin boasts a small cowboy town where, at the end of the working day, office workers can transform themselves into marshals, cowboys, and Indians. Germany also has a national organization called the *Prairie Freunden* (Friends of the Prairie).

Artists have done much to fix the image of the cowboy in our minds. What George Catlin, Albert Bierstadt, Karl Bodmer, and John Mix Stanley did for the scenery, Indians, and mountain men, Frederic Remington, Charlie Russell, and Charles Schreyvogel did for the cowboy. Something about the cowboy appeals to a basic spirit within each of us. Unlike the mountain man clad in buckskin or the Indian cast as Rousseau's noble savage, which reflect particular historical periods, the cowboy as solitary hero seems somehow timeless.

But what is the truth of the cowboy? How authentic is the strong and silent Shane of Jack Schaefer's novel or the nameless Virginian of Wister? Does the real cowboy have anything to do with the "reel" cowboys of the silver screen or the characters created by the prolific pens of Western writers? Strangely, we may come closest to the cowboy of history in the now-familiar songs that he sang—"The Old Chisholm Trail," "The Cowboy's Lament," and "Little Joe, the Wrangler," among others.[15] The rigors of his life, his humor, and his fatalism are expressed there.

Some of the early movie cowboys actually had seen life on the range, Tom Mix and Buck Jones among them. Tex Ritter, one of the more authentic singing cowboys, was a collector of Western folklore and music. Their films, and others of the 1920s and 30s, offer tantalizing glimpses of a remembered reality. Later productions came to depend on formulas and stereotypes played out in a Western never-never land. One actor who started his career in dusty films, where at least the stuntmen were genuine Western riders, went on to become the world's ideal of a cowboy hero. He was John Wayne, who starred in one of the few screen epics that in fact concerned the business of herding cows—*Red River*.

The writings of in-the-flesh cowboys are much less well known than the romantic fictions and morality plays. Teddy Blue Abbot wrote the masterpiece *We Pointed Them North*. The literate Andy Adams detailed a fifteen-hundred mile trail drive from Texas to Montana in his *Log of a Cowboy*. And old Charlie Siringo wrote of his life in *A Texas Cowboy*.

Today the cowboy era is virtually over. Those few who still work the trade now use a technology vastly different from that of the nineteenth century. Now six men can brand fifty-five cattle in less than an hour. Present-day roundups are more likely to be directed by a man in a helicopter than by a trail boss on a horse. Great herds have been replaced by feed lots. Western fashions, however, remain. Levi jeans, rodeo belt buckles, and cowboy boots are still seen—in Chicago and New York as much as in Denver, Cheyenne, and San Antonio. As country singer Bobby Barea has observed, "Today, being a cowboy is more an attitude than an occupation."[16]

Of course, one cannot discuss the true cowboy without delving into the nature of the cattle who were his charge. Cattle, unlike buffalo, were not indigenous to North America. They were brought to North America by the Spaniards, "two years behind the gold-mad adventurers led by Hernando Cortez. They landed at Vera Cruz in 1521, six heifers and a young bull of sturdy Andalusian stock, sharp-horned fighters fast as wild deer."[17] Others were brought later and all multiplied, so that by 1540 Coronado drove fifteen hundred cattle with him in his search for El Dorado. Over the years, many of the cattle strayed and interbred, eventually producing the Texas Longhorn. Lean, mean, and stringy, it was so tough that it thrived on prickly pear cactus, together with the rich grama and buffalo grasses in the Southwest. Some had horn spreads that approached six feet. "The Longhorn was exceedingly slow in development, not reaching the maximum of weight until eight or ten years old. He was not considered mature until past four years old. Steers from four to eight years old averaged eight hundred pounds, while ten-year-olds and up weighed a thousand pounds or better, sometimes going to sixteen hundred pounds."[18]

In the early days of marketing, the beef of the longhorn was not sought as much as their hides, tallow, hoofs, and horns. Thousands roamed the plains unbranded and were there practically for the taking. A number of individuals treated unbranded stock as a public resource, rounding up cattle and applying their own brands. The less scrupulous might even alter existing brands freehand with a "running iron." Especially vulnerable were young calves, which normally were branded when they became older. Such cattle came to be called mavericks. The story is that a Texas lawyer named Samuel Maverick was given title to a herd in payment of a debt. He largely ignored his property, and the cattle roamed freely. When Maverick finally sold the herd, the new owner first had to find it. His men rounded up virtually all unbranded cattle in the area. If asked whose cattle they held, they replied "Maverick's," so hence the term maverick for unbranded cattle (or unconventional individuals). The roundup was very successful, bringing in about three times more cows than might have been expected by natural increase. This is not the only instance in which a herd was produced with a fast horse and a running iron.

Having few natural predators and a potent weapon in its horns, the longhorn increased until it outnumbered two-legged Texans six to one. A small number of ranchers were experimenting to produce a faster-growing and meatier breed. Most Texans, however, were too busy tending to political affairs to look to the future of the cattle business. Becoming a republic in 1836 and a state in 1845, Texas was soon involved in the Civil War.

With the close of that conflict, a new clamor for beef arose and demanded attention. The population of the East was burgeoning. Californians were fed up with the mutton available to them from the south. The Army in the West and the Indians on government reservations were a ready market. With the completion of the transcontinental railroad and spur lines under construction, a vast market for beef emerged with overwhelming suddenness. Thus was born the cattle industry. The supply was in Texas, which had over five million cattle at the end of the war. The demand was nearly everywhere else, and the problem was how to get the cattle to rail centers still far removed from Texas. Cattle worth perhaps two dollars a head in Texas would sell for as much as twenty dollars if they could be brought to a railhead.

Texas was faced with a great opportunity. Some far-sighted ranchers had been building up their stock, not only of longhorns but of other breeds as well. The largest single ranch owned by one man was that of John S. Chisum (not to be confused with Jesse Chisholm of Chisholm Trail fame) with sixty to a hundred thousand head of cattle. The biggest of the ranches was the xit operated by B.H. Cambell but owned by a partnership. Despite its size, it never made a cent.

Richard King, the steamboat tycoon, ran perhaps the most profitable ranch of all. His land covered more than a million and a half acres. It was King who bred the famous Santa Gertrudis, a blend of Brahman and shorthorn. Last, there was old Charlie Goodnight, one of the few cowboys who worked his way up; he became co-owner of the ja ranch with its one -and -a -third million acres.[19]

To get their beef to the railheads up north, cowmen could use trails blazed in pre–Civil War days. The Shawnee Trail, for example, had been pioneered partly by Oliver Loving, later a coworker with Goodnight. It went northeast from Fort Worth to Joplin and St. Louis and even extended to Chicago. Used until 1878, the trail was long and dangerous, exposed to constant Indian depredations. Loving was struck on the trail by Comanche arrows and died from his wounds (he was not helped by the inadequate care offered by the hospital he was taken to). There also was the old Spanish Trail to California that led out of Fort Sumner, New Mexico. Using it, Kit Carson had delivered a herd of sheep to the Golden State.

The need for new trails was apparent. The problem was that the routes had to avoid both large white settlements and areas controlled by Indians, so setting up a good one took careful planning. Goodnight and Loving responded with the Goodnight-Loving Trail which conspicuously avoided Indian territory. The trail moved from west central Texas into eastern New Mexico, going up Raton Pass to Pueblo, Denver, and Cheyenne. It was extensively used for nearly two decades, from 1866 to 1885. Long before that time, of course, spurs had been

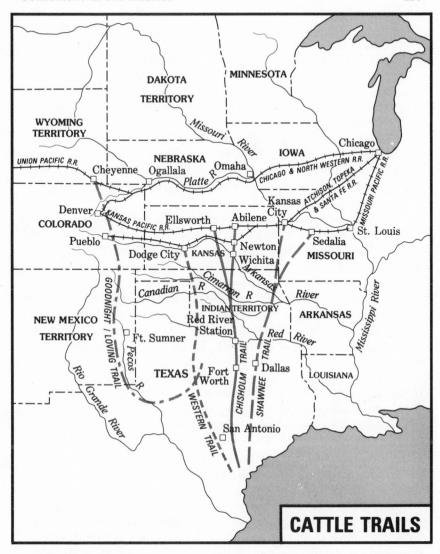

CATTLE TRAILS

built by the railroads. Yet because of the high costs of the nearer connections, many drovers continued to go farther to find cheaper shipping charges.

Another major trail was the Western Trail, which went to Dodge City and then all the way to North Dakota and Montana. Finally, there was the major trail popularized in song and founded by Jesse Chisholm, a tough mix of Scotch and Cherokee. The trail, extended and perfected by Joseph McCoy, led to Abilene, Kansas. From 1867 to 1871, it was the most heavily used of all.

Trailing herds required cowboys, but no one knows how many

cowboys were employed in the West at any time. As one author observed, it was cattle that were counted, not cowboys. Some estimates have put the number of cowboys at fifty thousand, with about a third of them blacks and another third Mexicans. Others say that Mexicans and blacks made up only two-sevenths of the total. There is no way to verify these projections and most likely both figures are exaggerated.[20]

Indeed, many of the cowboys didn't want to be counted and for various reasons were known only by their nicknames. No one inquired too closely about another's identity, for Texas was a refuge for lawbreakers. At the time, any lawbreaker a sheriff couldn't find might be said to be GTT, "Gone to Texas."

The cowboy trade was pioneered by the Mexican *vaquero*, a term that was corrupted in English to "buckaroo." Yet the Texans and others who followed the vaqueros became something quite different; they became American cowboys. Cowboys, especially Texans, didn't like the Mexicans much, and the feeling was mutual. The differences were cultural as well as political. The cowboy saw his Mexican counterpart as unnecessarily cruel to his animal. The razor-sharp Mexican spurs bled and scarred a horse's sides and, after a short time, the equally cruel bit tore out the horse's mouth. To the cowboy, the horse was more a friend, one that should be treated as such.

Although the nineteenth-century western cowboy did not dress in the elaborate styles of his twentieth-century movie imitators, he did have his own peculiar dress—as much as he could afford. Because of low wages, many worked in whatever was available—baggy shirts and equally baggy pants, with a rope around the waist serving as a belt. But when they could, cowboys spent money on certain items of apparel that helped them in their work—or helped them look the part they wanted to play.

The cowboy dressed from the top down, and his most prized possession was a fine Stetson hat, or anything reasonably close. Hats were distinctive and told those in the know where the wearer hailed from and what work he did. A bull rider's hat, for example, had a much higher crown than that of a cowboy who worked in the mountains. The wrangler's hat had a twisted brim that rolled up on the sides.

Whatever the style, the hat served many functions. It was useful for shading the eyes and protecting the head from the blazing sun, as well as for fanning the embers of a dying campfire and for carrying water from a stream. Waving the big hat was a sure way to get attention, and, much like a matador's cape, it could be thrown in the face of a charging steer for distraction.

The cowboy's shirt generally was grey and the sleeves were held to their proper length by arm garters. A vest, with its many useful pockets, often was worn over it. A small knife might be carried in one pocket, some Bull Durham tobacco and cigarette wrappers might be in another. Perhaps the stub of a pencil with a piece of paper would find its way into another vest pocket.

Around the cowboy's neck was the ever-present large bandanna or "wipe." It could shade the back or front of the neck, be used for a washcloth, or be waved as a signal to others. When riding drag (behind the herd), the rider placed the kerchief over the lower part of his face, where it saved him many a mouthful of choking trail dust. (The same position was useful when robbing banks and stage-coaches.)

The most desired trousers were Levi's. They came in two colors, brown and blue, and usually were held up by large cavalry-type suspenders or a fancy leather belt with a fancy buckle. Life on the prairie was so plain that it called for some balancing finery.

Good boots were a must, and the best were Justine boots. Thin-soled, to allow a feel for the stirrup, they were tight fitting, and often getting them on or off required help. Their pointed toes were important for getting quickly into and equally quickly out of the stirrup. Getting loose was vital if the rider spilled and was dragged by one foot. Riders knew to make one body roll and hope that the foot would be released; if the maneuver worked, he might be considerably bruised but would live to tell about it. Being dragged to death with one foot caught in a stirrup was a cowboy's nightmare. The high heel of the boot curved inward to help the rider sit properly in the saddle without straining his back or putting pressure on his legs. Two types of spurs were worn, one for everyday work, the other for dress and showing off. The expression "being well-heeled" referred to expensive spurs, perhaps inlaid with silver and engraved with designs.

For riding through chaparral—thickets of scrub oak and other tough or thorny growth—a rider needed chaps to prevent scratches or severe lacerations to his legs. Chaps basically were heavy leather leggings worn over trousers. They differed according to need. In the high country or in the north where it was cold, they were lined with sheepskin to protect the rider's thighs against the bitter winds. These were called "woollies." One popular kind was the batwing chap, which flared outward. Other chaps featured a kind of stove-pipe leg and were known as "shotguns."

Not all cowboys owned a horse, but they all prized their saddles. A good one would ensure relative comfort during a twelve- to fifteen-hour work day. A bad one made both cowboy and horse ill at ease, and could mean painful blisters or saddle sores for each. Saddles differed considerably, but all cowboys agreed on the utter uselessness of the English saddle, which had no horn. Theirs were designed for work. They were not so much ridden on as lived in. Some had high cantles (upper backs) for more back support. The rider was intended to fit into the saddle, so that horse and rider were of one piece. Cowboys were in their element on horseback. They declared, "If God wanted man to walk, he would have given him four legs!" Or, "A man without a horse taint no man atall!"

The lariat (from the Spanish *la reata*) at first was made of braided horsehair. With use, it weakened and would break. Over the years it evolved into two strands of rawhide closely woven and eventually into a number of such strands. The leather ones sailed better into the wind, giving a unique whistling sound as the loop or honda whirred toward its target. Good ropers were hard to come by and generally were given the job of wranglers with the outfit. One talented twentieth-century rope artist was Will Rogers, who was part Cherokee. His remarkable feats took him to the Broadway stage and then to movie fame.

One of the cowboy's worries was that a rattler might crawl into his bedroll at night. If snakes, being cold blooded, liked to rest on warm rocks, why wouldn't they be attracted to a warm cowboy in the cool night? Most trailhands believed that snakes would not cross a horsehide rope. Hence, this extra item was often taken along on the drive and placed around the bedroll. Many a cowboy slept better because of it. Fortunately their protection was seldom tested, because research has found that rattlers show no compunction about crawling over such a rope.

A popular adage of the West was that it wasn't God that made men equal; it was Samuel Colt. Most cowboys carried a .44 or .45 with them on the drive. Seldom was it worn, however; it rode inside their bedrolls in the chuckwagon. In fact, shooting guns on a drive was strictly prohibited, as it was likely to produce a "stompede," as the Westerners called it. When stampedes did occur, guns were not used to turn them, as in the movies—the opposite effect was all too likely to be produced. The six-gun rather was used for shooting snakes or perhaps a horse which had broken a leg. Few cowboys were fast draws; they wore the gun in town primarily to project a macho image. Most cowboys couldn't afford the ammunition needed to practice and perfect a fast draw.

Many cowboys were illiterate, but they learned their alphabet by reading the brands. Many had a prodigious memory and could immediately recognize a brand and to whom it belonged. Brands were registered in Texas as early as 1848, and every trail man had a brand book. Almost anything could suggest a brand—something special about the owner or something geographical about his ranch. Variations were countless, and brands grew ever more complex to prevent thieves from altering them by adding a bar here or a semicircle there. The original brand, if burned correctly, left an indelible impression not only on the outside of the hide but on the inside as well. A rustler was in danger of receiving a "suspended sentence" when he was caught with animals whose brand's looked suspiciously doctored. A cow might be killed and skinned in order to examine the original brand on the inside.

Brands were commonly formed from standard parts. A horizontal line (bar) beneath a given letter, for example, B̲, would make a "B" brand into a "Bar B." A semicircle beneath the letter "B" would be called a "Rocking B." A "W" with arms carried farther or waved or curled a bit would be a "Flying W" brand [⌒W⌒]. Burning the "B" brand on its side [ㄓ] made it a "Lazy B." One owner with a sense of humor officially registered the "2 ᴎ P" brand. Interpretation: "Too lazy to pee."

In addition to branding, cattle were given other marks of identification. Various cuts were made on the ear; one of the most famous was John Chisum's, called the "jingle bob." This was produced by splitting the ear, so that the lower flap hung down loosely. Often, such marks could be seen at a distance easier than brands, since in perking up its ears, the cow revealed its mark. Some ranchers also cut the dewlap in various arrangements.

Among the cowboys, some were all 'round ranch hands and others were specialists. As I have mentioned, first-class ropers often became wranglers, roping the cowboys' remudas for a day's ride. (Remuda is American Spanish for "horse exchange"—the group of horses, perhaps ten of them, available to each cowboy for his day's work.)

Some cowboys who were good riders and knew horses instinctively became bronc busters. Usually, however, the rancher would hire a professional contract buster. He had other uses for his men than to risk their legs and necks in taming wild horses. A typical bronc buster was about twenty-four years of age, small and wiry. Although young, the riders grew old quickly. After getting repeatedly thrown, many suffered internal injuries and broken bones that required them to wear corsets and leg braces. Then they had to look for a grub line, or another line of work, if they could find it.

Before riding a fresh bronc, the would-be rider would size it up carefully—checking the way the horse walked, kicked, and ran, what it did with its head and how it arched its back, much like a bullfighter checking out his two-horned opponent.

The bronc was tied to a snubbing post with a very short tether to prepare it for riding. First, a blanket was thrown over its back.

Then, when the horse had calmed down, the saddle went on. If the horse was cantankerous, it might be blindfolded while being saddled. When the rider was ready to get on, one cowboy might grab the ear of the horse (perhaps even bite it), twisting it and bringing the head down as hard as he could. This distracted the horse while the rider mounted. Once he was aboard, the snubbing rope was removed and away went the horse, travelling as much vertically as horizontally. The tricks of a bucker were legion, but good bronc riders knew them all. As the saying had it, "never a horse that couldn't be rode"— always qualified by "never a rider that couldn't be throwed."

In a confined area like a corral, there always was danger that the horse would crash into a fence post or gate and injure himself or the rider. For protection some bronc riders used the old clumsy wooden stirrups. If the horse fell on the cowboy's foot, it wouldn't be crushed inside the heavy frame.

Some broncs were killers, willing to sacrifice their own lives to rid themselves of the rider, and cowboys did their best to avoid them. Some stiff-legged horses seemed to know how to break the rider's backbone. Instead of kicking the hind legs and then bucking with the forelegs, they would leap toward the sky and come down with a resounding bone-rattling thud on all four legs at once. No rocking or bucking, just a backbreaking jar and crunch.

After the first formal rodeo was held in 1888, bronc riders and some cowboys made extra money with their skills, although many ranchers frowned on the risk and some even forbade their hands to take part. On the rodeo circuit, neophytes were told how to be a good bull rider. Before his first ride, he was to fill his mouth with marbles. Every time he rode another bull, he was to spit out one marble. When he had no more marbles to spit out, he was recognized as a bull rider.

Cattle roundups on a ranch occurred twice a year. The first took place in spring to determine how many cattle had made it through the winter and how many calves had been born. This was the time for branding the new cattle and for castrating the males, making them into more docile and easily fattened steers. Gathering "Texas oysters," this process was called.

The second roundup took place in fall to organize the cattle for the trail drive ahead. Some herds were as small as five hundred but others numbered in the thousands. One drive to California over old Spanish routes had two hundred men working over fifteen thousand head of cattle. As the ranchers knew, the stronger the force on the drive, the less interference and robbing from rustlers, ex-Jayhawkers, and Indians. Smaller herds sometimes lost so many animals to robbers that the trip was profitless. But a cattle drive was hardly labor intensive, as each cowboy could handle from 250 to 300 cows.

When larger herds were being trailed, a few men had to ride drag, beating the stragglers or scaring them with yellow slickers to keep up with the main body. This was the dustiest and dirtiest job on the trail. Fortunately, it was rotated. Toward the rear of the herd but at its sides rode the several flankers, helping keep the cattle in a solidly moving phalanx. Others toward the middle sides of the group rode point, keeping the herd headed in the proper direction. Slightly in front and to one side of the herd would be the cook's wagon. He had to reach the end of the day's drive before the rest of the men so that he could set up his chow line. In front of him would be the ramrod of the outfit, the trail boss. His word was law and he was the enforcer. When he left his position to ride ahead to town or to a local watering hole, his "el secundo" took over, and the deputy was as much in command as the chief honcho. For the most part, drinking, gambling, and shooting were not allowed on the trail. Any violation was cause to send the offender packing; he might even be blacklisted and barred from other ranches' drives. The mighty King ranch had written rules covering cowboy behavior: there were to be no guns or big knives, no gambling, no liquor, no use of company horses for private purposes, and no owning of cattle on the property.[21]

Unlike movie cowboys with their wonder horses, many trail cowboys didn't own a mount, or, if they did, they did not take it on the drive. Instead, each was provided with his own company remuda to use for the entire trip, and only he was allowed to ride the horses in it. Even if the owner wanted to borrow one, it was customary for him to ask the cowboy's permission.

Each horse in a remuda was a specialist. One would have excellent night vision and a feeling for prairie-dog holes. The cowboy would feel relatively secure on night watch with such a horse. Another might be a good swimmer and be primarily used when helping the herd ford rivers. Still another would be a good "cutting horse" and help to keep the herd in order by changing the position of the troublemakers. Everyone also looked for a brush popper, a horse that would go fearlessly into the brush to retrieve cows that had broken from the herd and hidden there. Generally the remuda was made up of geldings, for stallions were too rebellious and temperamental and mares were considered to have their own problems. At the time, there were few quarter horses around and none on the trail.

On the first day of the drive, the trail boss sought to get as far as possible and tire out the cattle so that at the end of the day they would not try to return home. During the first ten miles, the cows always sought to go back, and cowboys had a tough time moving them forward. After several days of trailing, things would start to go smoothly and the drive could keep up a steady fifteen mile a day pace. Each animal would have found its own position in the herd, and there always were steers who fought for, took, and retained their position leading the herd. This animal hierarchy or butting order was a great help to the drovers.

Occasionally, some ornery steer would break from the herd, usually followed by a few others. If this happened several times, a ring would be put through its nose and a rope tied between it and the tail of the animal in front. The intense pain of this punishment usually brought it into line. If it was still contentious, its eyelids might be sewn tight.

Cowboys had to do more than keep the herd moving. They also had to doctor the animals for common problems, such as blowflies invading an open wound. They would deal with an overgrown calf that should have been weaned but was still pestering its mother. In such cases, they put a pinching device on the calf's nose so that it could eat grass but not suck its mother's milk.

Each day on the trail started about four in the morning as the cook clanged the dinner bell and yelled for everybody to "come and get yer vittles." The cook was one of the most important people on the drive, for good food made the men happy and poor cooking made them grumble and become irritable.

Cooks used regular wagons in the early days. Charles (Chuck) Goodnight changed things when he bought a surplus army wagon and modified it specifically for trail use. Dubbed the "chuckwagon," it was the sturdiest of vehicles, for it had iron axles. Previously, axle breakdowns were the major cause of delays. One of Goodnight's innovations was the compartmentalized cabinet built into the tailgate section. Lowered, it revealed a series of drawers into which all small essentials could be put and easily located. Raised, it held all its contents in good order with a minimum of tossing about. One compartment held medicine, for the cook served as doctor, barber, and father confessor. Another compartment held sewing utensils, and still another housed condiments and baking supplies.

The cook's authority in his domain was nearly as great as the trail boss's in his. Few complained directly to him about his cooking, least of all about his sonofabitch stew, for he had ways of getting even. He might dose a complaining cowboy's ration with a laxative that would make his next day uncomfortable, to say the least. One cowboy told the cook that his cookies were hard as rock, but quickly added, "and that's just the way I like 'em!" One of the cook's responsibilities was to keep a pot of coffee heated at all stops. Arbuckle's xxx was a favorite coffee brand and refreshed the cowboy like nothing else. Interestingly, many trail cooks were referred to as "Mary." This was never taken pejoratively but was considered a compliment. It was the cook's responsibility before retiring for the night to point the chuck-wagon tongue toward the North Star, giving direction for the morning drive.

While the men were eating breakfast, the wrangler was busy gathering in the remudas. All good horses had spirit, so each morning the cowboys had to "top off" their horses for ten to fifteen minutes to settle them down. Some minor restlessness and bucking were expected in that workout. During the drive, each horse would be ridden for about three hours and then changed for a fresh one. That way, each horse was ready whenever it might be needed.

In Indian territory, the cowboys had to be alert for raids on either the herd or the horses. Sometimes a few cattle were given to Indians to forestall such forays. Gangs of white outlaws also might try to cut some cattle from the herd. One way or another nearly every herd lost some cattle.

River crossings were always dangerous, especially when the animals had to swim. In crossing, many were reluctant to follow the leader. Some went upstream, others downstream, and, if there was an island nearby, many gravitated to it. When approaching rivers, the flankers would try to press the herd together to cross as one unit. Often cowboys would splash water on one side of a cow's face to get it to turn in the proper direction.

On some occasions, cattle toward the center of a herd would lose their sense of direction and start moving in tighter and tighter circles in the middle of the herd. This was known as *milling*. J. Frank Dobie noted, "While a mill was what wound up a stampede so tight that it could no longer move, in swimming water it resulted in pushing the inside, or center, cattle under it." Animals would keep crowding toward the center, forcing those caught in the middle to go under the water as they were squeezed from the outside. In this situation many would drown, and Dobie tells of one herd that "lost eight hundred head in a mill that could not be broken."[22]

One cowboy told how he broke up such an event in June 1871: "I stripped to my underclothes, mounted a big horse called Moore, and went to them. I got off the horse and right onto the cattle. They were so jammed together that it was like walking on a raft of logs. When I got to the only real big steer in the bunch on the yon side, I mounted him and he pulled for the shore. When I got near the bank, I fell off and drifted downstream to the horse who had come on across."[23]

At night, after a long day's drive, almost anything could spook the herd, especially when the weather was hot and muggy and there was plenty of heat lighting and St. Elmo's fire. Many Mexicans carried a ball of beeswax in their hat—a nonconductor of electricity—hoping to protect themselves from being hit by lightning. Those on night-watch had to be alert for any disturbance that could start a stampede. To soothe the herd, the nightwatch would hum or sing softly, letting the animals know he was still around. On meeting another night-watch, he would speak softly in order not to startle the herd. Each cowboy looked forward to the end of his watch and was glad to come in after his two or three hours of duty. The men knew the time from the position of the Big Dipper, which makes one full rotation around the North Star every twenty-four hours.

Constantly lowing and mooing, the cattle often became restless, with some deciding to move to another spot. Others would follow. All it took to cause a stampede at these times was a sudden noise—a dry twig breaking with a sharp crack under a cowboy's boot or a sap-rich piece of wood exploding in the fire. A lightning flash, a peal of thunder, a coyote's wail, or the scream of a "painter" (panther) could bring disastrous consequences. Each man's night horse was kept saddled and near the sleeping cowboy for speedy use.

When the cattle did stampede, gunshots were almost never used to turn the leaders. Rather, the yellow slicker was brought out and waved to direct the leaders into a circle. Every effort was made to avoid turning them too tightly, as milling was as dangerous on land as in water. A night stampede was the most dreaded experience for the cowboy. His horse could easily step into a prairie dog hole and throw both of them beneath the hooves of the maddened cattle.

As the herd neared the trail's end, it would be held some miles outside of town while the bossman rode ahead to announce to buyers that his animals were ready for sale. A number of buyers would ride out to inspect the herd and make offers. Finally the cattle would be driven into town and put into holding pens for shipment to the East. To obtain more money for their herd, some unscrupulous herders might "salt" the cattle, that is, feed them salt to give them an extra thirst. As they drank to quench it, their bellies would bloat, making them appear to be fatter.

Sometimes cattle that had become lean on the long drive were wintered over in northern grasslands to fatten up for spring shipment. But this was a gamble with the elements; more than one herd was decimated by harsh and icy northers that raked the high plains.

After spending perhaps three months on the trail and with the princely pay of a hundred dollars in his britches, the cowboy was ready for entertainment. The town was ready to provide it. The end of the trail was similar to the mountain man's rendezvous and pro-duced the same result—a happy man bereft of his earnings. Many towns posted a big sign that read, "Welcome all nations, except Carry!" (Carry Nation was the hatchet-wielding temperance crusader.) Dee Brown describes Abilene, Kansas, in 1870: "Abilene boasted ten boarding houses, ten saloons, five general stores, and four hotels. Here were the saloons, the honkytonks, the stores dealing in firearms, boots, hats, and horse blankets. Here waited the Calico Queens and the painted Cats, ready to entertain the cowboys from Texas."[24]

Many a young cowboy had his first sexual experience with a woman in these towns. An older and more experienced cowboy might accompany him, telling the woman, "I give you a boy. When he comes out, give me a man!" Sometimes referred to as "soiled doves," these were about the only women the cowboys knew. They felt ill at ease with respectable women, who in the cowboy's mind were on a throne beyond reach. As in boarding schools and the navy, where males associated only with males, there must have been a goodly number of homosexual relationships. But there was as yet no widespread concept of a sexual identity (the words *heterosexual* and *homosexual* were not coined until the 1890s), and whatever men did at night was never spoken of.

A few cowhands got into gunfights, like the one described in the moralistic epitaph: "Here lies Les Moore. Shot by a .44. No Les. No Moore." Gun fighting was not common, however, and there were more jokes about them than actual gunfights. In one story, a cowboy shot someone from a competing ranch. Asked why he did so, he replied, "He was a thief and a no-good varmint and *he was a little bit slow!*"

After doing the town, the regular cowboys went back to the ranch to take up tasks such as riding line fences, repairing them as needed, and helping out with general chores. Those who were extras had a choice between accepting a grub line, that is, getting free meals and housing in an understanding for doing future work, which their free spirits detested, and doing odd jobs anywhere they could get them. All they asked was something to tide them over until the next trail drive when they could be real cowboys again.

Despite the myth of the romantic cowboy life as constructed from our twentieth-century perspective, the truth is that "the Western way of life was a simple one. It dealt in cattle, grass, cowboys, horses, rain and the hope for rain. It accepted only the strong and had little time for the timid and the weak. It offered scant promise."[25]

Gradually, after ten million cattle had been driven north, the trails closed. One reason was the farmers' enthusiastic use of "bob" wire fences. Barbed wire was invented and first used by Joseph F. Glidden in 1874. It served its purpose so well that, by 1884, over 120 million pounds had been sold.

Another reason for the closing of the trails was that the longhorn carried a tick that caused Spanish fever among domestic cattle. The longhorn, itself unaffected, was a carrier and became unwelcome outside its home range. For some time there was political discussion of establishing a national cattle trail to which all cattle drives would be confined, but the idea was never put into practice.

Rather, the cattle industry sought new directions and developed more versatile and profitable shorthorn breeds. The cattle business became much like any other business enterprise, which looked for ever more efficiency and had ever less room for personal initiative. Nonetheless, the romance of the Western trail drive lives on, and our imaginations are the richer for it, for, if truth be told, there is a bit of the cowboy in each of us.

Epilogue
The Enduring West

Today, the spirit of the American West is evident all around us. The myth of the West gives meaning to our past and color to our present as we constantly relive it in symbol and ceremony.

On the most superficial level, the clothing of the West has gone beyond fashion to be the everyday apparel of people all over the world. Levi's and a shirt have been welcomed as the answer to the centuries' long search for garments that would stay on with a minimum of fuss, wear well, and enhance appearance. The full Western costume, including ten-gallon hats, heavily ornamented belt buckles, and leather boots, is no rarity on the streets of Chicago, Boston, New York—or Tokyo.

Varieties of the Western experience are available to aficionados everywhere. Dude ranches in Arizona and England are turning away customers for next summer. German *Prairie Freunden* reenact the Gunfight at the OK Corral in a Western town recreated in the heart of Berlin. People are purchasing models of the famous Hawkens' rifles to demonstrate their skill with powder and shot at latter-day mountain man rendezvous held throughout the United States.

Organizations beckon those who long to relive the old West. The Westerners' Club is one. California offers the Gold Prospector's Association of America and Texas the U.S. Horse Cavalry Association. The Frontier Skills Institute at Bent's Fort on the old Santa Fe Trail teaches present-day applicants to be mountain men. Those who tell the tales of the West for avid readers can belong to the Western Writers of America.

What accounts for the omnipresent appeal of the American West that so transcends geography? The answer is clear. Somehow, for a shining moment in history, the individual stood supreme, outside of society, class, and petty restrictions, and seemed to have all possibilities within grasp. It seems not to matter that it all was at the expense of the Indian, or that the mountain men, prospectors, and cowboys were quickly followed and overwhelmed by fur companies, mining companies, and cattle companies. There was a lightning flash, and the image of the heroic solitary individual, free of all restraints and able to reinvent himself at will, was burned into our imagination.

That image of self-reliance and rugged individualism is most often perceived as male; Teddy Roosevelt acknowledged this when he referred to a "masculine West." But although they have been idealized in paintings such as W.H.P. Koerner's "Madonna of the Prairie" and neglected in the stories that men have told to one another, women also gained strength and independence from their encounter with the West. They were full partners in the settling of the land, a fact expressed in their membership in the Granger movement. In the West they first won the right to vote and there the first woman was elected governor of a state. Only now are the writings and contributions of the women pioneers being reassessed and their achievements celebrated.

Where can we look today for contact with the renewing spirit of the American West? In works of art, certainly Remington's bronze representations of men and horses quicken our senses. The dreamy landscapes of Bodmer and Bierstadt and the intense and sympathetic portraits of the Mandans by Catlin enlarge our understanding. The stark desert scenes of Georgia O'Keeffe offer a vision of space and purity to viewers whose lives are constricted by obligations and walls. And Ansel Adams has captured the mythic image on film, in magnificent photographs like "Clearing Winter Storm" and "Moonrise, Hernandez, New Mexico."

Western history and fiction provide a respite from the rapid changes that confuse society and relationships today. In Bernard De Voto's *Across the Wide Missouri* or Jack Schaefer's *Shane*, it does not take a Philadelphia lawyer to distinguish right from wrong. Even though Zane Grey, Karl May, and Louis L'Amour may never be the focus of university literature classes, their books have instructed millions. Their work touches the longings and the better impulses of the common man.

The actual West also remains available to the pilgrim, displaying a largeness of vista that shames any smallness of soul. Generosity is everywhere, in the people and in the land. Monument Valley is monumental indeed, with godlike proportions. The Grand Canyon forever defines the concept *grand*. The Big Country with its Big Sky is bigger than life and challenges the human spirit forever to enlarge its vision.

If the West calls us to expand our horizons, it also brings us firmly down to earth. Rough realism guided those who passed through its wild beauty and named its features. Where else will one find Whiskey Gap, Hell's Half Acre, Rattlesnake Butte, Slumgullion Pass, Jackson Hole, Big Muddy, or Stinking Water? Where else do tombstones tell such pithy stories as "Born 1843. Died 1871. Drygulched by an unknown varmint"?

Perhaps the spirit of the West is best exemplified in the way it casts aside the unnecessary complications of life. In the mythic West, everyone has an equal start. Justice is simple but effective. We all have the opportunity to start afresh. In these ideals, we approach the heart of the American Dream.

Notes

Prologue

1. See my "A Proposal for a Philosophy of the American West," *Contemporary Philosophy* 10 (No. 6, 15 Nov. 1985): 10-13. Also see my "The American West: A Philosophical Interpretation," *Journal of Thought* 16 (No. 2, 1981): 11-24.

2. For a thorough discussion of this theme, see Henry Nash Smith, *Virgin Land* (Cambridge: Harvard Univ. Press, 1950). Also of interest is Ash Gobar's reflective piece, "The Significance of the Mountain Image for the Philosophy of Life," *Philosophy Today* 25 (No. 2-4, Summer 1981): 148-56.

3. Bruce Rosenberg, *The Code of the West* (Bloomington: Indiana Univ. Press, 1952), pp. 159-60.

4. Walt Whitman, *Specimen Days in America* (London: Folio Society, 1979), p. 186.

5. See Wallace Stegner, *One Way to Spell Man* (Garden City, N.Y.: Doubleday, 1982).

Chapter 1. Lewis and Clark

1. Jerome O. Steffen, *William Clark: Jeffersonian Man on the Frontier* (Norman: Univ. of Oklahoma Press, 1977), pp. 56-57.

2. Ibid., p. 56.

3. President Jefferson, "Secret Message to Congress, 1803," cited in *Original Journals of the Lewis and Clark Expedition*, ed. Reuben Gold Thwaites (New York: Arno Press, 1969), 7: 208.

4. Quoted by Thwaites in his Introduction to *Journals*, 1: xxvi.

5. Ibid., xxx.

6. Bernard De Voto, in his Introduction to *Journals*, 1, section 6.

7. Steffen, *William Clark*, p. 44.

8. The dog was strong, a Newfoundland weighing about 150 pounds but docile with the men. Where Lewis referred to it as "the dog" or "my dog," Clark called it "our dog" and Sergeant Ordway called it by name, Scannon. Scannon proved useful and prevented injuries to the party on several occasions. The dog probably did not attend Lewis's venture up the Marias, but experts are fairly convinced he made it back to St. Louis. The source for this opinion is a 9 Oct. 1982 letter from Robert Lange, editor of the journal *We Proceeded On*. He kindly referred me to a scholarly investigation of Scannon by Ernest Osgood in a supplement to that journal listed as WPO Publication no. 2, July 1977. The title is "Our Dog Scannon—Partners in Discovery," in 12 pages. To this article, Lange has appended all references to Scannon in the *Journals*.

9. For an interesting article which demonstrates this point, see Arlen J. Large, "The Leapfrogging Captains," *We Proceeded On* 8 (No. 3, July 1983): 4-5.

10. Lisa was one of the first organized fur traders and helped form the mighty

Missouri Fur Company, establishing forts farther north. He later employed a number of the men of the Corps of Discovery.

11. Smith, *Virgin Land*, p. 25.

12. *Journals* 1 (14 May 1804): 16-17. Note that some of the entries in the journals are copies. Sometimes Lewis copied Clark's entry of the day; sometimes it is the other way around.

13. This became the name of the magazine put out by the Lewis and Clark Trail Heritage Foundation—*We Proceeded On.*

14. *Journals* 1 (20 Aug. 1804): 114-15.

15. For years, Sacajawea has been a woman of mystery. To some extent she remains so, despite the uncovering of more facets of her life. The best scholarship to date indicates that her name is not a Shoshone one but probably of Hidatsan origin. This did not mean Birdwoman as Clark thought (he sometimes called her Janey) and there was no romantic attachment from Lewis or Clark. She helped Clark recognize passes on the way back from the Bitterroots to the Yellowstone. She left her husband, Charbonneau, sometime after their return to the Mandan village. Her son, Jean Baptiste, eventually was adopted by Clark and through Clark's connections travelled with high society throughout Europe, learning various languages there. On returning, Baptiste served as a mountain guide but never fit either of the two worlds in which he moved. He died in 1866. His mother, Sacajawea, probably died at Fort Union on the confluence of the Yellowstone and Missouri rivers on December 20, 1812. Previous research led most to believe that she had gone back to her own people (unlikely) and was buried on the Wind River Reservation after dying at the age of eight-four. In any event, a gravestone marks the Wyoming site, and the important thing is that deserved tribute was given her. Sculptor Harry Jackson created an outstanding bronze casting in her honor now featured in Cody, Wyoming, at the Buffalo Bill Historical Center. For a scholarly update, see Irving W. Anderson, "A Charbonneau Family Portrait," *American West* 17 (No. 2, March/April 1980).

16. Ibid., p. 1.

17. *Journals* 1 (7 April 1804): 284-85.

18. This is like a stuffed sausage made from the intestine of an animal, in this case, buffalo. For the recipe, see H. Jane Naumann, "Food of the French Explorers and Mountain Men, *American West* 20 (No. 1, Jan./Feb. 1983): 18.

19. Today, grizzles are rare in this area. "Fewer than 1,000 of the animals are left in the lower 48 states—about 200 of them are found in Glacier and another 200 in Yellowstone National Park." Earl Gustkey, "Space Age Approaches to a Grizzly Dilemma," *National Wildlife* 21 (No. 2, Feb./March 1983): 15.

20. *Journals* 1 (29 April 1805): 351.

21. *Journals* 2 (11 May 1805): 25.

22. Clark called it Maria's River, after a relative of his. Eventually the apostrophe was dropped and today it is known as the Marias

23. Established in 1872, Yellowstone was to be the prototype for national parks all over the world. The expedition heard strange sounds in the area but never entered. However, when Colter, one of the corps's hunters, returned at the end of the expedition, he did enter the area and this section (near Cody) came to be known as Colter's Hell.

24. For an excellent and detailed defense of Shannon, see Robert E. Lange, "Private George Shannon: The Expedition's Youngest Member—1785-1836," *We Proceeded On* 8 (No. 3, July 1983): 10-15.

25. *Journals* 2 (18 Aug. 1805): 368.

26. Dan Murphy, *Lewis and Clark Voyage of Discovery* (Las Vegas: K.C. Publications, 1980), p. 52.

27. *Journals* 3 (8 Nov. 1805): 210.

28. *Journals* 3 (22 Nov. 1805): 243.

29. *Journals* 3 (25 Dec. 1805): 290-91.

30. *Journals* 4 (20 March 1806): 192.

31. For an exact accounting, see Fitz Timmen, "The Men of Lewis and Clark," *Real West* (Jan. 1968), pp. 12 and 47.

32. Dale Morgan, "Opening of the West, Explorers and Mountain Men," in *The Book of the American West* (New York: Bonanza, 1963), p. 31.

33. Fitz Timmen, "Men of Lewis and Clark," pp. 12, 47, 74-75.

34. See Robert B. Betts, *In Search of York* (Boulder: Colorado Associated Press, 1985).

35. Ibid., 106.

36. Ibid., 108.

37. Quoted in Maurice Boyd, *Pioneer Trails West*, ed. Don Worcester (Caldwell, Idaho: Caxton Printers, 1984), p. 56.

Chapter 2. The Mountain Men

1. See Maria Sandoz, *The Beaver Men* (New York: Hastings House, 1964), p. 137.

2. For a pictorial study of beaver, together with a running commentary, see Des Bartlett and Jen Bartlett, "Beavers: Master Mechanic of Pond and Stream," *National Geographic Magazine* 145 (No. 5, May 1974): 716-32.

3. Beaver hat making is a little-known art today. The first step was to separate the coarse, rough, and long hairs of the pelt from the fine and soft hairs closest to the skin. These were like a short-napped wool. Next, the fine wool was shaved from the pelt and mixed with water almost to a paste consistency. (The discarded skin was used for glue.) The paste was blown onto a perforated metal cone form, where it was held by an inner air suction while it was being shaped and smoothed. When dry, the material was blocked, shellacked, and finely sanded. The hat took on a lustrous and glossy but soft appearance. It provided a warm and waterproof head covering.

4. Whitman, *Specimen Days*, p. 191.

5. Ibid., p. 195.

6. The Hudson's Bay Company, still extant, is one of the oldest continuously operating companies in the world. It publishes a magazine appropriately titled *The Beaver—Magazine of the North*. The publishers are "the Governor and Company of Adventurers of England Trading into Hudson's Bay, known as the Hudson's Bay Company." The magazine's title is a fitting one, for its employees in America were long known as *"les hommes du nord."*

7. The top men of the Nor'westers were long experienced in exploration and discovery, especially in the Canadian Rockies and the areas west and south. More important figures are Alexander McKay, Simon Fraser, and David Thompson, the latter one of the world's greatest practical land geographers.

8. The best overall treatment of the fur trade is Bernard De Voto, *Across the Wide Missouri* (Boston: Houghton Mifflin, 1947).

9. For a first-rate study on the different rendezvous sites, 1825-1840, including maps and pictures, see Fred R. Gowans, *Rocky Mountain Rendezvous* (Provo, Utah: Brigham Young Univ. Press, 1977).

10. The battle was precipitated by a number of Blackfeet and Gros Ventre Indians coming in full battle regalia to the rendezvous site. A Boston man and would-be fur trader, Nathaniel Wyeth, described what followed and I summarize his account. Antoine Godin, who was part Indian, and his Flathead Indian friend recognized the leading chief of the Blackfeet as the one who had killed Godin's father in a previous

quarrel. The two approached the chief as if in friendship and welcome. The chief, caught unaware, was killed and his blanket robe taken back to camp by Godin as a trophy.

11. This scene of debauchery was well and honestly depicted in the movie *The Mountain Men* with Charleton Heston and Brian Keith. Unfortunately, the public and the reviewers did not take to its rough and tumble portrayal, and the film disappeared from the theatres after only a few weeks of showing. Historical revisionism is still at work.

12. Dale L. Morgan, ed., *The West of William H. Ashley* (Denver: Old West Publishing Co., 1964), pp. 118-19. It is only fair to note that the trade involved tremendous risk of capital. On the first trip of Ashley's men up the Missouri, for example, their supply boat overturned in the muddy waters and $10,000 worth of merchandise was lost. Ashley immediately put up another $10,000 for merchandise and sent it upstream. This time it reached its destination.

13. Quoted from Lewis H. Garrard, *Wah-to-yah* (Norman: Univ. of Oklahoma Press, 1955), xv.

14. Howard Stansbury, Exploration and Survey of the Great Salt Lake, etc., quoted by Cornelius M. Ismert, "James Bridger," in *Mountain Men and Fur Trade of the Far West*, ed. LeRoy Hafen (Lincoln: Univ. of Nebraska Press, 1965), p. 263.

15. Donald G. Pike, "The Mountain Man," *American West* 12 (No. 5, Sept. 1975): 36.

16. Idem.

17. Idem.

18. Merrill J. Mattes, *Colter's Hell and Jackson Hole* (National Park Service: Yellowstone Library and Museum Association, 1962), pp. 13, 17.

19. Aaron B. Stevens, "Something Hidden Go and Find It," *American West* 3 (No. 6, Nov.-Dec. 1976): 42.

20. Ibid., p. 43.

21. Ibid.

22. For a brief description of the pros and cons of the evidence, see Mattes, *Colter's Hell*, pp. 3-17. The stone carving is on display (together with an interesting array of fur trade memorabilia) at the Grand Teton National Park Headquarters in Moose, Wyoming. Fittingly, it is located on the Snake River.

23. Dale L. Morgan, *Jedediah Smith and the Opening of the West* (Lincoln: Univ. of Nebraska Press, 1963), p. 7.

24. Harvey L. Carter, "Jedediah Smith," in *Mountain Men and Fur Traders of the Far West*, p. 91.

25. Morgan claims that "This was the worst disaster in the history of the Western fur trade." Morgan, *Jedediah Smith*, p. 56.

26. It was quite common to employ Eastern Indians as guides and trapper helpers. They were well experienced and accustomed to white men and their ways. Iroquois and Delaware were among the most popular. When missionaries invaded the area, many Protestant ministers and their wives were at first not credited by the Western Indian, for they were nothing like what the Eastern Indians had led them to expect. The true missionary, they had heard, was single, wore a cross and a black robe, and wouldn't make them farmers. The Indians, of course, were expecting a Jesuit.

27. McLoughlin recorded his sympathies for Smith, writing, "I am sorry to learn that your property is so scattered." McLoughlin said he would consider it a "favor" to be allowed to assist Smith in tracking down the culprits. McLoughlin further stated he had no "selfish motives" and that his offer was dictated "solely by feeling of humanity." The letter from McLoughlin to Smith is reproduced in Morgan, *Jedediah Smith*, p. 275. This letter is dated 12 September 1828.

28. Carter, "Jedediah Smith," in *Mountain Men*, p. 108. (My indebtedness to this fine chapter, indeed, to the entire book edited by Leroy Hafen, should be obvious.)

29. George Frederick Ruxton, *Life in the Far West* (Norman: Univ. of Oklahoma Press, 1951), p. 7.

30. Reported by a family friend of Bridger; Cornelius M. Ismert, "James Bridger," in *Mountain Men*, ed. Hafen, p. 271.

31. Stanley Vestal, *Jim Bridger* (Lincoln: Univ. of Nebraska Press, 1946), p. 60.

32. As quoted by Vestal, ibid., p. 315.

33. Dorothy M. Johnson, *The Bloody Bozeman* (New York: McGraw Hill, 1971), p. 116.

34. This is taken from part of Parker's journal reproduced in Gowan's, *Rocky Mountain Rendezvous*, p. 153.

35. This won many friends for the Whitmans, at least at the time. A decade later, Whitman and his wife Narcissa (one of the first two white women to cross the Oregon trail) were massacred at Waiilatpu. For further details, see Chapter 5.

36. Quoted by Ismert, "James Bridger," p. 257.

37. Kit Carson, *Kit Carson's Autobiography*, ed. Milo Quaife (Lincoln: Univ. of Nebraska Press, 1935), p. x.

38. "Kit Carson," in *The Reader's Encyclopedia of the American West*, ed. Howard R. Lamar (New York: Thomas Y. Crowell, 1977), p. 165.

39. One of the great restorations of the West is Bent's Fort. Authentically rebuilt, the fort is complete with supplies used for trading at the time of the mountain men and staffed by National Park Service personnel wearing period costumes.

40. There were three classes of trappers: hired trappers, skin trappers, and free trappers. Hired trappers were company men required to do any work requested of them. Skin trappers worked on credit for a company, promising to sell the company all the skins caught. Free trappers, who typified America's entrepreneurial spirit, were the men who trapped anywhere they could, sold their skins to the highest bidder, and worked alone or in small groups. The free trapper saw himself as the king of the trade.

41. Carson, *Autobiography*, pp. 42-44.

42. Parker, quoted by Gowan, *Rocky Mountain Rendezvous*, p. 154.

43. Jessie kept to the usual role of a woman of her time, but she felt keenly the excitement of going out into the mountains. Through her pen, she lived all the experiences her husband went through. After their marriage, she shared much of the writing of Frémont's *Memoirs*, and critics noted that "marriage improved the style of John Frémont's writing."

44. Quoted from Frémont's *Memoirs* by Quaife in *Kit Carson's Autobiography*, pp. 84-85.

Chapter 3. The Plains Indians

1. Research conducted at Stanford University, reported in *Chicago Tribune*, 1 Jan. 1984, sec. 5, p. 8.

2. Short noses and hooded eyes are favorable adaptations for cold, windy environments. One scholar proposes that the Mongols developed these features during several thousand years of living in northern Asia *after* rising sea levels had blocked migration across the Bering Straits. In his unconventional view, American Indians represent the original appearance of these peoples; it is the Mongols who have changed. See Robert Bunge, *An American Urphilosophie* (Lanham, Md.: Univ. Press of America, 1971), p. 5. This is a truly remarkable work reflecting an inside understanding of the Native American. The author teaches Lakota Sioux. My indebtedness to Bunge and to his publications is patent throughout this chapter.

3. John Byrde, *Modern Indian Psychology* (Vermillion: Dakota Press, 1971), p. 187. Of course, with intermarriage this no longer is the case. For further information that points to the overwhelming dominance of "O" type, see Clark Wislet, *Indians of the United States* (Garden City, N.Y.: Anchor Books, 1940), p. 12.

4. For an interesting study of the geometrical abilities of the Native American, see James A. Marshall, "American Indian Geometry," *Early Man Magazine*, Spring 1979.

5. M.R. Harrington, *Indians of the Plains*, no. 15 (Los Angeles: Southwest Museum, 1942), pp. 5-6.

6. Despite their love for horses, few Indians bred them. (An exception was a Northwest tribe, the Cayuse, whose name gave us the slang word for a horse.) Indian horses were small, wiry mustangs that lived off the land and were given minimum attention. The U.S. Cavalry used larger mounts that required more food and maintenance.

7. There was, in addition to the plains buffalo, a mountain or woods buffalo. The mountain buffalo was larger with woollier and darker hair. Their skulls have been found at elevations of twelve thousand feet. The last one was killed in 1897; one preserved by taxidermy can be seen in Canon City, Colorado. Today's buffalo is the product of interbreeding of the two types.

8. When telegraph poles appeared on the plains, the grateful buffalo used them as scratching posts. To discourage this damaging practice, sharp spikes were embedded in the poles. To the chagrin of the telegraph companies, this only made the poles more attractive. The buffalo's thick hide welcomed this white man's back-scratcher.

9. For further details, see Wislet, *Indians of the United States*, pp. 267-72.

10. Apaches used the intestines of horses as water-carrying tubes in their parched desert habitat. They draped these around the necks of the horses as they rode.

11. Quoted by Henry Inman, *Buffalo Jones' Adventures On the Plains* (n.d.; reprint, Magnolia, Mass.: Peter Smith), p. 255.

12. Pierre Jean De Smet), taken from his letters in *Western Missions and Missionaries* (Shannon: Irish Univ. Press, 1972), p. 72. By 1890 in the United States there probably were fewer than five hundred buffalo extant. A movement to save the beast got under way, however, and by 1983 there were sixty thousand in this country.

13. An original authentic hide tipi is on display at Pipestone National Monument in southwestern Minnesota. Canvas tipis, which became government issue, can be seen at the Fort Buford/Fort Union area in North Dakota. An excellent exhibit is on continual display in Cody, Wyoming.

14. Robert Bunge, "The Concept of Ultimate Reality and Meaning of the Teton Sioux," *Ultimate Meaning and Reality*, vol. 10 (No. 2, June 1987), pp. 83-100.

15. Angelo Calvello, "Lived Body and Personal Names" (Ph.D. diss., DePaul University, 1983), p. 100.

16. De Smet, *Western Missions*, p. 42.

17. For an extended discussion on marriage between Indians and whites, see Bil Gilbert, *Westering Man* (New York: Atheneum, 1983), pp. 161-66.

18. Ibid., p. 162.

19. Hafen, *Mountain Men and Traders*, pp. 340-41.

20. Gilbert, *Westering Man*, p. 163.

21. Sitting Bull, *I Have Spoken*, compiled by Virginia Irving Armstrong (New York: Pocket Books, 1972), p. 97.

22. Western Writers of America, Lenniger, *Water Trails West* (New York: Avon, 1978), pp. 142-43.

23. De Smet, *Western Missions*, p. 42.

24. For a fascinating account of the episode, see Dee Brown, *Fort Phil Kearny* (Lincoln: Univ. of Nebraska Press, 1962).

25. Quoted by Dorothy Johnson, *The Bloody Bozeman*, pp. 344, n. 35, 345.

26. For the mythic origins of this custom, see the Kiowa story "How Death Came to the World" in *American Indian Mythology*, ed. Alice Marriott and Carol K. Rachlin (New York: Mentor, 1968), pp. 223-25. This is one of the stories that ascribe the source of evil in the world to women. Comparable myths include Adam and Eve, Pandora, the Greek sirens, the German *Die Lorelei*, the *femme fatale*, and Mata Hari.

27. See the vivid description of the hunt given by De Smet, *Western Missions*, p. 147.

28. This account is summarized from K.C. Tessendorf "Red Death on the Missouri," *American West* 14 (Jan.-Feb. 1977): 48-53.

29. Ibid., p. 50.

30. Marriott, "Saynday and Small Pox: The White Man's Gift," in *American Indian Mythology*, pp. 173-77. The Kiowa god Saynday is a typical trickster-hero figure. A Kiowa myth tells how Small Pox was coming to plague the Kiowa. Saynday, however, directed Small Pox to their enemy, the Pawnees, and so saved his tribe while decimating his enemy. The story offers no real explanation of why Small Pox was coming. It simply "was willed." Instead of admitting our ignorance, we humans often mask it under the explanation of "the will of God." The seventeenth-century philosopher Benedictus Spinoza called any explanation by the will of the deity an "asylum of ignorance."

31. For a thorough and lucid explanation of pemmican, see Tom McHugh, *The Time of the Buffalo* (New York: Alfred A. Knopf, 1972), pp. 88-92.

32. William Tomkins, *Indian Sign Language* (New York: Dover, 1969), p. 7. This is a simple but excellent book with copious illustrations. It also explains pictographs and petrographs.

33. Roberta Carkeeh Cheney, *The Big Missouri Winter Count* (Happy Camp, Calif., Naturegraph Publishers, 1979). This covers the years 1796 to 1926, reproducing the pictographs and presenting their interpretation by Kills Two.

34. Bunge, "Ultimate Reality," p. 10. Also see his "Awareness of the Unseen: The Indian's Contract with Life," *Listening: A Journal of Religion and Culture* 19 (No. 3, Autumn 1984): 186.

35. Scott Momaday, "I Am Alive," in *The World of the American Indian* (Washington, D.C.: National Geographic Society, 1974), p. 14.

36. For a full description of this ceremony, see Andrew Weil (a physician), "The Indian Sweat," in *American West*, March-April 1982, pp. 42-49.

37. For an explanation and description of this ritual and the six others that are sacred to the Sioux, see Bunge, "Awareness of the Unseen," pp. 181-91. For an insight into spiritual aspects of the Sweat Bath, and meditations to accompany these, see Paul Steinmetz, *Lakota Spirituality* (Santa Fe: Bear and Co., 1984).

38. Steinmetz, *Lakota Spirituality*, pp. 11-12.

39. Mircea Eliade, *Myth and Reality* (New York: Harper and Row, 1963). Also see his *Patterns in Religion* (Cleveland: World Publishing, 1963). See also Claude Levi-Strauss, *Triste Tropiques* (Paris: Plon, 1955).

40. Paul Steinmetz, "Christian Meets Lakota Sioux," *Listening* 19 (No. 3, Autumn 1984): 220-29.

41. Gerald F. Kreyche, "Structures," *New Scholasticism* 58 (Summer 1984): 336-56.

42. "The Man Who Called the Buffalo" in George Bird Grinnell, *Pawnee Hero Stories and Folk Tales* (Lincoln, Neb.: Bison Books, 1961), p. 141. This collection also has a story parallel to Peter's denial of Christ, "Pa-hu-ta-ka-tawa," pp. 142-46.

43. Says Locke, "Yet every man has a property in his own person. . . . The labor of his body and the work of his hands, we may say are properly his. Whatsoever then he removes out of the state that nature hath provided, and left it in, he hath mixed his labor with, and joining to it something that is his own, and thereby makes it his property." John Locke, *Two Treatises on Government*, vol. 2, ch. 5, sec. 27.

44. See Aldo Leopold, *Sand County Almanac* (New York: Ballantine, 1966). This is

a virtual bible of the ecology movement and provides a clear outline for a possible structure of a badly needed land ethic. See especially pp. 237-95.

45. Of course, the whites now claim ownership of the air, as in "air rights" over buildings, countries, an solar power sources.

46. The remarkable movie *Heartland* caught this sense of oneness with the land. It was based on the diaries of a widow who went West with her child to keep house for a rancher and grew to feel herself a part of the land. They have been published as Elinor Pruitt Stewart, *Letters of a Woman Homesteader* (Boston: Houghton Mifflin, 1982).

47. Here I summarize views of Robert Bunge, "Land Is a Feeling," Institute of Indian Studies *Report of Papers Presented at the Spring Conference*, April 19-21, 1979 (Vermillion: Univ. of South Dakota, 1979), pp. 2-15.

48. For a history of the struggle to establish and preserve this first of all national parks, see Richard A. Bartless, *Yellowstone: A Wilderness Besieged* (Tucson: Univ. of Arizona Press, 1985).

49. This was the reply of a Canadian tribe to its government. Davis S. Bayer, "Ontario: Canada's Keystone," *National Geographic*, Dec. 1978, p. 782.

50. Chief Sealth (Seattle) in *Chief Sealth's Testimony* (Edinburgh: St. Andrew Animal Fund, n.d.).

51. *Washington Post*, 30 Sept. 1973, p. 5. See also Gilbert, *Westering Man*, pp. 35-36, 190.

52. Gilbert, *Westering Man*, p. 191.

53. Sitting Bull, *I Have Spoken*, p. 146.

54. George Catlin, *The North American Indian*, quoted by Jack Forbes, *The Indian in America's Past* (Englewood Cliffs, N.J.: Prentice-Hall, 1964), p. 22.

55. Ibid., p. 24.

56. George Catlin, *Episodes from Life among the Indians and Lost Rambles*, ed. Marvin C. Ross (Norman: Univ. of Oklahoma Press, 1959), p. 336.

57. For a further discussion of the Indians' demise or possible renaissance, see Gerald F. Kreyche, "Commentary on Bunge's 'The Concept of Ultimate Reality and Meaning of the Teton Sioux,' " *Ultimate Meaning and Reality*, vol. 10, (No. 2, June 1987), pp. 140-42.

Chapter 4. Gold and Silver

1. T.H. Watkins, *Gold and Silver in the West* (New York: Bonanza, 1971), p. 11.

2. Sutter, quoted by Richard Dillion in "Captain John Augustus Sutter," *American West* 17 (May-June 1980): 55.

3. *Encyclopedia of the American West*, p. 1152.

4. Rodman W. Paul, *California Gold* (Lincoln: Univ. of Nebraska, 1947), p. 15.

5. B.A. Botkin, *A Treasury of Western Folklore* (New York: Bonanza Books, 1975), p. 310.

6. Quoted in Watkins, *Gold and Silver*, p. 25.

7. Quoted in Botkin, *Western Folklore*, p. 322.

8. Daniel R. Phillips, ed., *The West* (Chicago: Henry Regnery, 1973), p. 104.

9. A. Delano, *Life on the Plains and at the Diggings* (Auburn and Buffalo: Miller, Orton, Mulligan, 1854), p. 242.

10. Ibid., p. 241.

11. See Monaghan, *Book of the American West*, p. 146.

12. Botkin, *Western Folklore*, p. 337.

13. Paul, *California Gold*, p. 264.

14. Ibid., p. 199.

15. *Encyclopedia of the American West*, p. 449.

16. For an interesting discussion on this issue, see Paul, *California Gold*, p. 69.

17. For the uses and abuses of these courts, see Ray Allen Billington, *The Far Western Frontier* (New York: Harper & Row, 1956), p. 239.

18. *Encyclopedia of the American West*, p. 741.

19. Ibid.

20. Watkins, *Gold and Silver*, p. 278.

21. Ibid., p. 279.

22. Paul, *California Gold*, p. 178.

23. Ibid., p. 21.

24. Ibid., pp. 119-20.

25. *Encyclopedia of the American West*, p. 447.

26. Watkins, *Gold and Silver*, p. 28.

27. Paul, *California Gold*, p. xi.

28. Monaghan, *Book of the American West*, p. 158. Billington cites a slightly different figure: *Far Western Frontier*, p. 254.

29. Stephen M. Voynick, "Those High Grade Miners," *True West* 34 (August 1987): 24. At the Homestake Mine in South Dakota today, each miner works in company clothes and must shower before leaving the plant, have his hair rinsed, nails checked, and the like. The residues of gold that drip into a false shower floor amount to thousands of dollars a year.

30. For a history of the Cornish miners, see A.L. Rouse, *The Cousin Jacks: The Cornish in America* (New York: Charles Scribner's Sons, 1969).

31. Frank A. Crampton, *Deep Enough* (Norman: Univ. of Oklahoma Press, 1956), p. 71.

32. See Monaghan, *Book of the American West*, p. 160, and *Encyclopedia of the American West*, p. 735.

33. For exciting and first-hand experience of this, see Crampton, *Deep Enough*, p. 69.

34. See Arthur W. Thurner, "The Western Federation of Miners in Two Copper Camps," *Montana*, Spring 1983, pp. 38-42.

35. Watkins, *Gold and Silver*, p. 90.

36. Johnson, *The Bloody Bozeman*, p. 100.

37. Quoted by Paul, *California Gold*, pp. 204-5.

38. The Bighorns are among the least commercialized mountains in the United States. Three northern passes offer unparalleled scenery: motorists may take Route 16 through Ten Sleep; Route 14 through Shell Canyon; or Route 14A, a serpentine descent.

39. Frank Marryat, *Mountains and Molehills* (London: Longman, Brown, Green and Longmans, 1855), p. 315.

40. Watkins, *Gold and Silver*, p. 55.

41. Ibid., p. 60.

42. Monaghan, *Book of the American West*, p. 169. Stephen M. Voynick supports the higher grubstake sum. See his "The Tabor Opera House" in *True West* 34 (No. 6, June 1987): 22. The article on the opera house is extremely informative.

43. Watkins, *Gold and Silver*, p. 234.

44. Voynick, "Tabor Opera House," p. 23.

45. Donald Jackson, *Custer's Gold* (Lincoln: Univ. of Nebraska Press, 1966), p. 9.

46. Ibid., p. 117.

47. For the exact wording of the treaty, see Jackson, *Custer's Gold*, p. 128.

48. See Ibid., p. 10.

49. LeRoy Hafen, *Fort Laramie and the Pageant of the West* (Lincoln: Univ. of Nebraska Press, 1938), p. 367.

50. Monaghan, *Book of the American West*, p. 154.

51. Watkins, *Gold and Silver*, p. 219.

52. See Arthur W. Thurner, *Rebels on the Range* (Lake Linden, Mich.: John Forster Press, 1984). This is the story of the Michigan Copper Strike of 1913-1914 and is especially concerned with the Western Federation of Miners.

Chapter 5. The Missionaries

1. William Brandon, *The American Heritage Book on Indians* (New York: Dell Publishing, 1961), p. 26.
2. De Smet, *Western Missions*, p. 120. The movie *Ulzano's Raid* portrayed a quest for power by a brave who, with some followers, left the reservation.
3. De Smet, *Western Missions*, p. 158.
4. Billington, *Far Western Frontier*, p. 85.
5. De Voto, *Across the Wide Missouri*, p. 201.
6. Monaghan, ed., *Book of the American West*, p. 78.
7. *Encyclopedia of the American West*, p. 1038.
8. Francis Haines, *The Nez Percés* (Norman: Univ. of Oklahoma Press, 1955); see pp. 61-70. See also his remarkable chapter "The Macedonian Cry," pp. 57-70.
9. Ibid., pp. 67-68.
10. Ellen Kelly, "In the Path of De Smet," *Listening: A Journal of Religion and Culture* 19 (No. 3, Autumn 1984): 192-93.
11. Haines, *Nez Percés*, pp. 61-62.
12. John D. Unruh, Jr., in *The Plains Across* (Urbana: Univ. ofIllinois Press, 1979), 29.
13. Quoted by David Lavender in *The Great West* (New York: American Heritage, 1965), p. 179.
14. Ibid., p. 176.
15. Haines, *Nez Percés*, p. 78.
16. Ibid., p. 79.
17. Ibid., p. 83.
18. For an illustration of such a page in Shahaptian, see ibid., p. 112.
19. Ibid., p. 86.
20. Ibid., p. 93.
21. This is taken from an unpublished manuscript by Lawrence J. McCrank, "Totem, Books, and Libraries," p. 8.
22. Ibid., p. 12.
23. Ibid., p. 13.
24. Blanchet was always looking ahead in a big way. Early on, he submitted a plan to Rome for dividing Oregon's huge area into dioceses, although there was virtually no white population at the time. Eventually, he did become the first bishop and vicar-general of the area, and his priest-brother became bishop of Walla Walla. Demers also became a bishop; his see was on Vancouver Island.
25. McCrank, "Totem, Books, and Libraries," p. 20.
26. For an illustration of these ladders, see Lavender, *Great West*, p. 209.
27. McCrank, "Totem, Books, and Libraries," p. 22.
28. Ibid., p. 54.
29. Gilbert, *Westering Man*, p. 178.
30. Western Writers of America, *Water Trails West*, p. 47
31. Quoted in Gilbert, *Westering Man*, p. 176.
32. De Smet, *Western Missions*, pp. 142-43.
33. Kelly, "Path of De Smet," p. 192.
34. De Smet, *Western Missions*, p. 109.
35. Ibid., pp. 70-71.

36. Ibid., p. 60.
37. Ibid., p. 92.
38. Ibid., p. 104.
39. Ibid., p. 105.
40. Ibid., p. 79.
41. Ibid., p. 110.
42. Ibid., p. 72.
43. *Encyclopedia of the American West*, p. 1039.
44. Ibid., p. 1038.
45. Unruh, *Plains Across*, p. 361.
46. The intrepid Ogden was one of the best of the Hudson's Bay men. Although he had his problems and once killed a man, he was an expert trapper, leading brigades as far south as Utah, whose city of Ogden is named for him.
47. Robert Utley and Wilcomb E. Washington, *The Indian Wars* (New York: Bonanza Books, 1977), p. 181.
48. Robert Utley, *The Last Days of the Sioux Nation* (New Haven: Yale Univ. Press, 1966), p. 31.
49. *Encyclopedia of the American West*, p. 100. The capsule summary of Black Elk is taken from this encyclopedia.

Chapter 6. Trails West

1. For an interesting account of waterways as trails, see Lenniger, *Water Trails West*.
2. This is paraphrased in "Castle on the Prairie." It is taken from Webster's senate speech "Objects of the Mexican War," March 23, 1848. This is cited in Edward Whipple, ed., *Speeches and Orations of Daniel Webster* (Boston: Little, Brown and Company, 1891), pp. 551-68.
3. A recent account of the history of the *Yellow Stone* can be found in Donald Jackson's *Voyages of the Yellow Stone* (Norman: Univ. of Oklahoma Press, 1987). See also my review of this work in *USA Today*, Sept. 1987, p. 97.
4. For a brief history of the steamboats and their trade in the West, see Paul O'Neill, *The River Men* (Alexandria, Va.: Time-Life Books, 1977).
5. Don Worcester, ed., *Pioneer Trails West* (Caldwell, Idaho: Caxton Printers, 1984), p. 4.
6. Ralph Moody, *The Old Trails West* (New York: Thomas Y. Crowell, 1963), p. 4.
7. For the debate on the pros and cons of mules, oxen, and horses, see Randolf B. Marcy, *The Prairie Traveler* (New York: Harper Brothers, 1859), pp. 25-30.
8. Moody, *Old Trails West*, p. 192.
9. *Council Grove and the Historic Kaw Mission* (Council Grove, Kansas: Old Kaw Mission, n.d.). This is a brochure written to honor the pioneer woman. In the center of Council Grove is a large statue, "Madonna of the Prairie," one of many such monuments in the West.
10. For an interesting yet scholarly history of the famous place, see David Lavender, *Bent's Fort* (New York: Doubleday, 1954).
11. Susan Magoffin, *Down the Santa Fe Trail and into Mexico: The Diary of Susan Magoffin* (Santa Fe: William Cannon, 1975).
12. *Encyclopedia of the American West*, p. 87.
13. Josiah Gregg, *Commerce of the Prairies* (Lincoln, Neb.: Bison Books, 1967). Gregg's father accompanied Becknell on his second trip, and Gregg, a Harvard-educated physician, took to the trail and was active in its commerce in 1831-1840.

14. Moody, *Old Trails West*, p. 219.

15. Narcissa Whitman quoted in Fred Gowan, *Rocky Mountain Rendezvous*, p. 162.

16. For a nice summation of this, see Worcester, *Pioneer Trails West*, pp. 132-35.

17. See Boyd Gibbons, "The Itch to Go West," *National Geographic*, Aug. 1986, p. 154. For an interesting account of the story of Willie Keil, see Catherine Mary Weidem, "On the Trail with Willie Keil's Coffin," *American West*, June 1987, pp. 67-68.

18. Narcissa Whitman recounts many overturnings of her wagon: "It was a greater wonder that it was not turning somersaults continually!" Quoted in Worcester, *Pioneer Trails West*, p. 132.

19. George R. Steward, *The California Trail* (New York: McGraw-Hill, 1962), p. 84.

20. Ibid., pp. 106-17, gives a graphic account of these procedures, complete with drawings.

21. Various journals give accounts of trail routine. This one follows the report of Jesse Applegate, a wagon train leader bound for Oregon. See Worcester, *Pioneer Trails West*, p. 140 ff. See also Steward, *California Trail*, pp. 64-68.

22. Marcy, *Prairie Traveler*, p. 208.

23. John D. Unruh, Jr., *The Plains Across* (Urbana: Univ. of Illinois Press, 1979), p. 185.

24. Marcy, *Prairie Traveler*, chap. 11.

25. Sally Zanjani, "Phantasmagoric Visions on Western Plains," in *American West*, July-August 1986, pp. 58-59. The author presents photographs of mirages and explains, "These wondrous illusions on the Western plains occur when light rays are bent as they pass through the atmosphere with an abnormal distribution of air density."

26. Rosenberg, *Code of the West*, pp. 79-80.

27. Quoted by Billington, *Far Western Frontier*, p. 193.

28. De Smet, *Western Missions*, p. 113.

29. Ibid., p. 132.

30. Ibid., p. 396.

31. Billington, *Far Western Frontier*, p. 199.

32. Ibid., p. 206.

33. Winther, *Book of the American West*, p. 113.

Chapter 7. The Military in the West

1. Evans S. Connell, *Son of the Morning Star* (Berkeley: North Point Press, 1984), p. 149. See my review of this interesting work in *USA Today*, March 1985, pp. 92-93.

2. Fairfax Downey, *Indian Fighting Army* (New York: Bantam Books, 1963), p. 140.

3. Robert M. Utley, *Indian, Soldier and Settler* (St. Louis: Jefferson Historical Association, 1979), p. 42.

4. See Paul Horgan's *A Distant Trumpet* (New York: Farrar, Strauss, 1960). A description of army life in the Southwest, it also is a thinly veiled account of a period in the life of General George Crook. See also Robert M. Utley and Wilcome E. Washburn, *The Indian Wars* (New York: Bonanza Books, 1977): life was a "ceaseless round of drink, hard work, bad food and a battle with boredom," p. 279, also pp. 279-88.

5. Ben Innis, *A Chronological Record of Events at the Missouri-Yellowstone Confluence Area from 1805 to 1896* (Williston, N.D.: Fort Buford Association, 1971), pp. 11-23.

6. Connell, *Son of the Morning Star*, p. 154.

7. See Don Rickey, Jr., *Forty Miles a Day on Beans and Hay* (Norman: Univ. of Oklahoma Press, 1963).

8. Downey, *Indian Fighting Army*, pp. 31-32.

9. Monaghan, *Book of the American West*, p. 202.

10. Ibid.

11. Downey, *Indian Fighting Army*, p. 144.

12. For an explanation of the treaty, see Leroy R. Hafen and Francis Marion Young, *Fort Laramie and the Pageant of the West* (Lincoln: Univ. of Nebraska Press, 1938), pp. 178-96.

13. For a balanced presentation of what actually happened, see ibid., pp. 221-34.

14. Robert G. Ferris, ed., *Soldier and Brave* (Washington, D.C.: National Park Service, 1971), p. 202.

15. *Encyclopedia of the American West*, pp. 747-48.

16. Benjamin Capps, *The Indians* (Alexandria: Time-Life Books, 1973), p. 187.

17. Utley and Washburn, *Indian Wars*, p. 235.

18. Quoted in Monaghan, *Book of the American West*, p. 218.

19. Ibid., pp. 219-20.

20. Hafen and Young, *Fort Laramie*, p. 346.

21. Margaret Carrington, *AB-SA-RA-KA, Home of the Crows* (Philadelphia: J.P. Lippincott, 1868), pp. 79-80. Urged by General Sherman to write this book, she provides excellent first-hand reports as well as helpful descriptions. See especially pp. 77-80 for the treaty scene. She was complimented by Oliver Wendell Holmes on her work.

22. Ibid., p. 75.

23. Monaghan, *Book of the American West*, p. 225.

24. Carrington, *AB-SA-RA-KA*, p. 201.

25. Paul Wellman, *The Indian Wars of the West* (New York: Modern Library, 1963), p. 46.

26. Dee Brown, *Fort Phil Kearny* (Lincoln: Univ. of Nebraska Press, 1962), p. 174.

27. Carrington, *AB-SA-RA-KA*, p. 201.

28. Monaghan, *Book of the American West*, p. 226.

29. Brown, *Fort Phil Kearny*, p. 191.

30. Ibid., p. 203. See also Downey, *Indian Fighting Army*, p. 47.

31. Carrington, *AB-SA-RA-KA*, p. 269. U.S. Senate document no. 13.

32. Monaghan, *Book of the American West*, p. 226.

33. *Encyclopedia of the American West*, p. 719. See also Nellie Snyder Yost, *Medicine Lodge* (Chicago: Swallow Press, 1970), pp. 22-35.

34. According to one story, the young Custer had trouble pronouncing his middle name, Armstrong. The best he could do was "Autie," and it stuck with him through life.

35. Quoted in Stan Hoig, *The Battle of the Washita* (Lincoln: Univ. of Nebraska Press, 1979), p. 82.

36. George Armstrong Custer, *My Life on the Plains* (Lincoln: Univ. of Nebraska Press, 1966), p. 321.

37. Ibid., p. 336.

38. Quoted in Hoig, *Battle of the Washita*, p. 164.

39. Quoted in Donald Jackson, *Custer's Gold* (Lincoln: Univ. of Nebraska Press, 1972), p. 8.

40. Connell, *Son of the Morning Star*, p. 188.

41. Carping and backbiting were nearly constant among officers, as each sought glory, publicity, and promotion. For example, Reno snidely referred to Custer's *Life on the Plains* as "Lie on the Plains."

42. The island disappeared when the river changed its course several decades back. A few houses and stores now hug the highway; a hundred yards to the west stands a monument honoring those who fought.

43. Hafen and Young, *Fort Laramie*, p. 367.

44. Quoted in Connell, *Son of the Morning Star*, p. 105.

45. Quoted in Jay Monaghan, *The Life of General George Armstrong Custer* (Lincoln: Univ. of Nebraska Press, 1959), p. 369.

46. Ibid., p. 386. See Chapter 6 for other details.

47. For a fascinating account of this final part of the story, see Edgar L. Steward, *Custer's Luck* (Norman: Univ. of Oklahoma Press, 1955), pp. 478-84. For a highly detailed and equally fascinating account of the spread of the news of the defeat and the transport of the wounded to Bismarck, see Ken Brooks, "Custer's Navy," *True West*, Oct. 1985. The trip piloted by Captain Grant Marsh was one of the most hair-raising and heroic incidents of the West. (Before the battle, the ship *Far West* had served as a field command post.)

48. For an accurate overview of the battle and battlefield, see Robert Utley, *Custer Battlefield* (Washington, D.C.: U.S. Government Printing Office, n.d.), Historical Handbook Series, No. 1. Also see my review of Douglas D. Scott and Richard J. Fox, *Archaeological Insights into the Custer Battle* (Norman: Univ. of Oklahoma Press, 1988), in *USA Today*, March 1988, p. 96.

49. This is the editor's paraphrase of Chapter 3 in Sigmund Freud, *The Future of an Illusion*, ed. and tr. John Strachy (New York: Norton, 1975), Introduction.

50. The date of this is a matter of dispute, since several eclipses took place during the period. See *Encyclopedia of the American West*, p. 438; James Mooney, *The Ghost Dance Religion* (Chicago: Univ. of Chicago Press, 1965), p. 13; and Ralph K. Andrist, *The Long Death* (New York: Collier Books, 1964), p. 337.

51. Quoted in Mooney, *Ghost Dance Religion*, p. 2. This is the classic work on the Ghost Dance religion. My indebtedness to it should be clear throughout.

52. Indian mythology held that man and many animals once dwelt in the bowels of the earth. (See my account of the Kiowa myth in Chapter 3.) The Indians believed that buffalo would emerge from caves in the earth because they could not conceive that the once vast herds of buffalo—numbering at one time between fifty and one hundred million—had been virtually eliminated. They must have gone into hiding.

53. Quoted in Mooney, *Ghost Dance Religion*, p. 27.

54. Quoted in Ibid., pp. 219, 222, 234, 226.

55. Wilcomb E. Washburn, ed., *The Indian and the White Man* (New York: Doubleday, 1964), p. 232.

56. For a detailed description of the decoration, see George Bird Grinnell, *The Cheyenne Indians*, Vol. 2 (Lincoln: Univ. of Nebraska Press, 1972), pp. 271, 280.

57. Mooney, *Ghost Dance Religion*, p. 5.

58. Quoted in Virginia Irving Armstrong, compiler, *I Have Spoken* New York: Pocket Books, 1972), p. 97.

Chapter 8. Settlement in the Interior

1. See Thomas D. Clark, ed., *The Great American Frontier* (Indianapolis: Bobbs-Merrill, 1975), pp. 109-12; Nelson Klose, *A Concise Study Guide to the American Frontier* (Lincoln: Univ. of Nebraska Press, 1964), p. 102.

2. Klose, *Study Guide*, p. 102.

3. *Encyclopedia of the American West*, p. 509.

4. Quoted in Keith Wheeler, *The Railroaders* (New York: Time-Life Books, 1973), p. 116.

5. Within the limits of Hollywood conventions, the movie *Heartland*, based on the diary of Elinor Stewart, offers an instructive depiction of the hard life of the pioneers and their love for the land.

6. Clark, *American Frontier*, p. 112.

7. See Everette Dick's classic, *The Sod-House Frontier* (Lincoln: Univ. of Nebraska Press, 1937). My indebtedness to this work is obvious.

8. Lavender, *Great West*, p. 346.

9. Dick, *Sod-House Frontier*, p. 223.

10. Quoted in Martin F. Schmitt with Dee Brown, *The Settler's West* (New York: Ballantine Books, 1955), p. 30.

11. Ibid., p. 34.

12. The one infamous exception was the Minnesota Sioux Uprising of 1862, mentioned in the preceding chapter. On this occasion, Sioux certainly killed "over four hundred settlers and soldiers . . . possibly as many as eight hundred." Robert M. Utley, *Indian, Soldier and Settler* (St. Louis: Jefferson National Expansion Association, 1979), p. 62.

13. For an informative synopsis of the sheep industry in the West, see Ogden Tanner, *The Ranchers* (Alexandria, Va.: Time-Life Books, 1977), pp. 85-127.

14. William Savage, Jr., *The Cowboy Hero* (Norman: Univ. of Oklahoma Press, 1979), p. 61. This theme is dramatized in the Clint Eastwood film *Billy Bronco*. A group of misfits find themselves in the fictional life of the West.

15. The best-known cowboy song of all, "Home on the Range," was first printed in 1911 to little notice. When it became popular years later, legal disputes erupted over its origins. Tex Ritter, jacket note, "Folk Songs of the Frontier," Capitol Record P-8332, n.d.

16. Quoted in Savage, *Cowboy Hero*, p. 79.

17. Dee Brown and Martin F. Schmitt, *Trail Driving Days* (New York: Ballantine Books, 1952), p. 1.

18. J. Frank Dobie, *The Longhorns* (New York: Grosset Dunlap, 1941), p. 82.

19. See Monaghan, *Book of the American West*, pp. 373-78. Charlie Goodnight was one of the early few who devoted himself to saving the buffalo.

20. Savage, *Cowboy Hero*, p. 6.

21. For details, see William H. Forbis, *The Cowboys* (Alexandria, Va.: Time-Life Books, 1973), p. 82.

22. Dobie, *Longhorns*, pp. 82-83.

23. Quoted by Dobie, *Longhorns*, p. 83.

24. Brown and Schmitt, *Trail Driving Days*, p. 17.

25. Caleb Pirtle, *The American Cowboy* (Birmingham, Ala.: Oxmoor House, 1975), p. 94.

A Short Representative Bibliography

Prologue. The West as History and Myth

Althearn, Robert G. *High Country Empire*. Lincoln: Univ. of Nebraska Press, 1960.
———. *The Mythic West*. Lawrence: Univ. Press of Kansas, 1986.
Bergon, Frank, and Zeese Pananikolas, eds. *Looking Far West*. New York: New American Library, 1978.
Bowen, Ezra. *The Old West*. Alexandria, Va.: Time-Life Book, 1973.
Lamar, Howard R., ed. *The Reader's Encyclopedia of the American West*. New York: Thomas Y. Crowell, 1977.
Lavender, David. *The Great West*. New York: American Heritage, 1965.
Monaghan, Jay, ed. *The Book of the American West*. New York: Bonanza Books, 1963.
Rosenberg, Bruce A. *The Code of the West*. Bloomington: Indiana Univ. Press, 1982.
Smith, Henry Nash. *Virgin Land*. Cambridge: Harvard Univ. Press, 1950.
Unruh, John D., Jr. *The Plains Across*. Urbana: Univ. of Illinois Press, 1979.
Webb, Walter Prescott. *The Great Plains*. New York: Grosset Dunlap, 1931.

Chapter 1. Lewis and Clark

Bakeless, John. *Lewis and Clark*. New York: William Morrow Co., 1947.
De Voto, Bernard, ed. *The Journals of Lewis and Clark*. Boston: Houghton Mifflin, 1953.
Goetzmann, William H. *Exploration and Empire*. New York: Vintage Books, 1966.
Salisbury, Albert, and Jane Salisbury. *Two Captains West*. New York: Bramwell House, 1950.
Steffen, Jerome O. *William Clark*. Norman: Univ. of Oklahoma Press, 1977.
Thwaites, Reuben Gold, ed. *Original Journals of the Lewis and Clark Expedition*. New York: Arno Press, 1969.

Chapter 2. The Mountain Men

Carson, Kit. *Kit Carson's Autobiography*. Ed. Milo Quaife. Lincoln: Univ. of Nebraska Press, 1935.

Clokey, Richard M. *William Ashley*. Norman: Univ. of Oklahoma Press, 1980.

De Voto, Bernard. *Across the Wide Missouri*. Boston: Houghton Mifflin, 1947.

Garrard, Lewis H. *Wah-to-yah*. Norman: Univ. of Oklahoma Press, 1955.

Gowans, Fred R. *Rocky Mountain Rendezvous*. Provo, Utah: Brigham Young Univ. Press, 1977.

Hafen, LeRoy, ed. *Mountain Men and Fur Trade of the Far West*. Lincoln: Univ. of Nebraska Press, 1965.

Leonard, Zenas. *Narrations of the Adventures of Zenas Leonard*. Ed. Milo Quaife. Lincoln: Univ. of Nebraska Press, 1978.

Morgan, Dale L. *Jedediah Smith and the Opening of the West*. Lincoln: Univ. of Nebraska Press, 1963.

———, ed. *The West of William H. Ashley*. Denver: Old West Publishing Co., 1964.

Russell, Carl P. *Firearms, Traps, and Tools of the Mountain Men*. New York: Alfred A. Knopf, 1967.

Russell, Osbourne. *Journal of a Trapper*. Ed. Aubrey L. Haines. Lincoln: Univ. of Nebraska Press, 1955.

Ruxton, George Frederick. *Life In the Far West*. Norman: Univ. of Oklahoma Press, 1951.

Sandoz, Maria. *The Beaver Men*. New York: Hasting House, 1964.

Chapter 3. The Plains Indians

Bunge, Robert. *An American Urphilosophie*. Lanham, Md.: Univ. Press of America, 1984.

Byrde, John. *Modern Indian Psychology*. Vermillion: Dakota Press, 1971.

Catlin, George. *Episodes from Life among the Indians and Lost Rambles*. Ed. Marvin C. Ross. Norman: Univ. of Oklahoma Press, 1959.

Cheney, Roberta Carkeeh. *The Big Missouri Winter Count*. Happy Camp, Cal.: Naturegraph Publishers, 1979.

Grinnell, George Bird. *The Cheyenne Indians*. 2 vols. Lincoln: Univ. of Nebraska Press, 1972.

———. *Pawnee Hero Stories and Folk Tales*. Lincoln: Bison Books, 1961.

McHugh, Tom. *The Time of the Buffalo*. New York: Alfred A. Knopf, 1972.

Marriott, Alice, and Carol K. Rachlin, eds. *American Indian Mythology*. New York: Mentor Books, 1968.

Sitting Bull. *I Have Spoken*. Comp. Virginia Irving Armstrong. New York: Pocket Books, 1972.

Standing Bear, Luther. *My People, the Sioux*. Lincoln, Univ. of Nebraska Press, 1975.

Steinmetz, Paul. *Lakota Spirituality*. Santa Fe: Bear and Co., 1984.

Tomkins, William. *Indian Sign Language*. New York: Dover Books, 1969.

Wislet, Clark. *Indians of the United States*. Garden City, N.Y.: Anchor Books, 1940.

Chapter 4. Gold and Silver

Botkin, B.A. *A Treasure of Western Folklore*. New York: Bonanza Books, 1975.
Crampton, Frank A. *Deep Enough*. Norman: Univ. of Oklahoma Press, 1956.
Delano, A. *Life on the Plains and at the Diggings*. Auburn, N.Y.: Miller, Orton Mulligan, 1854.
Paul, Rodman W. *California Gold*. Lincoln: Univ. of Nebraska Press, 1947.
Rouse, A.L. *The Cousin Jacks: The Cornish in America*. New York: Scribner's, 1969.
Watkins, T.H. *Gold and Silver in the West*. New York: Bonanza Books, 1971.

Chapter 5. The Missionaries

Billington, Ray Allen. *The Far Western Frontier*. New York: Harper & Row, 1956.
De Smet, P.J., S.J. *Western Missions and Missionaries*. Shannon: Irish Univ. Press, 1972.
De Voto, Bernard. *Across the Wide Missouri*. Boston: Houghton Mifflin, 1947.
Haines, Francis. *The Nez Percés*. Norman: Univ. of Oklahoma Press, 1955.
Lavender, David. *Land of Giants*. New York: Doubleday and Co., 1956.

Chapter 6. Trails West

De Voto, Bernard. *The Year of Decision*. Boston: Houghton Mifflin, 1942.
Gregg, Josiah. *Commerce of the Prairies*. Lincoln, Neb.: Bison Books, 1967.
Jackson, Donald. *Voyages of the Steamboat Yellow Stone*. Norman: Univ. of Oklahoma Press, 1985.
Lavender, David. *Bent's Fort*. New York: Doubleday and Co., 1954.
Magoffin, Susan. *Down the Santa Fe Trail and into Mexico: The Diary of Susan Magoffin*. Santa Fe: William Cannon, 1975.
Marcy, Randolf B. *The Prairie Traveler*. New York: Harper and Brothers, 1859.
Moody, Ralph. *The Old Trails West*. New York: Thomas Y. Crowell, 1963.
Parkman, Francis. *The Oregon Trail*. New York: New American Library, 1950.
Schlissel, Lillian. *Women's Diaries of the Westward Journey*. New York: Schocken Books, 1982.
Sprague, Marshall. *The Great Gates*. Boston: Little, Brown and Co., 1964.

Chapter 7. The Military in the West

Andrist, Ralph K. *The Last Days of the Plains Indians*. New York: Collier Books, 1964.
Brown, Dee. *Fort Phil Kearny*. Lincoln: Univ. of Nebraska Press, 1962.
Custer, George Armstrong. *My Life On the Plains*. Lincoln: Univ. of Nebraska Press, 1966.

Hafen, Leroy R., and Francis Marion Young. *Fort Laramie and the Pageant of the West*. Lincoln: Univ. of Nebraska Press, 1938.

Hoig, Stan. *The Battle of the Washita*. Lincoln: Univ. of Nebraska Press, 1979.

King, Charles. *Campaigning with Crook*. Norman: Univ. of Oklahoma Press, 1964.

Miller, David Humphreys. *Ghost Dance*. Lincoln: Univ. of Nebraska Press, 1959.

Monaghan, Jay. *The Life of General George Armstrong Custer*. Lincoln: Univ. of Nebraska Press, 1959.

Mooney, James. *The Ghost Dance Religion*. Chicago: Univ. of Chicago Press, 1965.

Rickey, Don, Jr. *Forty Miles a Day on Beans and Hay*. Norman: Univ. of Oklahoma Press, 1963.

Scott, Douglas D., and Richard A. Fox, Jr. *Archaeological Insights into the Custer Battle*. Norman: Univ. of Oklahoma Press, 1988.

Utley, Robert M. *Indian, Soldier and Brave*. St. Louis: Jefferson Historical Assoc., 1979.

———, and Wilcome E. Washburn. *The Indian Wars*. New York: Bonanza Books, 1977.

Chapter 8. Settlement in the Interior

Adams, Andy. *The Log of a Cowboy*. Lincoln: Univ. of Nebraska Press, 1964.

Dick, Everette. *The Sod-House Frontier*. Lincoln: Univ. of Nebraska Press, 1937.

Dobie, J. Frank. *The Longhorns*. New York: Grosset Dunlap, 1941.

McDowell, Bart. *The American Cowboy in Life and Legend*. Austin: Univ. of Texas Press, 1972.

Pirtle, Caleb. *The American Cowboy*. Birmingham: Oxmoor House, 1975.

Savage, William, Jr. *The Cowboy Hero*. Norman: Univ. of Oklahoma Press, 1979.

Stewart, Elinor Pruitt. *Letters of a Woman Homesteader*. Boston: Houghton Mifflin, 1982.

Index